T0328134

John Brown and the Era of Literary Confrontation

Studies in American Popular History and Culture

JEROME NADELHAFT, *General Editor*

John Brown and the Era of Literary Confrontation

Michael Stoneham

Routledge
Taylor & Francis Group

New York   London

First published 2009
by Routledge
711 Third Avenue, New York, NY 10017

Simultaneously published in the UK
by Routledge
2 Park Square, Milton Park, Abingdon, Oxon OX14 4RN

Routledge is an imprint of the Taylor & Francis Group, an informa business

First published in paperback 2013

© 2009 Taylor & Francis

Typeset in Sabon by IBT Global.

Library of Congress Cataloging in Publication Data
Stoneham, Michael.
  John Brown and the era of literary confrontation / by Michael Stoneham.
    p. cm.—(Studies in American popular history and culture)
  Includes bibliographical references and index.
    1. Brown, John, 1800-1859—Influence. 2. Brown, John, 1800-1859—In literature. 3. Antislavery movements in literature. 4. American literature—History and criticism. 5. Antislavery movements—United States—History—19th century—Sources. 6. Authors, American—19th century—Correspondence. 7. American letters. 8. Abolitionists—United States—Biography. I. Title.
  E451.S885 2009
  973.7'114—dc22
                            2008051939

ISBN13: 978-0-415-99682-2 (hbk)
ISBN13: 978-0-203-87643-5 (ebk)
ISBN13: 978-0-415-84551-9 (pbk)

This book is dedicated to all those who have bravely confronted hypocrisy, duplicity, and oppression; I am convinced that those who embrace Henry Thoreau's sense of duty and confront their errant contemporaries are worthy of our admiration. However, I also believe that they may be worthy of our fear, since they may feel compelled to offer support to radically violent agents of social change. This book, therefore, is specifically dedicated to those whose work is the reduction of the sense of moral indignation that inspires dutiful scholars to justify the radical freedom fighters who have been compelled to violence.

Contents

Acknowledgments

With deepest appreciation for his kind guidance and strong influence, I want to acknowledge the help of Professor Marty Bickman at the University of Colorado; Professor Bickman's patient counsel and enthusiastic support allowed this project. I'd also like to acknowledge the support, wisdom, and kindness of my wife, Ellen, and my two daughters, Katsume and Dorothy, without whose understanding and encouragement, this book might not have been possible.

1 Introduction

> I believe John Brown to be the representative man of the century, as
> Washington was of the last—the Harper's Ferry affair, and the capac-
> ity shown by the Italians for self-government, the great events of this
> age. One will free Europe, and the other America.[1]
>
> George Luther Stearns

Radical abolitionist, freedom-fighter, and terrorist John Brown inspired literary America during his short but dramatic career as public figure in ante-
bellum America. Emerging from obscurity during the violent struggle to
determine whether Kansas would enter the Union as a slave or free state in
1856, John Brown captured the imagination of the Eastern intelligentsia in
reports of his exploits on behalf of the Free State settlers during the chaotic
summer of 1856. He was a bold guerilla fighter committed to ensuring that
slavery did not succeed in Kansas, and prominent members of eastern emigration societies and Kansas committees were thrilled by the stories of his
heroism at Blackjack and Ossawatomie and eager to entertain the Kansas
veteran when he journeyed east during the winter of 1857. Men like Thomas
Wentworth Higginson, abolitionist Free Church minister and future mentor to poet Emily Dickinson, was genuinely excited to meet Brown; before
a Boston audience gathered to celebrate the twenty-fifth anniversary of the
Massachusetts Anti-Slavery Society at Faneuil Hall that January, he likened
Brown to a "genuine warrior of the Revolution." [2] According to Higginson,
John Brown was the "Ethan Allen, the Israel Putnam" of the day.[3] He was
a bold man unflinchingly committed to liberty in Kansas, and his fearless
opposition to Pro-Slavery Border Ruffians on remote battlefields thrilled
attentive eastern opponents of slavery desperate for a victory against the
powerful Southern slave caucus. John Brown came to represent the struggle
against slavery in Kansas. He became the representative of liberty in the
contested territory, and he earned the appreciation and the approbation of
prominent eastern intellectuals when Kansas became a free state. As Henry
Thoreau would later remark, "it was through [John Brown's] . . . agency,
far more than any other's, that Kansas was made free" (262).

Regardless of the considerable liberty that Thoreau exercised when he
made this statement, there is no doubt that John Brown inspired many of
his countrymen by his resolute commitment to oppose the illegal and often
ruthless efforts of Pro-Slavery forces to make Kansas a slave state. Special
correspondents for the New York *Tribune* sent dispatches east reporting
the "old man['s]" willingness to endure both depravation and suffering in

order to ensure the eventual triumph of principles in Kansas.[4] John Brown, himself, sent an account of his forthright conduct at the battle of Black Jack to the New York *Tribune*.[5] As Franklin Sanborn records, "all of Concord had heard . . . of Brown's fights and escapes in Kansas; and Thoreau, who had his own bone to pick with the civil government . . . was [particularly] desirous of meeting Brown."[6] So were many other leading men and women in Concord: Emerson, Alcott, Hoar, and Sanborn, and Thoreau all attended Brown's evening lecture in Concord and were moved to contribute toward Brown's future efforts. After meeting Brown at Thoreau's dining room, Emerson even invited the captain to his home for a discussion of both his views and experiences, evidently learning to both admire and respect the forthright character who had whole-heartedly dedicated himself to abolition. Likewise, many other men and women in Massachusetts were impressed by the fifty-seven year old man who had dedicated himself to liberty in the contested territories. They eagerly attended events where the Kansas veteran was invited and attentively listened as he narrated accounts of his efforts to oppose the outrages of the Pro-Slavery Border Ruffians.

During the winter of 1857, Brown appealed to individuals as contentious as abolitionists Theodore Parker, William Lloyd Garrison, Wendell Phillips, and George Luther Stearns and addressed audiences as diverse as the Massachusetts state legislature. Committed to the end of slavery and convinced that if "slavery goes to Kansas, it goes to all the territories," Parker even hosted Brown at his home in Boston and joined in his debate with outspoken non-resistance champion William Lloyd Garrison on the biblical injunction "resist not evil with evil."[7] Not only did the Reverend Parker believe that "carnal weapons" were absolutely necessary in the fight against those whose will to impose slavery's stamp on the Kansas territory knew no limits, Parker, like his fellow divine Henry Ward Beecher, had actively supplied Free State settlers with weapons and funding for nearly a year by the time he met Brown.[8] Unsuccessful in converting his friend, Garrison, to a more violent perspective, Parker was none-the-less not at all disappointed with the opportunity that he had to gain a greater appreciation for the man who had inspired a revolution in sentiment in Kansas and a newfound willingness to combat slavery in New England.

In fact, Parker was so impressed by John Brown and his militant willingness to oppose the inertia of Southern slavery on the battlefield that he committed himself to Brown when the freedom fighter revealed his intention to attack slavery itself. Joining five other ultra-abolitionists in 1858, Parker became one of the primary financial supporters for the event that would electrify the nation—the attack on Harper's Ferry. He was joined by Worcester reformer Thomas Wentworth Higginson and Concord schoolmaster Franklin Sanborn, both men whose commitment to abolition informed their literary efforts for the next five decades.

However, when news that John Brown had initiated his attack reached the North, these men, like many other Northern abolitionists, did not emerge from the security of their covert complicity to sing Brown's praises and challenge the inertia of negative public opinion inspired by the conservative press. Instead, they either fled the country or silently—and safely—observed the response of an outraged populous.

Henry Thoreau was appalled by their behavior. Indignant over their behavior and offended by the public response to John Brown's failed effort, he determined to speak on behalf of John Brown. Disregarding the advice of his well-intentioned neighbors, on Sunday, 30 October, 1859, he announced that he would lecture on the character and actions of Captain John Brown to his Concord neighbors. Having been inspired by reports of Brown's forthright responses to queries of the government officials and outraged by the paucity of favorable public commentary concerning Brown's motive, Thoreau confronted his Concord contemporaries that night with a powerful address condemning their collective renunciation of Brown's actions and demanding a revaluation of Brown's actions—and their own. Over the next week, the indignant Concord naturalist gave his lecture on two more occasions. Each time he read "On the Character and Actions of John Brown," he confronted an audience with a strong historical abolitionist sentiment and a significant connection to one of the more prominent abolitionists among Brown's primary supporters.

Both incisive and disconcerting, Thoreau makes his nineteenth century listener understand the vast difference between the passive social role that he or she may have played in the fight to end slavery and the active confrontational role that John Brown played at Harper's Ferry. The one, Thoreau intimates, does little more than ensure stasis; the other, he insists, compels individuals to re-examine their own moral fiber and commit to an activism that denies compromise.

Acknowledging the appropriateness of Thoreau's speech on John Brown, Emerson did not take long to proclaim his own sympathy with the Kansas veteran.[9] On 8 November, he publicly proclaimed that John Brown was a "new saint awaiting his martyrdom" to a packed audience at the Parker Fraternity, the same forum that Henry Thoreau had explored during the second of his three presentations of "On the Character and Actions of Captain John Brown."[10] Emerson's brief reference to Brown during his lecture on "Courage" was not, however, altogether satisfying for the Concord sage. Inspired by Brown and convinced that the conditions that had compelled the "pure idealist" were brought on by the culture of compromise that had dominated American public life for the past ten years, Emerson spoke most poignantly at the meeting to "Aid John Brown's Family" on 18 November, 1859.[11]

Using the freedom fighter as a kind of touchstone, Emerson perspicaciously confronted his errant contemporaries with their complicity in the enslavement of four million African-Americans in the United States. He insisted that each American was responsible for the existence of slavery and its paradoxical presence in a nation established upon the principles of liberty and justice. Collectively, Emerson assured the Tremont Temple audience, Americans had had many opportunities to ensure the end of slavery; however, they failed to eradicate the blight upon the nation because they were more interested in political power, material wealth, and social influence than in moral righteousness. Juxtaposing Brown with the "men of talent" who occupied positions of political power in America, Emerson exposed both the elected and the appointed representatives who had brought the nation to ruin by their devotion to compromise, appeasement, and convention.[12] Asserting that they had consistently privileged political expediency at the expense of morality, Emerson suggested that they imperiled the lives of the citizens throughout the nation by securing a government that demanded the enforcement of immoral laws, hence compromised the future of the nation by denying the validity of the primary philosophical premise upon which the nation was established—that government exists to secure the "unalienable rights" of men.[13] For Emerson, John Brown embraced an incorruptible morality gained not by political association or fawning admiration of existing legal precedent, but by a right reliance. He was, according to Emerson, a model self-reliant man who acted upon his uncorrupted convictions for the universal good, hence offered a model of moral engagement for all of America. Indeed, Emerson constructed Brown as a kind of restorative who, by his commitment to universal laws and public demonstration of virtue, could inspire the errant mass of American representatives to right public engagement.

Emerson and Thoreau were not the only literary figures inspired to confront their contemporaries as a result of either their intimacy with or awareness of John Brown's willingness to violently confront slavery. There were many other contemporary literary figures who found themselves inspired after encountering John Brown. Harriet Beecher Stowe was one of them. Perhaps the most well-known abolitionist author in the 1850s, Stowe makes Brown central to her exploration of abolition in her second major novel, *Dred: A Tale of the Dismal Swamp*. Written during the summer of 1856 when news of the struggle for bloody Kansas dominated the press, *Dred* is an exploration of the efficacy of the kind of violence that John Brown embraced in his effort to defend the rights of Free Soil settlers against the abuses of Border Ruffians in Kansas. Informed by what was occurring on the frontier and conscious that a degenerate atmosphere must exist in order to inspire men like John Brown to murderous mid-night reprisals, Stowe attempts to demonstrate both the corruption inherent in slavery and the degenerate influence that it exerts upon those subject and witness to its effects. It cannot, she attempts to demonstrate, be the method that abolitionists embrace to end slavery; instead, it is clearly the choice of brutes—not enlightened men privileged by education, religious discourse, and morally informed social engagement. Civilized men and women, Stowe asserts, do not resort to violence except in self-defense.

Confronting her own fears that slaves might eventually adopt the degenerate violence that both Pro-slavery and Free-State militiamen embraced in their fight to win Kansas, Stowe attempts to convince her readers that something must be done to end slavery before the Southern slaves embrace the brutal methods that the violent advocates of slavery had adopted on the frontier. Neither the real violence on the border nor the narratives of slave violence that Stowe knowingly evokes for her less-than informed readers are acceptable. She cannot embrace the "John Brown way" that Frederick Douglass celebrated in Boston almost four years after the publication of *Dred*, nor can she advocate the degenerate violence inherent in armed insurrection that Nat Turner modeled nearly thirty years before. To embrace violence, Stowe opined, was to embrace brutality. Certainly, it was not the choice of intelligent Americans. John Brown, and men like him on the fringes of civilization, brought Stowe to this realization. The "John Brown way" could not be the only way to reverse the inertia of slave power in America; however, as Stowe reluctantly recognized, it was both the most dramatic and the most likely way that slavery might be brought to an end in America.

Harriet Beecher Stowe did not approve of John Brown, but she did approve of his purpose. In a sense, John Brown tormented Stowe; he represented the violence that slavery inspired, but he also represented a conscious willingness to act against the moral wrong that Stowe had devoted herself to eradicating. He was noble, and he captured the attention of the nation in his devotion to a noble cause. John Brown radicalized Harriet Beecher Stowe; he inspired her to consider advocating violence; he also radicalized Henry Thoreau inspiring him to boldly confront vacillating abolitionists with their cowardly failure to acknowledge the value of John Brown's attack at Harper's Ferry; and he inspired Emerson to pointedly challenge the entire political system and demand the renunciation of the corrupt practices that resulted in what Theodore Parker appropriately termed the "national crisis" of 1859. He also compelled countless other contemporary literary figures to defy the inertia of condemnation that initially overwhelmed the nation when news of Brown's attack first escaped the remote town in West Virginia where Brown chose to begin his guerilla campaign. Henry Wadsworth Longfellow translated Brown into an American hero whose date of execution, the "Second of December, 1859 . . . [was] the date of the new Revolution: quite as much needed as the old one."[14] John Greenleaf Whittier celebrated Brown's visible martyrdom by translating a New York *Tribune* account of Brown's tender gesture toward a "negro child" whose "poor slave mother [Brown had] . . . striven to free" into a poetic tribute to the heroic abolitionist.[15] Herman Melville penned a tribute to the fearless abolitionist champion—the man he termed a "*meteor of war*," as did Walt Whitman, William Dean Howells, and Julia Maria Child.[16]

Many of these tributes to John Brown appear in *Echoes of Harper's Ferry*, the 1860 companion book to James Redpath's biography of Brown, *The Public Life of John Brown*. What distinguishes most of these tributes from Thoreau's "Plea for Captain John Brown," the title his John Brown lecture assumed when it appeared in Redpath's text, are the form, force, and direction of the work. Thoreau's lecture, much like Emerson later "Speech at a Meeting to Aid John Brown's Family," is an attempt to confront an errant citizenry with their moral complicity in the culture of compromise pervasive in America during the decades that preceded John Brown's attack on Harper's Ferry. Both Emerson and Thoreau confront their listeners with the example of John Brown—an idealist who "believed in his ideas to the extent that he put them into action" (119). Both addresses are also distinct petitions calling for individual social reform and moral courage in opposition to the cowardice displayed by public figures charged with guiding the nation toward its millennial destiny. And both Emerson and Thoreau implicitly confront their readers with the question, do you believe in any ideas to the point that you would risk all in order to attempt to put them into action?

Absolutely committed to translating his ideas into reality, John Brown was willing to die in order to demonstrate his belief that slavery was a "great wrong against God and humanity."[17] He was also willing to commit the lives of other men, some absolutely innocent of any wrong-doing, in order to advance his cause. At Harper's Ferry, Brown and his men killed five innocent men, wounded nine others, captured and held over forty hostages, terrorized what had been a peaceful civilian community, and inspired fear, anger, and chaos in the citizenry riotously attempting to understand and deal with the armed assault in their homeland. After his capture, Brown skillfully manipulated the press, offering himself as a both a victim of injustice and champion of the oppressed, in the process achieving both mythic and martyr status within a community ripe for violent social change.

Not unlike Osama bin Laden, the mastermind of the September 11 attacks on America, John Brown charismatically violated the sensibilities of mid-nineteenth century America in a dramatic raid on a prosperous nation divided by notions of individual liberty, personal rights, race, and morality. Like Brown, bin Laden achieved instant renown, immediately securing the enduring attention of the press, compelling both literary and public figures to boldly speak out on behalf of justice and oppression, and inspiring a sustained and violent war in the name of liberty. His method, although inconceivable in both its lethality and scope for his nineteenth century predecessor, dramatically changed the political environment of the United States accelerating the acceptance of limited but brutal violence as the appropriate solution to religiously supported differences in right living.

Like Brown's raid at Harper's Ferry, Osama bin Laden's raid was a paramilitary failure; even though it was devastating, it failed to immediately inspire a revolution of oppressed proselytes in either the world or in the United States. Consistently, the revolution that Brown envisioned would never come to pass. Brown did not escape the federal armory with wagon-loads of weapons and follow through with his plan to successively liberate all of the African-Americans kept in bondage in the Southern United States.[18] Except in the liberal adaptations abolitionists like Thomas Wentworth Higginson would construct as commanders of black units in the latter half of the Civil War, John Brown also failed to inspire a revolution in race relations between the blacks and whites.

Osama bin Laden, quite impressively, has succeeded in inspiring scores of new terrorists in various guerilla campaigns throughout the world in the wake of the airborne attacks on the World Trade Center and the Pentagon; perhaps more successful than Brown, bin Laden has also avoided both capture and extradition to face charges of murder in the United States.[19] However, neither his army of Al Qaeda freedom fighters nor his zealous fundamentalist supporters have escaped from the violent and determined response to his attacks on 9/11; many, like those of Brown's men who escaped the close quarters of the Armory Engine House, have been captured and now face the retributive justice that their enemies embrace. For them, universal *jihad* against the Western forces of oppression is a distant myth; perhaps, just as anti-abolitionists violently reacting against the radical abolitionist effort Brown embraced actually made Northern cities dangerous for free blacks in the aftermath of the raid and trial, bin Laden's efforts will be felt by militant fundamentalist Islamic forces only for a short period of time before there is a far more cataclysmic confrontation between nations so ideologically distinct.

What we have yet to determine is whether the myth which currently surrounds Osama bin Laden will inspire devotees to the kind of holy civil war that John Brown—and the literary figures who embraced his radical revolutionary notions—inspired in America. bin Laden has perhaps inspired University of Colorado Professor Ward Churchill to examine, just as Emerson did, the complicit role many empowered representative Americans may have played in the September eleventh bombings; like the "official gentlemen" that Emerson lambastes in his November 18, 1859 speech at the Tremont Temple, Churchill condemns the "technocratic corps at the very heart of the America's global financial empire" whom, he asserts, "willingly and knowingly" profited from the military campaign of oppression and genocide in Iraq.[20] They were complicit, Churchill maintains, in the deaths of 500,000 Iraqi children—what a former United Nations Assistant Secretary General termed a "systematic program . . . of deliberate genocide."[21] Churchill asserts that the men who flew the planes into the World Trade Center and the Pentagon on the eleventh of September were neither insane nor fanatics, both labels applied to John Brown and his men when American newspapermen attempted to understand why twenty-two men were willing to attack the federal armory at Harper's Ferry; instead, he claims that the men who piloted the planes were "desperate . . . secular activists," men inspired to sacrifice themselves by their desire to liberate those oppressed by the chains of a brutal United States policy of oppression. These radical activists could no more envision the possibility that peaceful protest to United States' engineered UN sanctions would result in abolition of harsh limits to their political, economic, and social liberty than John Brown's men could envision successful abolition of chattel slavery by adopting the rhetoric of moral suasion. The decade of oppression that followed the first United States first war in Iraq inspired the champions of Iraqi liberty to believe that there was no option, at least according to Churchill, but violent confrontation with the author of their subjugation.

Likewise, successive decades of oppression in America inspired select champions of abolition to believe that the time had arrived to leave the doctrine of peaceful non-resistance and embrace violence as the means of ending slavery in America; John Brown led the assault. Initially targeting a federal installation on October 16, 1859, Brown began a campaign to purge the nation of its immoral institution and herald the birth of a new government dedicated to the liberty of all people.[22] John Brown, a man we now recognize as nineteenth century terrorist, inspired the most notable literary figures of his day to forcefully engage their contemporaries in public discourse on the most contentious issue of the day—slavery. Frustrated by the failure of decades of Garrisonian rhetoric, Emerson and Thoreau rallied around the fiery Calvinist John Brown and celebrated his program of practical abolition.

Harriet Beecher Stowe, whose ambiguous abolitionist romance *The Minister's Wooing* had just been published in book form, paradoxically responded to news of Brown's "noble effort" with words of praise for the "witness slain in the great cause."[23] She had not been so adulatory in her second major textual effort to determine the appropriate abolitionist response to slavery in the United States. In fact, in *Dred*, she overtly rejects the violent methods that John Brown adopted in order to confront the advocates of slavery in Kansas. She subtly condemns Brown for his decision to conduct a brutal mid-night raid along the Pottawatomie Creek by suggesting the degree to which he compromised his accomplices in the murderous reprisal. Brutal violence, Stowe intimates, only begets more brutal violence; it does not inspire enlightened men and women to reject immoral institutions like slavery. Instead, it inspires depravity. This cannot be the recourse of good African-American men and women, nor can it be the choice of "brave, good" white men.

Yet Stowe makes John Brown a "brave, good man" in her New Years Day, 1860 *Independent* column.[24] Dead, John Brown embodied the will to act, not violently but righteously, in the cause of abolition. In Stowe's translation, John Brown "calmly gave his life up to a noble effort for human freedom and died in a way that is better than the most successful selfish life;" like Christ, Stowe suggests that he died to show others that human liberty belonged to all believing men and women.[25] John Brown, a man who literally translated himself from a wool merchant to an abolitionist hero, became an American martyr on 2 December, 1859. As Thoreau poetically mused,

> On the day of his translation, I heard, to be sure, that he was *hung*, but I did not know what it meant; I felt no sorrow on that account; but not for a day or two did I even *hear* that he was *dead*, and not after any number of days shall I believe it. Of all the men who were said to be my contemporaries, it seemed to me that John Brown was the only one who *had not died*. I never hear of a man named Brown now,—and I hear of them pretty often,—I never hear of any particularly brave and earnest man, but my first thought is of John Brown, and what relation he may be to him. He is more alive than ever he was. He has earned immortality. He is not confined to North Elba nor to Kansas. He is no longer working in secret. He works in public, and in the clearest light that shines on this land.[26]

Despite Thoreau's eloquent assertion of John Brown's ascension to abolitionist sainthood, his commitment to the liberation of African-Americans was neither universally recognized by his contemporaries nor validated by scores of successive literary historians. In fact, Thoreau's characterization of John Brown as a "simple," "straightforward," "principled" idealist perfectly willing to act upon his convictions, has been repeatedly deconstructed by pragmatic critics attempting to understand why intelligent men and women respond so enthusiastically to militants who commit extreme acts of violence in order to advance a cause.[27] They have shown that John Brown was anything but simple. Insightful, intelligent, manipulative, and extremely charismatic, John Brown was able to inspire some of the most enlightened men and women in his society to express their approval of dramatic and arbitrary violence in the name of morally justified social change. Extreme acts of arbitrary violence are justifiable, according to both Brown and his celebrants, if its authors can convincingly articulate their dedication to an unassailable principle—the principle of justice for all men.

John Brown maintained that he initiated the attack on Harper's Ferry because he was firmly committed to eradicating the injustice inherent in the American system of slavery. It was "perfectly right [,Brown asserted,] for any one to interfere [with the celebrants of slavery in order] to free those . . . wickedly h[e]ld in bondage."[28] Committed to a higher law, John Brown and his literary celebrants justified the violent attack on Harper's Ferry as the perfect right of morally informed men outraged by the injustice pervasive in their society. Interestingly, Osama bin Laden suggested that the attacks on September eleventh were inspired by his own unswerving commitment to the universal principle of justice and his absolute dedication to higher law.[29] It will be interesting to see, if we can accept a rather loose adaptation of transcendentalist rhetoric, if Ward Churchill chooses to embrace the eloquent prose of either Thoreau or Emerson and defend the actions of the living Islamic martyr as the justifiable response of an idealist acting to herald the end of oppression in the Muslim world. Either way, in all probability, we can expect to hear from Osama bin Laden again. Like John Brown, "[he] is more alive [now] than he ever was. He has earned [a kind of] immortality. He is not confined to . . . [Afghanistan] nor to . . . [Somalia]."[30] He is larger than life, and he clearly exists in the mind of every attentive American in this land.

It will also be interesting to see if any of his celebrants suggest that he will "make the gallows glorious" should he end up trapped in some remote metaphorical Engine House during his next dramatic attempt to end the oppression he believes that the United States embraces in its engagement with the Arab world.[31]

2 John Brown
"A Muse of Fire"

O for a Muse of fire, that would ascend
The Brightest heaven of invention,
A kingdom for a stage, princes to act,
And monarchs to behold the swelling scene!
Then should the warlike Harry, like himself,
Assume the port of Mars, and at his heels,
Leash'd in like hounds, should famine, sword, and fire
Crouch for employment. But Pardon, gentles all,
The flat and unraised spirits that hath dar'd
On this unworthy scaffold to bring forth
So great an object.[1]

Shakespeare, *Henry V*

On May 22, 1856, John Brown decided to "strike terror in the hearts of the Pro-Slavery people" of Kansas.[2] Enlisting the aid of seven hand-picked men, four of whom were related to him by blood, Brown proceeded to Pottawatomie Creek to see a bit of "radical retaliatory" justice done.[3] In the killing spree that followed, Brown and his men brutally hacked five men to death with their razor sharp broadswords. At the time of the murders, Brown had been in Kansas for only seven months, having made the arduous journey from his home in North Elba, New York during October of the previous year. He came to Kansas to join five of his sons who had been lured there by "glowing accounts of extraordinary fertility, healthfulness and beauty of the territory."[4] The promotional literature of Ohio's emigrant aid societies suggested that the territory would be a paradise for Eastern settlers if "honest, free-soil men could keep it from the grasp of the South."[5] Intrigued by the opportunity to both aid his sons in their claims of good land and advance the Free-Soil cause, Brown arrived in Kansas mentally prepared for armed conflict.[6]

Brown's sons had primed their father for the atmosphere he would encounter when he arrived in Kansas. In letters depicting the conditions they discovered following their own arrival five months before, Brown's sons informed their father of the atmosphere of oppression that Free Soil settlers endured when attempting to establish a home in the territory. Not only were there "Annoyance Associations" of Missourians living along the border who had organized to terrorize Free-State settlements in Kansas, there were "hundreds and thousands of the meanest and most desperate men, armed to the teeth with Revolvers, Bowie Knives, Rifles & Canon . . . under the pay from Slave-holders" ready to descend upon Free Soil Settlers on a moments notice.[7] The result, Brown's son John Jr. asserted, was that the "people . . . [in Kansas] exhibit the most abject and cowardly spirit, whenever their dearest rights are invaded and trampled down by lawless bands of Miscreants which Missouri has ready at a moments call to pour in upon them."[8]

Missouri, John Jr. was quick to point out, was not the only state commit-ted to terrorizing the Free Soil settlers in the territory; "[e]very Slaveholding State from Virginia to Texas is furnishing money to fasten Slavery upon this glorious land."[9] Petitioning his father to proceed at once to Kansas armed with "Colt's large size Revolver[s]," "*Minnie rifle*[s]," and "heavy Bowie Kni[ves]," which he claimed, free state settlers in Kansas needed "more than they do bread," John Brown Jr. emphasized the willingness of Free State setters to resist if they had the means. Referring to a petition recently sent to Congress, John Jr. connected the fight for liberty of those enslaved for generations by their Southern masters with his own fight for economic and political liberty: he suggests that "it is no longer [simply] a question of Negro slavery, but it is the enslavement of ourselves."[10]

Outraged by the reports of vigilante tactics that Pro-Slavery advocates felt at liberty to visit upon his sons and indignant at the apparent want of fortitude among the settlers, John Brown put aside all other business, to include settling the remainder of his large family at their new home in New York, and "resolved to proceed at once to Kansas."[11] In order to secure enough money to arrive in Kansas with the supplies necessary to the defense of the Free State settlers, Brown resolved to petition the anti-slavery community for funding so that he might be able to arrive in Kansas with arms sufficient to allow his sons and their Free Soil neighbors the means to defend themselves. In late June, he made his first appeal to the "Radical Political Abolitionists" at their conference in Syracuse. Although he believed that the forum would be receptive to his appeal, Brown's petition for funds was not well received. The attendees were far more concerned with devel-oping strategies to empower black men and women to resist agents of the government in their effort to enforce the Fugitive Slave Law than with the armed self-defense of Free Soil settlers in remote Kansas. Only two of the principle speakers—Frederick Douglass and Gerrit Smith—were willing to offer support for the program Brown proposed.[12] Others—Lewis Tappan and Samuel J. May—expressed distinct reluctance to fund Brown. They were not prepared to commit to the kind of violent program of defense that he advocated. However, in spite of the overall disapproval of the tactics he embraced, Brown succeeded in Syracuse leaving the city with $60 for arms and ammunition as a result of his passionate plea.

Undaunted by the relatively poor demonstration of support he was able to inspire in New York, Brown continued to petition for contributions dur-ing his journey West. In Akron, Ohio, he successfully appealed to his former neighbors by describing the desperate conditions in Kansas and appealing for contributions for its defense. Eager to support Brown and arm the Free Soil settlers they believed were vulnerable to the vigilante rampages of the Pro-Slavery Border Ruffians, the residents of Akron formed committees of aid and contributed several cases of guns, powder, caps, broadswords, clothing, and money to the future guerilla leader.[13]

As he approached Kansas, Brown's efforts to amass a supply of arms for the defense of Free-Soil settlers in Kansas seemed not only prudent but absolutely necessary. In his autobiographical sketch of his journey to Kansas, Brown recalls "companies of armed men, and individuals [who] were constantly passing and repassing Kansaswise [sic] continually boasting of what deeds of patriotism; & chivalry they had performed in Kansas."[14] Observing those whom he would soon recognize as "Border Ruffians" and hearing of "their cruel treading down & terrifying of defenseless Free State men," Brown felt both righteous and vindicated in the militant posture he had embraced while journeying West.[15]

Arriving at Brown's Station, the collection of claims that his sons had established west of Ossawatomie on the seventh of October, Brown discovered that the Border Ruffians were not the only threat to his sons' prosperity in the territory. Ill with malaria, demoralized, and suffering from extreme cold in makeshift tents, four of Brown's five sons had learned that the climate in Kansas could be just as hostile as the Border Ruffians.[16] Not withstanding their condition, after unloading his supplies, to include the weapons that he had gathered during his journey, Brown thoroughly interrogated his sons about the conditions in Kansas. Not only did he discover that there were both Pro-Slavery and Free State settlers in the area immediate to his son's claims, he learned that there was a great deal of difference in the perspectives of their new neighbors. Some, like brothers William and Dutch Henry Sherman believed in slavery and routinely provided shelter to Missouri Border Ruffians in their crude tavern on the Pottawatomie. Others, like recent arrival Theodore Weiner and James Townsley, were proclaimed Free-State men; however, their crude behavior barely distinguished them from their Pro-Slavery neighbors. Both were men known for their "bloodthirsty" temperaments and violent inclinations.[17] These were not, according to Brown's sons, Salmon, Frederick, Jason, Owen, and John Jr., the only frequent visitors they enjoyed. They told their father that they were also visited by marauding Missourians to whom they boldly admitted both their Free-State and abolitionist sympathies.[18] This, of course, set the Browns apart from the majority of their neighbors who were either Pro-Slavery or Free-State settlers, the majority of the latter objecting to slavery but also objecting to the idea of allowing free negroes as settlers in the territory.[19]

From his initial conversations with his sons, John Brown learned that in three days, there was going to be an election for delegates to the Free-State Constitutional Convention scheduled to be held in Topeka. Excited by the prospect and anticipating the presence of disruptive and well-armed Missourians, Brown and his sons went "powerfully armed" to the Pottawatomie precinct to both assert their own civil rights and defend those of their free-state neighbors.[20] Despite their history of overwhelming every Kansas voting precinct with armed citizens, stuffing ballot boxes, and expelling Northern election officials, no Border Ruffians showed on the ninth of October in Pottawatomie.[21] Assuming some personal responsibility for the peacefulness at the polls, John Brown declared that Kansas's prospects were "brightening every day."[22]

This was not the first time that Brown had militantly exerted himself to protect an oppressed segment of the population, nor was it the first time that he advocated armed resistance in response to those he considered tyranous and immoral. He had first demonstrated his willingness to embrace violent confrontation six years before while living in Springfield, Ohio. Incensed by the enactment of the Fugitive Slave Law in 1850, Brown helped organize the local black community into a defensive league dedicated to foiling the efforts of slave catchers in the conduct of their business. Aided by leaders of the Zion Methodist or "Free Church," so-called because of its commitment to black leadership and its strong anti-slavery sentiment, Brown organized the local black population into a small defensive army dedicated to fighting the efforts of any slave-catchers who might pursue their business in Springfield. The "United States League of Gileadites," Brown directed, would go about their daily business prepared for confrontation at any moment. According to their constitution, which Brown authored, Gileadites achieved strength through unity; therefore, "at first threat" by either fugitive hunters or marshals, members were encouraged "to attack [en masse], making 'clean work'" of their immoral opponents.[23] Recognizing that federal marshals and slave-catchers would not anticipate armed opposition, Brown encouraged every Gileadite to go armed in public, though he thought it best that each man and woman conceal his or her weapon in order to avoid attention.[24] Commitment to immediate opposition, Brown assured his black neighbors, would both surprise their enemies and discourage their zealous pursuit of the repugnant Fugitive Slave Law. Building upon his belief that blacks could terrorize both the white population and the political order by violently opposing agents of the law, Brown also encouraged Gileadites to disrupt fugitive slave trials in order to save their brethren from the execution of immoral legal procedures.[25] Not only did he advocate the use of small bombs in the conduct of these attacks, Brown specifically counseled selectively killing agents of the government in the conduct of their immoral business in order to both dissuade similar efforts and deny the authority of a government committed to injustice.[26]

Although there is no record that any of the Gileadites ever acted upon any of the prescriptions embedded in their constitution, the forty-four men and women who signed the Gileadite charter made a clear choice to embrace both Brown and violence when they committed to the organization.

Unwittingly, they also inspired Brown to become both a leader and an architect of an organization established to oppose the existing government. Brown's position as revolutionary leader recognized and respected by a community of oppressed blacks and validated by representatives of the New England intelligentsia was firmly established in 1851 when, at his invitation, Massachusetts Senator and abolitionist Charles Sumner agreed to address the organization.[27] After decades of business failure, it may have appeared to Brown that the business of a revolutionary leader was one to which he was particularly suited.[28]

There is little doubt that the experience in Springfield inspired a more formidable desire to lead an organization in armed opposition to the government in power. In his revolutionary role, Brown tellingly expressed some of the operational methods that he would embrace both in Kansas and in Virginia. Embracing terror as a strategic tool, Brown committed to dramatic violence in Springfield in order to both inspire widespread fear in a populous accustomed to silent acquiescence to their government's exertions and to draw attention to those marginalized by blind acceptance of the exclusive right of a singular power structure. Demonstrating an understanding of the deterrent value of violent acts of defiance—and a more insightful understanding of their inspirational value to an entire community—Brown hoped that he had not only established a single revolutionary cell committed to violent defiance of the law, but the nucleus of an entire Gileadite movement that would proliferate throughout the North.[29] In Springfield, therefore, Brown established himself as a militant revolutionary leader committed to the efficacy of both violence and terror in the fight for recognition of the rights of the oppressed. Although the Gileadites did not proliferate as he had hoped, they did metastasize—in Brown's mind—and gradually overwhelm his entire consciousness as the conceptual means by which he would attack the corrupt arm of the government. Envisioning himself as a revolutionary leader in the fight against the oppressive mechanisms of the slave power, John Brown came to believe that he had a unique ability to plan, organize, and direct the efforts of a disempowered minority in the violent assertion of their right to liberty.

The Free Soil settlers that Brown's sons met when they arrived in Kansas were definitely a disempowered political minority. Although eastern emigration societies had been successful in establishing a steady flow of settlers into the contested territory by 1855, Pro-Slavery voters still vastly outnumbered Free-Soilers at the elections for the first Territorial Legislature in March. As a result, they overwhelmingly defeated the Free Soil settlers and held every seat in the territorial Legislature in Pawnee that Spring.[30] Meeting in Pawnee in July, the Pro-Slavery legislature decided to move their session to Shawnee Mission, a site more conducive to Pro-Slavery legislation since it is nearly in Missouri, the home of many particularly energetic Pro-Slavery activists and the source of the legal statutes that would become the general law of the territory.[31] According to the modified statutes that the Pro-Slavery Kansan's adopted, it soon became illegal for anyone but Pro-Slavery men to hold office, and "only those who recognized the right of slavery could sit on juries;" further, anyone who contested the rights of slave owners or "circulated abolitionist literature" was subject to five years imprisonment at hard labor; anyone aiding a fugitive slave was subject to ten years in prison, and anyone who incited a slave insurrection was destined, by law, to hang.[32]

Indignant over the blatant contempt for the election process and appalled by the subsequent adoption of Missouri's odious Pro-Slavery statutes, Free Soil settlers responded by calling for a series of conventions to both denounce the Shawnee legislature and organize a Free State party. During the first of the five conventions conducted in Lawrence, Free State leaders proclaimed the laws and statutes adopted by the Pawnee legislature invalid, and members of the convention "resolv[ed] that they were bound by no laws whatsoever of its creation."[33]

In subsequent meetings, however, Free State representatives were neither as daring nor as righteous as they were in their first indignant response. Instead of adopting a position that allowed both white and free black settlers in the territory, they adopted a position that reflected the will of the majority of their constituents proposing the adoption of "stringent laws excluding all negroes, bond and free from the Territory."[34] Additionally, the Free State delegates embraced a platform that consented to "any fair and reasonable provision in regard to slaves already in the territory."[35] Attempting to clarify these apparently contradictory positions, Free State party delegates distanced themselves from abolitionists declaring "the stale and ridiculous charge of Abolitionism so industriously imputed to the Free State party . . . is without a shadow of truth to support it."[36] In a clear compromise to maintain cohesion among the Free-State opposition, Free State delegates adopted the position that would establish Kansas as a free white state, not a free state.

Despite the concessions that the Free State delegates made during their last convention, John Brown Jr., a member of the "Territorial Executive Committee," returned from the final Free State convention in Big Springs excited by the prospect that the 9 October Free State elections presented.[37] Confident in the Free State repudiation of the laws adopted by the Pawnee legislature, John Jr. even challenged one of the most offensive of the statutes by boldly proclaiming that "no man had a right to hold a slave in Kansas" to a Pro-Slavery man at Pottawattamie on 14 September.[38]

With his son subject to both arrest and five years hard labor for voicing an opinion contrary to the law, John Brown boldly positioned himself as an opponent to the empowered Pro-Slavery government when he accompanied his sons to the Pottawatomie precinct on 9 October. Armed and prepared to resist any attempts to either arrest his son or violate the Free State polls, Brown was disappointed by the quiet at Pottawatomie. However, he would not remain disappointed for long. Following the publication of the election results, Free State delegates assembled in Topeka on 23 October to draft a constitution, which they intended to submit for popular vote on December 15, 1855.

Aware that their ideological rivals had established a second government in the territory, elected their own congressional representative, and drafted a constitution, which they intended to submit for popular ratification in December, Pro-Slavery leaders began to become concerned about their here-to-fore uncontested authority over the territory. Ably led by Pro-Slavery Governor Wilson Shannon (an appointee of President Franklin Pierce), Pro-Slavery leaders responded to the Topeka Convention by establishing the "Law and Order Party" and announcing a constitutional convention of their own. With the political situation degrading and tensions between the rivals increasing, armed conflict seemed inevitable.

The murder of a Free State man south of Lawrence in late November provided the spark necessary to bring the ideological opponents to battle. Responding to the failure of local Pro-Slavery law officials to arrest the murderer, Jacob Branson (the murdered man's land-lord) called a protest meeting in Lawrence; County Sheriff Samuel J. Jones promptly and paradoxically arrested Branson for disturbing the peace. Outraged by the Pro-Slavery sheriff's actions, local citizens from Lawrence demonstrated their refusal to recognize the authority of the Pro-Slavery law by capturing both the sheriff and his posse and liberating Branson. Indignant over the affront, Jones called on "border Missouri for help and notified Governor Shannon of the 'open rebellion against the laws of the Territory.'"[39] Shannon responded by ordering the newly appointed Adjutant General of the militia to raise as many men as he could and assemble them in LeCompton, two miles from Lawrence. Meanwhile, Governor Atchison of Missouri, and several other Missouri border captains, began to raise their own forces, which they subsequently led toward Lawrence on December 6, 1855. They encamped along the Wakurusa River, just south of the bastion of Free State Power in Kansas—Lawrence.

Incensed at the news of the invasion and reports that drunken Border Ruffians had vowed to "exterminate the abolitionist 'outlaws of Douglas County,'" John Brown gathered his four healthy sons and prepared for combat.[40] Arriving in Lawrence on the seventh of December, he found a town transformed for battle. According to Brown, over five hundred Free State men had been "busy fortifying the Town with Embankments; & circular Earthworks."[41] Reporting to the nominal heads of the Committee of Public Safety, Charles Robinson and James Lane, Brown offered his services and was at once commissioned a captain in the First Brigade of the Kansas Volunteers, his company of twenty men designated the Liberty Guards.

Despite their newfound status and their eagerness to enter into a fight with the Missourians, the Liberty Guards found no outlet for their enthusiasm in the beleaguered city. Intent upon avoiding bloodshed, Robinson and Lane focused their attentions upon negotiating a peaceful settlement to the situation rather than upon the tactical opportunities that their now fortified town offered them. Quite to his chagrin, John Brown and his men were not able to fire a shot.

When the peace treaty was announced, John Brown had been in Lawrence for less than forty-eight hours: yet during that time, he established himself as a leader of men willing to commit to battle against Pro-Slavery forces in Kansas. Not only had he openly defied Pro-Slavery forces by overtly passing through their ranks during his march to Lawrence, he had achieved momentary prominence by publicly advocating offensive action— a surprise attack under cover of darkness—against the assembled, though disorderly, Missourians.[42] He had been empowered by an official commission and authorized by the Governor to use force should armed Missourians again invade the territory; as a result, Brown's role as militant champion of the oppressed was guaranteed.[43]

Upon his return to Brown's Station, the new captain of the Liberty Guards was enthusiastic about his experiences in Lawrence lauding the performance of the Free State forces who had responded to the call of freedom.[44] Anticipating the ratification of the Free State Constitution on 15 December, Brown confidently suggested that "the Territory is now entirely in the power of Free State men."[45] However, the relative calm that followed the end of what became known as the Wakarusa War did not long last. Reports of violence at the Free State polls in Leavenworth ignited the tension that had seemingly been diffused in Lawrence. In the tense atmosphere in Leavenworth, a Pro-Slavery man was killed and two others injured. Once again, the vitriolic Pro-Slavery press demanded war.[46] News of the violence even reached Washington, and President Franklin Pierce, a Pro-Slavery advocate, openly blamed the unrest in Kansas on the emigrant aid societies of the East warning that organized resistance by Free State settlers to the Pro-Slavery government would be "regarded as treasonable insurrection."[47] Writing his wife in late February, John Brown acknowledged Pierce's overt support for the Free State opponents by remarking, "[w]e hear that Franklin Pierce means to crush the men of Kansas. . . . I do not know how well he may succeed; I think that he may have his hands full before it is over."[48]

When federal troops arrived in Pottawatomie in late February, John Brown did not display the same confident defiance that he had in his 1855 letter to his wife. In fact, the troops greatly concerned the militia captain since their arrival indicated that the collusion of the federal government with its Pro-Slavery territorial counterpart was not all political rhetoric. More ominous than the soldiers ostensibly sent into the area to remove "*intruders* from certain Indian lands," however, was the announcement of the immanent arrival of both a tax collector and a Pro-Slavery magistrate in April.[49] Anticipating that the circuit court judge might attempt to enforce

Pro-Slavery laws and that the tax assessor might try to collect funds supporting the Pro-Slavery government, Brown angrily joined fellow settlers at a meeting called by local men to determine what they ought to do on 16 April. Rising to address the group of settlers, John Brown declared that as an abolitionist, he "would rather see the union drenched in blood than pay taxes to a pro-slavery government;" additionally, he swore to kill any officer of the government—territorial or United States—who attempted to make him obey Pro-Slavery laws. [50]

On 21 April, when Pro-Slavery Judge Sterling G. Cato opened the district court, Brown consistently proceeded to challenge the authority of the court that had indicted several Free-State men in Pottawatomie. In the company of the unarmed Pottawatomie Rifles—John Brown Jr.'s company of free-state militia—Brown walked to Dutch Henry's tavern and informed Cato that the local Free State settlers did not consider the Pro-Slavery laws valid, therefore would resist all decisions of the court. [51] He also presented Cato with a letter containing the defiant resolutions to which he and his neighbors had agreed five days before. [52] Evidently non-pulsed by Brown's resolution but unwilling to test Brown's will in Pottawatomie during this session of his court, Cato left Pottawatomie that day without confronting any of those who had signed the treasonous resolution.

Confrontation, however, was not long in coming. On 23 April, Sheriff Jones, the same man who had been at the center of the uprising that had resulted in the invasion of Lawrence in November, was shot outside of Lawrence as he and a posse of U.S. troops arrested six Free-State citizens for "contempt of court." [53] Once again, Pro-Slavery newspapers loudly proclaimed war upon the abolitionists, and leaders of militia units in Missouri began mobilizing their forces along the border. [54] In the tense atmosphere that followed, two Free State men were murdered. To add to the atmosphere of indignation that the Free State settlers felt when they learned of the abuse of their fellow citizens, militia units from Alabama and Georgia began to arrive in Kansas, one encamping along the Pottawattamie Creek—right in Brown's extended back yard. [55]

If that were not enough, Pro-Slavery Judge S. D. Lecompte chose to flex his legal muscle by directing a grand jury in session at LeCompton to indict all members of the Free State government for "high treason" since all "laws passed by the Shawnee Legislature were of United States authority." [56] Further charging the already volatile atmosphere, Federal Marshall J.B. Donaldson asserted that unruly citizens in Lawrence had obstructed a deputy marshal while he was serving summons on several Free State settlers in that city. Calling for a posse of law-abiding citizens to enforce the law, Donaldson set the stage for the second invasion of the Free State enclave.

Responding to Donaldson's command, companies of militiamen from border towns in Missouri streamed across the Missouri River in anticipation of the opportunity to "exterminate the 'freedom shriekers'" in Lawrence. [57] Joined by John Buford's Georgia and Alabama militiamen, they formed a formidable force; Buford commanded four hundred militiamen and David Rice Atchison held sway over seven hundred-fifty.[58] On 21 May, in an atmosphere of increasing lawlessness and civil unrest, this unopposed force sacked Lawrence, a free-state enclave—"looting stores, destroying the printing presses, and setting fire to the Free-State Hotel."[59]

John Brown was indignant. Responding to information that the Missourians and Southern militiamen now occupied Lawrence, Brown join the assembled the Pottawatomie Rifles anticipating that he would once again reinforce Free State forces in the fight against the marauding Pro-Slavery ruffians. However, before they were able to get more than five miles from his sons' claims, Brown received word that U.S. troops from Fort Leavenworth had taken charge of the town; he also learned that they were allowing Pro-Slavery Missourians to depart without charging them with any violations of the law. If this were not enough, Brown then heard that Senator Preston Brooks of South Carolina had brutally caned Massachusetts Senator Charles Sumner on the floor of the United States Senate.[60] Incensed, Brown determined to show both the Pro-Slavery vigilantes and the federal authorities who supported them that abolitionists and Free-State men would not stand idly by while their rights were abused.

Determining, "[s]omething must be done to show these barbarians that we, too, have rights," Brown assembled seven volunteers for a secret mission.[61] Brown informed his men that he was going back to Pottawattamie to "break up Cato's court and get away with some of his vile emissaries."[62] After ordering his men to prepare their weapons, to include putting a fine edge on their heavy broadswords, Brown conferred with H.H. Williams, who lived along the Pottawatomie Creek, and identified the "slave hounds" who would feel the righteous anger of the Free-State militia who had been too late to defend Lawrence.[63] Departing the camp with James Townsley (who, according to John Brown's son Salmon, had volunteered "in high glee" to "haul all [of] our crowd back in his lumber wagon"), John Brown led his men to a copse of trees and subsequently revealed the entirety of his plan to "sweep the creek . . . of all the proslavery men." All were not enthusiastic.[64] Brown spent the rest of that night and much of the next day attempting to convince his men that this kind of bloody reprisal was the only option that they had. According to Townsley, Brown proclaimed that it was time "to strike terror in the hearts of the Pro-Slavery people," explaining that it was "better that a score of bad men should die than one man who came here to make Kansas a Free State should be driven out."[65] He was successful.

As night fell on the evening of 24 May, Brown and his men descended upon the quiet cabins on the Pottawatomie and began to "regulate matters."[66] Committed to the notion that it was time to "strike terror in the hearts of the proslavery people," Brown and his volunteers made their way toward the first of his retaliatory targets, J. H. Menting. However, when they approached his cabin, they clearly heard the sound of a rifle being pushed through the space between the logs in the cabin wall and scattered.[67] After regrouping, they proceeded to the cabin of James Doyle, a relatively recent arrival from Tennessee. Knocking on Doyles' cabin door at about eleven o'clock, Brown inquired if the unwitting respondent could provide him directions to the Wilkinson's. When James Doyle obligingly opened the door, John Brown forced his way into the cabin demanding that Doyle and his sons surrender. Salmon Brown later recalled that Mahala Doyle began "raving at her men" insisting that she had told them what would occur if they continued "along the course they had been taking."[68] Evidently recognizing the fate that her husband and his elder sons were facing, Mrs. Doyle then tearfully appealed to Brown to spare her fourteen year old son. Respecting Mrs. Doyle's emotional appeal, Brown decided to call out only "old man Doyle" and two of his elder sons from the house. Brown's men took them a short distance from the house, whereupon they fell upon the Doyles killing the three men and leaving their bodies where they fell.

According to Townsley's account, John Brown shot James Doyle in the forehead, and his youngest sons killed Doyle's sons, William and Drury, by hacking them to death with their "short two-edged swords."[69] After completing their grizzly task, Brown and his murderous entourage proceeded down Musquito Creek, a tributary of the Pottawatomie, to the house of Allen Wilkinson. Informing him that they would break into his cabin if he did not open the door, they forced Wilkinson to leave his wife and children, marched him some distance from the house and killed him with several blows of their broadswords.[70] They then crossed the Pottawatomie arriving at the cabin James Harris rented from Henry Sherman. After ransacking the house and taking two rifles and a bowie knife that they found there, Brown and his "northern army" compatriots proceeded to successively interrogate the four men whom they had discovered sleeping peacefully in the one room cabin. According to James Harris, William Sherman was the third man that Brown and his men called outside during the course of their interrogation.[71] Fifteen minutes later, Harris heard a cap burst and the men who had accompanied Brown departed the cabin. The next morning, when he looked for Sherman, he discovered the man's dismembered corpse in the creek.[72]

The next night, when Brown and his "northern army" joined John Jr.'s Pottawatomie Rifles, they found that the news of their midnight murders had already reached the free-state militiamen.[73] The men in John Jr.'s company were convinced that the report they had received was true when they saw several horses that they recognized as property of those reported to have been slain the night before. John Brown and his men must have murdered five men on the Pottawatomie, just as they had heard. Confronting his father, Jason Brown demanded to know if the old man had had a role in the murders. Brown pointedly informed him, "I did not do it, but I approved it."[74] According to Jason, John Brown later asserted, "God is my judge . . . It was absolutely necessary as a measure of self-defense, and the defense of others."[75]

Brown's prescience was not universally acknowledged among his neighbors in Kansas. When Owen Brown approached his uncle's cabin at Brown's station seeking shelter shortly after the murders, the Reverend Samuel Adair told him to get away; "[y]ou are a vile murderer, a marked man!"[76] Others in Ossawatomie were similarly appalled by Brown's actions. Three days after the murders, they held a public meeting to address the "outrage of the darkest and foulest nature" pledging that they would oppose similar actions and hand over "to the criminal authorities the perpetrators for punishment."[77] On 27 May, 1856, reports of the murders of "eight Pro-Slavery men" appeared in the Westport *Border Times*. Soon thereafter, newspapers throughout Missouri were carrying reports of the Pottawatomie murders.

Calls for war, vigilante justice, and retaliatory murder dominated the press.[78] Remarking on the "extraordinary state of excitement" that descended upon Kansas, Governor Shannon expressed great fear for the territory in his letter to President Pierce.[79] Rumors that "Buford's Southerners were going to kill every free-state settler in the Ossawatomie-Pottawatomie area" permeated Southeastern Kansas creating an atmosphere of terror and indignation.[80] Alarmed by the murders, both Free State and Pro-Slavery forces were in arms. In the Leavenworth *Herald*, Pro-Slavery authors proclaimed war on abolitionists demanding that "the knives of the Pro-Slavery men [not] be sheathed while there is one Abolitionist in the Territory."[81] In an effort to avoid all out war, Governor Shannon sent a company of Regular Army soldiers to Ossawatomie and requested immediate reinforcements from the commander of Fort Leavenworth.

When the federal troops arrived in Ossawatomie, they discovered that eager militia units from Missouri were much swifter to respond than they were. Alarmed by news of the murders, militia companies from Missouri entered the territory and proceeded at once toward Ossawatomie. By this time, witnesses to Brown's brutal murders had identified the old man, his four sons (Frederick, Salmon, Oliver and Owen), Thomas, Townsley, and Weiner as the authors of the massacre. On 28 May, therefore, Judge Cato issued warrants for the arrest of each of the men that had taken part in the murders. Two days later, deputy marshals proceeded toward Brown Station with a warrant to arrest a total of ten men. In the hunt for the killers that ensued, John Jr., Jason, H.H. Williams, and four others were captured, chained "like a gang of slaves" and forced to march twenty-five miles a day until they reached the jail at Tecumseh.[82] Although the others were released after examination, John Jr. and Williams remained in custody for nearly three months before being released.

John Brown, surprisingly, escaped capture, and, after a period of hiding, commenced a guerilla war against the increasingly zealous and violent roving bands of Pro-Slavery militia. During the next five months, Brown played what he imagined to be a critical role in the increasingly violent war that erupted in Eastern Kansas. Using the horses and equipment that he captured from his Pro-Slavery enemies, Brown engaged in skirmishes with various Pro-Slavery guerilla units around Ossawatomie reporting his victories to the Eastern press as remarkable tributes to his military skill.[83]

Brown's accounts were understandably not objective. In his narrative of the battle of Black Jack, printed in the July 11 New York *Tribune*, Brown regales his readers with a tale of bravery and tactical skill that highlighted his own role in the battle, glossing over the fact that he achieved success at Black Jack by exploiting his enemy's confidence under a flag of truce.[84] In another self-proclaimed victory, Brown informed eager readers of his singular bravery and remarkable leadership during the battle of Ossawatomie—where he fended off an attack of over four hundred Pro-Slavery men with a force never numbering more than thirty; noting that he was slightly wounded during the fight at Ossawatomie, Brown remarks that his band "killed & wounded from 70 to 80 of the enemy" suffering only one killed (his son Frederick) and two or three wounded.[85] He did not mention that in the meantime, he stole cattle, looted Pro-Slavery stores, and freely disposed of captured horses and equipment to support his roving band of guerillas.[86]

Eastern audiences eagerly followed news of the war in Kansas. Accounts of the battles varied widely depending on the perspective of the respective authors. In the New York Daily *Times*, Captain Pate's account of his capture at Black Jack Point was second page news on 17 June. Narrating the story of his capture, Pate remarks that he "fell into the hands of the very party of assassins whom [he and his men] were in search of;" he was *"taken prisoner under a flag of truce, a barbarity unlooked for in this country and unheard of in the annals of honorable warfare."*[87] Not only did Pate assert that "BROWN had violated the most sacred rules of warfare," he forcefully concludes his account of the battle by exposing John "BROWN and his confederates [as the] . . . men [who] were engaged in the Pottawatomie massacre."[88]

However, Pate's recognition of Brown's complicity in the murders on 24 May does not seem to have impressed many Eastern readers; in fact, there is very little evidence to suggest that any of the members of the Eastern intelligentsia that Brown subsequently met, courted, and—some claim—manipulated during his 1857 fund-raising campaign had any intimation that they were entertaining the attentions of either a murderer or what we might now term a terrorist. Although Brown's ruthlessness seems to have been well-recognized in Kansas, most of his unsavory guerilla activity seems to have been ignored by the Eastern press. Many of those who read newspaper reports in the East seem to have been completely willing to accept sanitized versions of Brown's exploits, since a noble, courageous, altruistic, and principled champion was far more appealing than one who was ruthless, fanatical, and deceitful. Committed to radical change and responding to the charismatic abolitionist guerilla leader, prominent intellectuals and social reformers in New England did not acknowledge any consciousness that Brown was anything but a noble hero committed to the cause of liberty in Kansas.

When he came East to raise funds for the force that would continue to defend the rights of Free State settlers in the winter of 1857, they did not note any awareness of his activities on the Pottawatomie in May.[89] This is a bit surprising, given the fact that ever since Congress had approved the 1854 Kansas-Nebraska Act stipulating that the settlers in the territories of Kansas and Nebraska would determine by "popular sovereignty" whether their territory entered the union as a slave or free state, prominent citizens throughout New England had eagerly attended to news from the West. Charles Edward Stowe recalled that his famous mother "kept herself informed of the minutest details of the struggle" believing that the events in Kansas indicated a "desperate crisis in the nation's history."[90] Ellen Emerson remarked that "Kanzas [sic] is all the interest out of doors now."[91] She later recalled her family's excitement when Franklin Sanborn would drop by to discuss Kansas, noting that he knew "everything about Kansas" and "tells all to father."[92] In his excellent biography of Emerson, Len Gougeon notes that Emerson was particularly attentive to the events in Kansas, frequently visiting his abolitionist friend, George Luther Stearns, to learn first hand details of the events in Kansas.[93] Stearns, chairman of the Massachusetts State Kansas Committee, was often the first to learn of developments in Kansas.

Franklin Sanborn, as committee secretary, was just as informed as Stearns and just as informative in Concord circles. In July, 1856, Sanborn, then secretary for the Middlesex County Kansas Committee, even took an investigatory journey to Kansas to assess the needs of the Massachusetts citizens emigrating to the troubled territory.[94] Although he never actually entered Kansas, Sanborn returned to Concord proclaiming that the contested territory was the "most practical form in which the struggle for freedom has ever presented itself."[95]

Emerson and Sanborn were not the only citizens of Concord keenly interested in the developments in Kansas. As Henry Thoreau reveals in his 1856 journal, he too was very much concerned by what was happening in the territory:

> For only absorbing employment prevails, succeeds, takes up space, occupies territory, determines the future of individuals and states, drives Kansas out of your head, and actually and permanently occupies the only desirable and free Kansas against all border ruffians.[96]

Dining at Thoreau's mother's house, Sanborn certainly contributed to Thoreau's awareness of the tumultuous events occurring in Kansas in 1856.[97] As Thoreau's singular journal entry on Kansas indicates, the news from Kansas was so overwhelming that it could completely occupy the attentions of those who did not willfully exclude it from their minds. This was certainly the case with young Franklin Sanborn; increasingly agitated by the events in Kansas, Sanborn gave over the stewardship of his newly founded private school to his sister Sarah while he dedicated himself full-time to the business of the Massachusetts State Kansas Committee.[98]

Thoreau seems to have been more successful than the Concord schoolmaster in temporarily pushing the news of the civil strife in Kansas from his mind. He focused on botany and regularly recorded his observations in his growing journals. He was not, however, ignorant of the social tensions inspired by the events in Kansas, nor was he reluctant to express his concern for citizens of Massachusetts who had been illegally "seized, robbed, and held as prisoners by the citizens of the state of Missouri" in the Fourth of July letter that concerned citizens sent to the Governor of Massachusetts.[99]Nor was he reluctant to occasionally retreat from his deliberate ramblings in the fields around Concord. In June, 1856, he chose to attend a Kansas Aid Meeting. Like Emerson, he had been profoundly offended by the Compromise of 1854 and spoken strongly against the encroachment of slave power during that year.[100] Although there is no record that he joined Emerson on the podium during the Kansas Aid Meeting in 1856, Thoreau was moved on the occasion to contribute a small sum to the effort in Kansas. He did not, however, remain particularly engaged with the business of Kansas. However, as Sanborn recalls, "all of Concord had heard . . . of Brown's fights and escapes in Kansas: and Thoreau, who had his own bone to pick with the civil government . . . was desirous of meeting Brown."[101]

When Sanborn escorted John Brown to Concord in an attempt to gain support for Brown's efforts to violently oppose the Pro-Slavery ruffians in mid-March, 1857, Thoreau was particularly pleased to have the opportunity to meet the freedom fighter.[102] In fact, when Sanborn had to attend to disciplinary duties at his Concord School, Thoreau enjoyed the privilege of hosting the forthright Kansas freedom fighter in his mother's dining room. Later, attending Brown's lecture at the Town House in Concord and listening to a litany of crimes and abuses committed by citizens of Missouri, the U.S. government, and the proslavery forces of Kansas, Thoreau gained a distinct appreciation for the righteous Free State man.[103]

Brown was a captivating speaker. Charismatic, energetic, and completely committed to the righteous power of the individual man armed with conviction and strengthened by principles, he quickly enthralled his like-minded listeners (which, in a short time, included Emerson). Contending that the righteous individual man was worth a hundred of his enemies since he could triumph in the struggle against oppression because he was empowered by both his righteousness and his self reliance, Brown won his audience completely. That afternoon, he made a strong appeal to the key figures in the transcendentalist community, and he impressed them with both his dedication to the fight against immoral laws and his absolute commitment to his own convictions.

Brown seems to have particularly impressed Emerson; after meeting Brown at Thoreau's home, Emerson invited the Captain to his home for a discussion of his views and experiences. With Thoreau, he also attended Brown's lecture at the Town House that evening.[104] Emerson was inspired by Brown; he noted in his journal that

> Captain John Brown of Kansas gave a good account of himself in the Town Hall, last night, to a meeting of Citizens . . . He believes on his own experience that one good, believing, strong-minded man is worth a hundred, nay twenty-thousand men without character . . . and that the right men will give a permanent direction to the fortunes of the state.[105]

Self reliant, virtuous, manly, and supremely confident in his own voice, Brown was a fascinating study for Emerson. Brown, Emerson later noted, was an "idealist . . . [who] believed in his ideas to that extent that he existed to put them all into action."[106] Emerson saw Brown as a true patriot; he was also impressed by the man's personal belief in "two articles—the Golden Rule and the Declaration of Independence."[107] Appreciating a man able to articulate his values with such clarity, Emerson paid Brown tribute in both words and kind; by the year's end, had directly "solicited money for rifles" for the freedom fighter during his "Speech on Affairs in Kansas."[108] Although he may not have consistently valued a literal understanding of Brown's contention that it was "better that a whole generation of men, women, and children should pass away by violent death that that one word of either should be violated in this country," Emerson did not allow what some might call a rather casual willingness to sacrifice lives to trouble him in his subsequent efforts on the freedom fighter's behalf.[109] Perhaps it is important to note that Emerson, a dis-unionist, had never here-to-for embraced such a literal and brutal conviction that violence was acceptable in the pursuit of a principled nation of individuals. John Brown was the catalyst who seems to have radicalized the Concord sage and propelled him toward a new understanding of the value of violent action in the struggle for the liberation of the nation from the chains of slavery.

Brown impressed many other influential people while he was campaigning for funds for the defense of Kansas in the winter of 1857. Not only did he captivate the attention of the influential citizens in Concord, Brown succeeded in both gaining access to and earning the admiration of many other abolitionists in the various philanthropic societies dedicated to making Kansas a free state. Already an acquaintance of abolitionist Gerrit Smith, the Peterboro capitalist who had sponsored the black community in North Elba, New York, Brown met and befriended *Liberator* publisher William Lloyd Garrison while he was in Boston. More importantly, through the efforts of the enthusiastic Franklin Sanborn, Brown met New England Emigrant Aid Society director and industrialist Amos Lawrence, Unitarian minister and outspoken abolitionist Theodore Parker, Medford businessman and chairman of the Massachusetts State Kansas Committee George Luther Stearns, medical innovator and ardent abolitionist Samuel Gridley Howe, and Worcester County Kansas Committee secretary and radical abolitionist Thomas Wentworth Higginson. These men would eventually form the nucleus of Brown's covert support network and provide him with the preponderance of financial backing and logistical support that he would require in the conduct of his very personal war on slavery.

Franklin Sanborn provided Brown access to these men. After first meeting Brown in the offices of the Massachusetts Kansas Committee in early January, 1857, Sanborn was convinced that he had found a man with the experience, character, and insight to inspire the Free State citizens to victory in the struggle to defeat the forces of slavery in Kansas. Within a few days of their introduction, Sanborn had coordinated meetings with the most influential abolitionists in his acquaintance for his radical champion. Actively campaigning to win Brown the two-hundred Sharp's Rifles and $30,000 that he had explained were necessary in order to form a company of fighting men in Kansas who could resist the aggression of the corrupt Pro-Slavery Border Ruffians, Sanborn eagerly escorted the Captain to a series of meetings with Howe, Parker, Garrison, Stearns, Higginson, and Lawrence. Recounting his exploits during the defense of Kansas the previous summer and carefully explaining the means by which he intended to ensure Kansas became a free state, Brown was able to convince the abolitionists that he was both worthy of their trust and deserving of their philanthropy. Promised the two hundred Sharp's Rifles that the Massachusetts Kansas Committee had recently purchased, Brown pressed his success and began earnestly appealing for funds. Gaining a promise of $500 for "necessary expenses" from the Massachusetts Kansas Committee, Brown believed that he was well on his way to securing the kind of support he had envisioned for his future work.[110]

However, he soon discovered that his initial success in no way indicated the eagerness of the New England population to contribute funds for Kansas. The first indication that he may have been deceived occurred on January 9, 1857. Attempting to gain access to the sizable funds reputed to be in the coffers of the Worcester County Kansas Committee, Brown utterly failed. In fact, committee secretary Thomas Wentworth Higginson, engaged with the organization of the Massachusetts Disunion Convention, barely acknowledged Brown, despite his already demonstrated commitment to violent resistance to slavery.[111] When Brown approached Gerrit Smith, the same man who had donated $1000 per month to the Kansas effort during the summer of 1856 and announced that he was ready to put "slavery to a violent death" at the 1856 Abolitionist Convention in New York City, he discovered that Smith was unable to make any contributions in 1857. Smith explained that he had exhausted his "current means" in previous contributions to the effort in Kansas and was financially strapped.[112] Turning to the National Kansas Committee during their meeting in New York, Brown once again failed to gain any support for his efforts; the national committee cited the state of "public opinion," suggesting that its members did not believe that the anti-slavery community could raise sufficient money given the relatively quiet atmosphere in Kansas.[113] Undeterred, Brown approached the Massachusetts State Legislature with Sanborn in mid-February to help gain support for a $100,000 appropriation for Kansas. In a dramatic gesture, Brown even held up the chains that Pro-Slavery men had used to imprison his sons, hoping to impress the statesmen with the brutality of the Pro-Slavery forces and the righteousness of his own cause. [114] Although he was able to inspire Amos Lawrence to make a $70 contribution, Brown absolutely failed to convince the state representatives that their money would be wisely spent if they committed it to his future efforts.[115]

In part, Brown's failure can be attributed to his penchant for secretiveness. Responding to committee member's queries regarding his future plans, Brown characteristically responded:

> I am no adventurer. You all know me. You are acquainted with my history. You know what I have done in Kansas. I do not expose my plans. No one knows them but myself, except perhaps one. I will not be interrogated; if you wish to give me anything I want you to give it freely. I have no other purpose but to serve the cause of liberty.[116]

Perhaps, as a result of his complicity in the murders at Pottawattamie and his intense desire to further the atmosphere of both awe and respect with which the preponderance of New England philanthropists regarded him, Brown presented himself as an experienced freedom fighter who embraced secrecy as an operational imperative in the deadly game of guerilla warfare. Consistently, he embraced secretiveness in all of his fund-raising activity in 1857, emphasizing his expertise as a guerilla leader and abolitionist freedom fighter, his insight and authority about the environment and political atmosphere in Kansas, and his worthiness as an opponent to the unprincipled ruthless border ruffians who refused to submit to any legal authority in their efforts to ensure that slavery was victorious in Kansas. By remaining secretive, Brown effectively made himself both larger than life and remote from the possibility of any censure for his activities. He became, for his Eastern benefactors, a kind of mythic frontier figure emerging from the swamps of Kansas when Free-State rights were violated and fighting for liberty, justice, and individual freedom on the fringe of reality. He did not, in this guise, secure the purse that he felt necessary for an effective campaign against slavery.

Undeterred, Brown did not restrict his campaign for recognition as an author of liberty or champion of freedom in Kansas to benevolent organizations structured to provide support to emigrants; he also made strong appeals to certain affluent individuals in the abolitionist community. One of his more interesting appeals was not for arms or funding; it was for security. Hearing that a United States Marshall was traveling East to arrest him for his less than noble activities in Kansas, Brown appealed to some of his abolitionist friends in Boston for protection. With assurances that they could successfully hide him in their home, Massachusetts Superior Court Judge Thomas Russell and his wife sequestered Brown in one of their upstairs rooms for a week while the "US Hounds" pursued the free-dom fighter.[117] While he remained with the Russells, Brown penned "Old Brown's *Farewell*," a lament on his apparent failure to gain the support and recognition that he had sought in and around Boston. Presenting his lament to both Theodore Parker and George Luther Stearns, two of the more afflu-ent men who seemed to warm to his petitions, Brown prepared to return to Kansas a failure.[118]

Brown soon discovered, however, that personal appeals were far more successful than general ones. In fact, as a result of his personal plea to George Luther Stearns—aided, no doubt by his strong effort to win the con-fidence of Stearn's wife, Mary (who had been impressed by his *Farewell*), Brown gained an authorization to draw upon the committed abolitionist for $7000 for the "defense of Kansas."[119] In addition, Stearns influenced the other members of the Massachusetts Kansas Committee to authorize Brown $500 for his future endeavors and grant him the authority to sell one hundred of the rifles he had been given for $15 each.

Brown was elated.[120] He was, however, far from satisfied; tasting suc-cess, he attempted to press his other supporters for even more money in the month that followed. Traveling to Stearn's home, Brown made an impas-sioned plea for more money for his future effort in Kansas and for his long-suffering of his family in North Elba. His efforts nearly estranged his benefactor, but they were successful. Brown received a promise for addi-tional funding for both arms and for the purchase of 244 acres of land for his family in North Elba. Stearns generosity apparently affected fel-low abolitionist Gerrit Smith; in a reversal of his previous decision, Smith decided to make a contribution to Brown's Kansas work and gave him a total of $460 in cash. Confident in his newfound success, Brown journeyed West toward Kansas in June; he believed that he was returning to the ter-ritory with the means to fight the Missourians and Pro-Slavery settlers in style. He had cash, an expense account, and rifles, all of which offered him financial independence and a degree of personal affluence he had not seen since the days prior to his bankruptcy in 1837.[121]

During the summer of 1857, however, he discovered that his financial windfall was moot. The formerly chaotic Kansas territory was relatively calm, and in this disquieting environment, there was little for the exuber-ant freedom fighter to do. Despite the fact that there was another new Pro-Slavery governor, relative peace reigned in the territory. Free State elections had been held unopposed in August, and a continual flow of unmolested Free-State settlers arrived in the territory during the summer. With the guarantee of justice maintained by Governor Walker, it appeared to most that a peaceful political solution might be possible in Kansas.

John Brown did not believe that Walker would succeed. As a result, he established a training camp in Tabor, Iowa where he began preparations for the violent confrontation that he believed was inevitable in the contested territory. His conviction, however, was far from universal, and he only succeeded in inspiring one man—his son Owen—to join him in a training regimen for the inevitable return to civil war in Kansas. Despite the relative paucity of his force and the peace that settled on Kansas during the fall of 1857, John Brown sent missive after missive to his Eastern benefactors expressing his "*immediate* want of from Five Hundred to One Thousand Dollars for *secret service & and no questions asked.*"[122] Though he did not inform Stearns, Smith or Sanborn, or any others—for that matter—that his need was acute because he had enlisted the English mercenary and opportunist, Hugh Forbes, as drillmaster and tactician—and owed the self-proclaimed guerilla war expert money—Brown found himself in desperate need that fall. Forbes, who boasted of combat experience with Garibaldi during the Italian Revolution of 1848–1849, had impressed Brown with his knowledge of guerilla tactics when the two men met in New York during Brown's campaign to gain funds in March, 1857.[123] Agreeing to pay him $100 per month for his services, Brown hired Forbes as an expert lieutenant for his future efforts in the defense of freedom. To Forbes, he enthusiastically intimated that if certain "New England Humanitarians" agreed to support his efforts, he might count on a longer term of employment.[124]

Brown's enthusiasm for the Englishman did not last long. Within a month of his engagement, Forbes proved to be both an unwilling subordinate and a rather unstable ally in Brown's effort to decisively resist the Pro-Slavery forces in Kansas. Not only did he demand $600 in advance for his services, he approached his initial task (translating and condensing foreign guerilla warfare manuals for use on the border) with a degree of leisure incomprehensible to John Brown. When he arrived in Tabor in August, 1857—three months later than Brown anticipated—Forbes also proved himself to be both obstinate and disgruntled. He was not pleased with the two man army that he discovered in Iowa, nor was he pleased with the weapons that the Massachusetts Kansas Committee had provided them.[125] He also refused to blindly submit to Brown's whims, whom he considered his inferior in both experience and leadership ability and overtly challenged both Brown's authority and his methods.[126] The two men quarreled often; finally, in early November, protesting his lack of pay and expressing his absolute dissatisfaction with Brown's leadership, Forbes left Brown's camp and headed East. His departure was not amicable. Forbes contended that John Brown had promised him money that he did not produce. For the next year, Forbes attempted to convince the militant captain that he would not go gentle into the night.

Forbes, however, was not Brown's only problem during the fall of 1857. By the time he reached his training base in August, Brown had nearly expended all of the funds that he had gathered during his trip East. Since he had not yet entered Kansas, he did not feel at liberty to draw on Stearn's personal authorization, which the wealthy merchant had granted Brown for use in subsistence of one hundred "volunteer-regulars" in active defense of Free State Kansas.[127] Sick, plagued by continual concerns for money, and, perhaps concerned that he would be arrested in Kansas, Brown had done very little to satisfy either himself or his benefactors while he was in Tabor. He did, however, continue to press them for funding.

Finally, receiving some money from the Kansas agent of the Massachusetts Kansas Committee, Brown departed Tabor on 30 October for Kansas. Upon his arrival, he discovered that what the newspapers had been reporting about Kansas was true; relative peace reigned in the former war-torn territory. An atmosphere of political permissiveness existed. This allowed the October elections, which had been attended by both Free State and Pro-Slavery party members, to proceed unmolested. Governor Walker had guaranteed a fair election and set aside fraudulent returns. The result was a huge Free State victory; not only had a Free-State delegate been elected to Congress, but thirty-three of the fifty-two territorial legislature seats were now held by Free State men.

Unsettled by the dramatic change that had taken place in Kansas, but desperate to maintain the position of importance he had worked so hard to construct the previous spring, Brown sent anxious letters East acknowledging that although he did not anticipate that there was any use for "Arms or ammunition" in Kansas at the time, "matters are [still] quite *unsettled*" in the territory.[128] In order to maintain his benefactors' interest, Brown intimated that in his opinion, the relative peacefulness could not continue. Undoubtedly, he suggested, Pro-Slavery forces would resume their campaign of terror against the Free State settlers in the spring. Therefore, he confided, he would keep the weapons and ammunition in anticipation of the inevitable return to violence when he and his small army (not admitting that it now consisted of only two men) would once again staunchly oppose the Pro-Slavery vigilantes.

Recognizing that there was little opportunity to engage in any meaningful work in the peaceful environment in Kansas, John Brown recruited a half a dozen new men to serve in a company paradoxically dedicated to stopping the "aggressions of the Pro-Slavery forces" in Kansas and departed the territory in late November.[129] With John Cook, Aaron Stevens, Luke Parsons, Charles Moffet, John Kagi, and Charles Tidd, Brown and his son Owen set out for Springdale, Iowa where they would train to more efficiently fight the Pro-Slavery zealots. During their journey, these men also learned that their captain intended to extend the range of operations—his *"ultimate destination* [, he informed them,] *was the State of Virginia."*[130] After a few initial objections, Brown's new recruits chose to continue with him toward the site of their ad hoc military school. Along the way, they gained a further appreciation for the character of their leader; he revealed to them that he was convinced that "God had created him to be the deliverer of slaves the same as Moses had delivered the children of Israel."[131]

Despite this rather unsettling revelation, all of Brown's new men made it to Iowa. They arrived in Springdale in late December, after having traveling in the bitter cold on foot for over a month.

A quiet, remote Quaker community, Springdale pleased Brown very much; the townspeople were friendly, receptive, and decidedly anti-slavery.[132] Lodging his men in a farmhouse some distance from the village, Brown initiated a program of training that emphasized the skills he anticipated would be necessary in their future operations in Virginia. He also began to discuss further details of his Virginia plan with a few of his men.

The previous fall, Brown had had the opportunity to refine his plan in long discussions with Hugh Forbes.[133] He had explained his intention to end slavery in the South by initiating a guerrilla war against slave-owners with an army of former slaves armed with weapons captured by a nucleus of chosen men. The Englishman had not been receptive to Brown's notion that slaves would be prepared to immediately respond to news of an insurrection, assist in the capture of a federal arms facility, and then calmly wait while enlightened Northern intellectuals inspired the overthrow of the Pro-Slavery administration. He favored instead the organization of a series of "slave stampedes" which eventually would make slave property "untenable near the frontier;" the inevitable result would be the progressive destruction of slavery from the North.[134] Brown combined these two plans and matured them while in Springdale, and slowly revealed his ideas to his cadre of Free State zealots. When he departed the Quaker community to seek financial support for his plan in mid-January, conditions appeared to be favorable for the eventual execution of the "most *important* undertaking of . . . [his] entire life."[135]

However, during his journey East, Brown discovered that his vision of taking the fight to Virginia was in great jeopardy. At his son's home in Ohio, he received an angry letter from Franklin Sanborn indicating that Hugh Forbes had sent "abusive" missives to both Samuel Gridley Howe and Charles Sumner charging them with his reduction to poverty and his dismissal from Brown's service.[136] More importantly, Forbes accused Brown's New England supporters of knowingly failing to honor their financial obligation to him, since he had been engaged with the understanding that the New England men would provide the funds necessary for his retention.[137]

Forbes letters caused considerable concern among those privileged with Brown's confidence in the Massachusetts State Kansas Committee.[138] Not only had Brown exposed his friends to the abuses of a virulent opportunist, he had been disloyal to them by failing to make them aware that a former associate might attempt to blackmail them.[139] This was not the behavior that they expected from an experienced and trusted champion of liberty; it called to question Brown's judgment and his honesty.

Recognizing that he could not afford to lose the trust and confidence of his most ardent supporters, Brown devoted himself to silencing the voice that had threatened to compromise his venture. With the aid of his son, Brown sent Forbes a pointed and somewhat threatening letter indicating that he would not tolerate any other letters to his friends.[140]

3 Translating a Terrorist
The Business of Public Intellectuals

> The majority of the men of the North, and of the South, and East, and West, are not men of principle.
>
> Thoreau, "Slavery in Massachusetts"

Hugh Forbes, however, was not Brown's only concern in January, 1858; the relative peace that reigned in Kansas and the success that Free State settlers had achieved at the polls in October caused him considerable anxiety.[1] Realizing that a political solution in Kansas would compromise his ability to maintain a prominent position among the Eastern intelligentsia and effectively negate his ability to secure a legacy as a champion of freedom, Brown knew that he had to act quickly to secure support for the plan that Forbes had nearly compromised. His first stop was the home of Frederick Douglass. Just as he had on previous occasions, Douglass welcomed the radical abolitionist into his home and attentively listened as Brown revealed the details of his latest plan. This was not the first time that Brown articulated his ideas about a slave insurrection with Douglass, nor was it the first time that Douglass welcomed Brown's ideas about the necessity for violent confrontation in order to bring about the end of slavery.[2] Brown had first spoken to Douglass about a guerilla campaign to liberate Southern slaves in 1847 when they met in Springfield, Ohio. In his *Life and Times*, Douglass reveals that in 1847, Brown told him that from the mountainous region of the Allegany's, he believed that he could

> take twenty-five picked man, and begin on a small scale; supply them with arms and ammunition and post them in squads of fives on the line of twenty-five miles. The most persuasive and judicious of these shall go down to the fields from time to time, as opportunity offers, and induce the slaves to join them, seeking and selecting the most restless and daring.[3]

By this method, Brown believed that it was possible to "destroy the value of slave property . . . [since the losses of slaves would] render slave property insecure."[4] Impressed by both Brown's sincerity and his forthright commitment to the end of slavery, Douglass credits Brown with his loss of hope that the end of slavery might be achieved through peaceful methods; consistently, he gives John Brown credit for convincing him that "slavery could only be destroyed by blood-shed."[5] Acknowledging that they had visited one and other occasionally during the years following their initial meeting, Douglass notes that he and Brown often "talked over the feasibility of his plan for destroying the value of slave property," identifying the difficulties that the guerilla force might face after initiating a border campaign.[6] The significant obstacles to setting the plan in action, both men recognized, were men, money, and equipment.[7]

When Brown arrived at Douglass's Rochester home in January, 1858, he believed that he had formed the nucleus of men who would be willing to commit to his long-considered plan. If he could calm the anxiety that Hugh Forbes had inspired, John Brown believed that he also may have found a source for the funds and equipment he judged necessary for his attack on slavery. The first step to gaining the resources he required was the re-establishment of the trust and confidence of his wealthy New England supporters. Douglass was essential to this, since he both represented a black voice in the fight against slavery, and he enjoyed the confidence of the free black population of the Northeast. After reviewing the details of his latest plan with Douglass, Brown was hopeful that he might inspire his influential friend to commit to his effort and compel the free black community in the Northeast to join in the attack on slavery that spring.[8]

After much discussion, Douglass decided to support Brown; he agreed both to raise money and win recruits for Brown's provisional army.[9] Douglass's commitment was critical, Brown believed, since it would legitimize his plan in the eyes of his eastern benefactors.[10] Not only would he be able to demonstrate the confidence that Douglass had in him, he would also be able to confidently assert that blacks would gather to his standard in the fight for the freedom.

Brown was elated by Douglass's pledge and spent the remainder of the three weeks in Douglass's Rochester home writing letters to the men who might make his plan a reality. In "carefully worded" and individually "tailored" letters, Brown approached the six influential New England abolitionists who had access to funds sufficient to enable him to translate his plan into reality.[11] Proclaiming that he was preparing for the "most *important* undertaking of ... [his] whole life," Brown shrewdly solicited those who had demonstrated the most sympathy with his previous efforts in Kansas: Gerrit Smith, George Luther Stearns, Samuel Gridley Howe, Theodore Parker, Franklin Sanborn, and Thomas Wentworth Higginson.[12] In his 2 February letter to Higginson, whom Brown understood to have access to the $3000 then believed to be in the accounts of Worcester County Kansas Society, Brown craftily appealed to the Worcester minister's ego calling him a "true *man* and a true *abolitionist*," insightfully playing upon Higginson's personal history as an abolitionist willing to confront armed authority to effect change.[13] Appealing for "from $500 to $1000, for *secret service*," Brown attempted to inspire Higginson to commit some of the same funds that he had denied him in 1857. Higginson's immediate response gave Brown reason to believe that his effort was not without some chance of success. Indicating that "he was always ready to invest in treason," but had little to no funds available at the present time, Higginson pledged to look into the "trifling balance" of the Worcester County Kansas Committee, inquiring curiously if Brown intended to commit to some underground railroad business.[14]

Conceding Higginson's incisiveness, Brown claimed that the money was necessary for some "Rail Road business on a somewhat *extended scale.*" Brown failed, however, to provide any specifics about secret mission, but he did invite Higginson to Gerrit Smith's Peterboro residence where he promised to reveal the specifics of the *"secret service"* in detail. [15] Indicating that he had also approached Stearns, Sanborn, and Parker (whom Higginson held in the highest regard), Brown gave Higginson reason to believe that his presence was particularly important to the success of his effort. As if to underscore and accentuate Higginson's critical position to his future success, Brown emphasized, "I am very anxious to have *you come along,*"[16] in his letter.

Clearly intrigued, but reluctant to commit, Higginson cautiously avoided the meeting in Peterboro; instead, he chose to meet Brown in his rooms at the American House in Boston two days after Brown's return from Smith's home.[17] There, on 4 March, along with Sanborn, Stearns, Howe, and Parker, Higginson listened attentively as Brown revealed the scope of his plan. First addressing their concerns about Hugh Forbes, Brown calmly explained that Forbes recent actions were malevolent attempts to extort money from those most committed to the fight for liberty. Carefully detailing his relationship with Forbes, Brown explained that he had promised Forbes $100 a month for a period of six months. He made it clear that he had paid the Englishman in advance (for the entire six month period) in order to allow Forbes to take care of his pressing family obligations. He had not, he was certain, indicated that Forbes should expect an addition term of employment, nor had he suggested that there was anyone in either the Massachusetts State Kansas Committee or in the National Kansas Committee who would commit to such an agreement. Admitting that he had probably revealed the source of some of his own funds, Brown recognized that he had probably made an error by trusting the English revolutionary but assured his benefactors that he had not revealed details of his Virginia plan sufficient to jeopardize it.[18]

Recognizing the consistency of Brown's remarks with their own impressions, and admitting that Forbes's letters revealed a style of "insult and lunacy," Parker, Stearns, Howe, Higginson, and Sanborn agreed to "renew their commitment to Brown" and hear the details of the plan that they had become aware of following Franklin Sanborn's return from Peterboro.[19] Carefully explaining that he already had a nucleus of men committed to his guerilla campaign, Brown revealed his intention to inspire an insurrection of slaves by clandestinely taking his well-trained inter-racial provisional army into the heart of slavery, "beat[ing] up a slave quarter," arming those slaves who were willing to join him, and then retreating into the mountainous regions of Virginia. Brown then described how he would launch a series of attacks on slave-owners from his remote guerilla base eventually making slavery untenable in the region. As he succeeded, Brown explained, he would move operations progressively southward until slavery was extinct in America. Explicitly detailing his intention to involve the newly liberated slave population in the armed liberation of their brethren, Brown was quick to point out that he had already received assurances that the black population in the Northeast was both prepared to aid him and willing to fight in the effort to end slavery.[20]

After four days of discussions, the five men decided to join Gerrit Smith and support the radical abolitionist. Forming a committee to raise the money Brown believed necessary to commence operations in the spring, they committed to secrecy and pledged themselves to the end of slavery, the "John Brown way."[21] However, they did not do so without some serious misgivings. In his incisive assessment of the "secret six," Rossbach notes that most of the members of the secret committee were not completely convinced that slaves would be willing to fight for their own liberation. In fact, not two months before the March meeting with Brown, Theodore Parker had publicly articulated the racialist view that the African was the most "docile and pliant" of all races in an address entitled "The Present Aspect of Slavery and the Immediate Duty of the North." Explaining that blacks had "little ferocity" and were "little warlike," Parker suggests that the African was not at all like his combative Anglo-Saxon fellow man and had no natural inclination toward violence.[22] Others were of the same opinion.[23] However, they must have expressed their concerns less convincingly than Brown did during the enthusiastic defense of his plan to make a "dash against slavery" with an army largely manned by African-American men. Perhaps believing that "all peaceful alternatives had failed," Parker, Stearns, Sanborn, Higginson, and Howe decided to disregard their own misgivings and agreed to "trust in Brown's character and values."[24]

Parker, however, demonstrated the limits of his own support. Refusing Brown's covert request for two addresses, one directed to the "officers and Soldiers of the United States Army" and the other to the soldiers who would accompany Brown during the insurrection, Parker privately indicated that he would not provide potential captors with proof of his own complicity in Brown's war on slavery. Perhaps, revealing his doubts that Brown would be able to do anything more than enrage the slave-owning population of the South and inspire the abolitionists in the North, Parker chose to provide Brown with a copy of General McClellan's "Report on the Armies of Europe" as a substitute for the addresses he refused to craft.[25]

Most likely unaware of his benefactors' misgivings, Brown departed enthusiastically in early March to begin campaigning for support among the affluent free black population in both the United States and in Canada.[26] Visiting Philadelphia, Brown met with prominent black abolitionists Henry Highland Garnet, Stephen Smith, and William Still; when he departed that city, he did so with the confidence of man who had had his hopes for active involvement of the free black community enthusiastically affirmed. He proceeded to Syracuse with high hopes, meeting militant free black Jermain W. Loguen, who suggested that he seek out Harriet Tubman, whose intimacy with the communities of fugitive slaves then living in Canada might be of great advantage in the recruitment of black men for future employment as guerilla soldiers. Tubman, in turn, recommended that Brown seek Martin Delany, the strident black abolitionist who had forcefully asserted that "our elevation must be the result of self-efforts, and the work of our own hands" in his 1852 pamphlet, *The Condition, Elevation, Emigration, and Destiny of the Colored People of the United.* [27]

Receptive to Brown's entreaties, Delany agreed to organize a convention of black men in Chatham, Canada the following month. During this convention, Brown campaigned for support and for recruits for his forthcoming effort. He attempted to gain their confidence by calling attention to his experience in Kansas and his extensive study of guerilla warfare claiming that from the day he left Kansas, he had devoted his "whole being, mental, moral, and physical, all that he had and was to the extinction of slavery."[28] Emphatically maintaining that Southern slaves would "immediately rise all over the Southern states" at the first sign of a leader who demonstrated the will to liberate and lead them to freedom, he revealed his plan to initiate a successive uprising of slaves from the mountains of Virginia to the forty-six men who had gathered in the Negro schoolhouse. Confidently presenting his "Provisional Constitution" to the assembly after he had sworn them to secrecy, Brown attempted to demonstrate the thoroughness of his plan by outlining the organization of new states in the liberated territories. Not only would these states fully recognize the newly emancipated slaves as citizens "fully entitled to protection" under the Provisional Constitution, Brown asserted, the new black citizens would be eligible to serve in the government of the region. Schools would be established to teach "useful and mechanical arts and to instruct new citizens in "all the business of life;" families would be "kept together[,] . . . broken families encouraged to reunite, and intelligence offices shall be established for that purpose." [29] In the end, Brown asserted, the inertia of their enlightened efforts would make beleaguered officials in slave states realize that slavery was no longer possible in their states, and they would proclaim immediate emancipation of all blacks in their regions of influence. Eventually, Brown contended, there would be no region in the Untied States where slavery could exist.

At the convention's end, delegates to the secret meeting unanimously approved Brown's constitution and voted him as their Commander-in-Chief. However, only one Chatham resident (Osborn P. Anderson) demonstrated the enthusiasm sufficient to join Brown in his planned raid on slavery. This was a problem that Brown had not anticipated, and it was not his only problem. During the spring of 1858, Forbes, once again, made himself conspicuous by going to Washington and exposing part of Brown's plan to Senators' Henry Wilson, Charles Sumner, and William H. Seward. Maintaining that John Brown was "a reckless man, an unreliable man , [and] a vicious man" who must be restrained, Forbes not only identified several of Brown's key supporters, he revealed Brown's intention to inspire an insurrection in the South with the help of key members of the Massachusetts State Kansas Committee.[30] In the flurry of correspondence that followed, Samuel Gridley Howe, perhaps the most political of the secret six, assured his friend Henry Wilson that "no countenance has been given to Brown for any operation outside of Kansas *by the Kansas Committee.*"[31] He further assured Wilson that arms purchased by the Massachusetts State Kansas Committee would not be used for any other reason than the defense of Free-State settlers in Kansas. Attempting to dissuade Hugh Forbes from any future efforts, Howe wrote the desperate man and pointedly informed him that his assertions were incorrect and his efforts misplaced.[32] This succeeded, at least temporarily, in quieting the snubbed guerilla expert.

However, Forbes's compromise of Brown's plan, and the suggestion that he would reveal the identities of Brown's primary supporters, caused considerable concern among the "New England humanitarians" who had pledged themselves to support John Brown.[33] Fearful that Forbes' revelations would doom Brown's operation and implicate them as co-conspirators in a treasonous campaign, Howe and his colleagues demanded that the freedom fighter postpone his effort. Explaining his thoughts in a letter to Franklin Sanborn, Smith acknowledged, "I never was convinced of the wisdom of this scheme. But as things now stand, it seems to me it would be madness to attempt to execute it. Colonel Forbes would make such an attempt a certain and most disastrous failure."[34] Higginson alone was emphatically against any postponement suggesting that nothing would be gained from a delay: Forbes betrayal, Higginson was convinced, would simply *"increase* the panic" that Brown's raid would inspire. [35]

Ignoring Higginson's protests, five members of the "Secret Six" met in Boston's Revere House on the 24th of May and decided to postpone Brown's raid until things had quieted: Higginson, notably, was absent. They also determined that in order to foil Forbes, and convince those affected by Forbes' disclosures that the information that he had revealed was merely the product of an errant adventurer who had neither credibility nor insight into Brown's plans, Brown must return to Kansas. Seven days later, the five "major stockholders" in Brown's venture informed Brown of their decision and requested that he return to Kansas to validate their denial of Forbes' contentions.[36] In order to show their continued commitment to him, they presented Brown with $500 in gold for expenses.[37]

Disappointed, but not surprised by the committee's decision, Brown accepted his cautious benefactors' decision. He did not, however, fail to notice Higginson's distinct absence from the meeting at the Revere House and made a special—last ditch—appeal to his most militant supporter on 1 June. During their meeting, Brown lamented the committee's decision calling attention to the differences between the former Worcester minister and his fellow conspirators. Asserting that the others were not *"men of action"* and calling Smith a "timid man" while hinting that both Stearns and Parker lacked "courage," Brown ensured Higginson that he still needed his support.[38] Acknowledging that since "they held the purse he was powerless without them," Brown asked Higginson, a fellow man of action and courage, to conspire with him but remain silent as to his opinions of the others.[39] Reluctantly, Higginson acquiesced evidently enjoying both the distinction that Brown had conferred upon him and the confidence of the man he now recognized to be a "sly old veteran."[40]

With characteristic savvy, Brown then proceeded to Kansas under the pseudonym Shubel Morgan. He did not, however, abandon his plan. While in Boston, Brown dispensed most of the $500 he had received to his small cohort and instructed most of them to return to their homes until they were summoned. Several of the men, however, received special missions: Brown instructed Richard Realf to go to New York and watch Forbes for a while before proceeding to England to raise money among his affluent acquaintances; Brown sent Stevens, Gill, and Coppoc to Iowa and Ohio to solicit funds for future operations; and John Cook, the exuberant ex-law clerk and former Yale student, John Brown sent to Harper's Ferry with instructions that he should settle there and conduct a thorough reconnaissance of the target that Forbes had threatened to compromise.[41] Clearly not giving up the plan that he had carefully developed over the past two years, Brown departed for Kansas convinced that he would eventually recall his provisional army and initiate the end of slavery.

By 27 June, Brown was in Kansas. Once again, he was disappointed to learn that the territory remained relatively peaceful. Despite the recent attempted murder of eleven free-state men on the Marais de Cygnes River and the attempt by Free-State leader James Montgomery to burn a Fort Scott in retaliation, relative peace reigned over the contentious southeastern portion of the territory. The new territorial governor, James Denver, a recent appointee of President Buchanan, had been diligent in his efforts to maintain an atmosphere of fairness and honesty for all settlers, and the result was an atmosphere of peace throughout the territory.[42]

This was not a situation that John Brown relayed to his Eastern benefactors. In letters to "F. B. Sanborn & Friends at Boston and Worcester," Brown attempted to create the impression that an atmosphere of fear and tension pervaded the territory; in his August 6 letter, Brown described

> Deserted farms: [sic] & dwellings lie in all directions . . . & the remaining inhabitants watch every appearance of persons moveing [sic] about with anxious jealousy; & vigilance . . . A constant fear of new troubles seems to prevail on both sides of the line . . . Any little affair may open the quarrel afresh.[43]

Kansas, according to Brown, was still a war zone requiring a constant state of readiness. He therefore postured for immanent attack by hostile Pro-Slavery forces when he reached the area where armed confrontation had most recently occurred. Establishing his small company upon prominent terrain near the Marais de Cygnes, Brown, Tidd, and Kagi built a fort of logs and stone on the site in order to dissuade roving Pro-Slavery men from any thoughts of hostility toward the Free State efforts in the region. Aside from this engineering project, Brown did little else during the summer of 1858: he suffered a severe relapse of malarial fever and was bedridden throughout the warm months of July and August. He was cared for only by John Kagi, the man elected as his Secretary of War during the Chatham convention.

Following his recovery, Brown summoned the rest of his provisional army (excepting Cook, who had by now firmly establishing himself in Harpers Ferry) and began planning how he might satisfy the requirement that his secret supporters had revealed in the Revere House when they informed him that he must return to Kansas and quash any residual notion in the minds of Forbes' letter recipients that the Englishman's disclosures were legitimate. Brown revealed his eagerness to demonstrate the value of the support that his New England friends committed to him in an October letter to Sanborn. Appealing for funds so that the "little business can be accomplished," Brown anxiously indicated his readiness to demonstrate both his trustworthiness and his capacity as a militant leader.[44] Although he eagerly forwarded Brown's letter to the other members of the committee, none apparently felt particularly inspired to send Brown any money. As a result, Brown and his men could do very little; they spent a relatively quiet autumn improving Fort Snyder (the name he had given to the log fortress near the Marais de Cygnes), conducted reconnaissance of the border area, and petitioned the local agents of the Massachusetts and National Kansas Committee for arms, ammunition, supplies, and money.

Dissatisfied by the poor support he received from New England and aware that the relative quiet in Kansas would ensure more of the same, John Brown was excited when he received an invitation to join Free State leader James Montgomery on an expedition against Fort Scott, the same site that Montgomery attacked and attempted to burn the previous June. Brown saw this as an opportunity to demonstrate that there was still considerable danger in Kansas and to gain some attention in the territory. Responding to Montgomery's invitation, Brown excitedly prepared for the approaching operation eager to once again lead men in the Free State cause.[45] However, when Brown joined the "notorious Captain James Montgomery" on 14 December, he was disappointed to learn that Montgomery relegated him to a peripheral role in the raid. According to Montgomery's plan, Brown would provide Montgomery support while he liberated a captive Free-State man held in the Free State Hotel in town. This is exactly what occurred. However, despite the fact that Brown had been consigned a subordinate role in the raid, he and his men ended up gaining most of the credit for the "leadership and instigation of the Fort Scott outrage."[46] Hearing that John Brown was involved in the attack on Fort Scott where a man was killed and a store plundered, the new Governor, Samuel Medary, charged both Montgomery and Brown with responsibility for the raid and secured the authority to issue a reward of $250 each for their apprehension. This was not the kind of notice that Brown's benefactors had instructed the freedom fighter to gain.

In the immediate aftermath of the Fort Scott debacle, however, Brown found himself in a situation that did completely satisfy his humanitarian sponsors. During a routine patrol along the Missouri border on 19 December, one of Brown's men, George Gill, encountered a mulatto man named Jim who explained that he was a Missouri slave whose family was about to be sold and separated. Gill brought the slave to his captain and had him explain his predicament; elated, Brown determined that here was an opportunity to carry an attack against slavery itself.[47] The next night, Brown staged a two pronged attack on slavery across the Missouri border liberating two slave families and plundering the homes of their former owners. In the process, Aaron Stevens, the leader of the second raiding force, shot one Missouri planter dead. When the two forces united across the border in Kansas with a total of eleven liberated slaves, two captive white men, and an assortment of horses, oxen, mules, wagons, and various supplies plundered from the planter's homes, Brown learned of Stevens act and decided to lead his fugitive party to Canada some eleven hundred miles away. His trek was arduous, but after nearly three months travel through Kansas, Iowa, Illinois, and Michigan, Brown finally reached Canada and safety on 12 March, 1859.

Brown's raid was not universally celebrated. In fact, many Free State settlers, fearing that Brown's actions might once again herald a reign of lawlessness and terror, condemned the act.[48] Some settlers, anticipating reprisals, caustically criticized Brown remarking that the "retaliatory blow will fall on us:" it will not fall upon the author of the deed.[49] Brown ignored their claims casually observing that Pro-Slavery men had tried to kill eleven Free State men while he had freed eleven slaves. He defended his action as a retaliation for the May massacre on the Marais de Cygnes; he also pointed out that the two white men that he had captured were released within a few days of their capture.[50]

Implicated in Brown's raid, James Montgomery promptly distanced himself from Brown explaining that he knew "nothing of either . . . [Brown's] plans or [his] intentions" clarifying, for anyone who was not aware, that "Brown keeps his own counsels, and acts on his own responsibility."[51] This was not altogether true. On January 2, 1859, while he hid in a camp quite near Fort Scott, Brown sent a letter to Montgomery asking the "border chieftain" to be prepared to come to his aid "at a moments notice," should he require help protecting his newly liberated charges.[52]

This was not the only correspondence that Brown prepared as he readied his human freight for the arduous journey to Canada. Before he left Kansas, Brown sent a letter to the editor of the Kansas *Trading Post* explaining his decision to violate the tenuous peace that existed in the Kansas territories. Published in both the Kansas *Trading Post* and the New York *Tribune*, Brown proudly explained that during his raid,

> [e]leven persons were forcibly restored to their *natural; & inalienable rights*, with but one man killed; & all 'hell is stirred from beneath' . . . The Marshall of Kansas is said to be collecting a posse of Missouri (not Kansas) men at West Point in Missouri a little town about ten miles distant, to "enforce the laws" & all proslavery conservative Free-State, and dough-faced men & Administration tools are filled with holy horror.[53]

Brown's financiers were thrilled at the news. Gerrit Smith was particularly excited when he read of Brown's exploit; in his 10 January letter to his wife, Gerrit Smith enthusiastically inquired: "Do you hear the news from Kansas? Our dear Brown is invading Kansas and pursuing the policy which he intended to pursue *elsewhere*."[54]

On the whole, it appears that those outside of Missouri and Kansas reacted similarly to the news of Brown's attack on slavery. During the entire journey from the contested territory, the people Brown encountered seemed remarkably sympathetic with his effort. Citizens all along their route offered funding, protection, and transportation to the party, and not one law enforcement officer approached them during their overt escape. In his narrative account of Brown's exodus from Missouri, Stephen Oates identifies many individuals who aided Brown and his fugitives along the way: the Editor of the Des Moines *Register* who paid their ferry fees across the river bearing the town's name, the ministers in Grinnell who provided the party both money and supplies, and the well-known private detective Allan Pinkerton, who, in addition to hiding the slaves, provided them with $500 spending money and procured them a boxcar for their journey to Detroit.[55] In fact, during Brown's journey through Iowa, Illinois, and Michigan, there was only one poorly conceived attempt by either Pro-Slavery forces or bounty-hunters to capture Brown's party.[56] Evidently, very few people were inspired by the either the Kansas Governor's offer of $250 for the capture of Brown or the Missouri governor's offer of $75 for his arrest.[57]

When John Brown and his human freight reached Detroit—a short boat-ride from Canada—on March 12, he had reason to be pleased. During the previous eighty-two days of his journey, he had traveled 1100 miles with 11 fugitive slaves; he had also successfully quashed all concern about Hugh Forbes among his benefactors, and he had demonstrated his ability to successfully conduct guerilla operations in hostile territory. He was now ready to head east and begin his guerilla campaign[58] He felt confident that his plan to strike the heart of slavery would succeed; he also felt confident that he would be able to inspire overwhelming support for his effort to end slavery among the citizens in the North. His recent journey had provided ample proof that the country only needed a catalyst and slavery would forever disappear. The citizens of the Northwest had demonstrated their sympathy with the type of active pursuit of freedom that he embraced, and he felt confident that when he initiated his much more aggressive operation they would do so again.

When John Brown reached Cleveland, after sending the majority of his ten man army on to Ashtabula County, where John Jr. had established a cache for the weapons they would use at Harper's Ferry, his confidence only increased. He arrived in Cleveland during the trial of a group of the "Oberlin rescuers"—thirty-seven businessmen, college professors, students, and free blacks who rescued a fugitive slave from his captors in Oberlin. The town, Brown discovered, was in virtual uproar. Nearly every day, protestors arrived to "cheer the black rescuers in jail as loudly as the whites" establishing an atmosphere of "intense excitement" throughout the city.[59] John Brown exulted in the atmosphere of open defiance and even visited the jailed liberators.[60] Despite the presence of a United States Marshall in the city, Brown even gave a public lecture to raise money for his future operations in Cleveland and wandered freely through the streets meeting the people of the town. During his lecture, he revealed many of the details of his recent underground railroad operation and talked openly about his experiences in Kansas. He even acknowledged the $250 reward that President Buchanan had offered for his capture, and defiantly offered a reward of two dollars and fifty cents for capture of the President. [61] Covering the poorly attended event, a reporter for the Cleveland *Plain Dealer* did much to aid Brown in his effort to achieve public recognition. He insured that Brown's remarks were printed in the 22 March edition of the newspaper, noting that Brown "meant his invasion as a direct blow at slavery."[62]

Departing Cleveland, Brown went east through Ashtabula County. There, he met with anti-slavery Congressman Joshua Giddings (of Ohio) and regaled the congressmen with news of his recent successes in Kansas. On Giddings's request, Brown agreed to speak with local citizens about his recent experiences. Following his lecture, Giddings made "a special appeal for contributions, and 'every Democrat as well as Republican present gave something.'"[63] For Brown, this was a portentous occasion. With so many people celebrating his liberation of eleven slaves, he believed that the conditions were ripe for the liberation of millions.

After briefly visiting his son Owen in Ashtabula County, Brown stopped at the home of his benefactor, Gerrit Smith, who had recently told Brown that he was very pleased that the "Underground Railroad is so prosperous in Kansas."[64] In his 22 January letter to Brown, Smith informed the liberator that he would be thrilled to host the abolitionist in his home, since he was "most truly a Christian."[65] During the visit that followed, Smith rewarded Brown with over four hundred dollars and a promise of more in the future.[66]

Satisfied with the accolades he had received and ready to begin his real mission, Brown journeyed to the Adirondacks to see his family and rest prior to returning to the Northeast to raise funds for his greatest effort.

After a brief stay in North Elba, Brown proceeded to Concord where he visited with his most enthusiastic champion, Franklin Sanborn, and many in the influential transcendentalist community. He regaled an attentive audience—including Emerson, Thoreau, Alcott, Hoar, and Sanborn—with a rendition of his recent activities in Kansas at the Town Hall. Commenting on Brown's speech afterward, Bronson Alcott remarked that Brown is the "manliest man I have ever known—the type and synonym of the Just;" similarly impressed, Emerson invited Brown into his home and personally contributed to Brown's efforts in the name of abolition. Obviously taken with Brown, Emerson would later note that "everyone who has heard him speak has been impressed alike by his simple artless goodness, joined with his sublime courage."[67] In spite of his appreciation for the "idealist" and clear approval of his efforts, Emerson was not able to inspire many of his townsmen to offer Brown much pecuniary support for his future efforts; in part, this may have been a result of Brown's reluctance to explain the purpose of the funds he was raising.[68] It may also have been that they no longer believed that the conditions in Kansas merited a privately financed abolitionist army. Brown, therefore, left Concord a bit disappointed; he had only gained ten dollars in the center of intellectual liberty and self-reliance.

Nevertheless, Brown did not consider himself a failure when he left Concord. During his short stay, he had convinced his most enthusiastic supporter, Franklin Sanborn, that his plan to strike slavery in the South was now more viable than ever. Within two days of his departure from Concord, Sanborn had arranged a meeting for Brown with both Samuel Gridley Howe and George Luther Stearns in order to similarly convince the two affluent men. Agreeing that Brown's expedition into Missouri and liberation of eleven slaves had effectively neutered Forbes exposure, the men also agreed that favorable conditions now existed for Brown's more ambitious operation. Howe, however, seemed reluctant to embrace Brown's violent method: guerilla war. Explaining that he no longer believed it just to confiscate property—even from slaveholders—Howe told Brown that he could not bring himself to offer his unqualified support to the radical abolitionist; he had recently returned from a journey among wealthy slave-owners of North Carolina and learned to admire both the gentility of their lives and the beauty of their plantations. He could not now agree to destroy that which he had learned to appreciate.[69]

Recognizing Howe's reluctance, Brown made a special visit to the doctor's luxurious Boston home. There, he paid particular attention to Julia Ward Howe, the woman who would unite the immensely popular

Northern marching song "John Brown's Body" with her own words to become the poignant "The Battle Hymn of the Republic" in a few years. In a maneuver that he had executed successfully two years before—when he had appealed to Mary Preston Stearns and subsequently been promised sufficient funding to conduct operations in Kansas—Brown made a strong appeal to Julia Ward Howe in hopes that the outspoken woman would convince her husband to once again offer his unqualified support for his plan of liberation.[70] He was not disappointed in the result: during the visit, Samuel G. Howe realized the necessity for Brown's guerilla campaign and agreed to fully support the man he now introduced to his Boston friends as a man of the "'Puritan militant order' who had a 'martyr's spirit.'"[71]

When Brown left Boston, he was confident that he would be able to initiate his violent campaign to end slavery in the next few months.[72] He had over $2000, pledges of support from Smith, Stearns, and Howe, and introductions to several potentially influential sponsors: John A. Andrew, John Murray Forbes, and Senator Henry Wilson. However, during the brief visit to his family that followed his New England tour, his confidence suffered a blow. Two of his sons, Salmon and Jason decided not to accompany their father on "the most *important* undertaking of [his] . . . whole life."[73] Like their brother Henry, both Salmon and Jason told their father that they had sworn off fighting since their involvement in the executions at Pottawatomie and decided that they would not be a part of any more violent abolitionism. Disappointed with his sons' show of disloyalty, Brown argued with his boys for five days before he reluctantly accepted defeat.[74] Heartened, perhaps, that his other sons—Owen, Oliver, Watson, and Henry Thompson (a son-in-law)—felt no similar reluctance, Brown departed North Elba on 16 June, eager to begin final preparations for the attack on Harpers Ferry.

He arrived at Harpers Ferry, the small town situated at the confluence of the Shenandoah and the Potomac Rivers on 3 July, 1859; after conferring briefly with John Cook, the man whom he had ordered to Harpers Ferry the previous April, Brown set out to establish a base of operations in nearby Maryland.[75] Giving Cook, who had a penchant for casually revealing the most sensitive information, strict orders to remain silent about the arriving raiders, Brown began searching for a suitably private yet expansive residence for the numerous men he hoped would respond to his two-year-long recruiting effort.[76] Posing as a farmer, he rented a fairly spacious farm-house in Maryland six miles from his immediate target—the federal armory located on the west side of the Potomac at the edge of the small 2500 person town. In order to maintain the appearance of a normal home, Brown, who had assumed the name Isaac Smith, asked Martha, his son Oliver's seventeen year old wife, and Anne, his own fifteen year-old daughter, to come to Maryland to keep house.

Preserving the appearance of a normal family was not an easy task. During the course of the summer, seventeen men covertly arrived at the Kennedy Farm and took up residence in the cramped upstairs quarters of the main house and nearby cabin. Brown went to great pains to conceal his northern army from his rather inquisitive neighbors.[77] He purchased "a few things at a time or place," restricted most of his men to the upstairs of the house or the loft of the cabin during the day, and enforced strict noise discipline during daylight hours.[78] By encouraging quiet activities and maintaining discipline among his recruits, Brown was able to keep the presence of his inter-racial force secret, though one particularly troublesome neighbor did remark on the "right smart lot of shirts" that the Brown men appeared to possess on washing day.[79] Brown's ability to conceal his men during August and September is a true testament to his leadership, particularly when considering the scope of the effort to which he had dedicated himself. The summer was not, however, without periods of great turmoil. This was particularly true around the eighteenth of August when John Brown told his assembled freedom fighters the full details of the operation he envisioned.[80]

Until this time, many of the men believed that Brown simply intended to expand upon the success he had achieved in Missouri in 1858.[81] Brown, however, soon made clear that this was not to be the case. He explained that his real intention was to attack the arsenal at Harpers Ferry, take possession of the weapons stored there, and retreat to the mountains of Virginia to conduct a protracted guerilla war against slaveholders in the area; he expected that the slaves he liberated would rally to his standard, join the Provisional Army, and inspire successive rebellions throughout the South. When they had accomplished his intent in the northern slave states, he explained, his growing army would progress both southward and westward until slavery was eradicated in all of the territory of the United States. Producing maps of seven Southern states and 1850 census data indicating the number and concentration of slaves in each region, Brown sought to impress his recruits with both the thoroughness of his planning and the reasonableness of his design.[82]

When their charismatic newly-bearded leader finished explaining his plan, Brown's recruits were far from convinced that their captain was in any way reasonable. In fact, Brown's own sons forcefully objected to the plan; perhaps, most vocal, Brown's son Oliver objected to the choice of objectives since the terrain in and around Harpers Ferry was brutal; Harpers Ferry was located at the base of steep cliffs and difficult mountains 1200 feet tall; because the rivers surrounded the town, he noted, they might easily be trapped in Harpers Ferry and "cut to pieces."[83] Likewise, Charles Tidd vocally protested; he argued that an attack on Harpers Ferry was suicidal.[84] In clear opposition to these protests, John Cook, who had been in the area the longest, argued for Brown's plan. Having had the opportunity to observe the habits of the watchmen at the arsenal and learn the layout of the terrain, Cook maintained that the plan was viable and "favored the capture quite forcibly."[85] John Kagi, Brown's trusted Secretary of War, likewise favored the plan, but believed that it could succeed only if they were able to capture the armory both by surprise and with great swiftness; presciently identifying rapid withdrawal from the town as the key to success, Kagi pressed his comrades for approval.

In an atmosphere of tension, John Brown staged a dramatic resignation, and he achieved the result he desired; not only did all those present commit to the Harpers Ferry plan, they committed to John Brown.[86] He would now be able to fulfill his self-proclaimed destiny. In the weeks that followed the tense showdown, Brown's men prepared themselves for the mission that they now understood would begin with an armed assault on a federal arsenal. They recognized, however, that they had to remain confined, for the most part, to the interior of the farmhouse, so they had to limit themselves to activities that were fairly static. They spent a great deal of time quietly studying military tactics, preparing their weapons for battle, debating issues, and reading about the events that were occurring in Washington, not more than sixty miles away. In order to pass the time, they also wrote letters to many of their family members. Not surprisingly, many of these letters reveal—in explicit detail—the endeavor to which they had devoted themselves. Writing his mother, William Leeman clearly revealed that he was among a group of men who were "all privately gathered in a slave state, where we are determined to strike for freedom, incite the slaves to rebellion, and establish a free government."[87] Brown, himself, was frequently corresponding during this time. The vast majority of his letters, however, were either addressed to Northern allies or to remote members of his provisional army attempting to redress the logistical concerns that threatened to compromise his campaign. Short of money, manpower, and military hardware, Brown had reason to be concerned.

In mid-September, he still did not have all of the weapons that he believed necessary to conduct a protracted guerilla war. For one, the pikes that Connecticut blacksmith Charles Blair had manufactured for him were still in Chambersburg. Commissioned by Brown in March, 1857, Blair built one thousand steel pikes with the help of Brown's son, Jason, who had agreed to apprentice himself to the blacksmith during the two years that Blair labored on the rudimentary weapons.[88] Believing that it would be more effective to arm newly liberated slaves with pikes rather than rifles—since the rudimentary weapons could be immediately employed by the new conscripts—Brown made the last payment for the crude steel weapons that June. Then, he stored them alongside the 198 Sharps rifles and 200 revolvers that the Kansas Committees supplied him during his independent war in Kansas.[89]

Brown was also missing one other element for successful execution of his plan—"negro" men.[90] Although he had courted Harriet Tubman's favor in the spring of 1858, and convinced her to "use her influence among the Canadian fugitives" in St. Catherines, Canada, the year-long delay in implementation of his plan had resulted in the loss of any possible recruits from that area.[91] Keenly aware of the shortage of African-American men in his small force, he dispatched his son John Jr. in August to recruit negro men willing to fight for their brethren in the Northeast; John Jr., however, failed completely. Despite the assurances that affluent blacks had provided his father only fourteen months before, John Jr. was unable to inspire one man to leave the relative sanctuary of New York, Massachusetts, or Canada to fight for his enslaved Southern brother.

Aware of Brown's manpower shortfall, Franklin Sanborn also attempted to recruit men for Brown's impending mission; due to his commitments in Concord, however, he did not feel at liberty to travel in search of fugitive recruits. In his stead, Sanborn suggested that Thomas Wentworth Higginson should go to Canada with Harriet Tubman in order to win recruits from the fugitive slave population living there.[92] Evidently less than enthusiastic when he received Sanborn's 4 June letter, Higginson refused Sanborn's request, thus no one journeyed northward from Boston, and no one inspired recent fugitives to join Brown's provisional army.

John Brown even failed; in a last minute attempt, he invited Frederick Douglass to join him in his "special purpose;" Douglass refused. He would not "hive . . . the bees" who began to "swarm," or organize the newly liberated slaves for Brown following the initiation of Brown's guerilla war.[93] Brown's plan, Douglass asserted, was sheer suicide; Harpers Ferry was a "perfect steel trap and . . . once in [Douglass asserted, Brown] would never get out alive."[94] Further, Douglass argued, Brown's plan would be "fatal to running off slaves (as was the original plan) . . . It would be an attack on the federal government, and would array the whole country against us."[95] Brown spent the better part of two days arguing the merits of his plan with Douglass, attempting to convince his old friend that the effort "would serve as notice to the slaves that their friends had come, and as a trumpet to rally them to his standard."[96] However, in the end, Brown failed to convince Douglass that his plan had merit; as a result, he failed to enlist the most visible black abolitionist in the nation. He was not, however, entirely unsuccessful. When he and Douglass parted, fugitive slave Shields Green, one of the men who had accompanied Douglass to the clandestine meeting in Chambersburg, decided to join Brown and he accompanied Brown to the Kennedy farmhouse to prepare for the blow that he believed would "rouse the country."[97]

The absence of a notable African-American figure in his Northern Army was not Brown's only concern during the summer of 1859. A shortage of adequate funds plagued Brown. His need was especially acute after he had paid the balance of money that he owed Blair for his steel pikes, transported his weapons from their covert storage in Chambersburg, defrayed the cost of travel that he and his men had incurred in the process of their recruiting efforts, and payed for living expenses in Maryland. Brown knew that he needed money to initiate and sustain a protracted guerilla war.[98] Therefore, throughout the late summer and early fall, Brown persistently appealed to his Northern supporters for additional funds. His primary target was Franklin Sanborn, and he relentlessly petitioned Sanborn to provide him the finances necessary to "set his *mill* in operation."[99]

Sanborn attempted to convince Brown that he was doing everything in his power to satisfy the captain's needs. Responding to Brown's urgent request for $300 on August 27th, Sanborn informed Brown that he would "make up to you the $300, if I can, as soon as I can, but I can give nothing myself just now, being already in debt."[100] Attempting to coordinate the fundraising effort for Brown, Sanborn sent his secret associates urgent petitions for money on Brown's behalf; he was not always successful. Higginson, for one, refused all of Sanborn's entreaties. Even when Sanborn pleaded, "you must raise $50 if possible, [sic] you see the emergency and how others have met it," Higginson declined.[101] Only when George Luther Stearns made a personal appeal to Higginson's magnanimity did the Worcester agitator respond with $20 of the $50 asked of him.[102] Frustrated, yet undeterred in his commitment to Brown, Sanborn continued to urge Higginson and his fellow conspirators to support Brown throughout the month of September. As a result of his diligent efforts, Sanborn was able to send Brown a continual stream of small contributions. He was not, however, able to satisfy the needs of the agitated guerilla captain.

In order to begin his campaign, Brown told Sanborn, he required much more money than he had received to date.[103] Money was only one of Brown's concerns as the summer turned to fall; unbeknownst to John Brown, reports that the Kansas freedom fighter was planning a slave insurrection reached Washington in late August. Secretary of War John B. Floyd received a 23 August letter that clearly revealed John Brown's general plan to begin a slave insurrection in Virginia. According to the anonymous author, within a few weeks, "'Old John Brown,' late of Kansas" was planning on assembling a force of men in the mountains of Virginia to "arm the negroes and strike the blow" against slavery.[104] The author suggested that Brown would enter Virginia at Harper's Ferry and "rendezvous" with small companies of negroes who had been training in Canada. Further, he warned both that Brown's force of men had a "large quantity of arms . . . and are probably distributing them already." He even noted that they "have one of their leading men (a white man) in an armory in Maryland." [105] Perhaps fortunate for Brown, Floyd chose not to act on the letter. As he later suggested, the reference to the armory in Maryland led him to disregard the entire note, since, in 1859, there were no federal armories in that state.[106]

In hindsight, Floyd's decision to disregard the warning seems foolish. John Brown had achieved a national reputation as a warrior for the Free State cause in Kansas and he had attained recent notoriety as the liberator of eleven slaves from Missouri. A defiant militant with a public history of active opposition to the government, Brown's prominent name in a letter concerned with slave insurrection ought to have inspired more than a passing interest in the Secretary of War: however, it did not. Floyd filed the letter and evidently forgot about it until word that Brown was the author of the attack at Harper's Ferry became public knowledge on October 17, 1859.[107]

Floyd's awareness of a potential attack on an armory by John Brown was not singular. In his incisive study of John Brown, Stephen Oates suggests that over eighty people knew about Brown's plan to inspire an insurrection in the South, and many others had reason to believe that Brown "was planning some incendiary move against the South."[108] Brown's trusted benefactors revealed as much in their public engagements during the summer of 1859. In his 27 August letter to the "Jerry Rescue" Anniversary Committee, Gerrit Smith stated that for black men, "no resource is left . . . but in God and insurrections. *For insurrections* [he prophetically emphasized] . . . *we may look any year, any month, any day.*"[109] Smith proceeded to declare that it was "too late to bring slavery to an end by peaceful means—to late to vote it down;" The only option left blacks, Smith repeatedly emphasized, was "God and insurrection."[110] Made public on 20 October, 1859, a New York *Times* special correspondent would suggest that this letter was both a "prophesy . . . of the outbreak at Harper's Ferry" and an indication of Smith's complicity in Brown's violent attack on 16 October.[111]

Higginson may have similarly telegraphed Brown's future raid, though his audience was a good deal less public than Smith's; in November, 1858, Higginson cautioned Lysander Spooner, a Boston lawyer and abolitionist, to delay further publication of "A Plan for the Abolition of Slavery," since it resembled too closely the plan that Brown had articulated in March, 1858. In his plan, Spooner encouraged "non-slave holders of this country in their private capacity as individuals . . . to go to the rescue of the Slaves from their oppressors . . . by *force if need be.*"[112] Further, he advocated arming and training blacks for guerilla warfare in order to destroy the "security and value" of slave property.[113] Concerned that further publication might compromise Brown's efforts, Higginson wrote Spooner a revealing letter maintaining

> It is my firm conviction that, within a few years, that phase of . . . [a slave insurrection] will urge itself on general attention, and the root of the matter be thus reached. I think that this will be done by the action of the slaves themselves, in certain localities, with the aid of *secret* co-operation from the whites.

Were I free to do it, I would give you other assurance that what I say means something, & that other influences than those of which you speak are even working to the same end. I am not now at liberty to be more explicit.[114]

Later, in a personal meeting with Spooner, Higginson was more forthcoming. He explained the reasons for his concern in explicit detail and was able to convince Spooner that suppression of his manifesto was in the best interests of abolition.[115] Higginson, however, was not the only abolitionist to whom Spooner appealed. Theodore Parker had also received a letter from Spooner soliciting his advice about publication; much like Higginson, he too cautioned Spooner to refrain from further publication.[116]

Submitting to the requests of the prominent abolitionists, Spooner agreed to withdraw his "Plan." However, nearly two hundred copies had already been printed, and these had been distributed to "slaveholders themselves."[117] The potential damage to Brown's plan had already occurred; by preventing additional publication, Higginson and Parker were simply trying to limit its scope. Despite these apparent compromises, evidently very few in Washington, New York, or Boston anticipated that Brown would actually set his plan in motion on 16 October. After months of delays, Brown had not provided his New England sponsors with any satisfying indications that he was prepared to initiate operations when the leaves began to fall in Boston. Higginson's suggestion that the entire project was rather "chimerical" must have seemed frustratingly appropriate to Franklin Sanborn, particularly when the Concord schoolmaster considered Brown's constant requests for more and more money.[118] Concerned, perhaps, that Higginson's assessment had some validity, Sanborn responded to Brown's last request by sending the slight, one-eyed Francis Merriam (whom Higginson would later suggest was either "mentally unbalanced or severely retarded") to join Brown on 6 October.[119] On the advice of James Redpath, Merriam had presented himself to Sanborn and offered to contribute $600 if he could participate in the effort to liberate "slaves down South."[120] His arrival on 15 October removed the last obstacle to Brown's plan.

Having received the boxes of weapons from Chambersburg two weeks before and welcomed the last of his raiders—John Copeland and Lewis Leary—that same day, John Brown was finally ready to strike a blow against slavery. He had a force of twenty-one men, five of whom were African-American, an arsenal of weapons, a sum of $600 (in gold), and a firm conviction that he would succeed. If they failed, Brown told his men, "it will perhaps do more for the cause than our lives would be worth in any other way."[121]

Assembling his men on the afternoon of October 16, Brown reviewed his battle plan, made final assignments, and prepared to march on slavery. At eight o'clock that evening, Brown and eighteen of his men left the farmhouse prepared to initiate the end of slavery in the United States.[122]

Approaching the armory in the drizzle under cover of darkness, Brown's men surprised the night watchmen, captured the bridges into and out of the town, and took control of the federal armory. Herding his captives into the engine house near the gate of the facility, Brown and his men felt confident of their success. Not a shot had been fired and all appeared to be proceeding according to plan. He had captured the arms and ammunition that his guerilla campaign was dependent upon and had no reason to believe that anyone would oppose his withdrawal from the town.

Convinced that everything was going well, Brown then dispatched six men to seize notable hostages from the surrounding area: Colonel Lewis Washington, the grand-nephew of George Washington, was among the first captured.[123] During his tenure as a resident of Harper's Ferry, John Cook had briefly courted Washington's favor and learned that he had several relics of his revolutionary forefather. Among these was a sword that Frederick the Great had given General Washington and a pistol that Lafayette had presented the first Commander in Chief of the Revolutionary Army. Thinking that these might be appropriate weapons for his own commander, Cook confiscated both weapons when he took an indignant Washington—and several of his slaves—hostage. [124] After similarly making Washington's neighbor a hostage and dramatically arming several of the slaves that they had liberated, Cook and his compatriots returned to Harpers Ferry and presented their hostages to John Brown. Calmly welcoming Washington in the Engine House where he had temporarily established his headquarters, the Provisional Army commander informed his hostage, "I wanted you particularly for the moral effect [sic] it would give our cause having one of your name, as a prisoner."[125] Evidently, Brown felt quite confident that news of Washington's capture would both dissuade local citizens from arming against him and inspire them to consider his effort as the first steps in the new American Revolution. When Cook presented him with the weapons he had obtained from Washington, John Brown expressed particular pleasure that he would be able to "strike the first blow for the freedom of a race with them in his hands."[126] With the raid proceeding according to plan, he had no reason to doubt that he would have that opportunity.

It soon became evident, however, that Brown's failure to thoroughly familiarize himself with both the schedule of trains that serviced Harpers Ferry and the rotation schedule of the bridge watchmen might compromise his ability to dramatically flourish the sword that had been owned by the commander of the colonial army. Some time past one o'clock, a relief night watchman approached one of Brown's sentries on the wooden railroad bridge across the Potomac. Evidently unaware that there was anything wrong, he was surprised when someone demanded his surrender—and even more surprised when he heard the sound of a gunshot and felt a sharp pain along the ridge of his skull.[127] Wounded, the watchman retreated to one of the nearby houses and began to alarm the local citizens. About the same time, an express passenger train from Wheeling arrived at Harpers Ferry and attempted to cross the bridge; though wounded, the watchman saw the train and was able to signal the conductor to stop before informing him that men armed with rifles were in the town and had just had shot him. Concerned that they might endanger their passengers by proceeding, the train engineer and the baggage master went forward on foot to investigate the night watchman's strange tale. When they too heard gunshots, they quickly returned to the train and inspired the conductor to move the passenger cars out of rifle range. At nearly the same time, Hayford Shepherd, a free black man serving as baggage master for the train station, failed to respond to the commands of one of Brown's men and received a fatal bullet wound in the chest.[128]

By now, the inhabitants of Harpers Ferry were becoming aware that something was absolutely wrong in their quiet town. The distinct report of Sharp's carbines was not normal in the middle of the night in peaceful Harpers Ferry. Alarmed by sporadic sounds of gunfire in the darkness, residents armed themselves with whatever weapons they had available and assembled in the streets.[129] By morning, rumors that a slave insurrection was occurring at Harpers Ferry had reached nearby towns and local militiamen were preparing for battle.[130]

Seemingly oblivious to the events occurring outside of the Engine House, John Brown did not demonstrate any concern about the disorganized townsmen who were beginning to shower the armory with bullets. Instead, Brown calmly waited for word that local slaves, having heard the news, were preparing to join him, and watched the sun come up in Harpers Ferry in the company of his thirty hostages. He even allowed the conductor of the train to proceed safely toward Baltimore trusting that he would carry news of the attack to the world.[131]

Despite his good-will gesture, the people in Harpers Ferry seemed increasingly unwilling to offer the insurrectionists any quarter. As news of the attack spread throughout the local communities, incensed men descended upon the town and poured gunfire on both the Engine House and Hall's Rifle Works, where Brown's lieutenant, John Kagi, had taken refuge. With the arrival of the Jefferson Guards, the militia unit from nearby Charlestown, the foolishness of his Brown's decision to remain on-site was apparent to everyone; even John Brown realized that he and his men were trapped.

Recognizing the precariousness of his situation, Brown sent Will Thompson and one of his hostages under a flag of truce to negotiate a cease fire; the crowd, apparently, was not prepared for such a gesture and responded by seizing Thompson and taking him away at gun point.[132] Undismayed, and hoping that a more formidable party might succeed, Brown then sent Aaron Stevens, his son Watson, and the superintendent of the Armory out under a flag of truce to negotiate his escape. Evidently less than eager to consider his offer, the incensed mob responded by shooting both Stevens and Brown and liberating the terrified superintendent. Mortally wounded, Watson Brown painfully crawled back to the Engine House where he would repeatedly beg his father to shoot him and end his "agony."[133] Stevens, meanwhile, lay in the gutter outside of the Engine House bleeding profusely. He survived only because one of Brown's hostages bravely volunteered to bring him to medical attention, then return to captivity.[134]

Despite this singular act of compassion, neither the incensed residents of Harpers Ferry nor the increasingly numerous militia-men who responded to word that "one-hundred fifty insurrectionists" had descended upon Harpers Ferry offered Brown's men much quarter.[135] In fact, as both the Wager and the Galt House liberally dispensed liquor to the men who made up the increasingly irate mob, the tenor of the town turned menacing as the afternoon matured.[136] Inspired by drink and encouraged by the arrival of the men from Charlestown, many of those present at Harpers Ferry on October 17 determined that justice would be theirs and loudly shouted, "Kill them, Kill them" from the outskirts of the armory.[137] Terrified by what he heard, William Leeman, one of Brown's young soldiers, fled for his life. As he crossed the Potomac, two men caught him, killed him at point blank range, and then left his mangled body to serve as a target for irate riflemen for the remainder of the day.[138] Inspired by their success, another group of incensed men charged nearby Hall's Rifle works where John Kagi, William Copeland, and Lewis Leary had barricaded themselves. Forced to withdraw from their position and attempt an escape across the Shenandoah, both Leary and Kagi were instantly killed as they ran towards the river. Copeland—a Negro raider—was captured as he attempted to wade into the Shenandoah and only escaped lynching because a good Samaritan happened by and protected the terrified raider until a policeman brought him to safety.[139]

As the situation deteriorated and five more companies of militia arrived in Harpers Ferry, John Brown made yet another attempt to negotiate out of his predicament. Sending a note bearing his signature, Brown offered to release his hostages if he and his men were offered free passage to Maryland. Confident that Brown had no chance of escape and cognizant that federal troops would soon arrive, Colonel Baylor, the senior militiaman on site, refused Brown's request outright. He did not, however, restrict the knowledge that it was the notorious John Brown of Kansas who had attempted to instigate a rebellion among the slaves in Virginia; the next day, news dispatches that revealed that John Brown was the leader of the men who had violated the sanctity of the South confronted the nation.[140]

President Buchanan, sixty miles away in Washington, was informed by telegraph of the insurrection at Harpers Ferry on the morning of 17 October. He responded by requesting that three artillery companies then stationed at Fort Monroe be immediately dispatched to Harpers Ferry. Later, he also ordered the "only United States force then in Washington—a small company of marines" under Lieutenant Israel Green to march on the beleaguered town.[141] Choosing among the senior officers present in Washington, President Buchanan directed Brevet Colonel Robert E. Lee to take charge of the situation.[142] When Lee arrived at Harpers Ferry in the company of the Marines on the night of 17 October, it did not take long for him to assess the situation and determine that he would attack at first light. Out of concern for the prisoners that Brown held in the Engine House, however, Lee decided that he would first offer Brown an opportunity to surrender.[143]

As he observed from an elevation some forty feet away, at dawn on 18 October, Lee sent J.E.B. Stuart, his temporarily appointed Aide de Camp, under a white flag of truce toward the Engine House. Presenting Brown with a note "demanding the surrender of the persons in the armory," and, at the same time, promising their safety—if they were to immediately comply with his terms—Stuart bravely waited as Brown read his commander's demand.[144] As Lee had anticipated, Brown refused his terms, responding that he would surrender only if his men were allowed to escape.[145]

In all probability, Brown did not expect that Lee would be any more willing to entertain his request than Colonel Baylor had been; however, he probably hoped that the Regular Army officer might respect his effort to negotiate and offer his men some quarter during the fight that might ensue. Regardless, he was not prepared for Stuart's curt explanation that his commander would not "accede to any terms but those he had offered," nor was he prepared for the Marines' assault that immediately followed Stuart's departure from the door of the Engine House.[146]

Armed with bayonets and light swords, the storming party of twelve Marines attacked on Stuart's signal. From the concealed positions that they had assumed while Stuart was talking to Brown, the Marines quickly approached the Engine House, breached the doors with a heavy ladder, and proceeded to either kill or capture all of the armed men who resisted them. As Colonel Lee succinctly noted in his report, "the insurgents that resisted were bayoneted. Their leader, John Brown, was cut down by the sword of Lieutenant Green, and our citizens were protected by both officers and men. The whole affair was over in a few minutes."[147] After Green's men secured all of the hostages, he instructed his men to take the dead and wounded raiders outside of the Engine House. When they completed the task, there were four severely wounded men (to include John Brown) and two cadavers lying on the grass. At Colonel Lee's directive, John Brown was carried to the paymaster's office where he was provided medical attention.[148]

Sequestered with the gravely wounded Aaron Stevens, Brown did not demonstrate any remorse for his failed effort. Instead, displaying the same "cool, collected, and indomitable spirit" that Lewis Washington had noted during the defense of the Engine House, Brown exuded a quiet confidence when he found himself confronted by an assembly of incensed politicians, military officers, errant civilians, and eager reporters who demanded an immediate interview on the afternoon of his capture. During that interview, Brown's deft responses to the queries of Colonel Lee, Senator Mason of Virginia, Congressman Vallandigham of Ohio, Congressman Faulkner of Virginia, and Governor Wise of Virginia, clearly demonstrated that he recognized that his military failure did not mean defeat; he knew that he still could achieve a political and moral victory if he used the opportunity that his audience provided him. Not only would his responses to the questions the assembled congressmen posed him reach the highest levels of government, Brown understood that because reporters from both the New York *Herald* and the Baltimore *American* were present, there was a good probability that his responses might reach a far more significant audience—an eager and impressionable public. Brown astutely recognized that he now had a platform more significant than any lyceum in America. In fact, when the *Herald* printed the full transcript of the interview on 21 October, Brown had the very public opportunity to "make his motives understood to all of America."[149]

During the course of the three hour interview, not only did Brown use the opportunity to express his own belief that those who defended slavery were morally corrupt, he cleverly manipulated the language of his interrogators to expose their hypocrisy as defenders of slavery in the United States. When Senator Mason intimated that he had attacked the federal armory for some personal gain, Brown clearly articulated that his only objective in conducting the raid on Harpers Ferry was "to free the slaves, and only that."[150] Asked to justify his actions, Brown cleverly turned the tables on his inquisitors charging them with "great wrong against God and humanity."[151] Explaining his actions, Brown suggested that it was the perfect "right in anyone to interfere with you as far as to free those you willfully hold in bondage."[152] Asked to reveal the names of those who provided him the resources for his expedition, Brown responded, "No man sent me here; it was my own prompting and that of my Maker, or that of the devil, whichever you please to ascribe it to. I acknowledge no man in human form."[153] Further elaborating his motive for attacking Harpers Ferry, Brown remarked, "I want you to understand that I respect the rights of the poorest and weakest of colored people, oppressed by the slave system, just as much as I do those of the most wealthy and powerful."[154] After he made this comment, Brown turned directly to the reporter for the New York *Herald* and informed him, "you may report that."[155]

Throughout the entire interview, Brown consistently challenged his inquisitors with his forthright responses. Clearly recognizing the opportunity that he still had to strike a philosophical blow against slavery, Brown deftly used the interview to turn his military failure into a public relations success. Brown's performance during the 18 October interview seemed to make a distinct impression upon his interrogators. Perhaps most vocal, Virginia's Governor Henry Wise remarked that Brown was a

> man of clear head, of courage, fortitude and simple ingenuousness. He is cool, collected and indomitable, and it is but just to him to say that he was humane to his prisoners . . . and inspired me with great trust in his integrity as a man of truth. He is a fanatic, vain, garrulous, but firm, truthful and intelligent.[156]

Clearly, he was not the only man impressed by Brown; a reporter for the Baltimore *American* noted that "in reply to every question, [Brown] gave answers that betokened the spirit that animated him."[157] Many in the reading public were as impressed by Brown as his interrogators had been. Newspapers throughout the country carried reports of Brown's invasion, subsequent capture, and testimony. For radical abolitionists throughout the country, Brown's forthright defense of his actions at Harpers Ferry and staunch refusal to compromise his financial supporters indicated a bold new era in the movement toward the emancipation of slaves. For slaveholders, Brown represented the type of destructive subversion that abolitionists had been talking about for the last three decades. Brown confronted America with the reality of slavery anew; he represented a new era in abolition marked by a willingness to attack slavery with both violent acts and violent words.

However, Brown's 18 October performance was compromised when Lieutenant Stuart, responding to information that Brown had rented a farm in Maryland only six miles from Harpers Ferry, discovered a carpet bag full of incriminating correspondence carelessly left there. Not only did these letters clearly reveal that Brown had not acted independently, they suggested the identities of four of the six of his most significant supporters. They also exposed both the detail and scope of Brown's intention to initiate a rebellion in every slave state in the Union. Published in both the New York *Tribune* and New York *Times,* these texts had a significant impact upon both the men they implicated and men they exposed as conspirators.

The publication of Brown's plans, taken from the sheaf of papers found in the Maryland farmhouse, inspired general hysteria in the South. Concerned that slave revolts might erupt within their communities or invading abolitionists might cross their borders to liberate their human property, citizens from Virginia to Louisiana alerted their militia units, increased their security measures, and anxiously awaited signs of an invasion.[158] In Virginia, Governor Wise activated nearly four hundred militia-men to keep the peace in Charlestown, where Brown and Stevens had been moved to ensure that they were neither rescued nor lynched by the volatile local population; one hundred and fifty militia-men were called to Harpers Ferry to guard the now peaceful armory. As Oates points out, Brown's raid created a "Great Fear" comparable the atmosphere of terror prevalent in France in 1789.[159]

Throughout the South, Northern men who had been residents of local communities for years were arrested, forcibly removed from their homes, and physically tortured on the assumption that their sympathies were with the northern abolitionists who had just been captured at Harpers Ferry. In the American Anti-Slavery Society's *Annual Report*, accounts of abuse and forcible expulsion of Northern merchants, teachers, and intellectuals in Southern cities confirm the widespread alarm that Brown's raid caused. For instance, local vigilantes in Savannah called out shoe dealer Sewell H.

Fisk in the middle of the night, gagged the native of Massachusetts, placed him in a wagon, drove him from the city, then stripped, tarred, and covered his entire body with cotton in response to his "known Abolitionist proclivities."[160] This was not an isolated occurrence. Throughout the South, vigilantes accosted northern men—or those who had displayed any sympathy for abolition—and made examples of them. In the Atlanta *Confederacy*, the anonymous editors boldly proclaimed:

> We regard every man in our midst an enemy to the institutions of the South, who does not boldly declare that he believes African Slavery to be a social, moral, and political blessing. Any person holding other sentiments, whether born in the South or North, is unsound, and should be requested to leave the country.[161]

Governor Wise, capitalizing on the nation's focus, proclaimed Brown's raid an "extraordinary and actual invasion, by a sectional organization, specially upon slave-holders and upon their property in negro slaves."[162] Calling upon slave states to maintain the temporary unification that Brown's invasion had inspired in the face of the northern aggressor, Wise further proclaimed that the "non-Slave-holding States are in nearly solid array against us."[163] Brown had accomplished, it seems, the exact opposite of his intention; he had given Southern slave-holders a singular event around which to rally and establish solidarity. Many southern Democrats confirmed this sentiment when they asserted that the "Harper's Ferry Insurrection is certainly very opportune, quite a God-send, for the Southern Democracy and all Pro-Slavery Partisans." They also claimed that "the very agitators whose conduct gave rise to the Republican party, originated and fostered it, and is still furnishing it aid, and comfort and sustenance."[164]

In the North, reactions to Brown's capture and interrogation were mixed. Many prominent citizens regarded Brown and his associates as mere criminals who had broken the law and deservedly faced severe punishment.[165] Like their Democratic brothers in the South, these Northern Democrats attempted to make political capital of Brown's raid. Stephen A. Douglas, New York Senator and aspiring presidential candidate, asserted that the invasion "was the natural, logical, inevitable result of the doctrines and teachings of the Republican Party."[166] Abraham Lincoln, distancing himself from the abolitionist effort, declared "John Brown was no Republican, and you have failed to implicate a single Republican in his Harper's Ferry enterprise."[167] However, as news of Brown's behavior continued to reach the reading public, many changed their minds and began to admire the fifty-nine year old freedom fighter for his willingness to translate principles to action and then staunchly defend those actions, even though they had resulted in his own capture.

Among Brown's closest Northern supporters, however there was no consistent response. In the immediate aftermath of Brown's capture, Howe and Stearns, like Sanborn, fled the country rather than face possible legal censure for their complicity in Brown's activities.[168] Frederick Douglass, likewise, fled the country. Gerrit Smith, whose name had been prominently paraded before the public as one of the men who had been most active in providing John Brown with support, was committed to the Utica Asylum immediately following Brown's capture for a condition of insanity termed "exaltation of the mind."[169] He remained institutionalized until John Brown was dead.

Of Brown's most significant supporters, Thomas Wentworth Higginson was the only man who quietly remained in the country refusing to either consider flight or privilege Franklin Sanborn's repeated requests that he immediately destroy all letters that might be used to prove their complicity in Brown's attack.[170] Since no correspondence bearing his signature had been found at the Kennedy farm, he was not pressed to make a public declaration of sentiment with regard to Brown. Privately, however, Higginson called the outbreak at Harper's Ferry "the most formidable slave insurrection that has ever occurred and it is evident, through the confused and exaggerated accounts, that there are leaders of great capacity and skill behind it."[171]

Notwithstanding Higginson's assertion that the leader of the raid had great skill, it did not take long for authorities to account for most of the twenty-two men who comprised Brown's Provisional Army. Within a few days of Brown's capture, federal authorities had accounted for fifteen of Brown's army: ten were dead or dying; five were in captivity; and seven were on the run—two of that number would be captured in Pennsylvania within a few days; five others would escape. None of the slaves that John Brown had liberated during the raid had rallied to his standard, although some did, with frightened expressions, hold the weapons that were forced upon them in the Engine House; none, however, actively engaged in any fighting once the shooting began around the armory.[172]

Despite reports of vandalism in the countryside immediate to Harpers Ferry, there did not appear to be any slaves who chose to desert their masters' homes at news of Brown's attack and rally to Brown's call to arms. Governor Wise attempted to make political capital out of the fact that "faithful slaves refused to take up arms against their masters; and those who were taken by force from their happy homes deserted their liberators as soon as they could dare to make the attempt."[173] He denied John Brown any immediate success suggesting that his effort had been a complete failure.

Describing his act as "wanton, malicious, [and] unprovoked," Wise determined that he would prosecute his prisoner in a Virginia Court.[174] Urging a speedy trial for the men who had challenged both the sovereignty of Virginia and the will of her slave-owning citizens, Wise ordered Brown to stand trial one week after his capture in the circuit court in Charlestown. Arraigned on October 25, 1859, Brown was charged with five counts of murder, conspiracy to incite rebellion among the slaves, and treason against the state of Virginia.[175] To the delight of the Northern press, Brown characteristically responded to these charges by denying the legality of the trial, and asking for a dismissal so that he would "not be foolishly insulted" by the "mockery of a trial."[176] Judge Richard Parker was not impressed, but he was fearful that the atmosphere in Charlestown was too volatile to delay Brown's trial; as a result, Parker determined that he would hear opening arguments on 27 October, two days after Brown's arraignment.

On the 27th, Brown captured the attention of the court as he was carried into the court on a stretcher. Wounded badly, but not cowed, Brown inspired both awe and hatred in the gallery. He did not, however, awe his court-appointed counsel, Lawson Botts. After accepting the case, Botts had initiated some very practical measures to ensure that his client did not stand trial. Much to Brown's surprise, Botts' first motion was to attempt to prove that there was sufficient evidence to claim that Brown was insane during the raid. Citing a significant history of insanity in Brown's family, Botts suggested that Brown was—in all likelihood—insane during his attack on Harper's Ferry, and, therefore, could not be held responsible for his actions there.[177] Indignant over Botts's assertions, Brown publicly challenged his lawyer and asserted that the plea of insanity was a "miserable artifice and pretext of those who ought to take a different course in regard to me."[178] Clarifying his refusal to privilege a plea of insanity, Brown forcefully asserted, "I reject, so far as I am able, any attempt to interfere in my behalf on that score."[179]

He did not, however, reject Bott's motion that the court delay the trial until his own counsel might arrive from Cleveland; Andrew Hunter, the special prosecutor for the state of Virginia, did. Arguing that there was no evidence to suggest that the counsel Brown had requested would arrive, and calling to question whether Brown's private counsel came as a legal representative or as the "head of a band of desperadoes" intent on liberating the prisoner, Hunter vigorously opposed delay.[180]

Perhaps concerned about the antagonistic crowd that gathered outside his court room during the trial, Judge Parker agreed with Hunter and refused to consider Bott's petition for a delay in Brown's trial. Even the arrival of attorneys George Hoyt from Boston, Samuel Chilton from Washington, and Hiram Griswold from Cleveland (on the second and third days of the trial) did not inspire Judge Parker to delay the progress of Brown's trial, nor did Brown's dismissal of his court appointed attorneys and subsequent assertion that the trial was decidedly unfair, since his attorneys had not ensured that the witnesses he desired would appear in his defense.[181] There-fore, after only four days of testimony, the trial concluded on 31 October.

Instructed to "acquit the prisoner if you can; but if justice requires you by your verdict to take his life, stand by that column [of justice] uprightly, but strongly, and let retributive justice, if he is guilty send him before that Maker who will settle the question forever and ever," the jury recessed.[182] Within forty-five minutes, they returned and proclaimed Brown guilty.

Just prior to sentencing on 2 November, Judge Parker offered Brown the opportunity to address the court. In what may have been his most poignant public statement, Brown rose from the pallet that he had occupied during the preponderance of the trial and addressed the packed court-house. Clearly making the most of the opportunity, Brown asserted:

> I believe to have interfered as I have done, as I have always freely admitted I have done in behalf of His despised poor, is not wrong, but right. Now if it is deemed necessary that I should forfeit my life for the furtherance of the ends of justice, and mingle my blood further with the blood of my children and with the blood of millions in this slave country whose rights are disregarded by wicked, cruel, and unjust enactments, I say let it be done.[183]

Shortly thereafter, Judge Parker pronounced the sentence of death, specifying 2 December, 1859, as the date of Brown's public execution.

In the outcome of the trial, Governor Wise had to deal with an onslaught of correspondence and press regarding his prisoner. Appeals for clemency were frequent, some recognizing that Brown's execution would add to the power of the abolitionists by providing them a martyr and others maintaining that Old Testament justice would only flame the embers of vengeance and further strain the tense relationship between the states. In spite of both the private and public warnings that to "HANG A FANATIC is to make a martyr of him, and fledge another brood of the same sort," Wise determined to carry out Judge Parker's sentence and hang Brown and his fellow conspirators in Charlestown.[184] Explaining his decision to the legislature on 5 December, 1859, Wise remarked

> I know of no magnanimity which is so in-humane . . . which would turn felons like these, proud and defiant in their guilt, loose again on a border already torn by a fanatical and sectional strife which threatens the liberties of the white even more than it does the bondage of the black race."[185]

Although able to pardon Brown, a course he was frequently counseled to adopt, Wise would not consider it.

John Brown would not consider it either. Recognizing that his death was far more valuable to both his own legacy and the cause he so poignantly championed, Brown acknowledged, "I am worth inconceivably more to hang than for any other purpose."[186] To reports that several of his supporters, to include Thomas Wentworth Higginson, were in the process of preparing plans to rescue him, Brown was equally adamant; he wanted no such thing. To achieve the martyrdom that was both feared and prophesied by Pro-Slavery newsmen, John Brown recognized that he had to hang.

Brown also recognized that to ensure his own legacy, he had to actively commit himself to the eager public in the last thirty days of his life. From his Charlestown jail room, therefore, John Brown dedicated himself to the public. He entertained a steady stream of visitors during the ensuing month, actively courted newspaper reporters' favor, and embarked on a prolific letter writing campaign to ensure that he achieved the end that his Pro-Slavery enemies feared. To all, he was cordial, forthright, and considerate.[187] Summarizing his brave conduct in both prison and on the battlefield, James Redpath, reporting for the Boston *Atlas & Bee*, proclaimed that "[l]iving he acted bravely, dying, he will teach us courage."[188]

Reporters from the Charlestown *Independent Democrat* made Redpath appear like a conservative when they printed Brown's assertion, "I feel no shame on the part of my doom. Jesus of Nazareth was doomed in like manner. Why should I not be?"[189] Likewise, New York *Times* reporters noted that "John Brown speaks for himself and for the cause to which he had given his life and the lives of his children, as calmly, as openly, and as earnestly as he could have done in the supreme hour of victory itself."[190] Eager to sell papers, they made Brown a nineteenth century icon—a saintly figure of both national and religious significance. Brown, of course, guided them to this realization by repeatedly associating himself with Christ and ensuring that his willing sacrifice on behalf of slaves was closely associated with Christ's sacrifice.

Brown was most effective, however, in the prolific personal correspondence that he carried on during his month-long incarceration at Charlestown. Not only did he write letters to family members, friends, and fellow abolitionists, he penned poignant letters to members of an increasingly sympathetic public whom he had never had the opportunity to meet. Often published in newspapers, these letters helped Brown achieve symbolic status as the courageous champion of the oppressed that he had yearned for, and it helped him promote the cause of abolition. In a letter addressed to his wife, Brown wrote, "I have been whipped as the saying is but am sure I can recover all the lost capital occasioned by that disaster; by only hanging a few minutes by the neck; & I feel quite determined to make the utmost possible out of defeat."[191]

Paying close attention to the newspaper articles daily covering responses to his efforts, Brown crafted the enduring and symbolic public figure that both reporters and intellectuals would celebrate. Responding to a Quaker woman who had expressed both her sympathy and her profound respect for his actions, Brown likened himself to Peter, the apostle who once had gone armed at the behest of Jesus.[192] To the son of a business friend, Brown likened himself to Christ suggesting that he would go "joyfully in behalf of Millions that 'have no rights' that this great and glorious . . . Christian Republic' is bound to respect."[193] And to Lydia Maria Child, who asked Brown if she could come South and serve as his nurse, Brown graciously asked only that she interest herself in the plight of his poor wife.[194] Perhaps, manipulating the sentiment of the well-known female abolitionist, Brown carefully drew a picture of his suffering wife, and the suffering wives of all the men who had died in the effort to end slavery at Harper's Ferry. Like Christ, Brown told Child, he had absolute "trust [in the] 'peace of God which passeth all understanding'" and awaited his execution concerned only for those who suffered still on earth. However, Brown's comment, "you may make just use of this [letter] as you see fit" suggests that he was just as concerned with his own legacy as he was with the temporal fortunes of the woman whose fortune it had been to marry a Harper's Ferry raider.[195] Child, responding to Brown's request, published the letter in the *Liberator* making very *public* use of the missive in the effort to demonstrate Brown's pure motives and saintly disposition.

Brown's carefully worded attempt to prevent his wife from visiting him in his Charlestown prison cell (cleverly sent through Higginson) may have been motivated from the same desire. In his 4 November letter to Higginson, Brown not only suggests that he is concerned that a trip from North Elba would "use up the scanty means she has to supply Bread & cheap but comfortable clothing, fuel, & for herself, and Children *through the winter,*" he also points out that her visit "cannot possibly do me any good," intimating that a visit might diffuse the foci of public attention from the figure he was busy creating for posterity, a singular selfless man of courage, vision, and godliness.[196] Recognizing that his reputation as the new George Washington committed to the revolution that would liberate all men in America depended upon the public image that he was creating, Brown denied his wife the opportunity to visit him; he needed no first lady to diffuse his own position as the liberator of America. Mary would appear as a suffering wife who had given her future prosperity to the abolitionist cause, but she would not share the public eye; Brown wanted it all.

Not only did he want to achieve singular recognition that martyrdom might bring, Brown wanted to ensure that his martyrdom had a distinctly America flavor. In order to achieve this, Brown presented himself as a patriot with a distinctly American pedigree. Perhaps hoping that his cousin, the Reverend Luther Humphrey, would have his letter published by the local Ohio press—as others had frequently done with his correspondence—, Brown recorded his remarkably American heritage in a 19 November missive to the religious man. In this poignant farewell letter, Brown crafts himself as the new revolutionary martyr of America. He reviews the lineage of his family and asserts that his forefathers not only included an original pilgrim, Peter Brown—who arrived in American on the Mayflower—but a revolutionary martyr, Capt. John Brown—who died fighting to establish the United States in 1776.[197] Building his own history with this letter and employing the same series of stock phrases he had employed while campaigning for funds in 1857 and 1859, Brown constructed himself as a modern revolutionary hero.

Emerson, like many others, accepted Brown's pedigree without challenge and re-inscribed the freedom fighter's own words in both his journal and in his Tremont Temple address in Boston on 18 November. Calling Brown a "representative of the American Republic," Emerson celebrated Brown by opening his lecture with a review of Brown's pedigree. He noted that the imprisoned abolitionist was "the fifth descendant of Peter Brown, who came to Plymouth on the Mayflower, in 1620 . . . [and that] his grandfather, of Simsbury, Connecticut, was a captain in the revolution."[198] Emerson then proceeded to make Brown an American hero dedicated to the country his forefathers had established affirming Brown's belief "in the union of the United States, and [emphasizing his conviction] . . . that the only obstruction to the union is Slavery, and for that reason, as a patriot, he works for abolition."[199] Likewise, Thoreau integrated Brown's ancestry into his powerful 30 October lecture "On the Character and Actions of Captain John Brown," which he later renamed "A Plea for Captain John Brown." Establishing Brown's character, Thoreau not only notes his grandfather's service in the Revolution, he establishes Brown's intellectual independence and devotion to the principles upon which the country was founded. Explaining Brown's decision to never engage in war "unless it were a war of liberty," Thoreau makes a powerful statement about the righteousness of Brown's war on slavery and the end he hoped to achieve: liberty for all human beings, regardless of skin color.[200] Brown, Thoreau asserts, is a "man of rare common sense, and directness in speech, as of action; a transcendentalist above all, a man of ideas and principles." He is a principled man of honor whose actions reveal only the noblest intent and the most American virtues.

Brown's American pedigree, he had decided, was informed by his own Puritan instinct to reform his society. An independent Calvinist, Brown continually emphasized his purely Christian motives attempting, as Stowe had in *Dred*, to reform the corrupt American clergy on his way to the gallows. In a 10 November letter to his wife, Brown makes his failed abolitionist effort at Harpers Ferry the cause of God. Calling attention to "the sacrifizes [sic] you; & I have been called to make on behalf of the cause we love the cause of God; & of humanity," Brown proceeded to admit that he was "quite determined to make the utmost possible out of defeat."[201] Clearly writing for the newspaper audience, who, by this time, was accustomed to reading his missives, Brown instructed his wife to have their daughters Ruth and Anne "send copies (when they can) to their deeply afflicted brothers, of all I write."[202] Brown was certainly not literal in this request: he clearly intended his letter to go to his metaphorical brothers who might be able to take his message and translate it into reality. These included J. Miller McKim and Lucretia Mott, the prominent Abolitionists and Philadelphia residents with whom Mary Brown was temporarily lodging.[203]

Informed that she was staying in Philadelphia with Mott and the McKims by George Hoyt, Brown was aware of the immediate audience who would read his letter and hopeful of the much larger one that would appreciate his magnanimity. Attentive to press reports during his incarceration, Brown diligently read the news reports (that included his letters) and chronicled the comments of his supporters while he awaited his execution; he wanted to ensure that his message was clear and unadulterated when it became public.[204] Lambasting the Southern clergy who had winked at and justified slavery for years, Brown sent letters to numerous religious leaders hoping to expose the complicity of the corrupt clergy in the institution he attempted to end. Writing to the Rev. James McFarland, whom he had never met, Brown acerbically comments that there are "no ministers of Christ here. These ministers who profess to be Christian, and hold slaves or advocate slavery, I cannot abide by them. My knees will not bend in prayer while their hands are stained with the blood of souls."[205] Assuming the role of the persecuted martyr surrounded by Pharisees, Brown prophetically points the finger of condemnation at those whose corrupt brand of Christianity has sustained slavery. Their salvation, Brown poignantly suggests, is reliant upon both their acknowledgement of the wrong of slavery and their public rejection of it as Christian men. As the day of his execution approached, Brown continued his campaign to reform the clergy and "make the utmost out of a defeat." Writing George Luther Stearns, Brown acknowledged that he had

> asked to be *spared* from having any *mock; or hypocritical prayers made over me*," when I am publicly *murdered*;" Instead, Brown suggested that on his execution day, "my only *religious attendants* be poor *little, dirty, ragged, bareheaded, & barefooted Slave boys*; & *Girls*: led by some old *grey headed Slave Mother*.[206]

In a testament of the way in which his private letters became public property and succeeded where he had failed, the image of Brown's canonization by impoverished slave children appeared almost immediately in public forums throughout the Northern states. [207] Three days after his execution, the New York *Tribune* ran a story that presented this image to the eager reading public.[208] According to the column, when Brown stepped outside of the jail-house, he met a black woman holding a child and stopped for moment "with the tenderness of one whose love is as broad as the brotherhood of man, [and] . . . kissed it affectionately."[209] James Redpath, Brown's first biographer, included the scene in his 1860 narrative of Brown's life, emphasizing the religious significance of his two black attendants by allowing the black woman to proclaim, "God bless you, old man."[210] Abolitionist poet John Greenleaf Whittier inscribed the scene his poem "Brown of Ossawatomie" first published in the *Independent*. In Whittier's version, Brown "stooped between the jeering ranks/ And kissed the negro child!" who had stopped there "with some poor slave mother whom [Brown had] . . . striven to free."[211] Inspiring newspapermen, poets, and visual artists alike, Brown's enduring affront to Southern clergyman helped him achieve the significance of an American icon.

Brown articulated his understanding of symbolic poses in a grander scheme as well. In his letter to his boyhood teacher, the Reverend H. L. Vaill, Brown expressed himself most clearly; he proclaimed, "before I began my work at Harpers Ferry; I felt assured that in the *worst event*; it would certainly PAY."[212] Noting that like him, "Christ was a great Captain of *liberty*," Brown acknowledges that he saw the opportunity for both public acknowledgement and enduring personal and social significance at Harpers Ferry. In his tactical failure, Brown commanded the attention of America and had the opportunity to champion abolition as he never had before. A captain who championed liberty in the face of his oppressors, Brown's success in death was strategic; it would far exceed any success he had achieved during life.

As the date of his execution approached, John Brown continued to "recover lost capital occasioned by" his capture at Harpers Ferry.[213] On 30 November, he wrote his "BELOVED WIFE, SONS: & DAUGHTERS, *EVERYONE*" what he thought might be his last letter. After encouraging them to live their lives as true Christians, Brown ends his letter with an insistent prescription: "John Brown writes to his children to abhor with undiing [sic] hatred, also: that 'sum of all villainies;' Slavery."[214] Clearly appealing to an audience beyond his wife and remaining seven children, Brown affectionately closed his letter hoping that his words would inspire an attentive public to commit to the cause for which he anticipated dying.

Mary Brown was not idle while her husband was managing his strategic victory. While she stayed at the home of Lucretia Mott in Philadelphia, Mary became the subject of intense public interest. A reporter from the *National Anti-Slavery Standard* who came to observe the beleaguered matriarch as she awaited her husband's death described the woman as "brave without insensibility, [and] tender without weakness."[215] Denied the opportunity to visit her husband (by Brown, himself) until two days prior to his execution date, Mary accepted her fate and petitioned Governor Wise for the bodies of her husband and sons.[216] Humane but shortsighted, Wise consented to Mary Brown's plaintive letter. Unknowingly, he had agreed to provide American abolitionists with a visible symbol—a martyr's body—to fete from Charlestown to New York. This was exactly the course of action that many of Wise's correspondents had advised him not to take.

Releasing Brown's body to his widow for a triumphant funeral procession "through the Eastern States," one New York physician suggested, would "tempt to vanity . . . many another scoundrel," and "they will make a hero martyr of him:" a more appropriate manner of disposing of Brown's corpse, he suggested, was donating it for dissection, since it would further degrade the man who had violated all of Virginia.[217] A professor at the College of Virginia suggested adding Brown's head (and the heads of his fellow conspirators) to the museum collection of his college.[218] Perhaps the most vitriolic suggestion was featured in the 4 November New York *Times*: John Brown, the author asserted, "should be hung on the gallows as high as the Washington Monument that is to be, and afterward chopped into small pieces, in the Chinese manner, and distributed *in terrorum* all over the land, a fragment of flesh impaled in every square mile of our mighty nation."[219] Refusing to consider either the wisdom of Dr. Sayr, the outraged New York physician who had presciently explained what would occur when Brown's body slowly traveled North following his public execution, or entertain the more ghoulish suggestions of his own statesmen, Wise unknowingly provided abolitionists in the North with a symbol they could load with the rhetoric of offended liberty when he authorized release of John Brown's body to his wife.

This, in addition to his execution, is exactly what many abolitionists desired. In death, they knew that Brown would become an abolitionist saint. His body would offer an indignant Northern abolitionist public proof of the South's commitment to brutality and inhumanity. Many Northern abolitionists, therefore, looked forward to his execution date and forcibly advised against any suggestion of a commutation of Brown's sentence. Henry Ward Beecher, in his 31 October letter to the New York *Herald*, maintained that Brown would do the abolitionist cause far more service on the scaffold than in prison; approving Beecher's sentiment, Brown noted on the side of Beecher's published proclamation, "good."[220] Perhaps seeing the tremendous opportunity in Brown's execution for symbolic advances in the cause of abolition, Thoreau maintained the same opinion asserting: "I almost fear that I may yet hear of his deliverance, doubting if a prolonged life, if any life, can do as much good as his death."[221] He was not alone in this sentiment. After meeting with Sanborn, Emerson, and Channing, Bronson Alcott privately recorded his conviction that "the spectacle of martyrdom . . . will be of greater service to the country, and to the coming in of righteous rule, than years of agitation by the Press, or the voices of partisans, North or South."[222] Even Longfellow maintained that Brown's death "will be a great day in our history: the date of a new Revolution."[223]

Brown, of course, confessed his own desire to serve as a martyr for the cause. In his 30 November letter to his family, Brown wrote, "I am waiting for the hour of my public murder with great composure of mind and cheerfulness."[224] He knew that his public execution would "ultimately result in the most glorious success."[225] In a letter to his brother written on 12 November, Brown acknowledged that "I am quite cheerful in view of my approaching end,—being fully persuaded that I am worth inconceivably more to hang than for any other purpose."[226]

Brown's more vigorous radical abolitionist sympathizers, however, were not confident that Brown's willing martyrdom at the gallows best served the abolitionist cause. Convinced that they had to "redeem the honor of the Free States," John W. LeBarnes and Thomas Wentworth Higginson began to consider what would become a series of rescue plans within days of learning of Brown's capture. [227] Le Barnes, perhaps more impulsive than Higginson, even began to investigate the possibility of a rescue attempt while Brown was still on trial. He sent twenty-one year old lawyer George H. Hoyt to Charlestown on 27 October under the pretense that he would provide legal counsel to Brown. [228] In reality, LeBarnes instructed Hoyt to both gather information about the military situation in and around Charlestown and gain an appreciation for "other particulars that might enable friends to consult as to some plan of attempt of rescue." [229] According to Villard's account, when Hoyt informed Brown of the real reason that he had been sent to Charlestown, Brown "made it clear" that he "positively refused his consent to such a plan." [230] When Hoyt reflected upon the situation, he decided that Brown's reluctance did not seem altogether injudicious. After he had had the opportunity to gain an appreciation of the situation in the area immediate to Charlestown, Hoyt observed that the "country all around is guarded by armed patrols & a large body of troops are constantly under arms." [231] Given these conditions, Hoyt wrote LeBarnes and informed his employer that there is *"no chance* of Brown's ultimate escape . . . If you hear anything about such an attempt, for Heaven's sake do not *fail to restrain the enterprise."* [232]

However, neither Brown's entreaty nor Hoyt's observation had any influence upon Brown's militant sympathizers. They were committed to liberating the captured freedom fighter. Higginson even traveled to North Elba in order to convince Mary Brown that she ought to personally convince her husband to consent to a rescue attempt. Brown, however, foiled the attempt by pointedly arguing that her visit would be painful, costly, and pointless, since it would do neither of them any good. [233] Although Higginson honored Brown's request, he did not cease in his efforts to conspire with other radical abolitionists to come up with a plan that would successfully liberate Brown and humiliate the South. Recognizing the truth in Le Barnes assertion that "success would be brilliant; defeat fatally inglorious," Higginson even considered Lysander Spooner's suggestion that they kidnap Governor Wise and hold him hostage until an exchange with John Brown might be arranged. [234] Unable to arrange adequate funding for the venture and aware of the potentially disastrous outcome of a poorly executed effort, Higginson and his associates determined that it was best to give up the bold idea. Undaunted, they continued to brain-storm rescue plans in late November even conspiring to capture Brown by boldly entering Charlestown with an armed band of one hundred men, breaking into his prison, then making off with the abolitionist on horses stolen from the local cavalry. Perhaps realizing that this plan, like the others, had relatively little chance of success, Higginson and his Boston associates abandoned the effort.

On 2 December, therefore, Brown prepared for the gallows. Passing his last correspondence to a guard, Brown quietly climbed upon the wagon in which he would ride to the newly constructed scaffold just outside Charlestown. In his last act of defiance, Brown asserted:

> I John Brown am now quite *certain* that the crimes of this *guilty, land*: will never be purged *away*; but with Blood. I had *as I now think*: vainly flattered myself that without *very much* bloodshed; it might be done.

Riding atop his coffin, Brown arrived at the site of the gallows where 1,500 militia men stood guard, sarcastically remarking, "I had no idea that Gov. Wise considered my execution so important."[235] After mounting the scaffold, and having his ankles bound by the executioner, John Brown placed his neck in the ready noose, and calmly waited for his martyrdom. Within ten minutes, he was dead.

Throughout the country, Brown's execution inspired expressions of sympathy, celebration, and relief. Throughout the North, memorial services were celebrated in churches, town halls, and in city streets. In Albany, New York, a one hundred gun salute was fired "in commemoration of the execution of JOHN BROWN."[236] In Boston, William Lloyd Garrison, who only two years before, had argued the superiority of moral suasion over violent and direct confrontation in the effort to advance abolition in America, read various letters and documents from John Brown to an audience in the packed Tremont Temple. In his closing remarks, he uncharacteristically proclaimed, "Success to every slave insurrection in the South, and in every slave country," even while acknowledging his continued strong belief in the non-resistance.[237] Two weeks later, Garrison would assert that "John Brown has raised up all the fierceness and diabolism of the pit of the South, and among a certain class at the North; but he has also inspired and strengthened millions to abhor slavery, and labor for its overthrow."[238]

In Concord, Emerson, Thoreau, Alcott, and Sanborn commemorated the abolitionist's life and paid tribute to the man who had lived and died in defense of his own ideas. Emerson read Brown's last words; Sanborn read a letter regarding Brown recently received from Theodore Parker (who was in Switzerland); Alcott read the martyrs service; and, after praising Brown, Thoreau read passages from a litany of poets before concluding the service with a selection from Tacitus's *De Vita Ilvi Agricolae*."[239]

Emerson, Thoreau, Alcott, and Sanborn did not express the sentiment of all of their townsmen. Many of the town's citizens were not at all pleased with the planned celebration of a man whose violent deeds had inspired such an outpouring of sympathy. Several of them demonstrated their discontent by hanging an effigy of John Brown from a tree in front of the town-hall on the morning of memorial service. Attached to the body was the last will and testament of John Brown which included the remarks,

> I bequeath to H.D. Thoreau, Esq., my body and soul, he having eulogized my character and actions at Harpers Ferry above the Saints

in heaven . . . I bequeath to Ralph Waldo Emerson all my personal property, and my execution cap, which contains nearly all the brains I ever had.[240]

Although a center of intellectual support and abolitionist fervor, Concord obviously did not universally embrace John Brown, nor did its citizens wholeheartedly confirm the preeminence of its well-known sage or his oft-disparaged disciple.

Neither did all of the citizens of Kansas, many of whom still harbored strong feelings of resentment toward the man who heralded an era of lawlessness during his tenure as a freedom fighter. Abraham Lincoln, campaigning in Troy, Kansas told a sympathetic crowd, "Old Brown has been executed for treason against the state. We cannot object, even though he agreed with us that slavery was wrong. That cannot excuse violence, bloodshed, and treason."[241] The less than celebratory attitude of the crowd that Lincoln addressed did not reflect the sentiment of all of the citizens of Kansas or the other western states in the Union. In Lawrence, church bells sounded and Free State settlers celebrated their now infamous patriarch; in Ohio, like almost all other free states, citizen's gathered to hear sermons on Brown's mighty effort.

Within weeks of his execution, Brown had succeeded gloriously; he had achieved literary and artistic immortality. Not only had Thoreau and Emerson written and spoken on the righteousness of the freedom fighter, contemporary poets to include Whitman, Melville, Whittier, and Howell's composed poems celebrating to the abolitionist's efforts and his plight. Even Harriet Beecher Stowe had praised Brown for his righteous effort to inspire the end of slavery.[242]

Six weeks after Brown's body made its historic voyage to his final resting place on the Brown farm in North Elba, James Redpath, the New York *Tribune* correspondent who first met Brown in his camp a few days after the Pottawatomie murders, published the first biography of the Kansas freedom fighter, *The Public Life of John Brown*. Brown achieved even greater renown during the Civil War. Union regiments marched to battle singing "John Brown's Body," the popular marching song that had been introduced by a quartet of sergeants of the 12th Regiment of Massachusetts Volunteer Infantry within weeks of the attack on Fort Sumter.[243] When Julia Ward Howe wrote new words for the tune in 1862, she commemorated her friend John Brown anew by associating his name with the cause of the entire Union Army. Published in the February, 1862 edition of the *Atlantic Monthly*, "The Battle Hymn of the Republic" both connected the John Brown who had "captured Harper's Ferry, with his minute men so few" with the effort to reunite the Union and made that effort a holy one.[244]

Not everyone who had the opportunity to meet John Brown before his execution was convinced of the man's magnanimity. James M. Mason, the Senator from Virginia who had authored the Fugitive Slave Bill, clearly did not have the same opinion that Whittier expressed in "Brown of Ossa-watomie" when he penned the line, "And they who blamed the bloody hand forgave the loving heart."[245] Intent upon exposing Brown's North-ern financiers as conspirators in Brown's raid, Mason initiated what he hoped might be a probing Senate investigation into the facts surrounding the attack on the sovereignty of Virginia three days after John Brown spoke his last words on the gibbet. Joining him on the five man committee were two distinctly Pro-Slavery senators, Jefferson Davis from Mississippi and G. N. Fitch from Indiana, and two Northern senators, Jacob Collamer of Vermont and James R. Doolittle of Wisconsin.

Appointed committee chair on December 14, 1859, Mason charged his fellow senators with four tasks: determine what had occurred at Harpers Ferry; determine if there was any intent to subvert the governments of any of the States of the Union during the conduct of the attack; determine if anyone had been complicit but not present in the attack "by contributions of money, arms, munitions, or otherwise," and recommend legislation to ensure that such an attack on federal property did not occur again.[246] Dur-ing the course of their six month investigation, the Mason Committee was able to gain a clear understanding of what had occurred at Harpers Ferry: they were not, however, able to determine much else. As William Lloyd Garrison would disparagingly comment, the "Mason Committee mountain labored and brought forth a mouse."[247] In their June report, the committee concluded that there was no evidence to suggest that there were "any other citizens than those there with Brown [who] were accessory to this outbreak or invasion."[248] Additionally, they found no evidence to suggest that "there was ever any conspiracy or design, by anyone, to rescue John Brown or his associates from prison in Virginia."[249] Acknowledging that "it is not easy to reconcile" the rather liberal business habits of either the Massachusetts State Kansas Committee or its chairman, George Luther Stearns, the com-mittee did call to question the testimony of the man, who, unbeknownst to them, had been Brown's most generous sponsor; they did not, however, confront Stearns with their concerns. Nor did they express any concerns about the testimony of the other thirty-one witnesses who agreed to travel to Washington to appear before them.[250] In other words, they absolutely failed to discover anything during their six month investigation. They implicated no one and sponsored no legislation to protect against future attacks on United States facilities. The only positive result of the commit-tee's six month's investigation was a recommendation to increase the guard on key federal installations.

Attempting to explain the apparent superficiality of the Mason Com-mittee, some critics suggest that that tenor of Congress during the 1860 election year was so tenuous on the subject of state's rights and slavery that the committee resolved to find that there was no evidence of complic-ity, which they did in the 15 June report. However, with such probing and militant committee members as Mason and Davis, it is not likely that the committee deliberately choose not to subpoena volatile personalities like Higginson, nor is it likely that they deliberately chose to phrase their questions in ways that would allow Howe and Stearns room to avoid perjuring themselves. [251] It is more likely that these apparent failures were a result of poor preparation, whether deliberate—since John Brown and the preponderance of his men were dead by the time they fully engaged in the investigation—or circumstantial—since 1860 was a particularly volatile political year.

Despite the committee's failure to determine much about Brown's support network, prominent Southern members of the committee did come to believe that the Republican Party was complicit in Brown's raid. Although none of the Republicans whom they summoned, like William H. Seward, Henry Wilson, John A. Andrews, and Joshua Giddings, revealed any prior knowledge of or active role in Brown's attack, Southern leaders believed that Northern Republicans backed Brown's attack in the South. Just as John Brown had constructed himself as a legendary liberator and prophet of freedom—a new biblical figure in the increasingly secular world—Southerners elevated him to the status of an archetype—a destructive crusader violently dedicated to eradicating their way of life. Representative of the common Northern political enemy, John Brown was the straw-man Southern leaders pointed to in order to unify and rally their electorate against an enemy dedicated to perverting their way of life. He became the nineteenth century bin Laden, a threat whose name inspired visions of arbitrary violence and terror. Lurking on the frontier, John Brown became the representative man of the evil Northern abolitionist empire.

This was not a phenomenon that abolitionists desired. He was useful as a symbol of righteousness, a model of virtue, and a figure whose name was synonymous with true dedication to liberty. Celebrated in song, defended in print, and feted from the lectern, John Brown achieved popular renown as Shelley's "Ozymandias" did not. Certainly, his name retained value while the names of his most vitriolic opponents faded to obscurity. Recognizing the enduring significance of John Brown's name in the tumultuous interim between his champion's death and the beginning of the Civil War, Higginson even proposed forming a military force under the command of Brown's son, John Jr., in order to guard the border of Pennsylvania. He believed that if he got the "name of John Brown rumored on the border . . . [it] will frighten Virginia into fits all the same."[252] Higginson's notion never became reality. Despite Governor Andrew's approval of his plan, there were no state funds available to finance such a force, and Higginson's efforts to privately raise the funds necessary for the unit were unsuccessful. Undeterred, Higginson championed a psychological campaign along the border; the Worcester *Spy* obliged him by running an article that reported that John Brown Jr. had an army in the field consisting of "400 Negroes with another 500 soon expected" intent on operating in Virginia.[253] There is no indication, however, that Higginson made any systematic effort to sustain his psychological campaign; certainly, John Brown Jr. made no effort to validate his idea. Far from the border of Virginia, John Jr. was serving as an agent for the Haitian Bureau of Emigration in Canada when Higginson concocted his plan.

John Brown Jr. did not, however, fail to recognize the value of his own name, nor did he refrain from putting it to use in the cause for which his father had died. On the third of December, 1860, he appeared with Franklin Sanborn and Frederick Douglass at the Joy Street Baptist Church in Boston and celebrated the anniversary of his father's martyrdom by encouraging free blacks to arm and violently resist slave catchers. Advocating what Frederick Douglass would incisively phrase the "John Brown way" of opposing slavery, John Jr. encouraged African-Americans to demonstrate the will to confront their enemies.[254] As Douglass aptly noted, sixty years of peaceful abolitionist appeals to the "magnanimity of the slaveholders of the nation" had failed to loosen the grip of the slave-holder; therefore, a more dramatic approach was necessary. To "reach the slaveholder's conscience," Douglass explained, it was necessary to make him feel personal danger.[255] This was possible, according to Douglass, only if slaves in the South make the slave-holder "uncomfortable"—if they confronted him with the truth of his own vulnerability, if they refused to bow down and accept his dominion. This was the approach that John Brown advocated.

Hoping to inspire the will to confrontation, John Brown Sr. had gone to Virginia in October, 1859 and attacked Harpers Ferry. From a tactical perspective, he utterly failed in his effort. He did not covertly withdraw from Harpers Ferry into the Allegany Mountains to initiate a guerilla war against slavery, nor did he inspire slaves from the surrounding area to reject their servitude and embrace the opportunity he presented for freedom. From a strategic perspective, however, Brown's success is undeniable. Inspired by his willingness to forthrightly confront slavery, and conscious of the distinct difference between his abolitionism and their own, many intellectuals in America were compelled to action by John Brown. As Theodore Parker aptly suggested, Brown's "noble demeanor, his unflinching bravery, his gentleness, his calm, religious trust in God, and his words of truth and soberness, [did not] fail to make a profound impression on the hearts of Northern men: yes, and on Southern men."[256] Brown certainly made a profound impression on Henry Thoreau and Ralph Waldo Emerson. Bravely confronting their contemporaries, both Thoreau and Emerson championed John Brown as they had no other living man; he was for them an idealist—one who believed in his "ideas to that extent, that he existed to put them into action."[257] Likewise, Brown significantly affected Thomas Wentworth Higginson. Inspired by Brown's unswerving commitment to liberty, Higginson confronted a skeptical Northern public with his own courage when he accepted command of the First South Carolina Volunteers, the first regiment of ex-slaves formed during the Civil War.

This was not the first time that Higginson demonstrated his agreement with Brown that blacks would both make capable soldiers and commit to violence in the assertion of their right to liberty. During the first year of the war, Higginson had published three narratives in the *Atlantic* demonstrating that fact.[258] Willingness to violently confront one's oppressors, Higginson clearly demonstrates in his accounts of the revolts inspired by Nat Turner, Denmark Vesey, and Gabriel Prosser, is not a faculty exclusive to whites. Clearly an inspiration to the militant abolitionist, John Brown motivated Higginson to engage in battle with both social prejudice and Southern soldiery. Likewise, he inspired others to combat the corrupt tendency to embrace political compromise and moral irresponsibility in the maintenance of the Union. Provoking his contemporaries to confrontation, John Brown inspired America's intellectual elite with the language of social responsibility, moral obligation, and justifiable violence. He also inspired them to social engagement and intellectual confrontation. This was one of John Brown's most significant achievements; he inspired intellectual America to action.

4 Confronting Conspirators
Re-Examining Thoreau's "Plea for Captain John Brown"

A man does a brave and humane deed, and at once, on all sides, we hear people and parties declaring, "I didn't do it, nor countenance him to do it, in any conceivable way. It can't be fairly inferred from my past career." I for one, am not interested to hear you define your position. I don't know that I ever was, or ever shall be. I think it mere egotism, or impertinent at this time. Ye needn't take so much pains to wash your skirts of him. No intelligent man will ever be convinced that he was any creature of yours. He went and came, as he himself informs us, "under the auspices of John Brown and nobody else.[1]

> Henry Thoreau, "A Plea for Captain John Brown"

When Franklin Sanborn brought John Brown to Thoreau's mother's house for lunch one cold day in March, 1857, he did not anticipate that Henry Thoreau would make John Brown a figure of legendary importance in the chronicles of American literature.[2] Thoreau certainly did not indicate that Brown had inspired him like no other man ever had. Though Brown's tale of the Battle of Black Jack and his exhibition of the chains that Border Ruffians had used to inhumanely restrain his captured sons inspired Thoreau to contribute a small sum to the campaigning freedom fighter, he did not motivate the prolific writer to enter anything enduring in his *Journal* about Brown during the freedom fighter's two day visit.[3] Likewise, when Brown returned to Concord and lectured about the affairs in Kansas a second time in May, 1859, there is no indication that he had captured Thoreau's enduring attention. Though Thoreau attended Brown's lecture and attentively listened as the Kansas freedom fighter told the story of his liberation of eleven slaves from their captivity in Missouri, he makes no mention of either Brown or his performance in his *Journal;* instead, he dwells luxuriously upon the early signs of spring and comments indulgently only upon "the swollen leaf-buds of the white pine."[4] Though Bronson Alcott noted that Brown told "his story with surpassing simplicity and sense, impressing us all deeply with his courage and religious earnestness,"[5] Thoreau mentions nothing about either Brown's sense or his courage in his extraordinarily detailed record of "incidents and observations" of the day.

Consistently, until Thoreau first recorded his desire to speak on "the character of Capt. John Brown" in a letter to his friend H.G.O. Blake,

Brown appears in none of Thoreau's correspondence.[6] In fact, despite the innate ability to inspire others "beyond their own expectations, hopes, and wishes"—characteristics that Sanborn ascribes to the Kansas veteran— Brown does not appear to have inspired Thoreau to any significant philosophical, intellectual, or moral consideration prior to his attack on Harper's Ferry.[7] Thoreau accords Brown no unique presence nor any significant position in his life until reports of Brown's failed raid began to reach Concord on October 19, 1859.

On that date, however, Brown emerged from the recesses of casual acquaintance to a position of intellectual and theoretical prominence for Henry Thoreau. He literally dominates Thoreau's intellectual life for a period of two months and inspires what may be Thoreau's most poignant engagement with political and social order in America. Not only did he celebrate John Brown in the lecture he gave to his Concord neighbors, Thoreau condemned those same neighbors for their superficial focus on the man John Brown, rather than on the moral wrong that Brown hoped to redress at Harpers Ferry. He defiantly challenged his neighbors to reconsider the virtue of Brown's militant statement of sympathy with the enslaved "four millions" (274) and bravely act upon their newfound consciousness of righteousness. Rejecting both the skewed focus of newspapermen— whom he had previously disparaged for their "servility" (187)—and the idea that it was wrong to forcefully oppose, indeed, attack a morally corrupt institution, Thoreau gave "On the Character and Actions of Captain John Brown"—the title he initially gave to his lecture—on three occasions.[8] He gave the first "John Brown" lecture to his Concord neighbors on Sunday, October 30. Addressing vocal abolitionists, prominent intellectuals, and curious townsmen, Thoreau impressed his neighbors with his forceful defense of the man he had seen maligned in news reports and diminished in conversation; more importantly, he impressed his listeners with a defense of the principles Brown had acted upon, suggesting not only that Brown was a representative of justice, but that he was a prescient visionary who recognized the injustice of the current government and courageously defied it, as was each man's moral obligation.[9]

Among his audience was Franklin Sanborn, the secretary of the Massachusetts State Kansas Committee and strident champion of John Brown who had just returned from Canada where he fled following the news that a carpet-bag full of incriminating letters had been captured near Harpers Ferry.[10] Sanborn's absence from Concord immediately following Brown's capture played a significant role in Thoreau's decision to speak in defense of Brown during the militant abolitionist's trial for insurrection, treason, and murder in Virginia.

Thoreau's second opportunity to publicly defend Brown occurred shortly thereafter. On 1 November, Thoreau addressed an eager Boston audience in the fifth of the Parker Fraternity Lectures at the Tremont Temple. Eagerly filling the vacancy left by Frederick Douglass, who had cancelled his scheduled lecture "Self-Made Men" due to fears that he would not be safe in Boston, Thoreau addressed an audience of twenty-five hundred at the forum Theodore Parker had initiated in order to air the more contentious subjects of the day.[11] Though he was not present, Parker might have enjoyed the performance, particularly given the fact that he, like Sanborn, had been involved in the secret conspiracy to provide Brown with the support necessary to execute a daring attack on slavery in the South.[12]

In his last public presentation of "A Plea for Captain John Brown," the title he adopted when he published his lecture, Thoreau addressed an audience familiar with vitriolic reform rhetoric—an audience accustomed to the forceful petitions of enthusiastic reformer Thomas Wentworth Higginson—at Washburn Hall in Worcester.[13] Committed to abolition, and, as Thoreau well knew, previously involved in a violent confrontation with the legal arm of slavery, Higginson ought to have been both a willing organizer and an eager attendee at Thoreau's lecture.[14] He was an outspoken radical abolitionist, and he had also been a member of the secret committee dedicated to providing John Brown with support in his practical effort to bring about the end of slavery in Virginia. Uncharacteristically, Higginson was quiet during Thoreau's speech on 3 November. He did not use the opportunity to either praise Brown's motives or celebrate his actions; instead, he refrained from making any public statement as Thoreau lambasted the slanderous "Newspaper editors" (278) and rebuked his craven countrymen for their inability to recognize John Brown's magnanimity.[15]

Interestingly, each time Thoreau presented "A Plea for Captain John Brown," it was in a location with a historic, social, and intellectual connection to one of the more prominent intellectual members of the secret committee of six men who had covertly dedicated themselves to John Brown. In Concord, that man was Franklin Sanborn, the enthusiastic scholar, the town schoolmaster, the ardent abolitionist secretary of the Massachusetts State Kansas Committee, and the primary coordinator of support of John Brown's attack on slavery. In Boston, it was Theodore Parker, the contentious Unitarian minister, prolific scholar, radical reformer, and staunch abolitionist whose oft-stated conviction that "the existence of Slavery endangers all our Democratic institutions" rang from pulpits and lecterns all over the East Coast during his fourteen year tenure as the leader of the 28th Congregational Society. [16] And in Worcester, it was Thomas Wentworth Higginson, the Worcester reformer and ardent abolitionist who, for the past ten years had been publishing radical abolitionist diatribes calling not only for immediate abolition, but celebrating the right of both fugitive slaves and whites alike to violently oppose the arm of slavery. Each of these men was publicly silent in the aftermath of John Brown's raid, and each of these men was guilty, in Thoreau's mind, of failing in his public duty to reverse the inertia of negative public opinion hastened by the press and maintained by the mass of unthinking men who condemned a singular principled champion of liberty in the conduct of an act Thoreau believed to be a public duty.

Emphasizing the distinction between the morally responsible active man willing to confront moral wrong where he sees it and the irresponsible passive man whose silent inaction perpetuates and strengthens the existence of current institutions, in each of his lectures, Thoreau distinguishes himself as both a principled citizen engaged in an act of moral and social importance and as a herald of righteousness who confronts others with their own timidity and inertness in the face of moral wrong. Confrontation, Thoreau implies, is worthy since it jars people from their timidity and inspires them to reassess their beliefs and their actions. He dismisses the idea that newspapermen somehow expressed the convictions of all Northern citizens in their claims that Brown was clearly insane in his attack on slavery. Clearly, that would suggest that strong opposition to slavery was insane. Then he asserts there are "two or three individuals to a town throughout the North" (266) who admire Brown and "his enterprise," but have remained silent in the face of what seems to be overwhelming public opinion against Brown. Attempting to universalize his own willingness to speak in opposition to what appeared to be universal condemnation of Brown and inspire those "two or three individuals" to recognize both the irresponsibility and the cowardice of their silence, Thoreau grammatically joins these silent allies by concluding his introductory paragraph with an inclusive first person plural subject. After claiming that it "costs us nothing to be just," Thoreau suggests that "[w]e can at least express our sympathy with, and admiration of . . . [John Brown] and his companions [my emphasis]" (261). He asserts that this is the least that responsible citizens can do—publicly proclaim their moral agreement with John Brown that slavery "was a great wrong against God and humanity."[17] Failure to articulate sympathy with Brown, Thoreau submits, is the non-response advocated by "stupid and timid chattels, pretending to read history and our bibles, but desecrating every house and every day we breathe" (266). Passivity, Thoreau explains, is akin to hypocrisy, since it suggests an abdication of an individual's obligation as a citizen, a socially aware singular man or woman with an intrinsic understanding of right and wrong; silence, consistently, suggests cowardice, since failing to assert an opinion in the face of public scrutiny denies the individual his proper position in society. By using the pronoun "we," Thoreau attempts to inspire his listeners from what he terms their "universal woodenness . . . [or] want of vitality" (268) to join him in his public act of responsibility—the celebration of a man who recognized not the authority of flawed human law but the universality of the higher law of liberty for all men.

Franklin Sanborn, Thoreau's Concord neighbor and frequent guest was one of the silent men whom Thoreau first confronted with his celebration of Captain John Brown. Having established himself in Concord almost four years before John Brown's fateful raid, Sanborn was one of the few men who could claim to be on intimate terms with Thoreau. Not only had Sanborn and Thoreau shared their noon meal at Thoreau's mother's table for just over three years, but they also had lived across the street from one and other in Concord for the majority of time that Sanborn was engaged in coordinating support for John Brown.

Franklin Sanborn's intimacy with Henry Thoreau began with a suggestion from Emerson. After seeking the Concord sage's counsel on several occasions, Sanborn had been inspired to move to Concord by Emerson in March, 1855. Concerned that the education offered by the local school was inadequate, Emerson proposed that Sanborn, then a senior at Harvard, open a private school in Concord. [18] After being assured that he would receive his degree, Sanborn left Harvard in late March, 1855 and established a progressive school for the sons and daughters of Concord's intellectual elite in town. [19] Both he and his sister Sophia took rooms at the Channing house across the street from Thoreau's mother's home, and soon made arrangements "to take their dinner each day at the Thoreau table—a practice they continued until April, 1858." [20] Sanborn met Thoreau for the first time shortly after moving to town and attempted to persuade the Concord native to lecture at his new school. [21] Well acquainted with the works of Thoreau—which he had read while at Harvard—Sanborn was eager to develop a relationship with the man who had boldly proclaimed his anti-slavery sentiment during the Fourth of July celebrations at Framingham and had admitted to aiding a fugitive slave in *Walden*. [22] Although he failed to convince his new acquaintance to lecture, Sanborn was able to interest the Concord native in occasional afternoon outings with his students. During these events, Thoreau would lead Sanborn's young pupils on rambling jaunts through the Concord fields explaining natural phenomena and teaching the eager youths "to admire and appreciate all that was impressive and beautiful in the natural world." [23]

Sanborn' efforts to court Henry Thoreau were not unique. Eager to develop a familiar relationship with all of the prominent intellects in Concord, Sanborn sought invitations from the parents of his progressive school students and established himself as a frequent visitor with Emerson, Hoar and Ripley. [24] Later, he acknowledged that living in the seat of transcendentalism "gave [him] . . . the opportunity of knowing the men who afterward had much to do with shaping the policy of the nation;" Sanborn was pleased with the opportunities that Concord presented him for expanding his social circle with the most notable American intellects of the day. [25] However, though he was inspired by the cerebral tenor of Concord—and excited by the opportunity to socialize with men who had expressed their forthright opposition to the encroachment of slavery upon the social fabric of Massachusetts—Franklin Sanborn was not satisfied with his own level of social engagement in 1856.

Morally outraged by the atmosphere of political compromise that potentially extended slavery to the Kansas Territory, informed by the "remarkable political insight of Theodore Parker" who had acknowledged that if "slavery goes to Kansas, it goes to all the territories," and inspired by men who translated their philosophical opposition to slavery to practical support for the Free State settlers in the territory, Sanborn began to involve himself in grass-roots efforts to influence the outcome of the most contentious issues of the day: the fate of Kansas in the wake of the Kansas-Nebraska Compromise.[26] Eagerly joining the Town Committee of Concord and Middlesex County Kansas Committee in 1856, Sanborn committed himself to supporting Massachusetts emigrants to the new territory. Convinced that if Free State settlers had the ability to defend themselves, they would be able to effectively oppose the brutes from Missouri, Sanborn actively promoted efforts to provide settlers with arms, ammunition, and supplies so that they might bring the spirit of Massachusetts to the contested territory. Appointed secretary of both committees in 1856, he soon began to direct committee affairs, organize fund-raising campaigns, schedule lectures about conditions in Kansas, and provide his interested neighbors with the latest reports of events in Kansas.[27]

Recognized as an authority on Kansas in Concord, interested citizens often sought out Sanborn for the latest news on events in the territories. As Ellen Emerson recalled, Franklin Sanborn was a popular guest in many Concord homes during the civil war in Kansas. In an 1856 letter, she notes, "Father and Mr. Sanborn talk about . . . [Kansas often]. Mr. Sanborn knows everything about it. He has been there and seen, and has constant information from there of what is going on, and he belongs to the State Committee of Massachusetts which takes care of all that is being done for it, and he tells all to Father."[28] As Ellen Emerson noted, Sanborn had made an investigatory journey along the emigrant route to Kansas in August, 1856; his purpose was to gain a better appreciation of the situation that Free State settlers faced when approaching the volatile territory.[29] Impressed by what he had seen and convinced that Kansas "was the most practical form in which the struggle for freedom has ever presented itself," Sanborn decided to devote himself full-time to the Free State effort in November, 1856. Petitioning Theodore Parker to use his influence to secure the position of secretary in the more influential Massachusetts State Kansas Committee for him, Sanborn soon found himself in routine contact with the leading abolitionist members of Boston society.[30] Due to the scope of their influence, these men gave Sanborn the ability to considerably influence the tenuous situation in Kansas; they also assured his continued role as an authority on Kansas within the Concord community.[31]

Ellen Emerson was certainly not the only Concord native to recognize Sanborn's authority on Kansas affairs. Many others in the small community sought out their enthusiastic townsman for the most up-to-date news on the efforts to exclude slavery from the new territory. Henry Thoreau and his family were certainly among them. The Thoreau's had a long anti-slavery history and were very quite interested in the question of slavery in Kansas. Both Henry's mother and his two sisters were charter members of the Women's Anti-Slavery Society in Concord; from its establishment in 1837, they actively engaged in local anti-slavery activities until the Emancipation Proclamation.

Interestingly, in 1839, the Concord Women's Antislavery Society raised more money for support of William Lloyd Garrison than any other society in New England.[32] They did not, however, restrict their efforts to fund-raising. Dedicated to ending the ignorance that allowed slavery, the Concord ladies attempted to raise the moral awareness of their neighbors with annual fairs, anti-slavery lectures, and commemoration rallies. Following the ratification of the Fugitive Slave Law in 1850, many even engaged in the Underground Railroad. According to Mrs. Edwin Bigelow, Concord's Underground Railroad leader, the Thoreaus were absolutely committed to the Underground Railroad; in fact, she suggests that Henry Thoreau, "more often than any other man in Concord looked after [the fugitive slaves who stopped in Concord] caring for them for the night, purchasing their tickets, escorting them to the station, . . . or for further protection accompanying them on the trains for a while."[33] Henry Thoreau, of course, was not as secretive in all of his statements of sympathy with the anti-slavery effort as he was in his own efforts to thwart the agents of the slave power. In fact, he was strident in his condemnation of the encroachment of slave power in Massachusetts and quite vocal about his opposition to the legal compromises that extended slavery to the frontier.

This is especially apparent in the aftermath of the ratification of the Kansas-Nebraska Act in May, 1854 when several prominent Massachusetts citizens were arrested for their role in the Anthony Burns riot.[34] Both indignant at the role that his fellow citizens had played in Burns's return to slavery and incensed by the injustice of a law that effectively extended the arm of slavery to Massachusetts, Thoreau expressed his outrage when he confronted his countrymen on Independence Day, 1854. Joining outspoken abolitionists William Lloyd Garrison, Moncure Conway, Sojourner Truth, Wendell Phillips, Stephen Foster, and Lucy Stone, Thoreau delivered his caustic lecture "Slavery in Massachusetts" during the annual Fourth of July celebration at the Harmony Grove in Framingham.[35] Thoreau's performance prompted Horace Greeley to comment that the soon-to-be published author of *Walden* was remarkable for his "profound abhorrence of the sacrifice or subordination of one human being to the pleasure or convenience of another" in his 2 August editorial.[36]

The direction of Thoreau's Independence Day address was both local and poignant. Not only did he charge his Boston neighbors with complicity in the execution of the immoral fugitive slave law, he charged them with cowardice and negligence in their acquiescence to laws they knew to be wrong. "What should concern Massachusetts," Thoreau asserted, "is not the Nebraska Bill, nor the Fugitive Slave Bill, but her own slaveholding and servility" (190). Calling his fellow citizens' attention to legal precedent immorally established seventy-nine years before, Thoreau focused the listeners' attention upon their own consciences and prompts them to embrace not an existent and somewhat dated human construction but their own undeniable understanding of right and wrong, which must both precede and supersede human law. As if modeling appropriate behavior, Thoreau expressed both his empathy with those arrested for devotion to higher laws—his contemporaries Thomas Wentworth Higginson, Wendell Phillips, Theodore Parker, and Martin Stowell—and his own willingness to join them, if somewhat vicariously, by "refusing [Massachusetts] . . . allegiance, and express[ing] contempt for her courts" (191). Confronting those unwilling to engage in the discourse of justice when injustice so flagrantly dominates political and popular rhetoric, Thoreau asked, "[w]ho can be serene in a country where both the rulers and the ruled are without principle? The remembrance of my country spoils my walk. My thoughts are murder to the State, and involuntarily go plotting against her" (193).

Distancing himself by implication from those who passively embraced the dictates of those they had empowered, Thoreau placed himself as speaker, citizen, and independently thinking man in an active role. His serenity impossible when his community was complicit in injustice, Thoreau challenged his fellow citizens to privilege higher laws and act upon them. Not only did he assert that doing so would restore the possibility of their own serenity, but he contended that it would allow his own.

In this bold challenge to institutional stasis, Thoreau demanded that his auditors re-examine inherited notions of the individuals' relationship with the government they empower. As he reminded his audience, "they are to be men first, and Americans only at a late and convenient hour" (189). Hence, just as he had in "On Civil Disobedience"—his earlier confrontation with a citizenry who abdicated many of their individual rights to a collective government that did not act from the collective empowering position of an engaged citizenry, in "Slavery in Massachusetts," Thoreau exhorted his contemporaries to individually examine the beliefs that inspired serene, hence morally satisfied living, and then demand consistent behavior from the government they both empowered and were part of. Thoreau affirmed that engaging in government allows the "right of revolution; that is, the right to refuse allegiance to, and to resist, the government, when its tyranny or its inefficiency are great and unendurable" (128).

Thoreau's ideas about the individual's moral right to resist the efforts of a government dedicated to injustice must have found an eager listener in Franklin Sanborn. This is especially true in the aftermath of James Buchanan's attempts to ensure that Kansas entered the Union as a slave state following his election in 1856. Not only did Buchanan appoint a Pro-Slavery governor to the territory, he "endorsed the Pro-Slavery government there" totally ignoring the existence of a democratically elected Free State legislature and pushing Congress to admit the territory as a slave state.[37] Attentive to political developments that might derail his efforts on behalf of the Massachusetts State Kansas Committee, indignant over the strong-arm tactics that the President embraced in order to ensure that the defeat of liberty in Kansas, and aware of his forthright neighbor's hatred of slavery, Sanborn certainly must have engaged in lively discussions with

Henry Thoreau on the subject of Kansas during his daily noon meal.[38] Since he and his sister had dined consistently at Thoreau's for nearly two years by the time he escorted John Brown to Concord for the first time in March, 1857, it is nearly certain that the two men often made both the affairs of Kansas and the activities of the more notable personalities in the territory the subject of their noon conversation. Indeed, in his 1909 autobiography *Recollections of Seventy Years*, Sanborn suggests as much; he notes that prior to Brown's 1857 visit, "all of Concord had heard . . . of Brown's fights and escapes in Kansas: and Thoreau, who had his own bone to pick with the civil government . . . was [particularly] desirous of meeting Brown."[39]

In March, therefore, Thoreau must have been pleased to meet the freedom fighter and very aware that Sanborn had recently been to Boston to introduce Brown to many of the more affluent men in the heart of Massachusetts abolitionist community. He also must have been aware of Sanborn's efforts to raise money and gain access to Sharp's rifles so that the well-known freedom fighter could continue to defend the rights of Free State citizens in Kansas.[40] Sanborn recalls Thoreau's meeting with John Brown in detail in his autobiography. According to his account, after a two hour lunch at Mrs. Thoreau's table, Sanborn left Brown with a very willing Henry Thoreau when he had to attend to disciplinary duties at his Concord school. Thoroughly enjoying the opportunity to hear about events in Kansas first hand, Sanborn records that Thoreau spent the early part of the afternoon listening to Brown narrate his rendition of the battle at Black Jack where, "with nine men, he captured twenty-odd men under the command of Henry Clay Pate, of Virginia."[41] He remained in discussion with Brown throughout the afternoon until Emerson—recently returned from a Western lecture tour—dropped by, and the three men retreated to his house for more conversation. From their discussions, and from Brown's evening lecture at the Concord Town Hall, Sanborn asserts, both men "came to . . . that intimate knowledge of Brown's character and general purpose."[42] Though this seems a bit overstated, Emerson was impressed with Brown's forthright assertion that "one good, believing, strong-minded man is worth a hundred, nay twenty-thousand men without character." [43] He recorded the comment in his journal before pondering whether Brown would be able to inspire Free-State settlers to successfully oppose the efforts of border ruffians, federal troops, and Pro-Slavery advocates in their effort to ensure that Kansas entered the Union as a slave state. Musing thoughtfully, Emerson noted "most men . . . promise <much more> by their countenance, & conversation, & by their early endeavor, much more than they ever perform."[44] He does not qualify this comment by mentioning whether John Brown was like "most men," but he does suggest that most men disappoint rather than satisfy the impressions that they initially make.[45]

Franklin Sanborn, evidently, had no doubts about Brown's ability to champion liberty on the frontier and bring about a victory for the Free

State cause. Throughout the winter months of 1857, Sanborn attempted to insure that Brown succeeded in his effort to secure both the weapons and financial resources he needed to win a victory against slavery. To that end, he actively petitioned the leaders in the Massachusetts State Kansas Committee to release the resources under their control to the Kansas veteran. In addition to introducing the freedom fighter to everyone in his acquaintance who might be able to provide resources for Kansas, he provided Brown with an opportunity to address the Massachusetts State legislature in order to secure a state appropriation for Kansas and jointly petitioned the National Kansas Committee in New York for Kansas aid.[46] On Brown's request, Sanborn even traveled to Pennsylvania, where he and Brown attempted to convince ex-territorial Governor Andrew Reeder to return to Kansas as both the leader of the Free-State militia and as an agent for the National Kansas Committee.[47] Failing in this effort, but not faltering in his support for Brown, Sanborn continued to encourage the most influential men among his growing acquaintance to commit to the man he referred to as the "bravest and most earnest man it has been my fortune to meet."[48]

In private, Sanborn informed Brown that despite their fund-raising failure, he "reckoned it an honor" to serve him and would do all in his power to ensure the continued support of New England for the Kansas veteran.[49] As the primary conduit for correspondence with Brown for the Massachusetts State Kansas Committee, Sanborn had plenty of opportunity to satisfy his promise. Throughout the spring, he diligently prodded Brown's Boston "friends"—notably George Luther Stearns, Thomas Wentworth Higginson, Theodore Parker, and Amos Lawrence—to continue to provide funding for the cause of freedom in Kansas.[50] He even took on the responsibility of ensuring that the $1000 subscription that the Massachusetts State Committee had agreed to provide Brown was fulfilled; he also personally assured Brown that his family would be "made comfortable" if the Free State defender met his demise upon his return to Kansas.[51]

In his capacity as the secretary of the Massachusetts State Kansas Committee, Sanborn also positioned himself in the center of the efforts to coordinate funding and equipment for Brown's anticipated 1858 guerilla campaign in the mountains of Virginia. Following the February, 1858 meeting at Gerrit Smith's Peterboro home, where Brown divulged his intention to bring the war against slavery to "Africa," it was Sanborn who coordinated the Boston meeting with Stearns, Howe, Parker, and Higginson, the men who were the nucleus of the secret committee dedicated to supporting Brown's efforts.[52] It was also Sanborn who diligently coordinated the collection of funds from the men who committed to Brown's enterprise, and Sanborn who ensured that all concerned parties remained aware of Brown's activities in preparation for his attack on slavery.[53] When Hugh Forbes threatened to expose Brown's plans in May, 1858, Sanborn remained the primary coordinator for the secret committee members—most of whom were very concerned by Forbes's threats. Not only did Sanborn attempt to convince Howe and Higginson, the two men who asserted that "any postponement [of Brown's Plan] as simply *abandoning the project*," of the wisdom of the delay that all other committee members advocated, he sided with Stearns, Smith, and Parker in their opinion that delay was the best means of allowing Brown the opportunity for future success.[54]

Although there does not appear to be any extant correspondence indicating Thoreau's knowledge of Sanborn's endeavors on the part of John Brown, it is likely that during their everyday intercourse at Thoreau's family home, or at Emerson's where both men were frequent guests, John Brown was frequently the subject of discussion. Both Thoreau's "small contribution" following Brown's 1857 visit and his expression of annoyance that Brown "would not say exactly what he wanted the money for" suggests a distinct interest in the future activities of the Free State champion.[55] Thoreau's willingness to attend to Brown during his second appearance at Concord in May, 1859 suggests as much, particularly in the aftermath of Brown's delivery "of a dozen [sic] human beings," whom he liberated and subsequently "walk[ed] off with them by broad daylight . . . through one state after another, for half the length of the North" (265). This event, widely reported in Northern newspapers, may have confirmed for Thoreau that his confidence was not misplaced.

Certainly, as Walt Whitman somewhat dismissively noted, if Brown had not impressed Thoreau as an exceptional individual, Thoreau would neither have attended the second Sunday evening lecture at the Town Hall, nor would he have considered responding to the failed revolutionary in his journal on October 19, 1859; Thoreau would have ignored Brown since, according to Whitman's rather curt but appropriate judgment, the Concord native expressed a distinct "disdain for [common] men" and would not afford them any of his time if they were not impressive in some way.[56] Clearly, as the first entry of six weeks of consistently emphatic journal entries indicate, Thoreau did not think that Brown was common in any way. Instead, he recognized Brown as "a superior man . . . [who] did not value his bodily life in comparison with ideal things; he did not recognize unjust human laws, but resisted them, as he was bid."[57] He was, according to Thoreau's 22 October journal entry,

> A man or rare common sense and directness above all, as of action; a Transcendentalist above all, a man of ideals and principles,—that was what distinguished him. Of unwavering purposes, not to be dissuaded by an experience and wisdom greater than his own. Not yielding to whim or transient impulse but carrying out the purpose of a life.[58]

Franklin Sanborn, Thoreau's Concord neighbor, was not at all like John Brown. When he learned that a carpetbag full of incriminating letters had been found at the farmhouse Brown used as his base of operations, he *wavered* in his support of John Brown and *yielded* immediately to his fears, impulsively fleeing Concord for George Luther Stearns's Medford home.[59] Fearful that they might be implicated as accessories in Brown's attack—since letters bearing both of their signatures were discovered at the Kennedy Farm—Sanborn and Stearns decided to flee the country.[60]

Explaining his actions in a letter to Emerson a day later, Sanborn reasoned that while his conduct might appear to be "inexcusable," it did not indicate that he had done anything for "which I or my friends need be ashamed."[61] Emerson was of a distinctly different opinion. After learning that Brown had been captured, he expected that Sanborn would have remained in Concord to both coordinate the "defense for the fallen hero" and arrange for the support of "Brown's needy family."[62] Reflecting upon conversations he had with townsmen during Sanborn's absence in a 26 October letter to a concerned friend, Emerson noted that "[w]e have all been all a good deal uneasy about Mr. Sanborn's absence, just at this time."[63] Emerson's concern prompted him to write Sanborn in Canada and imply that his absence suggested not prudence but the worst form of bad judgment. Short of suggesting Sanborn had acted in an irresponsible, indeed, a cowardly manner, Emerson implied that in order to avoid those criticisms, Sanborn ought to "return at the first hour wheels or steam would permit."[64] Keenly aware that his behavior might earn him the enduring disrespect of his more established neighbors, Sanborn decided to return to Concord that same evening.[65]

Shortly thereafter, he met with Emerson, Ellery Channing, and Bronson Alcott to discuss appropriate responses to Brown's impending trial. Surprisingly, there is no indication that Thoreau was in attendance at this meeting.[66] Perhaps, committed to refining the lecture that he would announce in a few short days, Thoreau chose not attend the strategy session. Or perhaps, he refused to attend any meeting because Sanborn had shown himself unworthy of his attention; he had both wavered in his support of John Brown and selfishly succumbed to fears for his own safety. Regardless, Thoreau's marked absence from Sanborn's homecoming suggests his distinct disapproval of the activist.

Thoreau's absence also left far less strident men in positions to influence the Concord schoolmaster; as Northern newspapermen labeled Brown an insane fanatic, Sanborn quietly returned to his home and passively agreed with Bronson Alcott that Brown's martyrdom "will be of greater service to the country, and to the coming in of a righteous rule, than years of agitation by the Press, or the voices of partisans, North and South."[67]

The only thing that the men who gathered at Emerson's appear to have actively done was to assuage Sanborn's lingering fears for his own security. As a result, he returned to his home and quietly observed his neighbor respond to John Brown. He did not rush to publicly challenge the right of Virginia to prosecute Brown, nor did he publish any statement of sympathy with Brown's effort. Aside from his quiet effort to inspire others among Brown's supporters to destroy all evidence of their association with the jailed abolitionist, Sanborn was both privately cautious and publicly silent about John Brown during the freedom fighter's trial and imprisonment.[68]

Thoreau was neither cautious nor silent. On October 30, he boldly announced that he would speak on the character and actions of John Brown to his Concord neighbors. Despite the tense atmosphere and considerable disagreement about the lawfulness and social value of Brown's actions at Harpers Ferry, Thoreau forthrightly proclaimed his intention to speak that evening. When both the Republican Town Committee and the Abolitionist Committee advised him that his subject might be too contentious to broach in a public forum, Thoreau forthrightly responded, "I do not send to you for advice, but to announce that I am to speak."[69] Likewise, when Franklin Sanborn heard of Thoreau's plans and advised him that he thought a defense of John Brown "would be better to wait until there was a better feeling among the people," since it might be "dangerous," Thoreau responded, "[t]ell Mr. Sanborn that he has misunderstood the announcement, that there is to be a meeting in the vestry, and that Mr. Thoreau will speak."[70] Neither concerned with the opinion of his subdued neighbor, nor interested in the advice of the cautious committee-men of Concord, Thoreau steadfastly determined to praise John Brown in the Vestry of the First Parish Meeting House that night.

Reading the address "as if it burned him," Thoreau confronted over one hundred of his townsmen (to include Sanborn) with their complicity in Brown's vilification and chastised them for their unwillingness to praise a man who had translated his principles into action in his effort to initiate the end of slavery in America.[71] In direct opposition to Franklin Sanborn's public silence, Thoreau both loudly and publicly offered a defense of John Brown. Thoreau's passionate presentation impressed many of his Concord neighbors. Edward Emerson noted that even those who condemned John Brown and "had come to scoff remained to pray" after Thoreau concluded his lecture.[72] Bronson Alcott, recording his impressions of the evening in his diary, noted that Thoreau "tells his story with surpassing simplicity and sense, impressing us all deeply by his courage and religious earnestness."[73] He further expressed his hope that Thoreau would "have opportunities of reading it elsewhere."[74]

Emerson expressed much the same opinion. Convinced that Thoreau's eloquent public challenge ought to reach a much wider audience, he wrote Charles Wesley Slack, chairman of the Fraternity Course of lectures that Theodore Parker had initiated only twelve months before, asserting

I understand that there is some doubt about Mr. Douglass's keeping his engagement for Tuesday next. If there is a vacancy, I think you cannot do a greater public good than to send for Mr. Thoreau, who has read last night here a discourse on the history & character of Captain John

Brown, which ought to be heard or read by every man in the Republic. He read it with great force & effect, though the audience was of widely different parties, it was heard without a murmur of dissent.[75]

Relieved to find an available lecturer whose speech might be topically consistent with Douglass's "Self Made Men," Slack, an ardent advocate of both the Free-State cause and abolition, responded with a telegraph addressed to both Emerson and Thoreau expressing his strong desire to provide Thoreau with an opportunity to address the Parker Fraternity. Phrasing his note, "Thoreau *must* lecture for Fraternity Tuesday Evening [my emphasis]," Slack provided Thoreau with the opportunity to speak in defense of the man whose most ardent intellectual champions had chosen cowardly silence.[76] Embracing the opportunity to not only to vicariously confront Theodore Parker and his congregation, but to address all of Boston with their complicity in Brown's vilification, Thoreau excitedly accepted Slack's invitation and prepared to journey to Boston the next day.

Though there is no extant record that Thoreau spoke to Emerson about his desire to address the forum that Theodore Parker had established only twelve months before, it is likely that Thoreau broached the subject with Emerson sometime during composition or immediately following the presentation of his lecture in Concord.[77] He was well aware of the large audiences who routinely packed into the Tremont Temple to hear speakers "who had something to say on the great humane subjects of the day, to which the ordinary lyceums in cities seldom tolerate any direct allusion."[78] He was also very well aware that no one had publicly defended Brown in front of the large crowd that routinely attended the Tuesday evening lectures that Parker had initiated in October, 1858. In fact, in his lecture, Thoreau acknowledges that previous to his own public celebration of John Brown, there was only one public expression of sympathy in Boston—what he terms "one noble statement, in a Boston newspaper" (269) since word that John Brown had invaded the South to liberate slaves had reached Massachusetts.[79]

Thoreau had good reason to believe that Emerson would support his desire to speak before the Fraternity audience. Only a few weeks before, Emerson had encouraged him to read "Life Misspent" to the regular Sunday morning parishioners of Theodore Parker's 28th Congregational Society in Boston knowing that this forum would provide Thoreau with a large audience accustomed to hearing stimulating reformist rhetoric and vitriolic abolitionist discourse.[80] Thoreau, much to Emerson's relief, had done well before "Parkerites" and impressed critics with a lecture that a Boston *Atlas and Daily Bee* reviewer suggested was "original, racy, and erratic [but was] . . . listened to the close with interest."[81]

Parker's Sunday morning Music Hall audience, much like Fraternity Course audience, was accustomed to hearing radical reformers defending their ideas on the more contentious issues of the day. Outspoken reformers and abolitionists had often addressed audiences from Parker's pulpit at the Tremont Temple during the course of 1859. Frederick Douglass,

Thomas Wentworth Higginson, Ralph Waldo Emerson, George William Curtis, Elizabeth Cady Stanton, and Henry Ward Beecher were among those who presented Tuesday evening lectures in 1859. Perhaps expressing the enthusiasm many of the lecturers felt as they addressed audiences at the Tremont Temple, Frederick Douglass noted that he enjoyed speaking from Parker's pulpit because it brought "fear and trembling" to the opponents of liberty.[82] Others felt similarly; the Tremont Temple pulpit that Parker first employed to sing the praises of Franklin—whom he distinguished as the author of the "first petition for the abolition of slavery"—carried with it a strong recollection of the Boston abolitionist who had vociferously contended that "[s]lavery is a flagrant violation of the institutions of America."[83]

Even in Parker's absence, the lectures conducted at the Tremont Temple retained a strong psychological association with its founder. Indeed, in their extant correspondence, both Emerson and Alcott refer to the forum as the Parker Fraternity.[84] Parker, himself, maintained an interest in the Fraternity Course even after he left the country in February, 1859. His July letter to Charles Wesley Slack indicates that he was both attentive to and interested in the topics and the speakers that Slack coordinated for the Fraternity Course.[85]

Writing Slack from Switzerland almost five months after he had departed Boston, Parker reluctantly informed the committee chairman that Charles Sumner, the outspoken abolitionist whose health had suffered so significantly as a result of Preston Brooks's attack on the floor of the Senate, could no longer lecture due to his deteriorating health.[86] He proceeded to express his real concern regarding the loss that Sumner's retreat from the lectern heralded, since he knew that Sumner's failure signaled the loss of not one, but two strong-willed abolitionist speakers to the community. Parker had recognized his own failing health and suggested that he would not, in all probability, return to the lectern to publicly denounce slavery.

An active reformer throughout his ministry, Parker had first publicly spoken against the slavery in 1838 when he delivered his *Thanksgiving* discourse to his first congregation at Roxbury. During the course of his sermon, Parker forcefully denounced chattel slavery asserting that "all men acknowledge that slavery is a curse, a sin," and all men were complicit in its existence if they do nothing in response to their cognition.[87] In his 1841 "Sermon on Slavery," Parker went further not only recognizing the "contamination and nameless abuse" inherent in slavery, but expressing distinct admiration for the control demonstrated by abolitionists in their dedication to pacifism, particularly when he acknowledged, "[w]hat wonder that their heart burns when they think of so many women exposed to contamination and nameless abuse: of so many children reared like beasts, and sold like oxen."[88] In this sermon, Parker called attention to the complicity of his congregation in the continuance of slavery by suggesting if "there is a crime in the land known to us, and if we do not protest against it to the extent of our ability, we are partners of that crime."[89]

Increasingly sympathetic with ultra-abolitionists like Garrison and May, Parker gave his most radical anti-slavery sermon to his Melodeon congregation in Boston in November, 1844 when he denounced the United States Constitution that made Massachusetts complicit in the support of the slavery, exposing political leaders (by name) who defended slavery, and declaring that the question is not "*shall slavery exist,* but *shall there be any Freedom*" in America.[90] Although he published this sermon in pamphlet form in 1845, and often included anti-slavery rhetoric in his weekly sermons, Parker did not openly declare himself an abolitionist until 1846 when he called on the

> men of Boston . . . the men of the old Bay State, to act worthy of their fathers, worthy of their country, worthy of themselves . . . to protest against this most infamous war [with Mexico and l]eave not your land cursed with slavery, extended and extending, palsying the nation's arm and corrupting the nation's heart[91]

at the annual meeting of the New England Anti-Slavery Society. Parker was never again silent in his opinion that "the existence of Slavery endangers all our Democratic institutions" and must be opposed at every opportunity.[92]

Not only did he often preach against slavery to the liberal attendees of his free church, he acted upon his convictions by twice confronting the Fugitive Slave Law.[93] In October, 1850, Parker led a group of sixty members of the Boston Vigilance Committee in a confrontation with the marshals charged with returning fugitives William and Ellen Craft to slavery. According to his journals, while other members of the Vigilance Committee guarded the entry-ways to the hotel where two slave-hunters had taken rooms, Parker personally confronted the two men and explained that though he had ensured their safety from "violence once, [he] would not promise to do it again."[94] They were not, Parker emphatically assured them, safe in Boston. Realizing the truth of Parker's cognition, the two men left the city that same night.[95]

News of Parker's effort soon spread among the abolitionist community in Boston. In the 6 December issue of the *Liberator*, Parker's personal effort to persuade the slave-hunters was clarified in an article authored by Willis Hughes, one of the two men whose efforts Parker had foiled. According to his account,

> a large crowd gathered at my hotel, for the purpose of insulting me . . . Before 6 o'clock [the] next morning they were around the house again in great numbers, with Rev. Theodore Parker at their head . . . I admitted Mr. Parker. He said he had come to give me a piece of friendly advice—that he had kept the mob off of me for two days, and was afraid he could do it not longer. I told him that I understood he was a minister of the gospel, and a great advocate of morals—in favor of

people's obeying the laws—but was sorry to find myself mistaken . . .
The crowd dispersed shortly afterward, and after transacting some
business, I left at 2 o'clock P. M. for New York.[96]

Emerson heard of Parker's forthright confrontation with the agents of
the new law. Recording the event in his journal, Emerson exults in the successful opposition to the corrupt Fugitive Slave Law, remarking: "A great
wrong is attempted to be done & the money power is engaged to do it. But
unhappily because it is criminal the feeble force of conscience is found to
set the whole world against it. Hallelujah!"[97]
Unsatisfied with the force of the statement that he had made in his defiance of the recently ratified Fugitive Slave Law, Parker proceeded to further challenge the Fugitive Slave Law by sending President Fillmore a letter
openly acknowledging his violation of a statute that made him subject to
a federal "fine of $1000 and imprisonment for six months" for the role he
had played in obstructing the efforts of slave-catchers in the conduct of
their official business.[98] Asserting that he would rather "live all . . . [his]
life in goal, and starve there, than refuse to protect one of these [fugitive
slave] parishioners of mine," Parker further suggested that violence was an
appropriate response to the Fugitive Slave Law. He acknowledged,

> I am not a man who loves violence . . . but this I will say, solemnly, that
> I will do all in my power to rescue any fugitive slave from the hands
> of any officer who attempts to return him to bondage. I will resist as
> gently as I know how, but with all the strength that I can command
> . . . I will serve as head, as foot, or as hand to any body of serious and
> earnest men, who will go with me, with no weapons but their hands,
> in this work.[99]

Parker's pledge was not inert. After Anthony Burns's capture in 1854,
Parker, like his Worcester contemporary, Thomas Wentworth Higginson,
dedicated himself to liberating another fugitive slave from the clutches of
the federal marshals in the heart of Boston. He would not, however, man
the battering ram with Higginson in the failed attempt to penetrate the
Court House to rescue Burns. Instead, according to Higginson's hastily
revealed plan, Parker would stir up the crowd at nearby Faneuil Hall with a
speech that inspired them to mob the Court House and enabled the assault
team to rescue Burns.[100] Engaging the crowd by addressing them as *"Fellow subjects of Virginia,"* indeed *"vassals"* of that state, Parker brought the
crowd to the point where they could effectively execute Higginson's plan.[101]
However, when the crowd yelled that they were ready to "Shoot, shoot!"
in order to free Burns, Parker backed away from his previous commitment
to violence and tried to convince the crowd that that murder was not yet
required.[102] Attempting to derail the increasingly agitated crowd from a
murderous rampage, Parker proposed two courses of action: first, that they

adjourn until the next day, and second, that they divert their efforts to a more significant public edifice, the Revere House, and stage a public protest there. [103]

His petitions failed, though they did succeed in dampening the combustive atmosphere that he had inspired only moments before. Therefore, when Higginson and his able cohorts rammed the courthouse door, they found themselves unsupported by the raucous crowd they had anticipated streaming from Faneuil Hall. Facing an armed force that they could not dislodge in the Court House entryway, Higginson and company retreated into the night disheartened by their failure. Famously, Thoreau's good friend and frequent companion, Bronson Alcott then ascended the Court House steps, faced the enervated crowd and confusedly asked, "Why are we not within?"[104]

Within days of the failed attempt, Parker, Higginson, Phillips, and Stowell were indicted for their role in what became known as the "Burns riot."[105] Perhaps responding to Sumner's suggestion that his indictment was a "call to a new kind of parish . . . and a pulpit higher than the Strasburg steeple," Parker determined to use his forthcoming trial as an opportunity to publicly attack both the representatives of the legal system who enforced the Fugitive Slave Law and the legality of the law itself, since it so plainly was not in accord with his own understanding of higher law.[106] Despite Parker's extensive preparation of a statement condemning the Fugitive Slave Law, he was not able to use the scheduled April trial as his new pulpit. Federal District Court judges charged with hearing the case dismissed the indictments and the scheduled trial never occurred.[107]

Edward Renehan, one of the more perceptive historians who have explored the relationships of the six men who secretly supported John Brown in his efforts to take his war against slavery to the South, suggests that in all probability, the judge dismissed the case on a technicality rather than allow Parker and his associates the opportunity to use a public trial to eloquently condemn the laws of the nation.[108] Parker was characteristically undaunted by the dismissal and published his argument the following August in pamphlet form as *The Trial of Theodore Parker for the "Misdemeanor" of a Speech at Faneuil Hall against Kidnapping, Before the Circuit Court of the United States, at Boston, with the Defense*. Arguing that any actions that "enforced and continued slavery were indefensible" and any "actions meant to bring down slavery were inherently correct," Parker made a strong public case for opposition—even violent opposition—to slavery.

Thoreau was surely aware of Parker's participation in the Anthony Burns riot and the subsequent publication of his *Defense*. Indeed, in Boston newspaper reports about the events on 26 May, Parker was one of two men most often cited as responsible for events that occurred in the Court House Square. In an article entitled "Who Are the Guilty," featured in the 9 June *Liberator*, an anonymous author attributes "to the Rev. Theodore Parker and Mr. Wendell Phillips the chief responsibility for the fatal proceedings on

Friday night."[109] The Boston *Courier* noted that the Boston "Court House [had been] assaulted, and a citizen stabbed to death [by] . . . an infuriated rabble of fanatics, hot from the seditious harangues of the Abolition mob-orators, Wendell Phillips, Theodore Parker, and the rest of that tribe of bed-lamites."[110] Indeed, in each of the five June issues of the *Liberator* in 1854, Parker was the frequent subject of feature articles dedicated to revealing the righteous bravery of abolitionist leaders who played a role in Burn's riot. The full text of his 28 May sermon on the righteousness of the attempt was included in the 2 June issue of the *Liberator,* and the entirety of his Faneuil Hall speech was included in the 9 June issue. Comparative essays on his character were even prominently set side by side in the 23 June issue.[111]

Parker certainly made no effort to conceal his role in the Burns's riot. In fact, he seems to have been eager to make political capital of the event and welcomed the attention of the press while he anxiously awaited his trial. It is not surprising, therefore, that in "Slavery in Massachusetts," Thoreau acknowledges that "though several of the citizens of Massachu-setts are now in prison for attempting to rescue a slave from her own clutches, not one of the speakers at that meeting expressed regret for it" (181). Indeed, Thoreau claims that his "sympathies in this case are wholly with the accused (191)" suggesting his clear understanding that Parker, Higginson, Phillips, and Stowell were the men anticipating legal censure for their roles at Faneuil Hall.

Thoreau's sympathy for Parker during the early summer of 1854, how-ever, did not reflect his overall sentiment for the popular Unitarian minis-ter. In fact, there seems to have been very little warmth between the two men whose similar socio-economic background, devotion to literature, and simultaneous residence at Harvard ought to have provided the ingredients for a close friendship.[112] Parker's caustic 10 August, 1840 journal comments on Thoreau and his first essay submission for the *Dial*, the transcenden-talist periodical both men contributed to during its four year publication, suggests that there was no love between the two men. Commenting on Tho-reau's essay on *Aulus Persius Flaccus,* Parker remarks, "I hope that he will write for the newspapers more & less for the Dial. I would recommend him to the editor of the New World to keep the youth out of mischief. I count this evening wasted—so few good things been said, by our Philosopher & Prophet."[113] Parker further contended that the value in Thoreau's work was "Emerson[']s, not Thoreau's, & so it had lived before."[114]

Parker's appreciation for Thoreau did not substantially change during the nine year period between his first vitriolic criticism of Thoreau and his equally uncomplimentary comments on Thoreau's first book *A Week on the Concord and Merrimack* in 1849. Responding to Emerson's request that he find a suitable critic to write a review of the work that Emerson somewhat ambiguously asserted "had rare claims" and "must [consistently] have an American claim, & ensign on it before it goes abroad for English opinions," Parker dismissively suggests that although the descriptions of natural objects are certainly uncommonly fine, there is a good deal of sauciness, & a good deal of affectation in the book, the latter seems to me to come from his trying to be R.W. Emerson, & not being contented with his own mother's son. Still, I think the book has its merits. It surpasses my expectations in some particulars, & makes me like the man better than I did before, & I have long liked him very well.[115]

Regardless of his personal reservations, Parker did agree to find a suitable critic; he paradoxically engaged James R. Lowell, whose satirical characterization of Thoreau as an "imitator" of Emerson in "A Fable for Critics" had been published only a year before.[116] Not surprisingly, the review that Lowell wrote was not altogether flattering. Lowell disparagingly asserted that the "great charm of Mr. Thoreau's book seems to be, that its being a book at all is a happy fortuity. The door of the portfolio-cage has been left open, and the thoughts have flown out of themselves."[117] He went on to note that Thoreau "looks at the country sometimes (as painters advise) through the triumphal arch of his own legs, and, though the upsidedownness [sic] of the prospect has its own charm of unassuetude, the arch itself is not the most graceful."[118]

Thoreau was not blind to Parker's less than enthusiastic response to his literary efforts. In 1847, when Emerson assembled thirteen friends at his home to discuss the possibility of establishing a new literary magazine, a "successor to the *Dial*," Thoreau immediately rejected the idea and attempted to convince those present (including Parker) that the idea was neither worth their while nor practical given the current publishing market.[119] When others decided to ignore his objections and found the *Massachusetts Quarterly Review*, appointing Parker as editor, Thoreau decided to have nothing to do with project.[120] He would neither submit himself nor his carefully-crafted work to a critic predisposed against him. Quite consistently, three years later, he rejected Emerson's suggestion that he contribute something in order save the failing *Review* when subscriptions signaled the doom of the periodical dedicated to the "momentous questions in science, politics, philosophy, morals and theology."[121]

Thoreau's refusal to contribute anything to the *Massachusetts Quarterly Review* while Parker remained the editor-in-chief did not, however, signal his refusal to consider the efforts of his transcendental contemporary. Indeed, he would have found it very difficult to ignore the multifarious efforts of the Unitarian divine following the passage of the Fugitive Slave Law. In the early 1850s, Parker was *the* radical abolitionist voice in Boston, and he used pulpit at the Melodeon and the Music Hall (where he moved his Sunday services in 1852) to vociferously attack the law claiming that it violated both Christian ideals and was a "threat to free institutions."[122] In his "Sermon of Conscience" (1850), he openly called for bold defiance of the statute publicly proclaiming that he would "do all in [his] power to rescue any fugitive slave from the hands of any officer who attempts to return him to bondage."[123] Parker's proclamation was not hollow; organizing like-minded men in Boston, he established the Boston Vigilance Committee and volunteered to serve as its chairman. In this position, he was active in both the successful effort to thwart slave-catchers bent on returning the Ellen and William Craft to slavery and the failed effort to secure the liberty of Thomas Sims.[124]

Parker's prominence was guaranteed by the press. His name was often featured in press reports about the Fugitive Slave Law, and his opinions were the frequent subject of editorials and debate: indeed, his name was even featured on posters in Boston announcing the commemoration of the first anniversary of the Sims's surrender, which stated that Sims's return was an "infamous deed of the City Government."[125]

Thoreau was, in all probability, absolutely aware of and receptive to the preponderance of Parker's activities during the first half of the tumultuous 1850s.[126] This was certainly true of Parker's widely reported May 26, 1854 speech about at Faneuil Hall. The full text of Parker's speech on the role that citizens of Massachusetts willfully played in Anthony Burn's rendition ran in the 9 June edition of the *Liberator*, the same periodical that published Thoreau's "Slavery in Massachusetts," and the same periodical that Thoreau deliberately cites in his jeremiad as one of only two papers in Boston "which made [itself] heard in condemnation of the cowardice and meanness of the authorities of that city" (188). In his Faneuil Hall address, Parker had forcefully confronted his contemporaries with their complicity in Burn's rendition. In fact, he begins his address by acknowledging that "[i]t was a Boston man who issued the warrant; it was a Boston Marshall who put it in execution; they are Boston men who are seeking to kidnap a citizen of Massachusetts, and send him into slavery for ever and ever. It is our fault that it is so."[127] Like Thoreau, Parker claimed that all men had the ability to reject the submissive position they had silently adopted in their previous failure to act against the agents of the Fugitive Slave Law; they did not have to be "subjects of the State of Virginia;" they could "be men first and Americans only at a late and convenient hour" (189) and oppose the corrupt arm of the law.[128]

Also like Thoreau, Parker was extremely disappointed when Anthony Burns was returned to slavery, but he was even more concerned by the ratification of the Kansas-Nebraska Bill and the subsequent congressional efforts to ensure that Kansas entered the Union as a slave state. In a January, 1856 letter to Charles Sumner, Parker expresses both his concern and his understanding that in the Senate, "the slave power has taken the committees, and fortified itself in that Sebastopol of despotism;"[129]further, he recognizes that if "slavery goes to Kansas, it goes to all the territories."[130] In order to make certain that did not occur, Parker chastened Sumner to do all that was possible to ensure the election of "a man thoroughly faithful to humanity" to the presidency. He was not optimistic that Fremont would defeat Buchanan and succeed in reversing the Pro-Slavery inertia evident in Washington. Anxiously awaiting the results of the election, Parker asserted that "[n]o Presidential election ever turned on such great questions. It is despotism or democracy which the people vote for."[131] To emphasize the potentially cataclysmic result of the struggle for the "national soul," Parker also dramatically informed Senator J.P. Hale that Buchanan's victory would result in "Slavery in Kansas," "Slavery in Cuba," "Slavery in all the Territories," "Slavery in all the Free States," "Bondage for niggers," "Bondage for poor whites," "Slavery for *greasy mechanics*," "No free schools," "No free press," "No free pulpit," "No free speech," "No free men."[132] Privately revealing his concern that Buchanan would triumph in the election, Parker also noted, "I am more than ever of the opinion that we must settle this question [slavery] in the old Anglo-Saxon way—with the sword . . . I make all my pecuniary arrangements with the expectation of civil war"[133] When Buchanan proved victorious, Parker was even more direct asserting that the choice was now between "slavery, or battle."[134]

Enter John Brown. In January, 1857, John Brown introduced himself to the Boston divine following his usual Sunday service at the Music Hall. The service, like most of those held by the 28th Congregational Society, was rather unconventional as it concluded with a debate on the appropriate method of combating the encroachment of slavery[135] Apparently inspired by what he heard, Brown sought out Parker, who had—eighteen months before—announced to his congregation that "while he ordinarily spent $1500 a year on books, he now intended to spend $1300 of that amount to . . . buy guns and ammunition for Kansas."[136] After Brown had introduced himself, Parker invited the freedom fighter to his townhouse. Although there are several accounts of the way that Brown earned an invitation to Parker's regular Sunday afternoon reception, it is most likely that it was arranged by Franklin Sanborn, who Brown had met a few days previously. According to Jeffrey Rossbach, the most thorough historian of the secret group of Brown's financiers, Sanborn wrote "Garrison, Howe, Phillips, and other well-known abolitionists" after he had first met Brown and spent several days discussing the freedom fighter's plan for the defense of Kansas, suggesting that they meet Brown at Theodore Parker's home. [137] Believing that they too would be impressed by the forthright abolitionist whom they all had read about in newspaper reports from Kansas, Sanborn escorted Brown to Parker's home on the fifth of January. During the course of the afternoon reception, Brown impressed Parker with the strength of his convictions and the forthright manner in which he revealed his hatred of slavery. William Lloyd Garrison, a frequent attendee of Parker's weekly receptions, provided Parker with an interesting opportunity to observe Brown. Soon after arriving, Garrison engaged the freedom fighter in a debate over the biblical injunction "resist not evil with evil."[138] Opposing Garrison's contention that there were no situations where "carnal weapons" were absolutely necessary, Brown argued that in the fight against those whose will to impose slavery's stamp on the Kansas territory knew no limits, violent resistance was absolutely necessary.[139]

Already committed to providing free-soil settlers with the means to violently resist the forces of despotism in Kansas, Parker sided with Brown.[140] Violent opposition to slavery, he intimated was the only means of effectively responding to those violently committed to imposition of slave power on both the new territories and the ideological geography of New England. Unlike his Worcester protégé, Thomas Wentworth Higginson, Parker rejected the growing popular notion that an effective response to the evolving rift between the North and the South was disunion. Although he appreciated the message of discontent that events like Higginson's 1857 Disunion Convention sent to the Republican representatives in Congress, he believed that abdicating moral responsibility for the "four millions of slaves and those four millions of 'poor whites'" living in the South was wrong.[141] The right solution, Parker asserted, would be to "bring the mixed multitude even out of the inner house of bondage, peaceably if we can, forcibly if we must."[142] Believing that the only morally correct solution for those bound in a union was the defeat of despotism as a Union, Parker embraced the notion of violent confrontation rather than peaceful dissolution. Over the course of the following year, Parker's position did not significantly change. He continued to argue in favor of confrontation echoing the prescient cognition he had so eloquently articulated in his letter to Higginson: "this question of freedom or slavery in America [will] not be settled without bloodshed."[143]

He also committed to become a stockholder in John Brown's personal war with slavery. Joining Sanborn, Higginson, Howe, Smith, and Stearns, Parker secretly pledged his support of Brown on 8 March, 1858.[144] He believed in John Brown, and he was willing to both raise funds for Brown's venture and to champion the inevitable violent confrontation that Brown would author. In fact, Parker delivered a speech on the day he met with his fellow conspirators in Brown's Boston hotel room confirming his belief in Brown's project. Affirming the conviction that there was no real possibility of a peaceful solution to slavery in America, Parker asserted that the "great charters of human freedom have been writ in ink very costly, very precious,—it is the ink that a man carries in his heart, . . . I believe that there is no other ink which will secure the freedom of the African people."[145] By 1858, Parker's public insistence that slavery's end would only be achieved through violence had become commonplace. His anti-slavery sermons were widely reported and often published in pamphlet form for the "serious consideration of all serious-minded men."[146]

Only a few months before he committed to support John Brown, Parker presented "The Present Aspect of Slavery in America, and the Immediate Duty of the North" to the Massachusetts Anti-Slavery Society in Boston. During this lecture, he boldly proclaimed that "we must attack slavery–slavery in the territories, slavery in the District, and above all, slavery in the *slave States*. Would you remove the shadow of a tree? Then down with the tree itself! There is no other way."[147] His speech, reported in the *Liberator* and offered to the public in a forty-four page pamphlet seems to signal both his frustration at the failure of peaceful reform and his eagerness to inspire more dynamic attacks on slavery than had here-to-fore been attempted.

Aware that many of his countrymen were reluctant to commit to or support radical abolition, Parker attempted to prod them with incendiary rhetoric during his May, 1858 presentation to the New England Anti-Slavery Society. In this stirring speech, entitled "The Relation of Slavery to a Republican Form of Government," Parker demands a public recognition that slavery is so incompatible with the republican government of the United States that it will inevitably cause its destruction. Slavery, he insists

> is the abnegation of the self-evident Truths of the Programme of Principles: it is the nullification of the Ends proposed in the Programme of Purposes:—it tends to destroy Union among the people; to Establish Injustice: to prevent domestic Tranquility: to hinder the common Defence [sic]: to disturb the General Welfare, and to annihilate the Blessings of Liberty, just so far as it extends. Not only is Slavery inconsistent with a Republican Form of Government, in the constitutional sense of the word, it is so utterly hostile thereto that the two cannot live together, but one must destroy one and other.[148]

Printed on the front page of the 4 June *Liberator,* Parker attempted to inspire his contemporaries to moral indignation and political engagement in a last effort to instigate a political revolution against the inertia of compromise and submission with the powerful advocates of slavery who dominated both Congress and the presidency.

He was, however, not very hopeful. In fact, toward the end of his address, he acknowledges the "time has passed by when the great American question of the 19th century could have been settled without bloodshed . . . I think now this terrible question must be settled as all the preceding ones, by bloodshed and the sword."[149] In July, during his last public proclamation against slavery, Parker addressed his 28th Congregational Society parishioners at the Music Hall with a sermon entitled "The Effect of Slavery on the American People." During this sermon, Parker reluctantly reiterates the conclusion that he acknowledged two months before: "Once I thought it [slavery] would end peacefully; now I think it must fall as so many another wickedness, in violence and blood. Slavery is a flagrant violation of the institutions of America."[150] Challenging each member of his congregation to act and "end slavery soon," Parker attempts to compel each of his parishioners to take a stand and actively engage in the business of abolition. If they did nothing, Parker assured his congregation, "it [will] ruin our democracy."[151] Perhaps less than certain that John Brown would ever bring his Virginia plan to fruition, Parker hoped that his own parishioners might act to end slavery.

He did not, however, retreat from Brown's plan for a violent and progressive revolution; recognizing that there could be no dramatic reversal to the progressive encroachment of despotism without violent opposition, he urged his listeners to embrace the faith of their "patriot fathers" dramatically suggesting the appropriateness of violent action to those committed to upholding the rule of "slavocracy."[152] As members of society committed to the end of slavery, Parker asserted, they ought to make their sentiment practical.

When John Brown initiated his attack on Harper's Ferry, Parker was no longer able to effectively lend his voice to the efforts of fellow abolitionists with carefully researched lectures and sermons on righteousness of Brown's actions. Increasingly debilitated by a long struggle with tuberculosis, Parker left America in February 1859 in what proved a failing effort to find a cure for his waning health.[153] When he learned that Brown had attacked Harper's Ferry, he was in Switzerland and it was mid-November.[154] In a letter to Francis Jackson, Parker privately expressed his sympathy for Brown asserting that Brown had acted in a morally just and courageous manner. As if excusing his own silence, Parker also expressed his indignation over the paucity of support for the freedom fighter and his desire to counter the "sayings of certain men in Boston" by speaking in *"defense of the True and the Right."*[155] Writing as if his private letter would be immediately made public, Parker rather belatedly challenged abolitionist leaders to speak out in support of John Brown and publicly recognize the righteousness of his actions. Evidently, he did not believe that the praise that Thoreau and Emerson offered Brown was sufficient for the man who had inspired the nation to a new understanding of liberty. As if recalling Daniel Webster's fall from political grace following his defense of the Fugitive Slave Bill, Parker challenged both Republican and Democratic politicians to leave the safety of cautious political discourse and embrace the man whose politics had been punctuated by the report of a Sharp's rifle. "America [,Parker recognized,] is rich in able men, in skilful writers, in ready and accomplished speakers. But few men dare to treat public affairs with reference to the great principles of justice and the American democracy."[156] Apparently agreeing with both Emerson and Thoreau that Boston's abolitionists and politicians had abdicated their responsibility to publicly recognize the moral value of Brown's action and immediately capitalize on the attention that it focused upon slavery, Parker subtly exhorts his friend and fellow abolitionist, Francis Jackson to take advantage of the opportunity and confront the defenders of slavery with the forthright boldness that moral wrongs demand.

Humbly acceding that "in my best estate, I do not pretend to much political wisdom, and still less now while sick; but I wish yet to set down a few thoughts for your private eye, and, it may be for the ear of the Fraternity," Parker then delineates his strong sympathy with Brown's decision to embrace violence in the armed confrontation at Harper's Ferry. He proceeds to offer five logical, though absolutely radical, maxims validating the right of both individual and collective violence in the rejection of slavery.[157] Based on natural law, and echoing the rhetoric of the *Declaration of Independence*, Parker proclaims the right of every slave to kill those who attempt to deny him liberty. Further, he asserts that it is the responsibility of every free man to aid slaves in pursuit of their liberty, hence establishing their right to kill in the effort to provide the slave with his freedom.

In his defense of Brown, whom he asserts, has "attempted to help his countrymen enjoy their natural right to life, liberty and the pursuit of happiness," Parker offers both a poignant vindication of Brown's violent conduct and a defense of future revolutionaries in the struggle for abolition. Killing to achieve individual liberty, Parker maintains, is the natural right of every American; Brown is simply the representative man of the moment. He is not, Parker proclaims, alone in the pantheon of American champions who have embraced violence to gain liberty from the yoke of oppression; he is only the latest model American. Parker then proceeds to proclaim that in the inevitable violent assertion of their will to liberty, slaves will soon become model Americans. In a process that anticipates Slotkin's theory of the regenerative and translational process of violence on the physical frontiers of the nation, Parker asserts that slaves will achieve a kind of regeneration and translation in their adoption of violence; by embracing the model of the revolutionary American willing to kill in order to establish their independence, Parker contends that slaves will achieve the ideological right to call themselves Americans. Insurrections, Parker insinuates, are the right of all Americans; they "will continue as long as Slavery [or any other significant injustice] lasts, and will increase, both in frequency and in power just as the people become intelligent and moral. Virginia, [Parker asserts] may hang John Brown and all that family, but she cannot hang the human race."[158]

Parker's letter to Francis Jackson is certainly as forceful as Thoreau's "Plea." It is, however, neither as courageous nor as poignant. Although Parker may have begun composition of his letter immediately upon receipt of the news of Brown's sentencing, he did not send it Garrison or Greeley for immediate publication. Instead, he sent it to his trusted friend, Francis Jackson, who—sensing the time was not yet ripe for publication—kept the letter and its contents far from public scrutiny. Perhaps sensing that anti-abolitionist sentiment in Boston was too virulent, Jackson also chose not to share the letter with the Fraternity, as Parker had suggested.[159] Instead, like other abolitionists who had gone underground immediately following Brown's capture, he kept his sympathy with Parker—and his correspondence having to do with Brown—private.

Parker's eloquent defense of violence in the pursuit of liberty, however, was too strong to remain unpublished; six months after John Brown's final statement at the gallows, George Ripley had Parker's letter published in the "all three editions" of the *Tribune*.[160] If Thoreau was aware of Parker's vicarious return to the public arena, he did not comment upon it in his extant journals. The time had passed when he was solely interested in the moral failure of his contemporaries to celebrate John Brown. He had spoken about

Brown from his own conscience—"practically and as a citizen, unlike those who call[ed] themselves [abolitionists]."[161] His role had been to confront men with their own abdication of individual responsibility; Parker, like Sanborn, had failed John Brown and failed his countrymen. He had been silent when his voice was urgently required to stem the stream of blind condemnation directed toward both John Brown and his radical desire to end slavery in the United States. Thoreau, a "majority of one" (133), had spoken for *and to* him at the Fraternity.[162]

Two days later, Thoreau spoke for *and to* another silent abolitionist whose voice was atypically silent in Worcester, Massachusetts. In this poignant address, Thoreau "celebrated . . . [John Brown's] courage and magnanimity" in Washburn Hall, Worcester's newest auditorium, impressing the audience with both his conviction and his presentation.[163] Thomas Wentworth Higginson, Worcester's most prominent abolitionist, was present; he was, however, strangely quiet as his friend, Henry Thoreau, took the pulpit. This was completely uncharacteristic of the Worcester reformer.

Higginson was a well known abolitionist militant in the Worcester community. In fact, since he moved to the community in 1852, Higginson had taken every opportunity to forcefully oppose the encroachment of the slavery in Massachussetts.[164] Higginson's commitment to social reform, particularly his commitment to anti-slavery, did not, however, develop in Worcester. By the time he moved to the Boston suburb, he had a reputation as a radical abolitionist and an energetic enemy of slavery. He had nurtured that reputation as a Unitarian minister in the predominantly Pro-Slavery community of Newburyport. Writing a daily column in the Newburyport *Union*, Higginson "openly advocate[d] nullification of the laws of the land" and fearlessly campaigned against both slavery and the Fugitive Slave Law in his daily column.[165] Finding a base of Free Soil supporters in Essex County, Higginson even accepted the party's nomination for Congress. Using his newspaper column to express his antipathy for the Compromise of 1850, Higginson articulated his opposition to the "intrinsic sin and wrong of Slavery" and his belief in the "intrinsic peril to Freedom from the Slave in the *Address to the Voters of the Third Congressional District*.[166] In his *Address,* Higginson advised those faced with executing the Fugitive Slave Law to "DISOBEY IT . . . and show your good citizenship by taking the legal consequences!"[167] Unlike Thoreau, who had asserted (in "Civil Disobedience") that it is "not a man's duty as a matter of course, to devote himself to the eradication of any, even the most enormous, wrong, . . . but it is his duty, at least, to wash his hands of it," Higginson suggested that it was each man's duty to forthright oppose the law in order to bring about eradication of what he considered the most enormous wrong.

Two days after Higginson delivered his *Address*, warrants for the arrest of William and Ellen Craft were issued in Boston.[168] Even before Theodore Parker had the opportunity to confront the agents of the law, Higginson boldly confronted the law itself. In an article he entitled "The Crisis Coming Now," Higginson publicly challenged the law by suggesting that the citizens of Boston had a moral obligation to disobey the statute since it required them to provide aid to federal agents in the conduct of their slave-catching duties.[169] Further, Higginson chastened his readers "in all cases [to] disobey the law and show [y]our good citizenship by taking the penalty."[170] He recommended that the Crafts "remain [in Boston] and then throw themselves on the sympathy of the people . . . to test the question at once—test it as peacefully as possible to do—and see whether the law of God or man is to prevail."[171] Openly challenging the law in court, Higginson proposed, is the only effective way to initiate its repeal.

Despite his apparent advocacy of the legal process, Higginson embraced a far more radical perspective when Fred Wilkins, also known by the biblically appropriate name Shadrach, was captured in mid-February, 1851. Celebrating the "colored men of Boston" both for their "real manliness" and their demonstration of courage in the peaceable abduction of Shadrach, Higginson expressed distinct approval when Lewis Hayden, one of the leaders of the local black community, defied the law and led a force of black men through the Massachusetts Court House to rescue the fugitive slave. [172] According to the account of the event that he wrote for the *Union,* the black men of Boston boldly demonstrated their humanity by refusing submission to a statute that was "inhuman," and they established their right to freedom by demonstrating their willingness to fight for it. They had, for all practical purposes, established themselves as American revolutionaries—just like the men who had dumped tea into the Boston harbor seventy years before.[173]

Two months later, when Thomas Sims was captured, Higginson was once again ready to assert his revolutionary belief that the citizens of Massachusetts must oppose the execution of an immoral law. A new member of the Boston Vigilance Committee, Higginson joined other incensed abolitionists at the *Liberator's* Boston office on the afternoon of April 3, 1851. Determined to force the liberation of Sims when legal efforts to free the twenty-three year old fugitive failed, Higginson and some of the more aggressive members of the Vigilance Committee covertly planned Sims' rescue. [174] However, their initial plan to help Sims jump from his third floor courthouse window onto a thick mattress, and then speedily escort him to freedom was compromised when bars were placed on his windows. Undeterred, Higginson proposed an armed assault on the ship commissioned to return Sims to slavery. However, he was unable to convince the other members of the committee that his plan would work in time to arrange for the vessel that he needed for the attack, and the bold plan died before it had a chance to be executed.[175] Disappointed by the effeminate demonstration that the Vigilance Committee decided upon—calling out "shame, shame" at the procession of policemen and soldiers as they marched Sims through Boston to the wharf for his return to Savannah—Higginson determined that he would not allow disorganization and lack of militant will to impede his desire to physically oppose the gross injustice of slavery again. He would not stand by as "Massachusetts ceased to exist & we seemed to stand in Vienna."[176]

The Kansas-Nebraska Bill accelerated Higginson's public association with the abolitionist movement. Preaching on the impact that the bill would have on the Union, Higginson asserted, "it will be a good thing that it does [pass and become law] for it will finally teach men who compromised in 1850 that you cannot compromise one day and then the next assert freedom."[177] Printed in the *Liberator*, Higginson's speech, like Thoreau's "Slavery in Massachusetts"—published in the same periodical five months later—was prescient in its recognition that "[n]ever, never, never will there be peace in this nation, until Slavery be destroyed."[178] Confrontation was inevitable and Higginson would play both a visible and a prominent role in the event that would serve as the most significant attack on slavery here-to-fore executed in the United States.

Anthony Burns' capture in Boston on May 24, 1854 marked Higginson's conversion to radical abolition. After learning of Burns' seizure, Higginson hastened to Boston to attend both a secret Vigilance Committee meeting and a far more public meeting scheduled at Fanueil Hall. Finding the Vigilance Committee disorganized and far from committed to action, Higginson and a select group of men formed a smaller executive committee to plan a rescue; however, disagreement on both method and location left them at an impasse. Before revisiting the executive committee's position prior to the public meeting scheduled later that night at Fanueil Hall, Higginson met with Martin Stowell, who had brought fifty men from Worcester with him, and agreed that there was no better time to rescue Burns than during the public meeting. After hastily reviewing the plan that Stowell had suggested to him, Higginson joined Stowell and Lewis Hayden in an effort to batter down the door of the Boston Court House to free the young fugitive held there. They failed. Though they were able to breach the door, they failed to overpower the "special" guards commissioned by the United States Marshall to protect the fugitive.[179] Additionally, the support that they expected from the crowd in Fanueil Hall never materialized, and they had to withdrawal. Despite his wound in the chin and embarrasment at his second failure as a liberator, Higginson emerged from the confrontation convinced that violent opposition was essential to the fight against slavery. Confirming his newfound conviction that moral suasion was the tactic of the deluded, Higginson asserted, "words are nothing—we have been surfeited with words for twenty years. I am thankful that this time there was action also."[180]

In the forceful sermon he entitled "Massachusetts in Mourning" and preached to his Worcester congregation and subsequently saw published in both the Massachusetts *Spy* and the *Liberator*, Higginson exhorted his parishioners to act upon the moral principles they knew to be right. Calling the nation an "oligarchy of slaveholders," Higginson urged his listeners to act in the defense of freedom and employ all of their assets in the fight against tyranny:

The way to make principles felt is to assert them—peaceably, if you can; forcibly if you must. The way to promote Free Soil is to have your own soil free; to leave the courts to settle constitutions, and to fall back (for your own part,) on first principles: then it will be seen that you mean something . . . Leave legal quibbles to lawyers, and parties to politicians, and plant yourselves on the simple truth that God never made a Slave, and that man shall neither make one nor take one here![181]

Despite the boldness of his rhetoric, Higginson was privately very concerned about his connection with the murder of Batchelder, the "special" guard killed in the Court House entryway during the attempt to free Burns. He waited restlessly for his arrest and was greatly relieved when he heard that he would be arrested only for assembling, alongside five hundred others, to "disturb the peace . . . and riotously beset and attack the courthouse."[182]

As his trial approached, Higginson sought the counsel of fellow abolitionists as to the best approach to the charge, since he considered it a concession to an immoral law to plead guilty.[183] Wendell Phillips characteristically advised Higginson to take advantage of the "opportunity of preaching to the jury [since it] is one of the things you fought for, perhaps the most important object."[184] Interestingly, this appears to be the advice Higginson felt most appropriate when anticipating a summons from the Mason Committee following that body's commencement of investigation into the John Brown affair in 1860. However, just as the public forum was denied him by the Mason Committee, the Federal District Court responsible for arraigning those responsible for the Burns' riot dismissed the cases against all participants, and Higginson did not have the opportunity to confront the State of Massachusetts with its complicity in the maintenance of slavery.[185]

In the aftermath of the Burns's case, Higginson put his desire to confront his fellow citizens with their responsibility to actively oppose immoral legal proceedings on hold. Concerned for his wife's health, he took a ten month leave of absence from the Worcester Free Church in order to accompany the invalid on a journey to the Fayal, a Portuguese Island in the Azores.[186] While abroad, Higginson remained attentive to events at home eagerly reading both the *Liberator* and the *Tribune* for news from the states.[187] The news reports that interested him most were the articles having to do with Kansas and the armed struggle for freedom there.[188] Both weeklies were particularly sensitive to the abuses committed by Border Ruffians on law-abiding Free State settlers attempting to make a new life in Kansas, and Higginson read these attentively. In January, the *Tribune* featured an article revealing the murder of Free State militia captain Reese Brown who was killed by "men, or rather demons, who rushed around Brown and literally hacked him to death with their hatchets."[189] Commenting on the deteriorating situation in March, Horace Greeley, editor of the *Tribune*, wrote that "a bloody collision is imminent" between the "diabolical" advocates of slavery and the Free-State men of Kansas."[190] In May, Greeley's prediction appeared particularly prescient when reports that

> Lawrence, the heroic focus and citadel of Free-State principles and efforts in Kansas, has been devastated and burned to ashes by the Border Ruffians: but most of its inhabitants still live . . . A few bare and tottering chimneys, a charred and blackened waste, now mark the site

graced the front pages of the *Tribune*.[191] Keenly interested in the battle for freedom taking place across the ocean, Higginson imagined himself in Kansas engaged in the battle for freedom.[192]

Upon his return to Worcester, it did not take him much time to translate his dreams of action to reality. In July, only one month after he converted the welcome reception that his Worcester congregation organized for him to a Kansas recruiting rally, Higginson accepted the commission of the Massachusetts Kansas Aid Committee to travel to Kansas in order to observe first-hand the difficulties that emigrants committed to settling in the territory experienced.[193] His inspiration was local. A group of thirty-nine Worcester men had been accosted by armed Border Ruffians from Missouri and disarmed before they could reach the territory; Higginson's charter was to determine what had occurred and recommend what to do to ensure that future emigrants to the territory did not suffer the same fate. What he discovered, Higginson knew might appear to be somewhat disconcerting: when challenged by an armed group of Missourians, the New England men had given up their weapons without a fight.[194] However, as Higginson paradoxically discovered when he "carefully questioned the members of the party," this fact did not suggest their cowardice. Quite to the contrary, it suggested the "caution, prudence, coolness and discretion" of Dr. Cutter, the leader of the party.[195] Clarifying the situation for outraged readers of the *Liberator*, Higginson characteristically reported that the Worcester men surrendered their arms and turned back only when they discovered their route opposed by *"from three to five thousand men,* distributed at different points, several hundred at each. At Waverly, Lexington, Delaware, Liberty, Independence, Plattville, Leavenworth, and Weston, there were these bands—commonly with cannon."[196] According to Higginson, the Worcester men were not cowardly but decidedly brave in their effort to penetrate the enemy territory and had lost their weapons only through "act[s] of treachery" on the part of the Border Ruffians.[197]

Inspired by what he had seen while working to ensure that a subsequent party from Worcester (led by former associate Martin Stowell) succeeded in reaching the territory, Higginson returned from the West committed to making Kansas a free state. Appointed as an agent for the National Kansas Aid Committee, Higginson diligently engaged in efforts to arm, supply, and fund settlers intent on making Kansas their home. He soon discovered that his endeavors increased his both popularity with the citizens of Massachusetts and his reputation as a man of action. The series of dispatches that he had sent to the *Tribune* during his trip had impressed a large number of readers, as had his fund-raising speeches on the part of the Emigrant Society.[198] In a letter to his mother, Higginson admitted, "I am particularly popular in private just now for what I am doing about Kansas, and it is rather pathetic to have them thank me for doing what they ought to have taken hold of themselves, but have not."[199] Higginson evidently made such an impression on the other members of the National Kansas Aid Committee that they decided to ask him to make another western trip. This time, however, he would do more than simply investigate the difficulties encountered by Massachusetts emigrants along the over-land route to Kansas; this time, Higginson would arm, supply, and accompany the emigrants into the hostile territory.

For two frantic months before his scheduled September journey, the Worcester minister excitedly devoted himself to amassing enough arms, ammunition, and equipment to supply the group of emigrants whom he planned to accompany to the contested promised land.[200] After his departure, he was attentive to his friends and often informed them of what he had seen. On 12 September, he wrote the first of a series of letters on conditions at the border for the New York *Tribune*, the Chicago *Tribune*, and the St. Louis *Democrat*.[201] In this dispatch, Higginson suggests the tension that all emigrants felt as they approached the border:

> As soon as one approaches the Missouri River, even in Iowa and Nebraska, he begins to feel as if he were in France or Austria. Men are very cautious in defining their position, and wait to hear what others say. Then perhaps, their tongues are slightly loosed, if they think that there are no spies about them. But it is no slight risk when a man may have to pay for his life, further down the river, for a free word, spoken at Counsil [sic] Bluffs or Sidney, both Pro-slavery towns.[202]

He was delighted by both the sense of danger and the sense of importance that his position afforded him. He also was delighted to meet those settlers who had lost everything, yet remained committed to a free Kansas and expressed their determination to make a life in the rich territory. Higginson reported being impressed by settlers whom he met upon entering Kansas in September. When he asked them, "Will you give up Kansas?" "Never" was the reply. "We are scattered, starved, hunted, half-naked, but we are not conquered *yet*."[203] His admiration was more pointed when considering those who placed their lives in jeopardy as bold leaders actively engaged in the struggle to defend the rights of Free-Soil settlers.

What Higginson discovered in Kansas, he told an assembled Massachusetts Anti-Slavery Society at their twenty-fifth anniversary celebration, was

> the history of the past, clothed in living flesh before me. I saw in Charles Robinson the Puritan soldier—the Hampden of Cromwell's army; so

modest, so absolutely noble . . . And if I wanted a genuine warrior of the Revolution where could I find him better than in the old Vermonter, Captain John Brown, the defender of Ossawatomie . . . Old Captain Brown, the Ethan Allen, the Israel Putnam of today, who had prayers every morning, and then sallies forth, with seven stalwart sons, wherever duty or danger calls, who swallows a Missourian whole, and says grace after the meat.[204]

Brown, for Higginson, had become the "genuine warrior of the Revolution" reincarnated.[205] A true Christian soldier, John Brown epitomized the righteous man fighting for independence from tyranny and oppression in America. Higginson's praise of Brown was not limited to the audience that attended the annual Fanueil Hall meeting. A much larger audience learned about Brown when Garrison included the entire text of Higginson's speech in the January, 1857 *Liberator*. Unknowingly perhaps, in his editorial decision, William Lloyd Garrison had established Higginson as both an uncompromising champion of the Free State movement and a celebrant of John Brown.

Regardless of the overwhelming approval for John Brown that he articulated in his speech before the Massachusetts Anti-Slavery Society, Higginson was not prepared to blindly embrace John Brown when Franklin Sanborn first approached him about committing the funds rumored to be in the coffers of the Worcester County Kansas Committee to the Kansas veteran. In fact, Higginson flatly denied Sanborn access to the $3000 that he reputedly controlled, and he refused to actively champion Brown in his effort to arm and equip a company of one hundred men for future operations in defense of freedom. Perhaps recognizing the trend toward lawfulness in Kansas during the early part of 1857, and hopeful that his own efforts to demonstrate the inertia of the disunion movement might inspire politicians to a new level of moral responsibility, he did not feel it appropriate to embrace Brown in 1857.[206] It was not until Brown contacted Higginson with a personal petition for funding for his "strictly confidential" future operation in February, 1858 that Higginson seemed intrigued enough to meet Brown in Boston, and then only after Sanborn had provided him with a sketch of Brown's radical plan to inspire a national revolution by attacking the heart of slavery. Agreeing to become a "stockholder" in Brown's venture, Higginson collected his $100 initial investment, submitted the money to Sanborn, and eagerly awaited word that Brown would soon begin operations.[207]

He was distraught when Hugh Forbes's threats of exposure succeeded in convincing the other stockholders that delaying Brown's operation was the wisest course of action and began to distance himself from his former associates.[208] He did not, however, distance himself from radical abolition. In fact, even while Franklin Sanborn was earnestly attempting to convince him of the wisdom of deferring Brown's venture, Higginson publicly advocated the type of violent rebellion that Brown intended to initiate in Virginia in a speech before the American Anti-Slavery Society in Boston on 12 May 1858.

Insisting that slavery is "destined, as it began in blood, so to end," Higginson explained that the American slave would inevitably embrace the kind of violence that the "heroes of Santo Domingo" had adopted and overthrow the yoke of bondage placed on them by their oppressors.[209] Although he did not mention anything about John Brown, Higginson asserted that the "white Anglo-Saxon . . . [was] too apt to assume the whole work is theirs," implying that whites would play a key role in the eventual confrontation with slavery, but that they would not take on the burden of liberty alone.[210]

No longer associated with the Free Church in Worcester, from which he had resigned in March, 1858, Higginson increasingly devoted himself to literature and to the lectern; John Brown's plan, however, was never far from his mind. His first essay for the *Atlantic*, "Saints, and Their Bodies," reveals his concern with the lack of vigor prevalent in Americans, which he clearly associates with the existence of "all perils,—financial crises, Slavery, Romanism, Mormonism, Border Ruffians, and New York Assassins."[211] Attacking the complacency he saw in his community, Higginson suggests that there is a direct correlation between physical and moral degeneracy. In a man like John Brown, whom Higginson increasingly regarded as a "sly old veteran," Higginson saw strength, wisdom, and conviction born of long consideration. Unlike almost every other man he knew, Brown carried himself apart from the moral and physical weakness prevalent in America. Therefore, even as Brown prepared to return to Kansas, Higginson expressed his trust that the man would carry out his slave insurrection, even if it had been delayed upon the advice of lesser men.[212]

In the days that followed Brown's capture at Harpers Ferry, Higginson privately expressed distinct pleasure that Brown had followed through with the bold insurrection he had planned.[213] He contended that the attack was the "most formidable insurrection that had ever occurred;" however, he did not embrace the opportunity to publicly defend Brown's effort.[214] Instead, like both Sanborn and Parker, he quietly observed the public response to Brown's raid and pondered how his confederates in Brown's endeavor could be so cowardly as to run off to Canada and try to destroy all evidence of their complicity in Brown's attack at Harper's Ferry.[215] In order to assuage his desire to do something to aid the Kansas veteran, he began a series of covert and ineffectual planning efforts to coordinate a rescue attempt for Brown, but he never once publicly proclaimed his sympathy for Brown.

When Thoreau decided to present his lecture on the character and actions of Captain John Brown in Worcester, and inquired if his friend H.G.O. Blake in Worcester could arrange an audience to hear his lecture, he queried, "[p]erhaps Higginson may like to have a meeting."[216] This was not a casual gesture toward the outspoken abolitionist. Thoreau was well aware of Higginson's long history of reform and his militant readiness to oppose slavery. He was also aware of Higginson's participation in the Anthony Burn's riot and his vocal condemnation of the citizens of Massachusetts following Burns's rendition.[217] Indeed, accounts of Higginson's arrest and the full text of "Massachusetts in Mourning" had been published in both the Massachusetts *Spy* and the *Liberator* within a month of the failed attempt to free Burns.[218]

In all probability, Thoreau was also aware of Higginson's role as one of the six men conspiring with his neighbor, Franklin Sanborn, to covertly provide Brown support in 1858 and 1859. Certainly, Sanborn must have informed Thoreau of Higginson's enthusiastic commitment to the efforts of both the Worcester County and Massachusetts State Kansas Committees. During his efforts to gain access to some of the resources held by these committees during 1857 and 1858, Sanborn is also very likely to have expressed his surprise that Higginson was reluctant to commit the committee funds that he controlled to Brown.[219] This is especially true in 1858 when, much to Sanborn's dismay, Higginson refused Brown access to the Worcester County Kansas Committee money a second time.[220]

In all likelihood, Sanborn was more than a little frustrated by Higginson's coy refusal and told Thoreau about the abolitionist's enigmatic behavior.[221] He desperately wanted to provide the Brown with the resources necessary to maintain freedom in Kansas, and he knew that Higginson could provide it if he really believed in Brown. Despite Higginson's radical abolitionist rhetoric, Sanborn probably informed Thoreau that his Worcester friend was not yet ready to do anything more than talk about fighting slavery.

When Hugh Forbes emerged from the fringe of society and threatened to compromise the identities of Brown's Boston supporters, Sanborn once again is likely to have expressed his frustration with Higginson at Thoreau's dining table. Among friends and known abolitionists who routinely defied the law by aiding escaping slaves, he had no reason to fear exposure. Quite to the contrary, he had every reason to believe that his efforts on behalf of Brown would be applauded. After all, the Thoreaus' had hosted the Kansas veteran in their home and attended his evening lectures at the Concord Town Hall.

In any case, there is no doubt that Thoreau was very aware of Higginson's failure to make any public gesture of support for John Brown following his capture at Harper's Ferry. Higginson did not respond to the Worcester *Spy's* claim that John Brown "has gone so far into madness, and become so wild with it, as to invade Virginia at the head of an army of seventeen white men, all as crazy as himself."[222] Nor did he respond to the *Liberator's* assertion that John Brown's effort was "a misguided, wild, and apparently insane . . . effort."[223] Inexplicably, the man who had both boldly led the attack on the Boston Courthouse in 1854 and claimed that the "way to make principles felt is to assert them peaceably if you can, forcibly if you must" was silent when John Brown was brought to trial and sentenced to death at the gallows.[224]

Higginson's behavior must have surprised Thoreau. Long acquainted, Thoreau had not known the outspoken reformer to demonstrate any reluctance to speak out in support of unpopular causes. Over the course of their ten year acquaintance, Higginson had publicly argued against the fugitive slave laws, unsuccessfully campaigned for a seat in the state senate proclaiming his devotion to higher law, actively championed armed resistance against slave-holders, used his pulpit to condemn those whose silence upon contentious issues contributed to the moral depravity of society, and published frequent articles advocating social reform and social responsibility. Silence was not the response that Higginson's acquaintances expected when reports of Brown's bold attack on Harper's Ferry began to filter North.

Thoreau's earliest acquaintance with the Worcester reformer suggested an altogether different response. In June, 1850, Higginson forthrightly presented himself to the author of *A Week on the Merrimack and Concord Rivers* "convinced that Thoreau knew more about nature than any man in American."[225] Thoreau, Higginson notes in a letter to his sister, was not at all like he anticipated. In fact, Higginson seems to have been surprised when he found Thoreau both "more human and polite than [he] . . . supposed."[226] In his account of their meeting, Higginson recorded that Thoreau

> is a little bronzed spare man; he makes lead pencils with his father on Mondays and Tuesdays and was in the midst of work. On other days he surveys land, both mathematically and meditatively . . . he talks sententiously and originally; his manner is the most unvarying facsimile of Mr. Emerson's but his thoughts are quite his own.[227]

Despite Thoreau's apparent affectation, Higginson was obviously impressed by him. Thoreau was a unique man, and he expressed the same kind of enthusiasm Higginson felt when exploring the wild. As a result, Higginson excitedly invited Thoreau to stay at his home when he heard that the Concord naturalist was planning on lecturing in Newburyport in December.[228]

Although Thoreau does not include any comments on either the success of his evening lecture ("An Excursion to Cape Cod") or the conversation that he most certainly had with Higginson following his early evening presentation (in his extant journals), it is certain that their discussion included a mention of the recent escape of William and Ellen Craft in Boston.[229] Indeed, the article "The Crisis Coming Now" that Higginson authored while the slave-catchers were searching for the Crafts only a month before Thoreau's visit would have found an eager celebrant in author of "Civil Disobedience."[230] Higginson's suggestion that the Crafts ought to remain in Boston and test "whether the law of God or the law of man is to prevail" distinctly echoes Thoreau's assertion that the right means of expressing dissatisfaction with the law is to challenge it directly, to meet "this American government, or its representative . . . directly, and face to face" in his recently published lecture.[231]

Two years later, Thoreau attended one of Higginson's lectures in Concord when the Newburyport minister spoke on Mohammed.[232] Although he was not impressed with Higginson's platform presentation—commenting both that Higginson was "not simple enough" and his "manner overbore, choked off, and stifled . . . the matter"—Thoreau did not refuse continued social intercourse with the newly installed Worcester Free Church minister.[233] In April, 1852, in response to Higginson's request that he provide the men of Boston with a lecture at Cochituate Hall, Thoreau entrusted Higginson with all of the lecture arrangements commenting, "I will leave it to you to name an evening next week—decide on the most suitable room—and advertise(?)—if this is not taking you too literally at your word."[234] Demonstrating his regard for the Worcester minister, Thoreau even accepted Higginson's invitation for tea before delivering his lecture, "Life in the Woods."[235] Sadly, no record remains of the conversation that the two men had over tea; Higginson did, however, leave a rather pointed affirmation of Thoreau's complete failure before the "young mechanics" who had braved the blizzard to sit in the reading rooms of the hall and leaf through their newspapers rather than entertain any of Thoreau's ideas.[236]

Despite the fact that neither man was overly impressed with each other at the lectern, both men agreed to appear in a "Course of Independent, or Reform Lectures" when the organizer for the Providence Lyceum requested that they join other notable anti-slavery activists and present a lecture "of a *reformatory Character* . . . whether Antislavery or what else" in the fall of 1854.[237] Perhaps impressed by the letter that he had recently received from Higginson praising his presentation of "Slavery in Massachusetts" as an essay that "surpasses everything else . . . which the terrible week in Boston has called out," Thoreau consented to lecture in Providence on 6 December.[238] However, he noted in his journal, "I feel that I am in danger of cheapening myself by trying to become a successful lecturer, i.e., to interest my audiences."[239] Thoreau was concerned about the tendency of audiences to categorize men of sympathetic opinion with one and other; he was also concerned that his own role as a featured speaker in the ten lecture series might indicate his retreat from the position of intellectual independence.

Thoreau's journal entry suggests his consistent concern with social critics who dedicated themselves to the reform of everything but themselves. Higginson's active role in various reforms to include abolition, women's rights, temperance, and education make him an obvious target of Thoreau's rather unspecific journal entry. Thoreau makes this criticism more specific in his reference to Higginson's decision to make a journey to Mount Katahdin in a rather rambling 1855 letter to H. G. O. Blake. After commenting on meeting Daniel Ricketson, whom he found refreshingly sincere and similarly devoted to simplicity, Thoreau remarks

> I was glad to hear the other day that Higginson and _____ were gone to Ktaadn; it must be so much better to go to than a Woman's Rights or an Abolitionist Convention; better still, to the delectable primitive mounts within you, which you have dreamed of from your youth up, and seen perhaps, in the horizon, but never climbed.[240]

Thoreau's implicit comparison of Ricketson, whom he found "singularly frank and plain-spoken," hence worthy company, and Higginson, whom he suggests was awkwardly formal and a bit pretentious, hence somewhat disagreeable company, is interesting.[241] For Thoreau, plainness seems to indicate trustworthiness and singularity forthrightness. On the other hand, awkwardly elaborate or complicated presentation intimates lack of sincerity and lack of real will to conviction. Higginson's willingness to engage in activities like a hiking trip on Mount Katahdin, which Thoreau intimates, necessarily simplifies one's perspectives and allows for the refinement of valuable personal perspectives, is worthy; merely attending conventions and demonstrating sympathy with an idea accomplishes nothing. In this short passage then, Thoreau suggests that the Worcester minister may have the potential to do some really valuable work, if only he would reassess the wisdom of devoting himself to a myriad of reforms and direct himself toward more productive arenas. As if anticipating his essay "Reform and the Reformers," Thoreau seems to suggest that in 1855, Higginson was part of the "class of *improvvisanti* more wonderful and amusing than the Italians."[242] He suggests that Higginson explore his own relationship to the universe and refine his activities to those pursuits consistent with well-examined principles, rather than every popular reform of the day.

Regardless of his concern with Higginson's tendency to over-indulge in popular reform movements and over-complicate his presentations, Thoreau was drawn to the Free Church minister. When in Worcester, he often called on Higginson; he evidently enjoyed his informal company and casual conversation much more than he did his formal platform manner.[243] Cognizant of Higginson's appreciation for his own work, Thoreau even gave Higginson an advance copy of *Walden* when he finally succeeded in gaining a publisher for his well-revised text. [244] Perhaps in recognition of their kindred love of nature, Thoreau valued the younger man's company and enjoyed his enthusiastic interest in the natural world. For his own part, Higginson found Thoreau fascinating, if a bit rustic. Reflecting on Thoreau thirty-five years after the Concord native died, Higginson noted:

> Thoreau came to take walks in the woods, or perhaps to Wachusett, with Harrison Blake, his later editor, and with Theophilus Brown, the freshest and most original mind in Worcester. . . . Sometimes I joined the party, and found Thoreau a dry humorist, and also a good walker.[245]

A fellow devotee of the outdoors, Higginson was also impressed by both *A Week* and *Walden* believing that Thoreau's intuitive understanding of nature and his ability to translate his intimacy was superior to every other author of the day. Commenting on Thoreau in a letter to Harriet Prescott Spofford, one of the women he had encouraged to authorship while in Newburyport, Higginson acknowledged Thoreau's genius:

The only thoroughly outdoor book I have ever seen is Thoreau's "Week ..., which is fascinating beyond compare to anyone who knows Nature, though the religion and philosophy are of the wildest. He has led a strange Indian life, the author, and his errors and extremes are on the opposite from most peoples ... Thoreau sent me his book [Walden], which I have enjoyed as much, I think as the other; it is calmer and more whole, crammed with fine observation and thought, and rising to sublimity at the last.[246]

Higginson's appreciation for Thoreau, however, was not entirely enthusiastic. Like many of his contemporaries, most famously Elizabeth Hoar, who once commented that she "loved Henry [Thoreau], but did not like him," Higginson appreciated Thoreau but did not necessarily always enjoy his company.[247] When chronicling notable individuals with whom he had established an acquaintance, Higginson noted somewhat paradoxically, "Thoreau is pure and wonderfully learned in nature's things and deeply wise, and yet tedious in his monologues and cross-questionings."[248]

By no means intimate friends in 1859, Higginson and Thoreau seemed to have enjoyed an interesting appreciation for one and other. Higginson respected the intimacy that Thoreau enjoyed with nature and had a distinct regard for both his ability to express himself in writing and his anti-slavery sentiment; he did not, however, pursue an active correspondence with the Concord native, nor did he attempt to make his relationship more intimate than their casual walks in Worcester might suggest. For his own part, Thoreau seems to have similarly appreciated Higginson's interest in nature and sympathized with his views on slavery. He did not, however, embrace the Worcester minister as a close friend, nor did he demonstrate any desire to join in Higginson's enthusiastic public commitment to reform all aspects of Massachusetts society.

Further, he did not remain silent when John Brown's effort to establish a bit of "Rail Road business on a *somewhat extended* scale" captured the attention of the entire nation.[249] As the news from Virginia filled the papers, and claims that Brown was insane dominated the headlines, Higginson, the ardent abolitionist and bold reformer, said nothing in public. Thoreau, indignant and unaffected by the cautious among his acquaintance, boldly proclaimed Brown a "man of rare common sense and directness of speech, as of action; a transcendentalist above all, a man of ideas and principles" (264) to a Worcester audience.

Thoreau's celebration of Brown was a direct response to the silence of men like Higginson; he could not stomach their hypocrisy. Unlike Brown, who had "the courage to face his country herself, when she was in the wrong" (262), Thomas Wentworth Higginson, Franklin Sanborn, and Theodore Parker—all vocal champions of the radical abolitionist movement—demonstrated cowardice in the wake of Brown's failed raid.

They did not courageously oppose the inertia of negative public opinion accelerated by eager newspapermen and maintained by cautious politicians. Instead, these Massachusetts men who covertly sponsored Brown silently observed the reaction of their countrymen and refused to sing praises of the man who had acted upon the principle that slavery was antithetical to the notion of liberty.

Thoreau did the exact opposite. Disregarding the hostile anti-abolitionist atmosphere that permeated Massachusetts in the immediate aftermath of Brown's capture, Thoreau passionately celebrated John Brown. Throughout his address, he confronted his silent countrymen with their cowardly behavior and modeled the forthright conduct that he expected of them. Thoreau's message is both pointed and unequivocal: he proclaims Brown's deliberate attempt to initiate the end of slavery as both worthy of the highest tribute and deserving of the greatest public honor; to fail to forthrightly recognize Brown as a principled champion of humanity and acknowledge him as modern day Christ is, according to Thoreau, both an abdication of social responsibility and a demonstration of cowardice. Committed to justice and offended by the silence of Brown's intellectual champions, Thoreau offered his defense of John Brown in Concord, Boston, and Worcester to confront Sanborn, Parker, and Higginson with their complicity in Brown's vilification and compel them to repudiate the ignorant remarks of their uninformed countrymen by celebrating the man who wholeheartedly committed himself to "the public practice of Humanity" (263) and the end of slavery in America.

Thoreau's lecture clearly indicates his confrontational intent. When he begins "A Plea for Captain John Brown," he does so uncharacteristically. He does not confidently assert his opinion that a "government is best which governs least" (125) as he did in "Civil Disobedience," nor does he recall an event in Concord where he felt disappointment that his townsmen were more interested in events occurring on the fringes of the nation than they were in the events occurring in their own state, as he did in "Slavery in Massachusetts" (181). He begins "A Plea" by unexpectedly asking for his listener's "pardon" (262), acknowledging the fact that his presence as a lecturer focused on the actions and character of John Brown, is somehow wrong. He suggests that he is not the most qualified citizen to defend Brown within the community. He is, however, the only person willing to speak on behalf of Brown, thus pointedly, and perhaps sardonically, Thoreau asks his audience for their indulgence. In the second sentence, Thoreau establishes an opposition that calls attention to the irony of his self-deprecating introductory sentence. He casually notes, "I do not wish to force my thoughts upon you, but I feel forced myself" (261). Thoreau's distinction, of course, is far from casual. By opposing the active "force" with the passive "forced," Thoreau indicates that he has been compelled to speak on behalf of Brown and believes that each man and woman in the audience ought to have been similarly compelled. Chastising his listeners for their unwillingness to publicly recognize the righteousness of Brown's actions, Thoreau returns to the *active* tense in the next sentence to bring his audience to an *active* appreciation of their folly.

> Little as I know of Captain Brown, I would fain do my part to correct the tone and the statements of the newspapers, and of my countrymen generally, respecting his character and actions. It costs us nothing to be just. We can at least express our sympathy with, and admiration of, him and his companions, and that is what I propose to do (261).

Recognizing his own limited knowledge of Brown, Thoreau successfully communicates the fact that he is not the most appropriate member of the community to celebrate John Brown. Others with far more intimate knowledge of the man could easily and more successfully correct the misrepresentations common in press reports; Thoreau could not. He did not know Brown well; he had only met the man on two occasions. However, unlike his more knowledgeable associates, he was unafraid to speak. Rejecting the passive role that he saw his friend Frank Sanborn in Concord, Wentworth Higginson in Worcester, and Theodore Parker assume, Thoreau assumed the active role of principled celebrant of John Brown that he witnessed his less righteous associates recently abdicate in their less than noble desire to save their own skins. Attempting to address the far from principled behavior of the men who fled the country when they saw their own names on the front pages of the New York *Herald* or silently observed while newspapermen denigrated Brown's effort, Thoreau attempted to correct the tone of his "countrymen,"—or, adjust their perspectives by publicly proclaiming his own sympathy with Brown and inspiring them to do the same; thus, instead of silently observing the defamation of John Brown, he hoped that he might inspire them to forthrightly defend the man as a principled champion of liberty—not passively retreat from the man when the opportunity to defend him was at hand.

Thoreau's fleeting transition, at the end of the first paragraph is both interesting and important. As if acknowledging the possibility of a community of active constituents, all individually committed to acknowledging higher law and consistently committed to acting upon their own intuitive understanding of right and wrong, Thoreau includes his entire audience in the transition to the body of his lecture when he remarks, "[w]e can at least express our sympathy with, and admiration of, him and his companions" (261). This is the least that a responsible citizen can do—publicly proclaim his moral agreement or disagreement with John Brown that slavery "was a great wrong against God and humanity."[250] However, as if recognizing that a community of individuals who courageously act upon their own convictions is far from reality, Thoreau suggests that at a minimum, he will do so when he returns to the first person singular. He will, in effect, model the transition to active principled man by singularly championing a man who was willing to devote himself to the cause of justice and humanity.

When he begins to review Brown's history, Thoreau, once again, calls attention to the abdication of individual responsibility he observes in his fellow citizens. He stresses the fact that he does not need to describe Brown for the members of his audience, since "most of [them] . . . have seen and will not forget him" (261). Diminishing any notion of his own uniqueness, Thoreau emphasizes the probability that others in the audience have as much or more personal knowledge of Brown than he does; therefore, he suggests that his position as singular defender of Brown is incomprehensible. This is particularly true for members of the audiences in Concord, Worcester, and Boston who maintained close contact with Brown from 1857 to 1859 and conspired to provide the abolitionist arms, equipment, and funding during his preparation for the guerilla campaign that he anticipated following his success at Harpers Ferry.

Thoreau continues to emphasize the degree to which his knowledge of Brown had been gained second-hand by employing passive verb constructions to describe Brown's early personal history. He uses the construction "I am told" when he begins his brief narrative of Brown's youth to suggest that he gained his knowledge of Brown's youth from conversations with someone other than Brown—someone who had developed a far more personal relationship with the man—someone like his neighbor Franklin Sanborn who committed himself to John Brown in 1857 and spent the next three years occupied in efforts to insure the Kansas veteran succeeded in his war on slavery. Thoreau's subtle shift to a slightly more active verb tense positions him as a general member of an audience to whom Brown recounted the experiences of his youth. Instead of suggesting simply that Brown had told him that his "father was a contractor who furnished beef to the army," Thoreau passively notes, "I heard him say that his father was a contractor who furnished beef to the army" (261). Thoreau presents himself to his audience as one listener among many, insinuating that he neither occupied a privileged position of trust nor a relative position of intimacy with John Brown. Instead, he was simply one man who had been privileged to witness the public remarks of an extraordinary man who was willing to commit himself to a "war for liberty" (262) and no other war.

Perhaps, uncertain that he had succeeded in his rather subtle effort to prod the silent majority from their eminently safe positions of psychological distance from Brown and his violent abolitionism, Thoreau recalls Brown's role in Kansas, only a few years remote in time for his listeners. He reminds his audience of their knowledge of Brown's forthright character. Emphasizing the degree to which all of his listeners knew about Brown and had an obligation to defend the man, Thoreau recalls how Brown stood ready to respond to the needs of his sons who had settled in Kansas as Free State men. Not only did his listeners have intimate knowledge of Brown's deeds in the battles for Kansas, many had been active in organizations which provided Brown weapons, ammunition, and financial support in order that he might be able to advance the cause of freedom on the frontier. As Thoreau acknowledges, when his sons requested his assistance, John Brown responded. He further emphasizes the familiarity of audience members with the abolitionists' willingness to champion the cause of freedom by remarking, "[t]his, *as you all know*, he soon after did; and it was through his agency, far more than any others, that Kansas was made free [my emphasis]" (262). Thoreau brings each listener to an awareness of his or her position of remoteness by calling attention to their intimate knowledge of Brown and his positive role in the extension of freedom in America. Each man and woman in his Boston audience *knows* of John Brown, and they *know* of the devotion to liberty and the "public practice of Humanity" he exercised in Kansas. They ought, Thoreau suggests, now embrace the man and consider his actions not like "wooden men" (127) who deny their own intelligence, but like active, informed, and intellectually engaged individuals who privilege not the reactionary rhetoric of the press, but their own well-considered, informed opinions of the man based upon his demonstrated commitment to freedom.

As he proceeds to celebrate the character of John Brown, Thoreau distinguishes the freedom fighter from both his cosmopolitan supporters and the more erudite in his audience. He refocuses the opposition he employed to initiate the lecture to contrast the active, principled, and admirably (though informally) educated man John Brown from those members of society who waited in apparent passive silence with the privilege of formal education and social position.

Thoreau spoke of Brown as

> A man of rare common sense, and directness in speech, as of action; a transcendentalist above all, a man of ideals and principles,—that was what distinguished him. Not yielding to whim or transient impulse, but carrying out the purpose of a life (264).

John Brown was completely unlike Franklin Sanborn, Thoreau's Concord neighbor who had recently graduated from Harvard, established a progressive school in Concord, devoted himself to the Free State cause in Kansas, then passionately dedicated himself toward coordinating support for John Brown. He did not yield to his fears when the possibility of capture, imprisonment, and prosecution arouse. Quite to the contrary, John Brown fixedly determined to demonstrate his opposition to slavery, regardless of the consequences. Unlike John Brown, Sanborn, the intellect, the ardent abolitionist secretary of the Massachusetts State Kansas Committee, and the primary coordinator for support of John Brown, yielded to his fears and impulsively fled the country when he learned that he might be arrested for his role in Brown's failed raid. Perhaps Brown's most vocal celebrant before the raid, Sanborn was one of the absolutely silent in its aftermath.

He was not alone. Thomas Wentworth Higginson, the Worcester reformer and ardent abolitionist who, for the past ten years had been publishing radical abolitionist diatribes calling not only for immediate abolition but celebrating the right of both fugitive slaves and whites alike to openly and violently oppose the arm of slavery, was also silent. Though he did not flee like Sanborn, Higginson failed to live by his own prescription when he remained silent during John Brown's trial. He did not place himself in a position of either physical or social risk, as he advised the readers of the *Liberator* in the aftermath of the Burns' affair, nor did he organize a public response to John Brown's rushed trial in order to reverse the "timidity of the majority, the irresolution of the rest," as he had suggested to Garrison in an 1855 letter.[251] Instead, while Brown was on trial for his life and in jail awaiting his execution, Higginson quietly sequestered himself in his Worcester home and occupied himself by planning a series of unrealistic rescue attempts for his principled champion. He did not bring any of these plans to fruition, nor did he make any gesture to publicly defend the man who "forcibly" promoted freedom by making "his principles felt" at Harper's Ferry.[252]

Nor did Theodore Parker, the long-standing abolitionist who had left both his Unitarian congregation and his work as a radical abolitionist to attend to his health in February, 1859, eight months before John Brown— whom he had sponsored and defended—brought his plan to attack slavery to fruition. Although his pulpit was temporarily filled by notable abolitionists like Garrison, Phillips, Emerson, Higginson, Sargent, Scherb, and Thoreau, Parker's absence as a lecturer and staunch advocate of abolition whose oft-stated conviction that "the existence of Slavery endangers all our Democratic institutions" was keenly felt.[253] His Sunday morning sermons routinely reached wide audiences of over one thousand citizens in Boston, and his Fraternity Lectures routinely attracted audiences of twenty-five hundred or more. A man of great intellect, energy, and social influence, Parker was a radical abolitionist force in Boston. Although certainly a man of "ideals and principles," Parker withdrew from public life due to failing health absenting himself from the field of public responsibility in a last effort to seek a climate which would reverse the onslaught of tuberculosis.

Only a few short years from his own withdrawal from public life due to the ravages of the same disease, Thoreau was strong, determined, and outraged by the failure of any public figure, excepting perhaps "Mr. Vallandigham" (273), to speak out on behalf of the man who had devoted himself to re-forming the consciousness of his fellow citizens and acting upon his own conviction that slavery wrong. An active man willing to boldly confront hypocrisy, Thoreau willfully prodded those whose passive silence suggested their indifference to John Brown's effort. Passivity, Thoreau suggests is an abdication of an individual's obligation as a citizen, a socially aware singular man or woman with an intrinsic under-standing of right and wrong; silence, consistently, suggests cowardice, since failing to assert an opinion in the face of public scrutiny denies the individual his proper position in society. By using the pronoun "we," at the end of his introductory paragraph, Thoreau attempts to inspire his listeners from what he terms their "universal woodenness . . . [or] want of vitality" (268) to join him in his celebration of a man who recognized not the authority of flawed human law but the universality of the higher law of liberty for all men.

Thoreau underscores the distance between those who are sympathetic, yet silent among his listeners, and the vocal principled man whom he has embraced as his ideal transcendental representative by distinguishing the potential gain Brown will achieve by his selfless act and identifying the impoverished position to which the inert have condemned themselves. Stressing the foolishness of his Yankee neighbor who cannot understand why any man would compromise his own safety if he did not stand the chance of significant pecuniary gain, Thoreau suggests that trivial valua-tions of a man's efforts are both short-sighted and blind. Far more valuable than transient pecuniary gains, Thoreau suggests that Brown "stands a chance to save a considerable part of his soul—and *such* a soul!—when *you* do not" (267). In his gesture toward conventional Christian rhetoric, Thoreau dramatically emphasizes the distinction between those few who live in accordance with their religious or ideological principles, and the much larger number of Americans who superficially claim faith or moral conviction, yet fail to act consistent with their professed beliefs. Thoreau is able to effectively denounce both his collective audience and his indi-vidual listeners by employing the pronoun "you" in negative opposition to Brown's model behavior. Implicitly condemning those who failed to speak in Brown's defense out of fear for either their social or financial positions, Thoreau calls attention to higher religious law in order to emphasize the poverty of the members of a society who collectively embraced or compro-mised with the forces of slavery to ensure the maintenance of a union based on economic advantage, not upon a common dedication to morality.

Directing his critique toward "[p]rominant and influential editors" whose opinions have been influenced by routine intercourse with lesser men, Tho-reau suggests that "they enlarge themselves to conceive" of Brown (271). Thoreau prompts both the literal editors of the newspapers—who had not included "one single expression of sympathy" (269) for Brown and his men during the week after their capture—and the metaphorical editors—the prominent and influential men who had revised Brown's 1858 plan and then helped him prepare it for final presentation on October 16, 1859—to understand the celebration of higher law—the law of personal liberty that Brown expressed in his attack on Harpers Ferry.[254] Both, Thoreau stresses, must stop concerning themselves primarily with their personal security, their reputations, and their financial prospects and selflessly enlarge their focus to adequately appreciate and celebrate John Brown, who, in his self-sacrifice, acted from a recognition of a far more important foci—the equality of all men. Thoreau tells his listeners, his own metaphorical editors who will *revise* and *re-present* his views, to leave their individual apolitical silent sanctity and celebrate the righteous actions of the man who acted from an understanding of a higher law that no man had a right to hold another in bondage.

5 "Self-Reliance"
Emerson's Antidote to Political Abdication and Judicial Compromise

When the American government and courts are false to their trust, men disobey the government, put it in the wrong; the government is forced into all manner of false and ridiculous attitudes. Men hear reason and truth from private men who have brave hearts and great minds. This is the compensation of bad governments,—the field it affords to illustrious men. And we have a great debt to the brave and faithful men who in the very hour and place of the evil act, made their protest for themselves and their countrymen by word and deed. They are justified, and the law is condemned.[1]

Ralph Waldo Emerson, "American Slavery"

Much like Thoreau, Emerson enthusiastically responded to John Brown during his visit to Concord in March, 1857. Having been particularly attentive to the affairs in Kansas the previous year, Emerson had often heard of the exploits of the Free State champion.[2] Frequent conversations with George Luther Stearns and Franklin Sanborn, both men who were intimately involved with the statewide effort to provide support for emigrants in the new territory, allowed Emerson to stay well-informed about the tumultuous affairs in Kansas and learn of the more notable figures who opposed the lawlessness embraced by the Pro-Slavery coalition.[3] In the aftermath of Charles Sumner's brutal caning on the Senate floor, an event that mirrored the outrages committed upon Free Soil settlers in Kansas, Emerson was even inspired to join other indignant Concord men and women to raise money for the defense of Kansas.[4] After urging his fellow citizens to provide the citizens of Massachusetts with the means to defend themselves against marauding bands of Border Ruffians, Emerson personally contributed $50 of the $962 raised in Concord, firmly establishing his commitment to liberty in Kansas.[5] In the months that followed, he did not limit his efforts to his home town; in September, 1856, Emerson traveled to Cambridge in order to raise additional funds for the oppressed Free Soil settlers. Indignant that "citizens of Massachusetts, legal voters here, have emigrated to national territory under the sanction of every law, and are set on by highwaymen, driven from their new homes, pillaged, and numbers killed and scalped . . . in loud defiance of all laws and liberties," Emerson urged individual citizens to aid emigrants and called upon the representatives of Massachusetts to confront the federal government regarding the creation of an atmosphere of injustice in Kansas.[6] John Brown, having committed to the defense of Free States settlers in October, 1855, was one of the most notable figures in the ongoing confrontation between the federally supported Pro-Slavery ruffians and the Free Soil emigrants struggling for control of the Kansas Territory in 1856.

Engaged financially, committed intellectually, and indignant philosophically over the "loud defiance of all laws and liberties" in Kansas, Emerson was pleased when he had the opportunity to meet the "hero of Kansas" at the Thoreau house in Concord in March, 1857.[7] After gaining an introduction to Brown, Emerson enthusiastically invited the captain to his own home for a discussion of Brown's experiences evidently learning to both admire and respect the forthright character who had whole-heartedly dedicated himself to liberty in America. Later, with Thoreau, he attended Brown's lecture at the Concord Town House and listened to a litany of crimes and abuses committed by citizens of Missouri, representatives of the federal government, and Pro Slavery settlers in Kansas upon those who were attempting to settle in the territory who did not embrace slavery.[8] Brown's performance seems to have impressed Emerson, who proclaimed the old man the "rarest of heroes . . . a true idealist, with no by-ends of his own," so much that he donated a small amount toward Brown's future efforts and campaigning for funds in his support.[9]

A few months later, when delivering his "Speech on Affairs in Kansas" in September of 1857, Emerson remembered Brown's appeal for the means to combat the well-armed Border Ruffians and directly "solicited money for rifles from his audience," tacitly expressing his support for violence in the fight against the extension of slavery to the new territories and clearly expressing his moral and political sentiments in the conflict that would increasingly engage his attention.[10] Two years later, in May, 1859, when the radical abolitionist returned from his second campaign in Kansas and told the story of his forceful abduction of eleven slaves from Missouri and their subsequent journey to freedom, Emerson once again welcomed Brown into his own home and personally contributed to Brown's efforts in the name of abolition.

Although Brown does not appear again in Emerson's extant letters or journals until sometime after his capture on October 18th, it is certain that the radical abolitionist remained important to Emerson. In his April, 1859 lecture "Morals," Emerson mentions a "pioneer . . . [who] was forced by our admirable government to fight against the scum of the human race for the protection of freedom, life, and property against brigands."[11] Clearly demonstrating his approval of the pioneer's singular stand against those who would deny the essential and uniquely American liberties established in the *Declaration of Independence*, Emerson both establishes and quotes Brown as archetypal American, one of the "right men [to] give a permanent direction to the fortunes of the state."[12] Emerson's trust in Brown may have been somewhat shaken, however, when he learned that the Kansas freedom fighter had attacked the federal arsenal in Virginia and been captured after having taking over forty hostages and killing five men at Harpers Ferry. In a letter to his brother William, Emerson commented that Brown "is a true hero, but he lost his head" at Harpers Ferry.[13] He did not, however, abandon the righteous abolitionist. In a 26 October letter to Sarah Forbes, Emerson defended Brown asserting that he "seems to have made this fatal blunder only to bring out his virtues."[14]

From that day forward, Emerson's defense of Brown, a man whom he had met on only two occasions, became increasing ardent. After attending Thoreau's first presentation of "On the Character and Actions of Captain John Brown" in the vestry of the First Parish Meetinghouse in Concord on 30 October, Emerson actively pursued a larger venue for his Concord protégé believing that "every man in the Republic" ought to hear Thoreau's tribute to the valiant freedom fighter.[15] Writing to Charles Wesley Slack the morning after Thoreau confronted his Concord neighbors with his celebration of John Brown, Emerson enthusiastically petitioned the chairman of the Fraternity Lecture Course in Boston to provide Thoreau with the opportunity to educate a much larger Boston audience on the social value of Captain John Brown. He explained, "you cannot do a greater public good than to send for Mr. Thoreau, who has read last night here a discourse on the history & character of Captain John Brown, which ought to be heard or read by every man in the Republic." [16] Slack's response to Emerson's request is telling; he wrote, "Thoreau *must* lecture for Fraternity Tuesday Evening [my emphasis]."[17] Inspired by the opportunity to vicariously support Brown that Thoreau provided him, Emerson decided to joined Samuel E. Sewall, Samuel G. Howe, and Thomas Wentworth Higginson in a separate effort to raise money to defray the cost of Brown's legal defense. In their public letter, dated 2 November, Emerson and his fellow abolitionists urged the Boston public "to contribute to the defense of Capt. Brown and his companions on trial for their lives in Virginia."[18] Emphasizing that "e*very moment is precious*," the legal defense committee encouraged potential contributors to immediately pledge money in the name of John Brown.[19]

Paradoxically, although Emerson eagerly committed himself to the service of John Brown, he did not dramatically alter his daily schedule. Even when he learned that Brown had been sentenced to death, he continued to work on his lectures and essays as he had done since leaving the ministry. This is not to suggest that his work was not influenced by the daily newspaper reports of Brown's eloquent public petitions or his forthright behavior in the Charlestown courtroom. When he lectured on "Courage" at the Music Hall on November 8th, Emerson revealed the extent to which he had been inspired by reports of Brown's righteous behavior. Beginning the process of translating the freedom fighter from a failed insurrectionist to what Gilman Ostrander terms a "transcendental hero," Emerson connects John Brown, "the hero of Kansas," with the quality of courage, which, he asserts, is the expression of the "perfect will."[20] He also makes John Brown a model of self-reliance whose "self-possession at the cannon's mouth, [and] cheerfulness in lonely adherence to right" guarantees him a place in the pantheon of American heroes.[21]

Emerson's most significant public celebration of John Brown, however, took place ten days after he addressed the citizens of Boston at the Music Hall. Joining abolitionists John Andrew, Wendell Phillips, and J. M. Manning at a fund-raiser for the "Relief of the Family of Captain John Brown" at the Tremont Temple on November 18, Emerson celebrated John Brown as an exemplum of courage and virtue in a country overwhelmed by corruption and cowardice. He constructed Brown as the "representative American," a self-reliant, principled, courageous man dedicated to the principles of liberty and justice in a nation corrupted by men who, he believed, had abandoned their responsibility toward those principles. Juxtaposing Brown with the "men of talent" (119) who occupied positions of political power in America, Emerson exposed the "official gentlemen" (118) who had brought the nation to ruin by their devotion to compromise, appeasement, and convention. He asserted that they had consistently privileged political expedience at the expense of morality. As a result, they had imperiled the lives of the citizens throughout the nation by securing a government that demanded the enforcement of immoral laws, hence compromised the future of the nation by denying the validity of the primary philosophical premise upon which the nation was established—that government exists to secure the "unalienable rights" of its citizens.[22]

For Emerson, John Brown embraced an incorruptible morality gained not by political association or fawning admiration of existing legal precedent, but by a right reliance. He is, according to Emerson, a model self-reliant man who acted upon his uncorrupted convictions for the universal good, hence offered a model of moral engagement for all of America. Indeed, Emerson constructs Brown as a kind of restorative, who, by his commitment to universal laws and public demonstration of virtue, can inspire the errant mass of American representatives to right public engagement. Following his short but powerful speech, Emerson demonstrated his commitment to the behavior that Brown embraced with a $50 contribution of his own money.

In the months that followed, Emerson would demonstrate that commitment again on three occasions. During the memorial ceremony for the executed martyr in Concord on 2 December, Emerson joined Thoreau, Alcott, and Sanborn in the celebration of the man he now regarded as a "pure idealist;" he read "Brown's last words . . . in his most touching and impressive manner" and paid tribute to the representative individual who had not abdicated his responsibility as a self-reliant citizen.[23] Two days later, during the 28th Congregational Society's memorial services for John Brown at the Music Hall, Emerson chose to present his lecture "Morals," once again underscoring the value of "one, good, believing strong-minded [self-reliant] man" in a nation where "politics are full of adventurers," or self-serving, unprincipled, weak-willed men who embraced the collective will of the immoral majority and stood for nothing.[24] The last time that Emerson publicly celebrated John Brown was on 6 January when he agreed to join Wendell Phillips in a fund-raiser for Brown's family.[25] In his speech on that date, Emerson constructs Brown as a "romantic character absolutely without any vulgar trait" and distinguishes him from his socially empowered contemporaries who selfishly dishonor themselves by their vulgar habit of repeatedly committing to compromise in order to secure their own prosperity, position, or privilege.

In his successive reconstructions of John Brown as a man of character whose individual revolution against tyranny is the result of a distinctly American heritage, self-reliant character, and egalitarian convictions, Emerson consistently emphasizes the distinction between Brown and the men who embraced legal precedent, political stasis, and political convention in their effort to attain social and political prominence. He intimates that they have divorced themselves from their revolutionary heritage and chosen to ignore the model that the authors of the *Declaration of Independence* established when they devoted themselves to higher law in the justification of their right to revolution. This is particularly evident in his most powerful tribute to Brown—his 18 November "Speech at a Meeting to Aid John Brown's Family." In this address, Emerson exposes the trend to moral dissolution in America established in political compromise and judicial abdication over slavery. He condemns the cowardly behavior of his countrymen and suggests that slavery, the "only obstruction to the union" (118), exists because of wrong reliance. Its advocates ought to have "learned to detect and watch that inner gleam of light . . . [which, inevitably would reveal the incongruity of slavery in a nation based on notions of individual liberty; his silent countrymen had privileged] the luster of the firmament of bards and sages" (145), or the superficial truths of legal and religious precedent, and had been led astray.

In order to salvage the union, Emerson suggests, politicians and judges alike must recognize their own failures as individual men, determine their own opinions exclusive of party position, economic consequence, or social outcome, and loudly advocate their unadulterated singular convictions. Contrary to John Carlos Rowe's assertion that in the 1850s, "Emerson clearly changed his mind regarding his earlier commitment to self-reliant men resisting the fashions and even the laws of his day," it is clear that in his 18 November speech, Emerson affirms that only self-reliant men can guarantee liberty and prosperity in the United States.[26] John Brown, the singular "representative American" who acted upon the dictates of his own conscience and modeled right reliance for the nation is, for Emerson, an exemplar of right political engagement. Largely ignoring Brown's violent tactics in his 18 November speech, Emerson employs Brown to inspire "gentlemen politicians" to revolt against the inertia of group think, singularly reconsider their public obligation to perfect the nation, embrace self-reliance as the proper American means of forming right opinions, and then fearlessly act upon those convictions in the public forum.

The central issue upon which Emerson believed the representatives of the nation had failed was, of course, slavery. In his 1855 lecture entitled "American Slavery," Emerson caustically points to the "well-born, well-bred, well-grown men among ourselves, not outcasts, not foreigners, nor beggars, nor convicts, but baptized, vaccinated, schooled, high-placed official men" who had made slavery an American institution, and those of the same privilege who had sustained it through the 1850s.[27] In their successive decisions to extend slavery, these men had failed the nation. Perhaps, foremost among these "men of talent in the executive" (119), Massachusetts Senator Daniel Webster inspired Emerson's considerable ire in his failure to "take the part of great principles, the side of humanity and justice" (78) when he insured that Senator Mason's Fugitive Slave Bill became law in September, 1850.

Emerson's reaction to Webster's extension of slavery was both vitriolic and powerful. In his address "To the Citizens of Concord" in May, 1851, Emerson condemned the man whom he had once recognized as the "one eminent American of our time" (66). A man of considerable talent, understanding, and eloquence, Emerson suggested that Daniel Webster was uniquely qualified to guide a flawed nation from its unnatural tolerance of slavery to its *natural* position as the herald of liberty. However, "in opposition to his education, association, and to all his own most explicit language for thirty years, he crossed the line [, abdicated his natural position,] and became the head of the slavery party in this country" (66). Distinguishing Webster's "powerful animal nature" as the force behind his political actions, Emerson calls attention to the orator's unnatural disregard of morality in his decision to compromise the lives of four million enslaved human beings in order to maintain the union. Such an action, Emerson suggests, makes man an animal; dedication to natural or moral law, in contrast, establishes the divinity in man. The proper devotion in a statesmen, Emerson intimates is to universal morality. As he had indicated in "Self-Reliance," Americans "want men and women who will renovate life and our social state," who will perfect our social institutions by recognizing universal moral law, not those who will maintain that which currently exists.[28]

As a scholar, concerned citizen, and devoted unionist, Emerson believed that it was his charter to "cheer, to raise, and to guide men by showing them facts amidst appearances."[29] In the aftermath of the Thomas Sims affair, he realized that the time for vigorous engagement in the corrupt political establishment had arrived.[30] The result was his "Address to the Citizens of Concord," an exposé of the trend toward political corruption in the service of slavery. Unsatisfied that this gesture was sufficiently significance, in May, 1851, Emerson took a further step by entering the political arena and actively campaigning for Free Soil candidate John G. Palfrey in his effort to win a seat in Congress. In order to inspire support for his candidate, Emerson repeated his "Fugitive Slave Law" speech on four occasions in various locations throughout Massachusetts. When it was certain that Palfrey had failed to gain the support of Massachusetts' voters, Emerson did not disengage from politics, though he did retreat from direct political involvement to the role he had defined in "The American Scholar."[31]

Incensed by the inertia that the Kansas-Nebraska Bill attained during the winter of 1854, Emerson demonstrated his commitment to scholarly political engagement on March 7 when he delivered his second address on the Fugitive Slave Law. Once again, he directed a considerable amount of his fury at Webster in his eloquent condemnation of the orator's leading role in the encroachment of slave power in America; unsatisfied with the scope of his previous address, Emerson greatly expanded his critique to include all "public men" whose "want of stamina" and failure to maintain philosophical and political independence resulted in the Compromise of 1850 and the subsequent Compromise of 1854.[32] These men had "failed to take the side of great principles, the side of humanity and justice, [in favor of] the side of abuse and oppression and chaos" and sided with slavery.[33] They were complicit in the advance of slavery in the United States, and Emerson was determined to demonstrate the degree to which their "party feeling and moneyed interest" contributed to the corruption of the nation.[34] Additionally, he wanted to lay bare the judiciary's failure to commit to "original jurisdiction" or "first principles" in the perversion of justice that made all of the citizens in the United States complicit in the hypocrisy legal slavery engendered.[35] However, his immediate effort to make political men aware of their errant ways and guide them to universal morality failed.

To Emerson's disgust, the Kansas-Nebraska Bill became law on May 30, 1854. Emerson reacted forcefully. Determined to expose the moral failures of his contemporaries, he lambasted those entrusted with justice for their abdication of responsibility in his lecture "American Slavery," which he first presented in January, 1855. By far his most pointed condemnation of those responsible for slavery's existence in the United States, Emerson plainly expresses his discontent with America's "dreary superficiality, ignorance, and disbelief in principles" (97) in the lecture he gave five times during the winter months of 1855. Impressing listeners in Boston, New York, Philadelphia, Rochester, and Syracuse, Emerson explained "how far our politics had departed from the path of right" and "forfeited the awe and reverence which always attaches to wise and honest government" in its acquiescence to slavery.[36] Noting that "private men who have brave hearts and great minds" are always ready to resist false government, Emerson presciently anticipates the violent resistance that John Brown embraced in his protest by "word and deed" four years later.[37]

Although Emerson expresses an insightful appreciation for the crisis that faced the nation in its "acquiescence in slavery," he did not anticipate the extent of the moral corruption that the Compromise of 1854 signaled. Preston Brooks brutal caning of Charles Sumner on the Senate floor after the Massachusetts Senator had denounced the "slave oligarchy" in his "Crime

Against Kansas" speech in 1856 changed all that. Responding to the apparent approval of Brooks's action among the constituents of South Carolina,
Emerson remarked, "I think that we must get rid of slavery, or we must get
rid of freedom." (107) Four months later, appalled by the abuse of Massachusetts settlers in the Kansas territory and offended over the support
that the abusive Missourians gained from the federal government, Emerson
indignantly addressed the citizens of Boston at the Kansas Relief Meeting
in Cambridge. Asserting that the "*Representative Government* is really
misrepresentative; *Union* is a conspiracy against the Northern states which
the Northern States are to have the privilege of paying for," Emerson caustically criticized elected and appointed representatives in the North suggesting that they had lost their independence and now served simply as
the tools of Southern slave-owners.[38] Emerson called this a "snivelling [sic]
support of slavery," since he believed it was the result of both cowardice
and lack of character on the part of those appointed or elected to represent
the citizens of the nation.[39]

In each of his successively more urgent lectures concerned with the
encroachment of slavery in the United States, Emerson emphasized the
need for individual introspection, self-trust, and singular bravery in the
moral battle for the soul of the nation. All around him, however, he saw
superficial gestures toward natural law, privilege of form, and cowardice in the actions of those appointed or elected as representatives of the
nation. Charles Sumner, who "took his [own] position" on issues and
"never faltered in his maintenance of justice and freedom" was a notable
exception to the inertia of corruption that Emerson believed was pervasive in the structure which maintained slavery in the United States.[40] As
Gougeon notes, Emerson admired Sumner because "he was an unpoliti-
cal politician, a welcome exception to the standard rule, a person capable
of independent thinking."[41] For his courage and his self-reliant rejection
of the politics of compromise, however, Sumner had been the target of
barbarity. Sumner's dedication to higher law and reliance upon the universality of natural truths did not result in the perfection of the Union
through the machinery of government; instead, it resulted in his practical
exclusion from the realm of politics in the United States and a ground-
swell toward disunion.[42]

Despite this rather painful example of the practical failure of an unswerving dedication to self-reliance, Emerson retreats to the principle that he had
first articulated in his 1832 journals and then fully celebrated in his 1841
essay "Self-Reliance" in his most poignant, though most troubling speech,
when he celebrated the failure of another self-reliant man and the apparent
success of his corrupt contemporaries. In his speech at the meeting to "Aid
John Brown's Family," Emerson juxtaposes John Brown, whom he trans-
lates into an exemplum of self-reliance and proper American citizenship,
with the legions of public figures who accelerated the dissolution of the
Union by their refusal to acknowledge their own intuitive understanding of

universal law. These public figures, Emerson asserts, are absolutely responsible for what he termed the "raging fever of slavery" plaguing the United
States and threatening its dissolution.[43]

John Brown, Emerson contends, is their antithesis. For Emerson, he
is a model of virtue who can inspire an errant citizenry to re-examine its
social behavior and act to perfect society. He is an example of righteous
social engagement. Emerson is not, in truth, solely concerned with the
man John Brown. Instead, he is concerned with the example that John
Brown provides to a citizenry whose collective ethical timidity has resulted
in a corrupt and infirm nation. Emerson's introduction to his speech pro-
portedly for the relief of the family of John Brown provides the first indication that he is far more interested in the forthright social engagement
that John Brown models, than with the man John Brown. Perhaps revealing his understanding that Brown could now serve most effectively as a
catalyst for individual and social change, Emerson acknowledges that he
is "very glad to see this sudden interest in the hero of Harper's Ferry, has
provoked extreme curiosity in all parts of the Republic, in regard to the
details of his history" (117). The rather obtuse syntactical construction of
this sentence, which privileges the first of two prepositional phrases "in
all parts of the Republic" instead of the latter "in regard to the details
of his history" suggests that Brown most importantly inspired interest in
the various component parts of the government of the United States. He
functioned as a sort of reflective lens for his fellow citizens clarifying the
current conditions of federal, state, and local government; in particular,
Brown "provoked" an examination of the elected and appointed representatives of the government and its spokesmen and exposed many of them as
dishonest, cowardly, and immoral.

Just as he does in his 6 January "John Brown" speech, Emerson distinguishes these men, whom he terms "political gentlemen," from the principled men and women who naturally feel the obligation to "protect the weak
and lowly against the strong oppressor."[44] The former have no "traits of
relation" to the man Emerson terms the true "representative of the American Republic" (117). Unlike John Brown, who is respectful of "men of
strong character," esteems "courage and integrity," displays "simple, artless goodness, joined with . . . sublime courage" and "is an idealist, with
"no by-ends of his own (118), these men are cowardly, unwilling to face
censure, selfishly motivated, and skillfully manipulative of public trust. In
his review of the all parts of the Republic, Emerson calls attention to the
history of false representatives of the American Republic, the "men of talent in the executive, on the bench" (119) who, in their abdication of self-
reliance, have not ensured that "life and freedom" is guaranteed to every
man and woman in the United States.

In the decade which preceded John Brown's attack on Harper's Ferry,
Emerson had been particularly attentive to the personal failures of public ser-
vants who had compromised their own principles or failed to privilege any

higher law than the law of man in the conduct of their duties. Emerson calls attention to the history of moral failure in America drawing heavily upon his previous ten years' lectures to inform his listeners of their representatives' pattern of moral failure in the face of the most significant moral issue of the day—slavery. Webster is perhaps the most notable of all of Emerson's "political gentlemen." As Emerson notes in "The Fugitive Slave Law (1854)," which is as much a condemnation of the moral cowardice of Webster as it is an clarification of the heinousness of the immoral law, at the end of an illustrious career during which he had distinguished himself as a champion of liberty, Webster revealed himself to be a coward and a failure who "did not take the part of great principles, the side of humanity and justice, [instead choosing] . . . the side of abuse and oppression and chaos (78)." Denying "the sanctions of morality" and the notion that it was man's duty to privilege a higher law than the existing manmade constructions, Webster had, according to Emerson, "by his personal influence, brought the Fugitive Slave Law on the country" (74). He reviled Webster for it, and offered the "brave man standing single, or with a few, for the right" (87) as an antidote to the political cowardice he saw evident in the culture of compromise that Webster heralded. Celebrating the spirit of liberty, which he insists "is the Crusade of all brave and conscientious men, the Epic Poetry, the new religion, the chivalry of all gentlemen" (88), Emerson challenges his listeners to deny political expedience and embrace liberty—the natural desire of "every noble and generous spirit."

Emerson, likewise, exposes the moral compromise of those entrusted with judicial authority in America in his 18 November lecture. Noting that "judges rely on forms, and unlike like John Brown, use their eyes to see the fact behind the forms" (119), Emerson directs his listeners to consider the role that they privilege a judge with in society. He had expressed his own ideas on judicial conduct four years before. A judge, he explained in "American Slavery"

> who gives voice, as a judge should to the rules of love and justice, is godlike: his word is current in all countries. But a man sitting on the Bench servile to precedent, or a windy politician, or a dangler trying to give authority to the notions of his superiors or of his set, pipes, and squeaks, and cheeps ridiculously. Judges are rare and must be born such.[45]

Emerson believed that the role of the judge was to dedicate himself to justice, not to precedent, in order to ensure natural, hence moral and enduring law. A judge's

> first duty was to read the law in accordance with equity. And if it jarred with equity, to disown law. All the great lawgivers and jurists of the world have agreed in this, that an immoral law is void. So held Cicero, Selden, and Hooker: and Coke, Hobart, Holt, and Mansfield, chief justices of England. Even Canon Law says, 'Neither allegiance nor oath can bind to obey that which is unlawful.'[46]

However, Emerson recognized that "in America justice was poisoned at its fountain [explaining that in] our northern states, no judge appeared of sufficient character and intellect to ask whether or not . . . [the Fugitive Slave Law] was constitutional, but whether it was right."[47]

Emerson's frustration with those entrusted with justice in America was well-founded. He had been a witness to Massachusetts' Chief Justice Lemuel Shaw's unwillingness to challenge the Fugitive Slave Law in both the Shadrach and Sims cases. Denying both men a writ of *habeas corpus*, Shaw anticipated Chief Justice Roger B. Taney's 1857 Supreme Court ruling that negroes were "so inferior that they had no rights which the white man was bound to respect" when he decided that the case of a fugitive slave was too insignificant to justify a writ.[48] Emerson was indignant when he learned of Shaw's decision commenting in his journal that a great moment had been lost "when Shaw denied the unconstitutionality of the Fugitive Slave Law."[49] Confident that the "overwhelming forces of conscience and culture would make the law a "dead letter,'" Emerson was appalled when members of his own community, "citizens of Massachusetts [were] willing to act as judges and captors" in the enforcement of what he caustically labeled the "most detestable law that was ever enacted by a civilized state."[50]

Emerson believed that Fugitive Slave Commissioner Edward C. Loring's decision against fugitive slave Anthony Burns in 1854 was a consistent abdication of moral responsibility. Loring had embraced a "substantial injustice" (119) and failed as a judge to "secure a good government"— the sole function, Emerson asserted, of those appointed to the judiciary. In his journal, Emerson noted that this was a time "when judges do not judge, when governors do not govern; when Presidents do not preside, but sell themselves to somebody who bargains to make them Presidents again."[51] Both elected and appointed officials had given up their moral independence, effectively negating their authority by compromising their intuitive understanding of right and making legal decisions based on precedent, or judicial form, in order to avoid the scrutiny of their contemporaries. Emerson intimates that they acted as cowards, not as self-reliant individual men who virtuously sought truth and unflinchingly proclaimed it.[52] The tendency toward conformity—or confirming current judicial decisions with existing laws—Emerson suggests is both unmanly and immoral.[53]

Chief Justice Taney's 1857 decision in the Dred Scott case was further confirmation that those entrusted with the highest positions within the American judiciary had abdicated their responsibility to act as independent thinking men dedicated to permanent higher laws.[54] Deciding that "no person of slave decent or blood could be considered a citizen of the US, therefore could not be entitled to sue in its courts" based on the flawed constitutional precedent which counted a male slave as three quarters of a man, Chief Justice Taney compromised his judicial heritage to the men who "believed in the ideal right, [and] strove to make it practical" and did not demonstrate the "sufficient character and intellect to ask [not] whether or not it was constitutional, but whether it was right."[55]

In the trial and sentencing of John Brown, Emerson saw a consistent perversion of justice when Governor Wise failed to consider the obligation that every just man must have to position himself in opposition to a government that embraced immoral laws. Pointing out the curious inconsistency that Governor Wise demonstrated in his determination to execute Brown while admitting that he was the "man of the most integrity, truthfulness, and courage he ever met" (119), Emerson calls to question both the wisdom, morality, and the judgment of the figure who insisted upon using the opportunity Brown created for political capital. His deliberate elision of the governor's surname in two references to the politician who took advantage of the fortuitous opportunity that Brown provided him to both gain national attention and assert his political authority is telling. Not only does Emerson suggest that Governor Wise acted in a manner that would disqualify the use of the adjective *wise*, he intimates that the man ought not be dignified by employing the adjective, since it suggests qualities he did not exhibit in his support for slavery. Certainly, Emerson suggests, the governor of Virginia showed very little *wisdom* when he refused to privilege his own recognition of the superior moral qualities that Brown possessed and determined to hang the man for treason against the state of Virginia. As he suggested in the letter which he drafted to the governor following Brown's sentencing (and then employed in his November 18th speech), Brown "will drag gentlemen into an immortality not desireable [sic]."[56] Emerson's prophetic assertion proved correct. In the aftermath of John Brown's execution, the attention Governor Wise gained while insisting upon his authority to both try and execute Brown did not earn him the national acclaim that he desired nor did it earn him the democratic nomination for president that he coveted;[57] quite to the contrary, it assured the end of his political career.

Emerson's decision to refer to Wise only by his official title also suggests the tendency of "official gentlemen" (118) to divorce themselves from their own opinions, or their right reliance upon themselves, and privilege instead some position maintained by a political party. Emerson emphasizes Wise's moral abdication by employing the passive voice in his description of the governor's decision to condemn Brown to death at the gallows. Emerson notes, "the governor of Virginia *is forced* to hang a man whom he declares to be a man of the most integrity, truthfulness, and courage he has ever met" [my emphasis] (119). Not only is there an absence of any identifiable subject, hence responsible agent in Emerson's sentence, there is a clear assertion that the object of the sentence, the governor of Virginia, has denied the validity of his own moral agency in his capitulation. His recognition of Brown's character is of no consequence; in a larger sense, Emerson also suggests that the "Governor of Virginia" is of no consequence. He is a hollow man, a political title, and a servant of an amorphous party. He is not an admirable representative of the nation.

John Brown, on the other hand, is "a representative of the American Republic" (117). Throughout his speech, Emerson ascribes to Brown the qualities appropriate for the individual citizen of America and identifies the conduct proper in a public servant in a republican form of government. Emerson was fairly comfortable making such broad assertions about the national character of a people. Only three years before, he had published a collection of essays on the English character that not only identified the qualities he believed essential to the English, but those that distinguished them from their American contemporaries.[58] Emerson similarly identifies the qualities he believes are essential to the American citizen in his 18 November speech on John Brown. However, he does limit his commentary to identify the qualities essential to an American citizen engaged in social and political discourse.

John Brown is Emerson's exemplum. Like his English contemporaries, John Brown is courageous, forthright, and honest.[59] However, unlike his more hierarchically established and historically entrenched fellow man, Emerson suggests that Brown felt no compunction to moderate his activities in order to pursue wealth, position, power, or influence. An idealist, he dedicated himself to the realization of a more perfect society—one that would not make one man a slave and another a master. For Emerson, Brown is the perfect statesman, though he did not occupy a conventionally recognized political position; committed, moral, and selfless, John Brown believed that by his own effort, he could translate his ideal into reality.

In John Brown, whom he had met on only two occasions, Emerson believed that he had found a man who might "give permanent direction to the fortunes of the state."[60] Committed to demonstrating Brown's value to his errant society, Emerson makes Brown a beacon of virtuous light, a model of positive social engagement, and an exemplum of right reliance in a culture corrupted by moral compromise, group think, and personal abdication. Brown is not, according to Emerson, a blinding figure. He is, instead, a common man whose "simple, artless goodness, with his sublime courage" (118) make him remarkable in a political culture marked by individual pretension, duplicity, and cowardice. Emerson notes that "[f]or himself, he is so transparent that all men see him through" (118).

At first glance, this somewhat awkward clause appears only to indicate that Emerson wanted to present Brown as a forthright man who simply acted upon his moral conviction that slavery was wrong. He clearly saw that slavery was both a desecration of Christian virtues, and it existed in direct violation to the basic premises of the United States; therefore, he committed himself to its end. Emerson's awkward sentence construction, however, provokes the attentive reader to dwell upon the idea of transparency and the act of seeing. Not only does Emerson intimate that John Brown has clarified the vision of "all men" of the inevitable confrontation that will result from the maintenance of immoral institutions like slavery, he suggests that "all men [will inevitably] see . . . [John Brown's desire to end slavery] through." Further, he suggests that it is inevitable that all men will see through John Brown the promise of their nation fulfilled. A salve applied to the eyes of the nation's leaders, Emerson hoped that John Brown would clarify the vision of his errant political contemporaries and inspire them to embrace universal liberty for black as well as white men.

Emerson's use of the word *transparent* to describe the man he had just proclaimed a "representative of the American Republic" also has a unique resonance for listeners familiar with his 1850 publication *Representative Men*. Not only does Emerson elevate John Brown to a position consistent with Plato, Swedenborg, Montaigne, Shakespeare, Napoleon, and Goethe by his classification of Brown as a representative American, he intimates that Brown, like his exemplary European forebears, is a both a great and a liberating figure in the history of Western thought. Great men, Emerson had explained are "a collyrium to clear our eyes from egotism, and enable us to see other people and their works."[61] They make clearly visible, or transparent, the corruption of men and the social institutions that those men have created. Indeed, Brown had done more than simply focus the public lens on a heinous institution; with Emerson's assistance, he had exponentially increased the public's scrutiny of their elected representatives and magnified the results of their decisions to maintain slavery as an American institution. Emerson's indirect assertion that Brown is a great American man is not, therefore, altogether surprising given his belief that great men "aid the individual in ascending out of his limits into a catholic existence."[62] He had personally witnessed the surge of interest in the incarcerated freedom fighter, read newspaper reports of Brown's forthright responses to members of the Circuit Court of Jefferson County, seen the magnification of public agitation upon the institution of slavery, and experienced the public swell of interest in abolition. In the days that followed John Brown's capture, Emerson also witnessed a revolution in sentiment in America; John Brown, Emerson's American representative man, was its impetus.

Emerson was neither careless nor casual in his classification of John Brown as a "representative of the American Republic" (117). He fully intended to suggest that Brown brought his contemporaries into a new realization of their individual role in the eventual abolition of slavery. His subtle reference to *Representative Men* suggests as much. In the first chapter of that work, Emerson clearly identifies the need for a representative or great man in the liberation of American culture from the scourge of slavery.

> I go to a convention of philanthropists. Do what I can, I cannot keep my eyes off the clock. But if there should appear in the company some gentle soul who knows little of persons or parties, of Carolina or Cuba, but who announces a law that disposes these particulars, and so certifies me of the equity which checkmates every false play, bankrupts every selfseeker, and apprises me of my independence on any conditions of country, time, or human body, that man liberates me;

I forget the clock, I pass out of sore relation to persons: I am healed of my hurts; I am made immortal by apprehending my possession of incorruptible goods.[63]

Although it recalls Emerson's denunciation of New England reformers in his 1844 essay by the same name—particularly in the intimation that conventions of philanthropists rarely result in any improvement of either the individual or of culture—this passage suggests that a representative individual or "gentle soul" has the capacity to create a new consciousness of liberty by first recognizing then enacting a natural law that "disposed of the particulars" of slavery in the Southern states, represented by Carolina, and in the territory then considered the next acquisition of the Untied States, Cuba.[64] In the resultant state where equity or natural law reigns, the individual is liberated from his tacit complicity in a corrupt institution, hence is truly liberated to the possibility of a higher state of being. Individual consciousness of the moral or natural laws, Emerson suggests, is tantamount to apotheosis.

In the successive abdications of both politicians and judges during the tumultuous decade preceding John Brown's raid on Harpers Ferry, Emerson's faith that some "gentle soul" might literally "announce a law" that made slavery illegal in the United States and release the nation founded upon liberty from its corruption of that concept must have undergone some real trials. Certainly, the failures of figures like Webster, Shaw, Loring, Pierce, and Taney challenged Emerson's trust in man. Eventually, however, Emerson's faith was restored. Not only did John Brown, a very different kind of "gentle soul," emerge from the frontier to demand liberty for all, he confronted the entire political establishment with their complicity in slavery.

Responding to Senator Mason's demand that he justify his acts at Harper's Ferry, Brown bluntly said:

I think, my friend, you are guilty of a great wrong against God and humanity—I say it without wishing to be offensive—and it would be perfectly right in any one to interfere with you so far as to free those you willfully and wickedly hold in bondage. [65]

Brown's humble, yet determined announcement clearly did not make slavery illegal in the United States. That would take another four years and another figure of vision and eloquence. [66] In John Brown, however, Emerson saw a prophet, a representative man who accelerated the process whereby the consciousness of the nation was renewed in liberty: John Brown, Emerson acknowledged, confronted the nation with an awareness of the violation her American roots.

In order to establish John Brown's representative American stature, Emerson emphasizes that Brown is a farmer descended from five generations of American farmers. Emerson's classification of Brown is far more than a

simple tribute to the Jeffersonian notion that Americans are properly independent yeoman farmers.[67] It is an affirmation of Brown's intimate relationship
with Nature and his intellectual, physical, and psychological independence
from the corrupt tendencies of industrial American society. Brown is a
proper "representative of the American Republic" because he embraces his
own intuitive understanding of right and wrong gained through "an original
relation to the universe." [68] As a farmer, Emerson suggests, Brown has had
unmediated access to the universal moral truths revealed in nature. As he had
indicated in his 1836 essay "Nature," "moral law lies at the centre of nature
and radiates to the circumference . . . nor can it be doubted that this moral
sentiment which thus scents the air, and grows in the grain, and impregnates
the waters of the world, is caught by man and sinks into his soul."[69] Through
close and habitual association with his natural surroundings, Emerson intimates, Brown gained an intuitive understanding of universal moral laws. His
opposition to slavery and his commitment to its end sprung from his atten-
tiveness to Nature, which Emerson suggests, "is the great organ through
which the universal spirit speaks to the individual."[70] Indeed, in his 1858
lecture "Farming," Emerson acknowledged that the farmer "stand[s] nearest
to God," hence has great access to universal truth.[71] For Emerson, Brown
was a natural prophet leading the blind to truth. The farm—what Emerson
termed a "mute gospel"—had given Brown divine understanding of the laws
of mankind and his role on the earth; it had also given him the judgment to
know how and when to reform societies of men.[72]

In addition to calling attention to John Brown's appropriate devotion to
divine—or natural—laws (which provided the authors of the *Declaration
of Independence* the philosophical basis for asserting their right to revolution), identifying John Brown as a farmer also suggests that the unnatural conditions present at the dawn of the nation once again are present in
his own society. In "The American Scholar," Emerson famously asserted,
"[m]an is not a farmer, or a professor, or an engineer, but he is all. Man
is priest, and scholar, and statesman, and producer, and soldier."[73] Reacting against the degeneration of man to his vocation, Emerson challenged
those who would singularize a man's contribution to society, hence make
a man a thing. In so doing, he also reveals the perversity of a social state
which would make a man a commodity, or a slave, or a piece of property,
or a fugitive. Such a state, Emerson intimates, is perverse: it defies nature
and limits man. Stating that John Brown is a farmer, therefore, inspires
the attentive listener to consider what else John Brown may be. Certainly,
Emerson suggests, John Brown is a liberator, a model citizen, a moral guide
for an errant nation, and an exemplar of political engagement. He may have
failed in his immediate goal to liberate slaves in Virginia, but he succeeded
as a liberator of men's consciences in America.

Emerson's recognition of Brown's heritage is another rhetorical move to
expand Brown's significance to America. Once again, however, it is a rhetorical move that seems, at first glance, inconsistent with Emerson's focus

upon the self-reliant individual. In his journal, Emerson noted that "the reverence for deeds of our ancestors is a treacherous sentiment," and in "Self-Reliance," Emerson diminished the notion that a man's heritage was critical to his own character. He had written:

> If therefore a man claims to know and speak of God and carries you backward to the phraseology of some old mouldering nation in another country, in another world, believe him not. Is the acorn better than the oak which is its fullness and completion?" Is the parent better than the child into whom he has cast his ripening being? Whence then this worship of the past? The centuries are conspirators against the sanity and authority of the soul. . . . history is an impertinence and an injury if it be any thing more than a cheerful apologue or parable or my being and becoming.[74]

Yet, in his November 18th construction of John Brown, Emerson notes that Brown was the "fifth descendant from Peter Brown, who came to Plymouth in the Mayflower, in 1620."[75] His grandfather "was a captain in the Revolution" (117) and his father "became a contractor to supply the army with beef, in the war of 1812" (117). Historically connected with the tradition of independence responsible for the formation and maintenance of the United States, Emerson suggests Brown is an heir to the spirit of liberty which inspired men to reject the dictates of state religion and embrace their own beliefs, even when in great peril. This same tradition inspired them to reject the government of an oppressive monarchy and pledge their futures to liberty. However, Emerson suggests that Brown's willingness to fight for individual liberty is not a tribute to his ancestors nor to their devotion to liberty; it is a function of his own right thinking. Emerson notes, Brown "cherished a great respect for his father as a man of strong character" (117). Emphasizing Brown's devotion, rather than his father's actions, Emerson focuses the reader upon Brown as the present champion of personal liberty, not as a reverent son focused upon the past. He suggests that Brown valued his father for the morality that he modeled, not for his actions, implying, somewhat uncritically, that the contractor of beef was a singular man of selfless virtue who independently committed to serve the army in its time of need out of recognition that his services were critical to the maintenance of the union. Devoted to the same virtues, Emerson implies that Brown's efforts on the part of the "despised poor" (118) deserve the same respect. Honest, courageous, and committed to "moral order," John Brown is for Emerson a model American.[76] His convictions are noble and his devotions appropriate to a nation founded upon natural or moral law.

Given Emerson's assertion that Brown is a man of character—a defender of moral imperatives—it does not seem inconsistent that he would include the statement: "Better that a whole generation of men, women, and children should pass away by violent death, than that one word of either [the

Golden Rule or the Declaration of Independence] should be violated in this country" (118) in his overt comparison of the anti-slavery champion with the political figures who had violated their obligation to privilege moral law before their own interests. It is, however, a bit jarring since it suggests that Emerson privileged moral law to the extent that he believed that its suppression justified total war—the only circumstance conceivable in which an entire generation might "pass away by violent death" (118). Considered from a larger perspective, however, Emerson's inclusion of Brown's statement presciently suggests that he believed that total war, hence massive violence on a scale that might result in the deaths of a generation of men, women, and children in the United States, was inevitable if representative men did not confront their own failure to privilege higher law and reform.

From another perspective, Emerson may have included this passage in order to confront the political representatives who had abdicated their role as self-reliant men with the natural result of their irresponsibility. Consider, Emerson, seems to suggest, what will be the outcome of all of your compromises and party politics: either the United States, founded by men who believed in the unalienable rights of all men, individual equality before the law, and a government which derived its power from the people, would privilege its founding principles or it would sink into the chaos of total war. By his inclusion of Brown's assertion, Emerson confronts the errant politicians of his day with their own political heritage and tacitly demands that they re-examine their commitment to the principles articulated in the *Declaration*.

Emerson's inclusion of this quote is also important because it is, to some degree, retrospective. Certainly, generations of men, women, and children had already died violent deaths as slaves in America in direct violation of both the golden rule and the *Declaration of Independence*. Denied humanity, unalienable Rights, and the right to participate in the government that kept them in bondage, African-American men, women, and children had, by natural law, the right to dissolve their bonds of allegiance to their captors and violently assert the natural right to achieve liberty. Emerson suggests that John Brown, idealistic champion of natural law and friend of the slave, asserted the right of all citizens bound by their common understanding of natural laws to violently confront those who would deny the law's practical application. He also asserts the right of slaves to violently throw off the yoke of oppression and declare their own independence. As subjects of an oppressive government, slaves had the same right to the violence authorized by the *Declaration of Independence* that the colonists had in their refusal to succumb to British colonial rule.

Within this context, Emerson's inclusion of Brown's assertion is a direct warning and an explicit call to conscience to the errant "men of talent" (119) serving in government: Recognize, he suggests, the universal truth of the moral laws your visionary forefathers imbedded within the *Declaration*; acknowledge the common humanity of men; deny the inertia of party politics that compels you toward compromise; and declare yourself a man who acts from his own unmediated understanding of moral law. Like John Brown, Emerson challenges those engaged in positions of political power to "believe in . . . [your] ideas to that extent, that . . . [you exist] to put them all into action" (119).

Emerson's interest, however, is not limited to those who represent the public in the federal government; he is also concerned with "everyman who loves the Golden Rule and the Declaration of Independence" or every person in the Republic who is able to recognize the threat that party politics and political abdication on the subject of slavery poses to his or her own moral condition. With these men and women, Emerson intimates, the fate of the United States lies. As always for Emerson, political reform must be local; it must begin with the individual, since the individual is true source from whom the government derives its power. The individual must demand right laws consistent with moral truths. These are the "necessary foundations" of the American government.[77] Local governments, in turn, must consistently defend those foundational moral laws from the perversions of pecuniary interest and power. Freedom and independence begins, Emerson asserts, with the self-reliant individual. Neither the state nor the party establishes the necessary conditions for liberty; the individual does.

Nearly eighteen years before John Brown captured the attention of the nation from his jail cell in Charlestown, Emerson had asserted, "[i]f the single man plant himself indomitably on his instincts, and there abide, the huge world will come round to him."[78] Despite the fact that he failed to inspire any slaves to enthusiastically join him in his attempt to initiate a revolution against their slaveholders—that he was an utter failure as a military leader who compromised both the lives of his men and the liberty of his most ardent supporters in his poor operational execution, and that he earned national attention in his capture, trial, and subsequent sentence to death—John Brown inspired the nation to "come round him" by his absolute dedication to the moral righteousness of his effort to end slavery. Not only did he call attention to the corruption inherent in the system of slavery in the United States, he called attention to the cowardice, complicity, and abdication of public figures in their duty to privilege permanent universal laws. For Emerson, John Brown was a model citizen because he steadfastly devoted himself to the higher laws and selflessly acted upon the truths inherent in them. Courageous, forthright, and unswerving in his devotion to liberty, Emerson celebrates Brown as a "representative of the American Republic" (117). In this construction, Emerson establishes Brown as model citizen of the United States, a man dedicated to the concepts of liberty and justice articulated in the founding document of the nation, the *Declaration of Independence*.

By November 18, 1859, Emerson is not, as I have attempted to demonstrate, primarily concerned with John Brown nor is he really concerned with raising money to aid Brown's immediate family, though he does make a contribution toward that end at the close of the meeting at the Tremont Temple. Instead, he is concerned with the state of the nation. In the decade preceding John Brown's emergence as a figure of national significance, Emerson had witnessed a series of judicial abdications and political capitulations that signified the triumph of greed, self-interest, and cowardice in America. In John Brown, Emerson believed that he had found an antidote to the inertia of corruption plaguing the nation. Contrasting Brown, the simple, self-reliant champion of the oppressed with the "men of talent" (119) who fail, in their privileged positions of power, to employ themselves to "secure good government" (119) or to "protect the life and freedom of every inhabitant not a criminal" (120), Emerson offers his listeners a simple alternative: just or corrupt government. The former, he clearly indicates, is available if representative men commit to and act upon the universal moral truths intuitively available to them; the latter, Emerson intimates, is the inevitable result of blind dedication to party politics and the current forms of law.

In his speech to "Aid John Brown's Family," Emerson poignantly identifies the cowardly complicity of Northern men in the extension of slavery and the maintenance of an immoral state. He suggests that the primary reason for the corrupt state of the union is the refusal of individual men to forthrightly stand against motions that are inconsistent with their well-considered beliefs. Failing to represent their own opinions, these men failed those they represented. John Brown, quite to the contrary, embraced the principle of liberty and equality, eloquently expressed it in the defense of his attack on Harpers Ferry, and, aptly represented the principles upon which the American Republic was founded.

Convinced that the "office of scholar is to cheer, to raise, and to guide men by showing them facts amidst appearances," Emerson attempts to guide his errant political contemporaries toward both a right reliance upon themselves and a renewed devotion to independence in their expression of opinions that will determine the course of the nation.[79] Right self-reliance, Emerson intimates, will inevitably result in the perfection of the union; moral cowardice and conformity, on the other hand, will just as inevitably lead to its destruction.

6 In the Shadow of John Brown
Refusing Violence in Harriet Beecher Stowe's *Dred*

"I do not think the subject could be clearer. If it were right in our war for liberty, we are wrong in making slaves, or keeping them."

"Oh I do not mean," said Mrs. Scudder, "that it was difficult to understand the subject; the *right* of the matter is clear, but what to *do* is the thing."[1]

In *The Minister's Wooing*, Harriet Beecher Stowe's rather sticky sentimental romance, slavery looms like a pestilent shadow over the quaint Newport cabin where Stowe's heroine, the saintly Mary Scudder, innocently entertains the attentions of an ascetic Puritan scholar, intrigues of an unprincipled U. S. Senator, devotions of a New England farm-boy, and curiosity of an errant but delightful French lady. A milk-white New England girl just awakening to the realities of her troubled post-revolutionary town, Mary bears silent witness to the initial articulations of moral indignation over the practice of enslaving Africans in America. Privy to the attentions of her mother's scholarly boarder, Dr. Hopkins, Mary observes the Puritan minister as he publicly declares his moral opposition to slavery. Confessing his new-found conviction, Dr. Hopkins reveals both his shame and his sense of complicity in the corrupt institution's presence in New England. Admitting the inconsistency of slavery in a nation dedicated to individual liberty, Dr. Hopkins tells Mary's practical mother—who understands that the Doctor is a "superior being, possessed by a holy helplessness in all things material and temporal"—that, despite the fact that the town is largely sustained by the slave trade, he must preach against the institution without delay.[2]

Recognizing the tenor of the community far better than her reclusive scholar, Mrs. Scudder reflects upon the immediate effect that his proclamation will have upon the population. She understands that not only will members of the small shipping community chastise the vocal clergyman for his opinions, many of them will refuse to continue to patronize Dr. Hopkins, attend his services, or consider his views on temporal conduct. Hence, instead of affecting a moral revolution in the community, the proto-abolitionist will effectively isolate himself from the community he hopes to influence and change nothing: only those with no significant financial investment in slavery will consider his message; those whose livelihoods depend upon slavery will do all in their power to ensure his silence. As if reflecting upon the conundrum faced by abolitionists in the decades preceding publication of her 1858 romance, Stowe confronts her reader with the central question abolitionists faced in America: "what . . . [ought abolitionists properly] *do*" about slavery in America.[3]

In her successive explorations of this conundrum, Stowe gives serious consideration to the entire spectrum of responses. In *Uncle Tom's Cabin* (1852), she famously calls for a sentimental revolution among the men and women of the North. Insisting upon each individual's ability to influence the social fabric of his or her community, Stowe petitions each Northern man and woman "who *feels* strongly, healthily, and justly, on the great interests of humanity" to re-assess his or her position on the subject of slavery.[4] The result, Stowe hopefully suggests, is inevitable: white Christian men and women throughout the North will recognize the error of their silent complicity with the slave-holders of the South and rise up to universally condemn the institution of slavery; abolition throughout the entire union, Stowe hopes, cannot long follow. In the interim, Stowe asks her countrymen to recognize their collective responsibility "for the wrongs that the American nation has brought" to the African and open their churches, their schools, and their purses in a responsible effort to prepare their fellow man for freedom.[5] Acknowledging the disadvantaged moral and intellectual position to which American slavery and racism have condemned many African-Americans, Stowe emphasizes the necessity for "the educating advantages of Christian republican society and schools" in the preparation of free blacks for liberty.[6] Education is particularly critical, Stowe asserts, in order to prepare former slaves for success in their new lives in a "redemptive black Christian republic in Africa," the site where Stowe believes former slaves will be able to carve a new, more enlightened democratic nation.[7] George Harris, the intelligent mulatto fugitive who escapes slavery with his family, gains a university education in France, and chooses to emigrate to Liberia is Stowe's fictive representative of the redemptive potential that this approach offers white America in re-establishing the liberated slave as a man in his own country.

In *Dred: A Tale of the Great Dismal Swamp* (1856), Stowe continues to advocate progressive educational programs in the preparation of African-Americans for liberty. She even has her gradualist heroine, Anne Clayton, construct a school on her plantation property in order to prepare her slaves for eventual emancipation. Anne soon learns, however, that her intention to teach her slaves to read and write does not bode well with her more conservative slave-owning neighbors. Having no interest in creating the conditions by which they might forfeit their entire fortunes, Anne Clayton's neighbors forcefully object to any effort to "start the minds" (530) of the local slave property and express their distinct disapproval of Anne's project; they will not, they inform her, tolerate a school for slaves in their vicinity (528). Educated slaves, they intimate, do not make good slaves; they make rebellion. Cognizant of the history of slave insurrections in the South, these men will not compromise their fortunes by allowing the idealistic whims of their neighbor to make vulnerable their own considerable fortunes. An ignorant, brutish, complacent slave population is for them a good thing; it ensures dominion; intelligent, inquisitive, energetic slaves challenge that dominion.

Stowe, of course, is very interested in challenging the dominion of the slave power. In order to "start the minds" (530) of her readers in *Dred*, she initially focuses upon the notion that there are slaves on every plantation that display both the social awareness and natural intellectual acuity to challenge the rule of the brutish master.[8] Reflecting on the failure of *Uncle Tom's Cabin* to inspire a sympathetic revolution and hasten the end of slavery, in *Dred*, Stowe crafts an informed narrative that acknowledges the intelligence of African-American slaves and pays tribute to their history of insurrection. Informed by her careful study of the injustices suffered by slaves, indignant over the continual encroachment of slave power, and discouraged by the apparent failures of principled men and women to successfully oppose its advances—evident during the summer of 1856 in the violent abuse of Free Soil settlers in Kansas and the brazen attack upon Charles Sumner on the Senate floor—Stowe explores the efficacy of violence and the threat of an armed slave rebellion as a social corrective in *Dred*. Capitalizing on frequent newspaper reports depicting the anarchic conditions present in Kansas, and conscious of "reports alleging the existence of plans for slave revolts" throughout the South in 1856, Stowe attempts to make the threat of violent slave revolt more immediate for her Northern readers by situating her novel within, rather than on the margins of, the established United States.[9]

However, in spite of the inertia toward violent confrontation that she explores in the narrative, and the threat of brutal degeneration that she suggests is inevitable in a social order based upon subjugation, Stowe clearly rejects the notion that violent confrontation is the right means of resolving the dilemma posed by slavery in America. Indeed, throughout a text where the rhetoric of violence seems both dominant and pervasive, Stowe rarely allows her characters to engage in any violent activity. The instances of offensive violence that occur in the narrative are perpetrated by ignorant white men who have either rejected or are ignorant of their moral nature.[10] No African-American character resorts to offensive violence. In fact, in her fictional presentation of Southern slaves, Stowe suggests that most African-Americans in the Southern states live in an uninterrupted state of moral indignation over the system of brutal offensive violence employed to maintain their plantation society; excepting her protagonist Dred, none truly embrace it. Offended by the violent abuse of power practiced by the Southern aristocracy, Stowe's African-American chracters are instead conscious of and exasperated by the injustice of their situation.

While it is certainly true that they occasionally embrace violence to defend themselves, and, in one instance, defend the life of Edward Clayton—Stowe's idealistic Southern social reformer committed to gradual emancipation—they never engage in offensive violence in the text. What Stowe's primary African-American characters do is refuse the romantic racialist categorization that suggests that they are incapable of violence because they are by nature complacent, child-like, and resigned to the position of social inferiority and servitude. On the contrary, Stowe asserts, many slaves are acutely aware of, and intensely dissatisfied with, their subject position. Further, she claims that they recognize their right to embrace violence and rebel against the injustice inherent in their subjugation. Employing the revolutionary rhetoric adopted successively by the Thomas Jefferson, Nat Turner, and William Lloyd Garrison, Stowe provides her most notable characters with the revolutionary discourse to express that right to rebellion. The right to violence, Stowe suggests, is implicit within the right to revolution; however, as she demonstrates throughout the course of her narrative, she is hopeful that it is not essential to it. Refusing to embrace the kind of ruthless and brutal violence that she had read about in contemporary newspaper accounts of the chaotic struggle in Kansas and studied in Nat Turner's *Confessions*, Stowe denies her reader the explosive denouement that she anticipates throughout the second part of her narrative. Instead of allowing the terrible retributive violence that her prophetic protagonist and titular hero anticipates, Stowe dismisses him from the narrative in a foggy scene that accentuates the degenerate atmosphere essential to the maintenance of Southern slave culture and emphasizes the inevitable failure that devotion to violence brings. She concludes the narrative with a series of blissful sketches of inter-racial harmony made possible by departure from the site of oppressive violence. Interestingly, at the narrative's conclusion, none of her African-American characters have any apparent recollection of the violent insurrection that they flirted with prior to their uneventful underground rail road trip to freedom. Apparently satisfied with the escape to their new lives, Stowe's fugitive slaves seem to embrace only the present. They have no memory of their revolutionary inclinations, nor do they exhibit any feelings of collective responsibility for the millions of other black men and women who still suffer in slavery.

Perhaps subtly expressing her dissatisfaction with many of her Northern neighbors in their silent acquiescence to the political intrigues that resulted in the extension of slavery to the new territories, Stowe compromises her snapshots of inter-racial harmony by recalling, for her reader, that empowered Southern men dedicated to maintaining slavery effectively determined the political fortune of the entire nation. As Stowe's pragmatic, though unprincipled character Frank Russell recognizes, the

> mouth of the North is stuffed full of cotton, and will be kept full as long as it suits us. Good, easy gentlemen . . . [of the North] are so satisfied with their pillows, and other accommodations inside of the car, that they don't trouble themselves to reflect that we [Southerners] are the engineers (537).

Acknowledging the vulnerability of every fugitive or free African-American in the Northern states, Stowe mockingly suggests that in America, there is no real possibility for liberty as long as Northern men continue to encourage their Southern neighbors by blindly embracing an economic system dependent upon slave labor in order to ensure their own comfort. Stowe's decision to situate the preponderance of her fugitives in Canada is, in one way, a tribute to this cognition, and in another, it is a subtle taunt to her hypocritical countrymen. Suggesting that the Canadian land that Harry, Hannibal, and Jim settled upon is a "land the most valuable for culture" (543), Stowe stresses both the culture and atmosphere of real liberty available in Canada and the potential that our northern neighbor freely offered its inhabitants for intellectual and psychological improvement. Canada, Stowe suggests ruefully, is the refuge of liberty; the hypocritical United States is not. As if she were echoing Emerson when he remarked, in an 1856 letter to his brother William, "I am looking at a map to see where I shall go with my children when Boston & Massachusetts surrender to the slave trade," Stowe looks at the map of the United States and recognizes that, for all practical purposes, it has effectively surrendered to the slave trade.[11] Liberty, she intimates, no longer reigns in the Union; it resides, instead, in Canada.

Although this suggests that Stowe has adopted shame as her weapon of choice in the didactic battle to turn her errant contemporaries from their acquiescence to the political will of their more aggressive Southern neighbors, her textual investment in this solution is so brevet that the discerning reader is compelled to dismiss it. Consistently, her textual investment in the idea of violent rebellion is so dominant that her readers feel compelled to dwell over the real possibility that violent confrontation over slavery is inevitable. The civil war in Kansas, which Stowe makes frequent reference to in the second half of her narrative, provided the nation with ample evidence that American citizens had arrived at the point where they were willing to engage in violence over the question of slavery. Stowe was fascinated—and a little terrified—by the violent struggle that she read about in the newspaper. Indeed, as her son Charles recalled, Stowe "kept herself informed of the minutest details of the struggle" believing that the events in Kansas indicated a "desperate crisis in the nation's history."[12] That desperate crisis informed *Dred*. Stowe's June 17, 1856 letter to the Duchess of Argyle reveals the extent to which *Dred* came directly from the swamp of brutal violence that overwhelmed Kansas. Commenting on her manuscript, Stowe tellingly remarks, "[t]he book is written under the impulse of our stormy times, how the blood & insults of Sumner and the sack of Lawrence burn within us I hope to make a voice to say."[13]

The eventual voice that Stowe gives liberty to is not absolutely clear. At once, she articulates a desperate approval of the impulse to violently oppose slavery; she will not, however, allow herself to advocate actual violent confrontation with slavery's local champions. The cost is too significant. Perhaps, as a result of the impression she gained from vicariously witnessing the brutal conduct of both Pro-Slavery and Free-State forces in newspaper reports of Kansas in 1855 and 1856, Stowe refused violent confrontation as a means of ending the reign of slavery in *Dred;* it simply did not offer the possibility of national redemption; instead, it clearly compromised the ability of nation to fulfill its providential promise. Violence, Stowe suggests during the narrative, is the recourse of brutes; men and women of moral sensibility demean themselves when they resort to it and utterly compromise the noble end they hope to achieve by embracing it.

Within this context, Stowe's singular reference to John Brown in *Dred* is both telling and crucial to an understanding of her rejection of violence. Situated within scenes of lawless brutality so graphic that violent retaliation seems both appealing and morally justified, Stowe makes John Brown's retaliatory murder of five men on the banks of the Pottawatomie Creek essential to an understanding of Harry Gordon, the mulatto fugitive central to her exploration of the abuses of slavery. When Harry learns that his "whole-souled [and] true-hearted" (499) friend and fellow slave Hark has been murdered because he would not provide his captors with any information about Harry's location, Stowe's narrator knowingly comments, "Let the associates of Brown ask themselves if they cannot understand the midnight anguish of Harry!" (499). The narrator then immediately explains that "careless about his own life," Harry's impulse is to embark on a murderous campaign to exact violent revenge upon the four men who had unhesitatingly tortured his friend to death.

However, Dred's reluctance to embrace Harry's craving for "immediate and precipitate action" (499) arrests the younger man's eagerness for vigilante revenge. Willingly submitting to Dred's authority, Harry quiets, considers the wishes of his inspired leader, and agrees not to act upon his instinctive desire. Although Stowe suggests that the emotional response Harry fictively experiences is to some degree consistent with the anguish she imagines that John Brown's "associates" experienced on the eve of their retaliatory murders on the banks of the Pottawatomie, both her use of ambiguous language and her refusal to allow Harry the opportunity to revenge his friend's brutal murder suggests that this may be too narrow of an interpretation of the meaning of such a telling exclamation. [14]

Stowe's failure to specify the instance when Brown's men might have felt "anguish" allows the sentence to suggest some other more significant meanings. Her omniscient narrator observes that Hark's "death weighed like a mountain upon . . . [Harry's] heart" (499). Filled with remorse because he had done nothing to ensure that Hark escape the wrath of Tom Gordon, whom he knew to be volatile, abusive, and prone to violence, Harry feels the anguish of a man who was complicit, to a certain degree, in an innocent man's brutal murder. Likewise, several of the men who heard John Brown say that he intended to "strike terror in the hearts of the Pro-Slavery people" of Kansas by seeing a bit of "radical retaliatory" justice done felt considerable remorse for their failure to forcefully oppose the will of their indignant leader. Indeed, one of Brown's own sons, Owen Brown felt so "conscience stricken because he had killed one of the Doyles . . . [that] he cried and took on at an agonizing rate" after he returned to the small community in Ossawatomie on 25 May.[15] Owen's brother, John Brown Jr., who chose not to accompany the retaliatory party and cautioned John Brown to "be careful and commit no rash act" while the old man was gathering volunteers for his "secret mission," was so affected by news of his father's midnight raid that he went "crazy" following the raid.[16] He felt complicit in his father's act since he had most vociferously petitioned his father to come to Kansas in the first place. Additionally, John Jr. knew that he had compromised the security of all of the Free Soil settlers in Ossawatomie, since he had failed to dissuade his father from committing murder and inviting the wrath of the entire Pro-Slavery population upon them.[17] John Brown Jr. knew that many of his neighbors would feel great anguish in the weeks following the raid. The Pro-Slavery militias would naturally extend the responsibility for the murders to all of the Free State settlers, particularly if they did not give up the men guilty of the murders, and the Pro-Slavery militias would seek vengeance for the outrage inspired by Brown.

In anguish, Brown's neighbors, including his brother-in-law, the Reverend Samuel Adair, called Brown's act an "outrage of the darkest and foulest nature" and pledged to hand over "to the criminal authorities the perpetrators for punishment" and oppose similar actions in the future.[18] They did not countenance the arbitrary murder of settlers who articulated Pro-Slavery sentiment; for the most part, they forcefully rejected the violent program that John Brown embraced on the night of 24 May. As intelligent men, however, they realized that their condemnation of Brown's actions was moot. Despite their moral revulsion and indignant renunciation of Brown's act, they recognized that as Free Soil settlers who had both welcomed Brown into their community and embraced him as a champion, they would appear complicit in Brown's mid-night murders. Even if they forcefully voiced their objection to the notion that the murders were absolutely necessary to demonstrate the will of Free Soil settlers, they knew that their history of association with Brown would inevitably result in their ill-treatment by roving bands of men ideologically committed to slavery.

Likewise, Harry's anguish may be understood to represent his real torment as a man of intelligence and ability at the thought of the brute violence that Hark's tormentors embraced. He is appalled by Tom Gordon's methods, but understands that he would be no better than Gordon if he allowed himself to seek immediate revenge on his master. He also understands that committing to revenge reduces him to the level of the brute he despises. Quite unlike Harry, the mulatto slave who counted as three fifths of a man by decree of the constitution, whole men in Kansas under the voluntary direction of John Brown did not, according to Stowe, experience the "midnight anguish" that Harry suffered when he heard of his friend's death. If they had, she intimates, they would not have embraced murder when they heard of their captain's plan to revenge the insult to Free-State men that the sacking of Lawrence and the attack on Sumner inspired. Demonstrating both his superior moral nature and his willingness to suppress his own violent inclinations, Harry does not allow his instinctual desire for revenge to overwhelm either his sense of justice or his sense of moral responsibility to his fellow fugitives. Unlike John Brown, Harry understands the immediate and compromising effect that revenge on Tom Gordon would have upon his community. Just as Free State settlers suffered the wrath of the empowered Pro-Slavery militias following Brown's brutal act of vengeance, both the innocent slave population and Harry's fellow fugitives in the swamp would feel the wrath of the enraged slave-owners. A truly moral man, Stowe suggests, does not succumb to his instincts and act without consideration of both the immediate result that it will have upon those in his own community and his own conscience.

Stowe further distinguishes Harry from the "associates of Brown" by suggesting, in her rather tortured syntax, that the men who accompanied John Brown on his murderous rampage "*cannot* understand the [kind of] midnight anguish [that] Harry [my emphasis]" (449) suffered. Supported by enthusiastic eastern emigration societies and armed with weapons sent to the territories in boxes occasionally marked "Bibles," the men who fought under John Brown in Kansas increasingly had both the means and the popular support to respond effectively to the abuses of "desperate men, armed to the teeth with Revolvers, Bowie Knives, Rifles& Canon . . . under the pay from Slave-holders."[19] They also enjoyed the legal right to defend both their families and their property from the abuse of tyrannous men. Fugitive slaves, like Harry Gordon, had neither the militant support of an emigrant aid society nor the legally sanctioned right to property which would have guaranteed their right to defend themselves. As Stowe was keenly aware, they were completely vulnerable: the Fugitive Slave Law of 1850 ensured that even in the nominally free states, slaves had no protections from their despotic owners. As a perceptive man, Harry recognizes the impotence of his position as a fugitive slave in the heart of the South; without either the effective Northern support for his efforts or the prospect of legal protection, neither he nor any of the slaves within the swamp community have any prospect for liberation in localized rebellion. If he pursued his desire for "immediate and precipitate action" (499) against his legally sanctioned tyrannical owner, he is aware that the result would ultimately be failure; acknowledging, "our case is utterly hopeless" (500), therefore, he knowingly acquiesces to Dred's request and does nothing.

Stowe's suggestion that the Brown's "associates" could not "understand the midnight anguish of Harry" (499) may also indicate Stowe's larger acknowledgement of the failure of most white Americans to begin to understand the social position that enslaved African-Americans occupied. Stowe's appreciation of her own ignorance had been heralded by African-American critics of *Uncle Tom's Cabin*. Following publication in 1852,

many critics had been quick to condemn Stowe for her racialist representa-
tions of African-Americans in *Uncle Tom's Cabin*. Despite his previous
inclusion of decidedly complimentary criticism of Stowe's 1852 narrative,
Frederick Douglass chose to include Martin Delany's vitriolic condemna-
tions of the text in issues of the *Frederick Douglass Paper* in April and May
1853. In the first of his published letters on *Uncle Tom's Cabin*, Delany
caustically suggested that "in all due respect and difference [sic] to Mrs.
Stowe, I beg leave to say that she *knows nothing about us*, 'the free Colored
people of the United States,' neither does any other white person."[20] In a
later criticism, Delany expanded his criticism and suggested that whites
"know nothing, comparatively, about us."[21] Perhaps, in view of Delany's
opinions, and in thoughtful consideration the respective psychological distance between whites and enslaved "Colored people," Stowe confronts her
predominantly white readers with the significance of their experiential difference in *Dred*.[22] Even the most sympathetic white middle-class reader,
Stowe insinuates, could not feel the true helplessness of the slave as he pow-
erlessly witnesses the legally sanctioned murder of a friend for whom he
has the highest regard; nor could a white reader understand the anguish of
the slave as he learns that his vile master has no intention of ever granting
him freedom, despite the written agreement that establishes the terms of his
liberty.[23] Free to pursue a trade, fight for a cause, settle in the new territory
or defend his right to develop a claim in that territory, white men *could not
know* the angst of an intelligent slave subjected to the abuse of a dissolute
master. Never having experienced the absolutely vulnerable position of the
slave, Stowe is quite literal when she suggests that John Brown's free white
men could not possibly understand Harry's anguish.[24]

Dred, on the other hand, could and does feel Harry's anguish throughout the text. In fact, he seems to emerge out of Harry's anguish and fuel the
fervor of Harry's frustration with his subject position. Entering the narrative as Harry furiously meditates upon the unlimited liberty of his entitled
white half-brother Tom Gordon when he capriciously strikes him across
the face and lasciviously teases him with the suggestion that he will make
the Harry's pretty wife his mistress, Dred taunts Harry with his complicity in his own subjugation. Stressing the fact that in his own willingness to
violently oppose the abusive behavior of the slave-owner, he has established
his own liberty, Dred awakens the "vague tumultuous, overpowering . . .
instincts" (200) that Stowe wants to insist are dormant within every slave.
Emphasizing the desire for liberty common to all of humanity, Stowe allit-
eratively explains that Harry felt the "waters of nature naturally noble"
(200) emerge within his soul connecting him with all other men in an
Emersonian acknowledgement of the "natural law of Justice, Truth, Love,
[and] Freedom."[25] In a flash, Stowe intimates that Harry both recognizes
the natural law, which establishes his right to liberty, and acknowledges the
unnatural law that denies him freedom. Perceptive, intelligent, and indignant over the violation of his natural right to the law, Harry emerges within

the text as an admirable man who has the natural right to deny the rule of his dissolute master. He also has the natural right to rebellion, but he recognizes that if he embraces that right, he will both embrace the repulsive behavior of his dissolute brother and compromise the security of the sister whom he has devoted his entire adult life to protecting.

In anguish once again, Harry, by chance, meets Milly—the character Lisa Whitney appropriately labels the "ideal slave of sentimental rhetoric—a mother, a Christian, a self-denying servant"—who temporarily assuages his anguish by pointing out that Tom Gordon, a dissolute, lascivious, and violent man, models no behavior worthy of emulation.[26] Admonishing Harry for entertaining any idea of violent rebellion against his degenerate master, Milly demonstrates that since Tom Gordon embraces violence, it cannot be the proper recourse of a good man. Embracing brute violence, she clearly asserts, makes the slave as depraved as his master.

However, in the series of increasingly offensive instances of Tom Gordon's depravity, Harry discovers his inability to repress both his anguish and the thought of violent rebellion against his oppressor. And, just as he had before, Dred appears in the moments when Harry's anguish over the injustices of slavery and the hypocrisy of Southern society are most severe. When Harry passes by a slave coffle on the margins of the camp meeting that he has just attended with his good mistress, Dred appears (269–270); when Harry learns that Tom Gordon has re-enslaved his twice-emancipated sister, confiscated her property, and revealed his intention to sell her and the two children that she has raised in freedom after twenty years of liberty, Dred appears (339–342); and when Tom Gordon vindictively asserts his unlimited legal rights as a slave-owner over Harry, Dred appears (389). As if he is the long suppressed embodiment of Harry's anguish, Dred appears at nearly every instance of insufferable injustice and beckons Harry to rebellion.

Harry, in turn, pragmatically articulates the impotence that every slave conscious of the injustice of his or her position feels. Without "any means, or combination, or leaders, [Harry recognizes, he] should only rush on to . . . [his] own destruction" (341) if he embraced the temptation to violence that he experiences when the injustice of his subject position is most evident. Harry's feelings of impotence are well-considered; as both he and the informed reader understands, no slave insurrection in the United States—not even Nat Turner's bloody 1831 uprising—resulted in any positive social change for the participants; in fact, in the atmosphere of indignation, anger, and hysteria that followed Turner's violent reign of terror, not only were all of the participants executed, at least one hundred-twenty other African-Americans were murdered by rampaging white mobs "[w]ound up to a high pitch of rage" at news that Turner had murdered sixty whites in Southampton County.[27] In their discussion of the efficacy of Turner's Rebellion, Dred dismisses the idea that slaves are impotent by underscoring the fact that Turner's rebellion inspired such fear in the slave-holders of Virginia that a motion to end slavery was introduced in the Virginia legislature. Acknowledging that the bill was only narrowly defeated (341), Dred confronts his pragmatic confederate with the fact that cultural change was at one time very possible through violent confrontation; it must, he logically insinuates, be possible now.

As Stowe worked on *Dred* during the summer months of 1856 and attentively read reports of the bitter atmosphere and chaotic violence that followed John Brown's retaliatory strike at Pottawatomie, she may have had second thoughts about the idea that positive cultural change was possible through offensive acts of violence.[28] If newspapers like the Leavenworth *Herald* can be used to illustrate the way in which violence over slavery tended toward complete chaos, Stowe's reluctance to allow Harry anything other than an impulse to violence seems understandable. After printing an account of the Pottawatomie killings, the Leavenworth *Herald* editors issued what historian Stephen Oates terms a "declaration of war:"

> The Abolitionists shoot down our men without provocation, wherever they meet them. Let us retaliate in the same manner—a free fight is all we desire! If murder and assassination is the programme of the day, we favor of filling the bill. Let not the knives of Pro-Slavery men be sheathed while there is one Abolitionist in the Territory.[29]

Closer to Andover, the New York *Daily Tribune* reported that in Kansas, "the Reign of Terror in the up-country continues in its most diabolical form. It is clearly their intention to hunt down the Free-State men, pursue them from point to point, terrify and drive off the timid . . . arrest and hold as prisoners the leading men, and thus keep out settlers."[30] In 29 May *Independent*, the Boston weekly that listed both Harriet Beecher Stowe and Henry Ward Beecher as "Special Contributors," the front page column simply entitled "Kansas Bulletin" acknowledged that "Free State citizens of Lawrence have fallen into the toils of tyranny as wily and inexorable as that of the famous Duke of Alva."[31] The same columnist noted that the "law of violence is the rule in the capital."[32] A week later, the *Independent* columnist revealed that "accounts of violence and brutality and recklessness of all humanity and property are not exaggerated, but fall below the truth."[33] In an even more inflammatory article in the 19 June edition, columnists suggested that the violence previously reported had reached new levels in its offensiveness: women had now become subject to the outrages of the Border Ruffians. In a front page column, editors for the *Independent* ran a story chronicling the abduction of a "matronly lady and her two daughters" reporting that Border Ruffians "VIOLENTLY ABUSED THE MOTHER IN HER OWN HOUSE, AND CARRIED THE DAUGHTERS TO THEIR CAMP, AND KEPT THEM THERE DURING THE INVASION!!"[34]

The only reason that the situation had not degraded to complete anarchy and absolute brutality, Stowe recognized, was that Free-State men were willing to oppose the brutal and anarchic efforts of men committed to the extension of slavery to the entire United States. In her own June 19 column, "Mothers of the Men in Kansas," Stowe indignantly noted that she heard "daily of the enormities perpetuated on our brave free settlers in Kansas."[35] Unable to refrain from prodding her readers to some sort of response, Stowe asked her readers, "shall these brave men be stricken down and defeated, while your voice can persuade one to go to their help—while you solicit material aid to send to their assistance?"[36]

Stowe's conundrum is clear. On one hand, she recognized the possibility of a positive social outcome in violent rejection of tyranny; on the other, she just as clearly recognized the tendency toward moral degeneration and brutal chaos in violent conflict. As she knew from her extensive investigation of the abuses of slaves in America, slave violence historically inspired only more and greater violence. Notwithstanding the positive outcome Frederick Douglass had achieved in his defiance of Edward Covey, Stowe also recognized that acts of defensive violence, or limited violent acts conducted by a slave to protect his own life or the life of a fellow human being, very often resulted in excessive and brutal punishments of other slaves by their white masters.[37] The power of the master, Stowe emphasizes in Judge Clayton's decision against Milly in her chapter entitled "The Legal Decision," is absolute.[38] His singular right to violence is equally absolute.

A slave, Stowe clearly points out, has absolutely no legal right to defend himself against the master's violent whims. However, she is insistent that the slave has a *natural* right to limited defensive violence in the preservation of the self and the community. Adopting both the form and the rhetoric of the *Declaration of Independence*, Harry succinctly articulates the natural right of the slave to both rebellion and violence. In the chapter entitled "The Slave's Argument," Harry claims the right to "fight and shed blood" (435) in response to the oppression slaves collectively endured under the system of slavery. Having physically articulated his refusal to submit to his immediate oppressor's tyranny by returning Tom Gordon's savage blow with one of his own, Harry articulates his philosophical right to violence by demonstrating the enormity of the injustice of his own position. If the revolutionary fathers had a right to armed rebellion, Harry argues, slaves have a far greater right to the same recourse. The injustice that slaves suffered is both more severe and more intolerable than the injustices that the revolutionary fathers of the nation revolted against.

Recognizing the validity of Harry's theoretical argument, and distraught over the illustration of slavery's injustice that he sees immediately following receipt of Harry's clearly articulated argument, Edward Clayton, Stowe's idealistic hero, declares himself a devoted abolitionist, and commits his life to the end of slavery. His efforts, Stowe reluctantly insists, are moot. Just like all other abolitionists committed to moral suasion, Clayton's endeavors to peacefully inspire the corrupt ministry to reconsider its duty to condemn slavery and motivate state officials with vested interest in slavery to initiate legal reforms that will bring about eventual emancipation absolutely fail to gather inertia. Slavery in 1856, Stowe, intimates, was more embedded in the social fabric of America than it had ever been. Regardless of the apparent reasonableness of gradualist strategies, Stowe acknowledges, they simply will not work in a society that privileges wealth and power before morality.

In her recognition of her protagonists' moot efforts, Stowe does not suggest that Clayton is without keen insight. Quite to the contrary, as Clayton is considering how he will respond to the clear logic of Harry's declaration of independence, Stowe has him acknowledge that in order to bring about abolition, "[p]eople have got to be shocked . . . in order to wake them up out of the old absurd routine. Use paralyzes us to almost every injustice; when people are shocked they begin to think and to inquire" (392). Within the context of Clayton's recent decision to dedicate himself to the abolition of slavery, this statement may simply reveal Stowe's understanding of the difficulties that morally enlightened Southerners (like the Grimke sisters) faced when they decided to openly advocate abolition.[39] Taken from a larger perspective, however, Clayton's cognition reveals Stowe's frustrated understanding that, given the atmosphere of corruption, self-interest, and moral infirmity she was personally witness to in the Northern states and vicarious witness to on the frontier, it might take something as shocking as a violent slave rebellion or a brutal reprisal on the banks of the Pottawatomie to trigger a productive examination of the culture of slavery in America.[40] Certainly, she was well aware that her own effort to inspire a sentimental revolution had failed inspire a productive social revolution, just as twenty-five years of Garrisonian moral suasion had failed. More dramatic engagement, Stowe recognized, was necessary to effect radical change.

Prior to the summer of 1856, Stowe had hoped that direct political engagement would be the means by which the country avoided violence. Incensed by the introduction of the Kansas-Nebraska Bill in January, 1854, she had engaged in the political battle over the bill by publishing "An Appeal to the Women of the Free States of America, On the Present Crisis in Our Country." In an attempt to inspire women to use their influence to ensure the defeat of the bill which effectively extended "the miseries of slavery. . . . all over a region of fair, free, unoccupied territory nearly equal in extent to the whole of the free states," Stowe urged American women to petition, to organize lectures, and to pray in order to ensure the bill's defeat when it reached the Senate in March.[41] Disappointed, but far from resigned when the Senate passed the bill, Stowe initiated two other petitions, "one for men & the other for women" to demonstrate the public discontent with the success of the bill and inspire congressmen to revolt against the inertia of compromise and moral cowardice; within two weeks, 3,050 Northern clergymen had signed Stowe's male petition.[42] Submitted to the House of Representatives by Massachusetts Senator Edward Everett in mid-March, Stowe's petition helped ensure the bill's delay, but it did not ensure its death. Resurrected in May, the bill succeeded in the House and became law within the month; the provision stipulating that the settlers in the new territory would determine whether the region would enter the Union as a free or slave state set the stage for the violent struggle that would capture the nation's attention for the next three years.

Expressing his concern over the bill, Stowe's dynamic brother, Henry Ward Beecher, acknowledged that the "whole nation lies spread out like a gamblers table."[43] A demonstrative and outspoken abolitionist, Henry Ward Beecher convinced his large congregation, and, in all probability, helped convince his well-known sister, that the success of the Free-State cause was essential to the success of the nation. Determined to offer tangible support, Beecher's Plymouth Church sent boxes of Sharpe's rifles in boxes marked "Bibles" to the Free State settlers in Kansas.[44] These rifles became popularly known as Beecher's Bibles.[45] Perhaps less overtly demonstrative than her theatrical brother, Harriet Beecher Stowe remained deeply concerned over the "desperate crisis" that was occurring in both Washington and in the territories of Kansas following the Compromise of 1854.[46]

Throughout 1855, she attentively followed news reports on events in Kansas. In order to understand the political dimension of the frontier crisis, Stowe also remained attentive to what was occurring in Washington. Maintaining a frequent correspondence with her friend, Massachusetts Senator and outspoken abolitionist Charles Sumner, she was able to gain an appreciation for the degree to which the federal government was complicit in the degenerate atmosphere in Kansas. Sumner, who read excerpts of *Uncle Tom's Cabin* on the floor of the Senate to demonstrate the corrupt behavior slavery engendered and to condemn the institution before his Southern colleagues, provided Stowe with regular updates from Washington on the status of both the violent confrontation in Kansas and the federal support of that effort.[47] When he learned that Stowe intended to write another antislavery novel, Sumner responded enthusiastically, urging Stowe to immediately commence with the project and continue to influence the abolitionist effort of America. In an 1855 letter, Sumner both praised Stowe for her past abolitionist efforts and urged her to remain steadfast in her determination to make the men and women of America painfully aware of the injustices inherent in slavery. He urged her to write another novel claiming, "I feel it will act directly upon the pending questions and help us in our struggle for Kansas, and also to overthrow the slave-oligarchy in the coming presidential election. We need your help at once on our struggle."[48]

Although Stowe refrained from openly engaging in public discourse on the violence current in Kansas following her effort to dissuade members of the congress from supporting the Compromise of 1854, she was not silent upon the right of certain men to commit to violence when they believed an oppressive power was encroaching upon their rights.[49] In October, 1855, Stowe provided the introduction to William C. Nell's "Colored Patriots of the Revolution." In her short, but poignant introduction to Nell's work,

Stowe both celebrates the African-American contribution to the revolution and recognizes the paucity of the racialist notion that blacks had "little [natural] ferocity" and were inherently deficient in energy and courage.[50] As if setting the stage for *Dred,* Stowe both encourages African-Americans to "emulate the noble [and violent] deeds and sentiments of their ancestors" and warns "their white brothers . . . [that] generosity, disinterested courage and bravery, are of no particular race and complexion."[51] Willingness to courageously commit to violence in order to secure liberty, Stowe emphasizes in her approval of Nell's work, is innate to all men; it is certainly not the particular domain of white men.

Arming Harry with the discourse of the American Revolution, Stowe seems to be preparing her reader for a violent rebellion more shocking, and more immediate, than the one occurring on the frontier. Informed by Nell's seamless integration of the narratives of Nat Turner and "Denmark Veazie [sic]" in his exploration of the black revolutionary patriots, Stowe constructs "Jegar Sahadutha," the loaded chapter that recalls Jacob's rejection of his abusive uncle Laban's rule, as an articulation of the slave's right to violent rebellion (Gen 31:43/52). As if preparing her reader to accept the kind of chaotic violence that Turner unleashed in Virginia, Stowe also arms her characters with a "long train of abuses and usurpations" (455) that convincingly establish their right to reject the authority of the law and rebel. With the *Declaration of Independence* as his model, Harry leads the clandestine assembly of "mulatto, quadroon, and negro" (454) men in an articulation of their "right and duty to throw off" (455) the government that authorized their abuse. Not only do they recall the despotism of their empowered masters in the conduct of everyday slave life, they pointedly recall the despotism of the law in the validation of the unlimited power that the master legally enjoyed over his slaves.[52] As if these abuses were insufficient to convince her reader of the cruel injustice the slave suffered under a government dedicated to liberty, Stowe re-inscribes the tyrannous power that the slave owner exercises over his slaves by intruding on the mid-night scene with news that Hark has been whipped to death (457). Clearly, Stowe suggests in this scene, slaves have the same right to violent rebellion that the white revolutionary fathers had.

However, Stowe does not allow Harry to take advantage of the atmosphere of indignation developed in this scene. Instead, she theatrically conjures Dred from the scene's periphery and focuses the reader upon the figure whose rhetoric has become as fantastic as his form. After allowing Dred a torrent of prophetic exclamations and making his figure both commanding and terrible, Stowe's narrator acknowledges that Dred "seemed . . . some awful form, framed to symbolize to the human eye the energy of avenging justice which all nature shudderingly declares" (458). He prophetically embodies the desire for vengeance, which is so *awful* that even nature *shudders* in its recognition, articulating Stowe's fear that the abuses of slavery will inevitably result in unrestrained violent acts of vengeance. However,

Dred does not articulate that desire physically. Instead of acting as John Brown did in Kansas, appointing himself as judge, jury, and executioner of those who appeared to embrace a particular social philosophy, Dred denies his own agency, defers to a higher authority than himself, and refrains from acting upon the right to violence he has recognized.

Cognizant of his authority, Dred commands the indignant assembly, "hold yourself in waiting, for the day cometh" (460). He clearly rejects Hannibal's inclination to respond to murder with more murder. Stressing the moral tenor of their future vengeance, Dred instructs his indignant fugitive confederates that in their revenge they will not allow their outrage to overwhelm their sense of propriety. Better than their dissolute white masters, they will not embrace the degenerate behavior that has inspired their indignation. Instead, Dred asserts, they will engage only in righteous and limited violence against their oppressors.

The first opportunity that Dred has to exercise that right occurs when Tom Gordon and his two comrades fall upon the lone Edward Clayton and strike him from behind with a "heavy blow of a gutta percha cane" (493). Re-inscribing Preston Brooks' attack on Charles Sumner, Stowe stages the scene in order to demonstrate both the hopelessness of moral suasion when confronting those who espouse a "might makes right" (168) philosophy and the failure of non-resistance as a viable response to brutes unencumbered by any sense of morality. Refusing to use the brace of pistols with which he has armed himself, Edward Clayton contemptuously condemns his attackers as cowards shaming them for their devotion to the ideology of ignorance. He does not, however, offer any physical resistance to his three attackers, and, when struck by the vile man who first hit him with the stout cane, falls critically injured to the ground at Tom Gordon's feet. Recognizing Clayton's peril, Dred appears and strikes Tom with a "violent blow" disabling the brute and protecting Clayton from a subsequent blow. Successful in his effort to protect Clayton, Dred withdraws into the forest, where he issues the degenerate a prophetic warning rather than killing him. True to the debauched character that Stowe has carefully crafted for him, Tom Gordon fails to recognize the wisdom of Dred's biblical injunction and attempts to locate the author of his pain. Displaying no capacity to understand the opportunity that Dred has given him to repent his impulsive devotion to violence, Tom demonstrates an instinctual dedication to brutality in his attempt to discover Dred's location. Recognizing his half-brother's intention to embrace his inclination toward violent retaliation, Harry fires two rifle shots over the heads of Tom and his flunkeys, exclaiming, "Tom Gordon, Beware! Remember Hark" (493)! Clearly demonstrating both his self-discipline and his moral superiority to his white brother, Harry allows Tom and his associates the opportunity to escape, and then immediately turns his attention to the wounded Clayton.

In Stowe's apparent reluctance to either allow her fugitive heroes to do anything but exercise the least degree of violence necessary to protect Clayton's life or to consider the opportunity that they have to rid the region of a ruthless despot, the reader can recognize Stowe's conviction that only dissolute brutes embrace unrestrained violence as a means of achieving social dominance. Although her fugitives clearly have the right to defend both themselves and their fellow man, Stowe seems to insist that if they did anything more than offer limited defense of the downtrodden, they will become as morally repugnant as their oppressors. When Dred dies in his effort to deliver his friend Jim from the "drunken, swearing, ferocious" (512) mob that Tom Gordon inspires, the reader can see Stowe's consistent willingness to only embrace limited defensive violence and her absolute condemnation of unrestrained violence. Dred's attempt to deliver his friend from the violent mob is praiseworthy and courageous, as is his willingness to risk his life in that pursuit; Tom Gordon's willingness to inspire the mob to uncontrolled violence in pursuit of his own desire for revenge, quite to the contrary, is despicable, just as his rag-tag mob of relentless brutes is despicable. Degenerate, drunken, and easily manipulated, they act not from devotion to principle but in mindless devotion to "violence and blood" (504). As the pragmatic Frank Russell points out, the "common people [who make up the mob] are so ignorant that they are in the hands of anyone who wants them. They are like a swarm of bees; you can manage them by beating on a tin pan" (468). Unrestrained violence, Stowe appears to suggest, is the resort of ignorant, narcissistic, base men under the influence of self-serving bullies. It does not result in a state of social perfection; quite to the contrary, she suggests, it inevitably results in a state of social degeneration.

The degenerate state of affairs in Kansas during the summer of 1856 was ample proof that unrestrained violence had very little potential as a method of ensuring positive cultural change; it only ensured chaos. As Pro-Slavery Governor Shannon indicated in his 31 May report on the state of affairs in Kansas to President Franklin Pierce,

> "The respectability of the parties and the cruelties attending the murders [at Pottawatomie] have produced an extraordinary state of excitement in that portion of the territory . . . I hope that the offenders may be brought to Justice; if so, it may allay to a great extent the excitement, otherwise I fear the consequences."[53]

Although several of those who were involved with Brown's "retaliatory justice" were indicted, Governor Shannon's concerns about the state of excitement that followed the murders on the Pottawatomie were well founded. As a June report by a correspondent from the St. Louis *Evening News* indicated, the consequences of Brown's unrestrained violence were dire: "The substance of the territory is devoured by the roving, roistering bands of guerilla fighters who, under the plea that war prevails, perpetuate deeds of robbery, rapine, slaughter and pillage that nothing can justify."[54] Summarizing the result of the chaotic violence embraced by both Pro-Slavery and Free-State guerilla forces, a reporter for the New York *Tribune* noted that "[a]ll over the territory, along the roadside, houses are deserted and farms abandoned, and nowhere are there evidences of industry."[55] The 3 July *Independent* provides an even clearer portrait of the anarchic conditions that violent confrontation had created in Kansas. Reviewing the "Outrages of the Ruffians," a correspondent suggest that it is "doubtful whether in any year in the history of savage warfare in this country, has witnessed so large a number of families thrown into so great terror and misery over so wide an extent of territory, as we have just seen among the peaceful and freedom loving settlers of Kansas."[56] Unrestrained violence on the margins of America, it appeared during the summer months when Stowe was preparing *Dred* for the publisher, led to chaos.

As such, in her fictional consideration of the alternatives open to abolitionists, Stowe will not allow it to be the method that enlightened Americans embrace. In order to direct her narrative away from the degeneration that she saw inevitable in the resort to unrestrained violence, Stowe provides Clayton with an understanding that "nothing but the removal of some of these minds from the oppressions which were goading them could prevent a development of bloody insurrection" (520). To avoid the chaotic backlash that insurrection would surely bring, Clayton guides Harry to an understanding of the "undesireableness [sic] and hopelessness, under the present circumstances, of any attempt to right by force the wrongs under which his class were suffering" (519). Violent reprisals, Clayton intimates, have no chance of bringing about the conditions of liberty; instead, they hasten an atmosphere of unrestrained and lawless butchery. In this recognition, crafted concurrent to and in recognition of the degenerate conditions in Kansas, Stowe concludes her narrative by scripting Harry's ready acquiescence to Edward Clayton's suggestion that he opt for the "safer way by flight" (519) along the Underground Railroad.

Reflecting momentarily on the service the Underground Railroad has done for the population of the South, Stowe's narrator acknowledges that this avenue "has removed many a danger from their dwellings" (520). Recognizing that it has offered those "men . . . who cannot be kept in slavery" (520) an alternative to violent rebellion, Stowe suggests that as long as there is slavery, there will be African-American men ready to commit to violence to escape their unnatural bondage. Certainly, she intimates, not all slaves are Uncle Tom's. Nat Turner, Denmark Vesey, Frederick Douglass, and William Nell had clearly proven that intelligent, resourceful, and vigorous African-American men would not accept the yoke of bondage nor would they submit to a position of subservience: they would rebel. Unless something is done to end slavery and end it soon, Stowe forewarns her readers, violent insurrection is inevitable in the South. If she could intuit anything from the chaos occurring in the Kansas Territory, Stowe clearly suggests that the resulting carnage will be more horrifying than anything the citizens of the nation had ever experienced.

Demonstrating the prescience of her understanding, Stowe revives Tom Gordon after she has delivered her African-American characters to liberty and brings him to renewed conflict with Edward and Anne Clayton. Stirring the discontent of the Clayton's North Carolina neighbors, Tom Gordon intrudes on the domestic bliss of their plantation, challenges their right to create a progressive atmosphere on their own land, and eventually leads a mob in the destruction of the schoolhouse that they have erected to educate their slaves. No longer convinced that they can pursue their work in the degenerate atmosphere of the South, Edward and Anne determine to flee the state to a location conducive to a domestic program of reform.

Although Stowe's exploration of violence in *Dred* seems distinctly at odds with the domestic role that nineteenth century women were encouraged to embrace by ladies magazines, domestic novels, and child-rearing manuals in the 1850s, her clear acceptance of the role of the nation's foremost female abolitionist following the publication of *Uncle Tom's Cabin* placed her in a unique national position to expand the role of "true woman" from the domestic bliss of the tidy, warm, well-regulated Stone Cabin in Andover to the metaphorical hearth of the entire nation. As Mary Ryan indicates in her exploration of the evolution of the woman's role in America, mid-nineteenth century women, empowered by their role as the "mothers of civilization" served society by guarding "the national soul and strengthen[ing] the moral fiber of America." [57] Believing that the events in Kansas indicated a "desperate crisis in the nation's history," Stowe embraced the role of civilizing mother and gently suggested that the passionate violence the nation witnessed on the frontier was a direct result of its collective failure to recognize the humanity of the African-American slave. Expanding the role of the mother from the socialization and transformation of infants to adults "suitable for the culture and society into which they were born," Stowe took it upon herself to transform the naïve understanding of the slave population that she had previously articulated as dependent, passive, and naturally subservient to a more mature perspective that recognized their desire for independence, capacity for violence, and willingness to reject the dominion of anyone who attempted to subjugate them. [58]

At the conclusion of *Dred*, however, Stowe seems to capitulate to the myth of domestic bliss popularized by Sarah Josepha Hale, editor of *Godey's Lady's Book* and countless other sentimental authors, by sketching portraits of tranquil scenes purified of all racial tension. [59] There is no threat of the slave-catcher in the tenement where Milly smiles over her inter-racial brood and happily points out that "De fust [set of orphaned children she has provided a nurturing home for] is all in good places" (546); there is no recognition of the strange privilege that Uncle Tiff enjoys in his role as guardian of two young white adults who have finally come into their inheritance (548); and there is no evidence of continued subservience or paternalism in the utopian community that Harry Gordon and Edward Clayton establish, though the reader does learn that Clayton "built for himself a beautiful residence, where he and his sister lived happily together, finding their enjoyment in the improvement of those [former slaves] by whom they are surrounded" (543). Each of these scenes records the kind of domestic harmony that mid-nineteenth century women were educated to believe it was their duty to create. Having exerted a "saving influence" over almost all of the slaves he had the opportunity to encounter within the narrative, Edward Clayton, Stowe's feminized hero, has succeeded in establishing several models of domestic inter-racial bliss on an international scale.

However, Stowe's discerning contemporary reader recognizes that the prospects for such a fairy tale ending are suspect. Not only was the Fugitive Slave Law still very much in effect in the North when *Dred* first appeared in book stalls in 1856, the likelihood that a slave-owner like Tom Gordon would simply give up his efforts to reclaim his slave property after they had reached the North—or Canada for that matter—is doubtful. Given his penchant for vengeance, it is unlikely that borders, private social welfare programs, or morally enlightened patriarchs would have curbed Tom Gordon's desire to feel the satisfaction of recapturing the human chattel he considered his own by law. As Stowe knew well, borders were no hindrance to men committed to the extension of their own wealth and influence; the welfare of poor Free Soil settlers or newly liberated slaves was of little consequence to those dedicated to ensuring their own political power; and moral arguments were rarely successful when trying to convince men who had enjoyed the power, affluence, and ease of the slaveholder to relinquish the source of that privilege.

Nearly every news report having to do with Kansas in 1856 provided Stowe with the evidence necessary to draw these conclusions: Pro-Slavery men from Missouri repeatedly crossed the border and threatened, murdered, and forced Free-State setters to flee their homes in an effort to ensure that settlers in Kansas embraced slavery when the territory entered the Union; contemptuous of the law, roving bands of Pro-Slavery vigilantes consistently overwhelmed polling locations and stuffed ballot boxes with votes for their Pro-Slavery candidates to ensure the same result; and decades of peaceful agitation absolutely failed to ensure that the perpetrators of these crimes considered their actions morally reprehensible.

Yet Stowe does not allow Tom Gordon to penetrate the scenes of domestic harmony that she so superficially constructs at the narrative's end. Like the Pro-Slavery agitators in Kansas, Stowe leaves Tom occupied with "some mischief" (526) in North Carolina near the scene of his latest debauchery, Edward Clayton's Magnolia Grove Plantation. Perhaps "insane with whiskey and excitement" (536) over his triumphant destruction of Anne Clayton's schoolhouse, a scene that distinctly recalls the debauched scene that succeeded the burning of the Free State Hotel in Lawrence, Kansas on May 22, 1856, Tom Gordon is "so completely under the power of liquor as to be incapable of mischief for the time being."[60] However, as the reader recognizes, neither the fictional despot Tom Gordon nor the real-life Border Ruffians that Stowe read about in the *Independent* disappear after they recover from their drunken mischief. Inevitably, they reappear on either the border of consciousness or on borders of Kansas to commit other heinous offenses. On the margins of domestic paradise, the Tom Gordons of America threaten the liberty of every fugitive and every peaceful citizen committed to the idea of liberty. The question Stowe seems to leave her reader with is: What are we to do about the Tom Gordons in America? Dissolute, empowered men who know nothing but a "[m]ight makes right" (168) philosophy will not bend to anything but force. As Stowe recognizes, they will not remain silent if freedom should triumph in Kansas, nor will they remain inert: they will, instead, embrace vengeance and respond with a degree of violence here-to-fore unseen in America. The only way to defeat these violent men, Stowe hopefully suggests, is to make their fellow slaveholders recognize their degeneracy, rebel against their leadership, and refuse their allegiance. The only other option, Stowe grudgingly seems to admit, is to commit to the same degree of violence that the "associates of Brown" did at Pottawatomie and anxiously anticipate the result.

7 Epilogue

> Self trust is the essence of heroism. It is the state of the soul at war, and its ultimate objects are the last defiance of falsehood and wrong, and the power to bear all that can be inflected by evil agents. It speaks the truth and it is just, generous, hospitable, temperate, scornful of petty calculations and scornful of being scorned. It persists; it is of an undaunted boldness and of a fortitude not to be wearied out. Its jest is the littleness of common life. That false prudence which dotes on the health and wealth is the butt and merriment of heroism.
>
> Emerson, "Heroism"

Harriet Beecher Stowe's momentary fascination with John Brown's terrorist tactics is indicative of the sense of helpless frustration felt by American abolitionists during the 1850s. Thirty years of moral suasion had failed to inspire a revolution of sentiment, and Daniel Webster's abdication had signaled the triumph of moral compromise and the inevitability of slavery's proliferation throughout America. Sensing that silence was complicity and devotion to scholarship was social myopia, America's leading intellects violated their apolitical inclinations and radically sounded the trumpet in support of a man who independently decided that society's ills were so significant that arbitrary murderous rampages were essential to reversing social inertia and midnight raids on sleepy government facilities were justified. They celebrated the freedom fighter—not for his murders or for his bravery—but for his righteousness. He gave them a champion—even a martyr—but he also gave them an impetus to expression—expression of their moral indignation and sense of powerlessness.

This is what terrorists do; they offer the disempowered and the morally indignant a very public voice of protest. Indeed, in the attention that their violent acts attract, terrorists bask in the momentary focus of their contemporaries and capitalize on the attention that a stunned—and often horrified—public provides them. The statements that terrorists issue—like the series of public statements that John Brown was able to situate in every major American newspaper in the month that followed his capture—are designed to legitimize their actions and themselves. They are claims of righteousness, since the actions which gained them public access are justified as correctives for an errant society. Their boldness is captivating—particularly in an era when offended sentiments are similarly privileged by significant segments of the population who have not been able to reverse what they believe to be the corrupt inertia maintained by both the empowered and the privileged of a society. Terrorists catalyze those whose frustrations mirror their own. When the sympathetic are public intellectuals—whose enduring efforts to bring about social change have been a series of failures—a new and far more mainstream agent of validation is created.

Ralph Waldo Emerson, Henry Thoreau, Harriet Beecher Stowe, Thomas Wentworth Higginson, Theodore Parker, Franklin Sanborn—these are just a few of the abolitionists who were moved to validate terrorism in 1859. The conditions that gave rise to their engagement varied, but in each case, it was their sense of moral outrage and indignation over the legally sanctioned encroachment of slavery on all of the citizens of the United States that inspired them to sing violent John Brown's praises. The hypocrisy of legal slavery in a nation devoted to liberty was not sufficient to inspire them to publically validate violent rebellion against the state; it was the hypocrisy of their acquaintances and those representative men whom they had admired that moved them to publicly declare their alliance with terrorist John Brown. It was also their recognition that the culture of moral compromise was so pervasive that it would no longer allow virtuous individuals the belief that their protests might reverse the tide of social inertia and correct social wrongs.

The sense of helplessness and the increasingly clear understanding that devotion to peaceful civil protest—or due political process—would only result in legally sanctioned moral hypocrisy moved individuals like Henry Thoreau and Ralph Waldo Emerson to rally around figures who advocated violent change; peaceful change was no longer possible in the America devoted to unifying compromise in 1859. The same conditions that inspired intellectuals like Thoreau and Emerson to celebrate and support John Brown in 1859 inspire intellectuals and businessmen to support contemporary terrorists in 2009. Individuals who feel that they cannot peacefully reverse the ideological encroachment of one culture upon another are offering support to those who violently—and arbitrarily—attack the signifiers of civil power and those who create their structures. Their moral indignation and sense of powerlessness is expressed by those whom they empower, and their own sense of righteousness is restored by their support.

By understanding the marginalized intellectuals who feel a distinct obligation to confront the encroachment of foreign practices that violate their moral code, we can work to reduce the probability that they will serve as cultural catalysts who accelerate support for violent terrorists. Privileging their shared perspectives and encouraging their inclusion in political dialogue diminishes their need for the kind of public exposure that radical violence achieves. Consistently, publicizing the investigations of practices antithetical to the professed ideology of a culture or a nation—and publically celebrating the condemnation of those practices—diminishes the impetus for radical violent protests and the subsequent statements of support that validate them.

Sympathetic intellectuals fuel terrorist bombs and make them lethal; they accelerate support for terrorist causes and provide a shocked population with an understanding of the issues that inspired a dedicated violent nucleus of committed individuals to act. Compelling this population to reject the kinds of arbitrary acts of violence that terrorists author reduces the likelihood of future terrorist acts. Without the public legitimacy that intellectuals proffer, terrorists cannot succeed. Intellectuals make terrorists effective; they can unmake them.[61]

Appendix A

(Ralph Waldo Emerson. Letter to Charles Wesley Slack, Chairman of the Fraternity Lecture Course)

Concord
Monday Morn
Oct 31

Dear Sir

    I understand that there is some doubt about Mr. Douglass's keeping his engagement for Tuesday next. If there is a vacancy, I think you cannot do a greater public good than to send for Mr. Thoreau, who has read last night here a discourse on the history & character of Captain John Brown, which ought to be heard or read by every man in the Republic. He read it with great force & effect, & though the audience was of widely different parties, it was heard without a murmur of dissent.

    I wish it to be heard in Boston, & if there is not room tomorrow night, can there not be next Sunday fore noon?

Yours faithfully,
RW Emerson

Mr. Slack

(Ralph Waldo Emerson. Letter to Charles Wesley Slack, 31 October, 1859. Charles W. Slack Papers, American Antiquarian Society.)

Appendix B

(Theodore Parker. Letter to Charles Wesley Slack, Chairman of the Fraternity Lecture Course)

Montreux, Canton de Vaud, Suisse
July 20, 1859

My dear Sir,

I thank you for your kind letter which came 14th inst.—I fear it would not be wise for Sumner to deliver the lecture you speak of. He had better not return to America till the end of Nov. & then with no public display or excitement & repair to Washington at once. Tho' much better than [word undecipherable] before since his assassins attacked him, he is still far from well, & I feel that a little over excitement might make him an invalid for life—while a proper caution may restore him for life to his friends or the nation. You know how dear I hold the Fraternity; I would do all in my power to promote its generous & noble works; but I think it had better let Mr. Sumner *slide* this winter. I shall tell him my opinion when I write him next, & know that you & your friends will appreciate my conduct tho' it is not the ghiste [sic] of your advice.—I rejoice in the evening lectures you have yet laid out. I hope by all means Phillips will speak & that too in his favorite theme. I wish I could give you a lecture on *the Causes* & *immediate* & *remote Results of the Present War in Europe,* & the authors in this *Conflict of Principles in European Politics* as I have *in the Conduct of the 5 Great Powers*. But it cannot be. I think Lowell has no deep & hearty interest in the great things the Fraternity aims at that I hope its Lectures will help forward. [Dr--elided] Holmes is much more on our side today. It will be a fine thing if *Whittier* stands up tall & valiant before you & gives one of his grand poems. I think John Weiss (now at Milton Hill) would give you a good lecture in the winter & a good Sermon anytime. He is a noble fellow—no minister in N.E, except Johnson of Salem, has so much *genius*. But he is a sick man with a feeble voice.

Of course the politicians are changing their stories. I trust Seward will be the Candidate in 1860—he is the Ablest Statesman (I think) in America, & tho' he is far enough from having all I want in a President, yet I know not where else to look for so much. Chase is a noble man—& I have great regard for him—personally & politically. But he has been Gov. of Ohio for years, & does not use the arm of the State to protect its innocent inhabitants; he does not *defend the Rights of his own State*! It may be Seward could do no better. But he has not been tried in the particular & found wanting. And with all my normal regard for Gov. C, I think he has shown the white feather when the red would have been more becoming to his office & his Character. We don't follow the lesson set us by the South—the Slaveholders stand to their Guns no matter who is before them–a school marm at Norfolk or the Supreme Court of the U.S. The So. will not punish a Slavetrader who steals men in Africa & sells them in Carolina, while Ohio & her Gov. *shut up in jail such as help a man honestly & peacefully to secure his unalienable right to Liberty*! While the Rep. Party pursues its present course of timid crouching to its masters at the South it will be beaten—& right to be beaten! "The World is ruled by boldness."—I thought Banks got out of the wrong side of his bed the morning he signed that amendment to the constitution of the US. But he is an able man with a fine future before him—if he remembers two things: (1) that the Eternal Law of Right overrides at length all the Statutes of Men; & (2) that Honesty is the best policy, & the People value *Integrity* above all the arts of Politicians & the Orators trick. It is that virtue which gives their reputation to Washington, Hancock, Saml Adams, & J. G. Adams. Many of whom had a high *brilliant* quality, the greatest of them not the least *skill in trickery*.

John A Andrew is a good fellow. We shall one day see him *Chief Justice of Mass.* There are better lawyers than he, much of abler mind, in the State. But he is a man of great integrity, if fair intellect, with a reasonable knowledge of law, & an intuitive perception of justice which is worth more than all the technical learning of Maine[,] skill of Mansfield, Selden & Coke. I am glad he did not take the Judgeship. Otis P. Lord is much judge to decide on the *strength of liquor* I take it; an expert to [decide—elided] tell what is *intoxicating* drink.—How is your little daughter's foot? Remember me kindly to your wife—& the neighbors about you. I often come into your house at night & see my friends sleep.

Yours faithfully,
Theodore Parker

Charles W. Slack, Esq.
Boston

(Theodore Parker. Letter to Charles Wesley Slack, 20 July 1859. Charles Wesley Slack papers. Department of Special Collections and Archives. Kent State University Libraries and Media Services.)

Appendix C

(Frederick Douglass, Letter to Charles Wesley Slack, Chairman of the Fraternity Lecture Course)

Rochester,
Aug. 26, 1859

My dear Sir:

Depend upon me. The Tribune is mistaken. I shall not leave for England before the middle of November. My appointment in Boston shall be fulfilled if life and health continue. If I speak in Theodore Parker's pulpit, it had better be on the Sunday succeeding my lecture.

To speak in Boston is a large undertaking but to speak in the pulpit of Mr. Parker is a huge undertaking. I shall come to the work with fear and trembling, but shall come nevertheless.

Very Truly Yours,
Fred. Douglass

Chas. W. Slack, Esq.

(Frederick Douglass. Letter to Charles Wesley Slack, 26 August 1859. Charles Wesley Slack papers. Department of Special Collections and Archives. Kent State University Libraries and Media Services.)

Notes

NOTES TO CHAPTER 1

1. George Luther Stearns assessed John Brown's enduring significance at the end of his testimony before the Mason Committee, the Senate committee charged with investigating the raid on Harper's Ferry. Quoted in the United States Senate, *Inquiry into the late invasion and seizure of the public Property at Harper's Ferry* (S. Rpt. 278), (Washington: Government Printing Office, 1860), 12.
2. In his 2 January, 1857 address commemorating the twenty-fifth anniversary of the Massachusetts Anti-Slavery Society in Boston, Thomas Wentworth Higginson commented favorably on Brown while reviewing his impressions of his recent investigatory journey to Kansas. *Liberator*, 16 Jan. 1857.
3. Ibid.
4. James Redpath, New York *Tribune*, 30 May 1856. Quoted by Oswald Garrison Villard, *John Brown 1800–1859: A Biography Fifty Years After* (Gloucester: Peter Smith, 1965) 199–200.
5. John Brown, letter to the Editor of the New York *Tribune*, 1 Jul. 1856. Quoted by Villard, 204–06.
6. Franklin Sanborn, *Recollections of Seventy Years* (New York: Gorham Press, 1909) 103.
7. Grodzins, Dean, "Why Theodore Parker Backed John Brown: The Political and Social Roots of Support for Abolitionist Violence." (Unpublished 1998, 2004) 4.
8. Oswald Garrison Villard. *John Brown 1800–1859: A Biography Fifty Years Later* (Gloucester: Peter Smith, 1965), 272.
9. Ralph Waldo Emerson, letter to Charles W. Slack, 31 October, 1859. Charles Wesley Slack Papers. Department of Special Collections and Archives, Kent State University Libraries and Media Services.
10. Ralph Waldo Emerson, "Courage" *Transcendental Log: Fresh Discoveries in Newspapers Concerning Emerson, Thoreau, Alcott and Others of the American Literary Renaissance.* ed. Kenneth Walter Cameron (Hartford: Transcendental Books, 1973) 136–27: In *Virtue's Hero: Emerson, Anti-Slavery, and Reform,* Len Gougeon notes that Emerson provided $50 and Thoreau $10 for the Brown Relief Fund. Len Gougeon, *Virtue's Hero: Emerson, Anti-Slavery, and Reform* (Athens: University of Georgia Press, 1990) 245.
11. Ralph Waldo Emerson, "Speech at the Meeting to Aid John Brown's Family (18 November, 1859)," *Emerson's Anti-Slavery Writings*, eds. Len Gougeon and Joel Myerson (New Haven: Yale University Press, 1995) 118.
12. Ibid.

13. Thomas Jefferson, "Declaration of Independence," *The Portable Thomas Jefferson*. ed. Merrill D. Peterson (New York: Penguin, 1975) 235.

14. Quoted by Merrill Peterson, *John Brown: the Legend Revisited* (Charlottesville: University of Virginia Press, 2002) 25.

15. John Greenleaf Whittier, "Brown of Ossawatomie." *The Complete Poetical Works of John Greenleaf Whittier* (Boston, 1892).

16. Melville's 1859 poem "The Portent" is the first poem in *Battle Pieces*; Whitman's 1859–1860 poem "Year of the Meteors" is included in the 1900 edition of *Leaves of Grass*; Howells poem "Old Brown," first published in the Ohio State Journal, was thereafter published in Redpath's *Echoes of Harper's Ferry* in 1860, and Child's poem "The Hero's Heart" was first published in the *Liberator* in 1860.

17. "A Conversation with Brown," *The Life, Trial and Execution of Captain John Brown* (1859, New York: De Capo Press, 1969) 45.

18. Brown's purported plan was to withdraw from Harper's Ferry with the weapons he had secured there and establish guerilla bases throughout the mountainous regions of what is now West Virginia from which to conduct a protracted war of liberation of the oppressed slaves in the American South, arming the successive flood of escaping slaves in the South against their former oppressors. Noted by Edward J. Renehan, *The Secret Six: the True Tale of the Men Who Conspired with John Brown* (New York: Crown Publishers, 1995) 128.

19. Jessica Stern. Terror *in the Name of God: Why Religious Militants Kill*, (Ecco: New York, 2003) 210.

20. Ward Churchill, "'Some People Push Back,' On the Justice of Roosting Chickens written by Ward Churchill 9–11–2001." 6 Apr. 2005, http://www.politicalgateway.com/news/read/html?id=2739.

21. Quoted by Ward Churchill, "'Some People Push Back,' On the Justice of Roosting Chickens written by Ward Churchill 9–11–2001." 6 Apr. 2005, http://www.politicalgateway.com/news/read/html?id=2739.

22. John Brown, "Provisional Constitution and Ordinances for the People of the United States," *The Life, Trial and Execution of Captain John Brown* 1859, (New York: De Capo Press, 1969) 51.

23. Harriet Beecher Stowe's novel *The Minister's Wooing* was first published in book form on 20 Oct. 1859, though it had been previously published serially in the *Atlantic*. Since she was on an extended European tour, she did not hear about Brown's raid until sometime in November; at the time she was in Florence. For the New Years Edition of the *Independent*, the Boston weekly that listed both Harriet Beecher Stowe and Henry Ward Beecher as "Special Contributors," Stowe submitted an assessment of world situation which included favorable commentary on John Brown, whom Stowe characterizes as "a brave, good man who calmly gave his life up to a noble effort for human freedom and died in a way that is better than the most successful selfish life." *Independent*, 1 Jan. 1860. Quoted by Forrest Wilson, *The Crusader in Crinoline: the Life of Harriet Beecher Stowe* (Philadelphia: J.B. Lippincott Company, 1941) 449.

24. Ibid.

25. Ibid.

26. Henry D. Thoreau, "The Last Days of John Brown," *The Essays of Henry D. Thoreau*, ed. Lewis Hyde (New York: North Point Press, 2002) 288.

27. Henry D. Thoreau, "A Plea for Captain John Brown," *The Essays of Henry D. Thoreau*, ed. Lewis Hyde (New York: North Point Press, 2002) 263.

28. Quoted by Thoreau, "A Plea for Captain John Brown," 280.

29. In his 29 Oct. 2004 videotape message to the people of the United States (entitled "Your Security is in your own Hands"), Osama bin Laden maintained

that America embraced injustice and oppression (of the Arab people) when it both approved and provided direct military aid for the Israeli invasion of Lebanon in 1982. Osama bin Laden, "Your Security is in your own Hands," CNN.com, 8 Apr. 2005, <http://www.cnn.com/2004/WORLD/meast/10/29/bin.laden.transcript/>. In his 24 Nov. 2002 "letter to the American people" bin Laden insists that the corrupt perversions of the world are a direct result of the Western failure to embrace Islamic higher law, what he terms the "Shariah of Allah." Osama bin Laden, "letter to the American people" 24 Nov. 2002, *Guardian Observer*, 8 Apr. 2005, http://www.observer.guradian.co.uk/worldview/story/0,11581,845725,00.html>.

30. Thoreau, "The Last Days of John Brown," *The Essays of Henry D. Thoreau,* ed. Lewis Hyde (New York: North Point Press, 2002) 288.

31. In his 8 November, 1859 lecture on "Courage" before a Boston audience at the Tremont Temple, Ralph Waldo Emerson asserted that John Brown, "that new saint . . . will make the gallows glorious, like the cross." Quoted in "Emerson on Courage," *Transcendental Log: Fresh Discoveries in Newspapers Concerning Emerson, Thoreau, Alcott and Others of the American Literary Renaissance.* ed. Kenneth Walter Cameron (Hartford: Transcendental Books, 1973) 136: bin Laden suggests that attacks against the United States are just since the United States deliberately influences Arab governments in direct violation of the Shariah. In his 2 Nov. 2002 "letter to America," bin Laden asserts, "under your supervision, consent and orders, the governments of our countries which act as your agents, attack us on a daily basis." He further suggests that these governments "prevent our people from establishing the Islamic Shariah, using violence and lies to do so . . . places us in a large prison of fear and subdual . . . steal our Ummah's wealth . . . and acknowledge the existence of [the Jewish state] . . . over the dismembered limbs of their own people." Osama bin Laden, "letter to the American people" 24 Nov. 2002, *Guardian Observer*, 8 Apr. 2005, http://www.observer.guradian.co.uk/worldview/story/0,11581,845725,00.html>.

NOTES TO CHAPTER 2

1. William Shakespeare, "The Life of King Henry V," ed. R. J. Dorius (New Haven: Yale University Press, 1955) Prologue, 1–11.

2. According to Stephen Oates, enraged by the sack of Lawrence and the caning of Sumner, John Brown determined to fight "fire with fire" and redress the wrongs done to Free Soil settlers on 24 May 1856 by killing Pro-Slavery settlers along the Pottawatomie. Stephen B. Oates, *To Purge this Land with Blood: A Biography of John Brown* (Amherst: University of Massachusetts Press, 1984) 133.

3. John Brown called his murder of five Pro-Slavery men a "radical retaliatory measure" in his frustration over the sack of Lawrence. Oates, *Purge this Land with Blood: A Biography of John Brown,* 128.

4. Oswald Garrison Villard, *John Brown: A Biography Fifty Years After,* 80.

5. Oates, *Purge this Land with Blood: A Biography of John Brown,* 84.

6. The Free Soil party, which John Weiss notes was the initiative of Senator Henry Wilson of Boston, was the original designation of the Republican party—derived from the question of Freedom and Slavery in the Territories. John Weiss, *Life and Correspondence of Theodore Parker,* Vol. II (New York: D. Appleton & Company, 1864) 209.

7. John Brown Jr. (hereafter JB Jr.), letters to John Brown (hereafter JB), 20, 24, and 26 May 1856. Villard, *John Brown: A Biography Fifty Years After,* 83.

8. Ibid.
9. Ibid.
10. Ibid, 84.
11. In the wake of his failed business trip to London and Liverpool in 1848, Brown convinced philanthropist Gerrit Smith to provide him with a homestead in the utopian community of free blacks that Smith began in the Adirondack Mountains of New York (in 1846). Smith donated nearly 100,000 acres of land in lots from 40 to 160 acres to Northern blacks willing to build independent lives based on agriculture after the defeat of the equal rights franchise in New York State. When Brown approached Smith, he contended that as a pioneer, he would be able to "show my colored neighbors how such work should be done." Louis A DeCaro Jr, *"Fire from the Midst of You;" A Religious Life of John Brown* (New York: New York University Press, 2002) 165–176.
12. Villard, *John Brown: A Biography Fifty Years After*, 85.
13. Ibid.
14. JB, "A Brief History of John Brown, otherwise (old B) and his family: *as connected with Kansas*; By one who knows." Quoted in Villard, *John Brown: A Biography Fifty Years After*, 87.
15. Ibid.
16. Oates, *To Purge this Land with Blood: A Biography of John Brown*, 97.
17. Ibid, 99, 121.
18. Villard, *John Brown: A Biography Fifty Years After*, 90.
19. Oates, *To Purge this Land with Blood: A Biography of John Brown*, 99.
20. The vote for the Free-State congressman and delegates for a constitutional convention occurred on Oct. 9, 1855, three days after Brown arrived at his sons' claims in North Middle Creek. Oates, *To Purge this Land with Blood: A Biography of John Brown*, 103.
21. See Villard, *John Brown: A Biography Fifty Years After*, 95–108 for a discussion of voting irregularities common in Kansas following its opening as a territory in July, 1854.
22. JB, letter to Mary Brown (hereafter MB), 13 October, 1855.
23. JB, "United States League of Gileadites," Quoted by Louis A. De Caro Jr, *"Fire from the Midst of You:" A Religious Life of John Brown* (New York: New York University Press, 2002) 192.
24. Ibid.
25. In the constitution of the league of Gileadites, Brown contended that by immediately massing and violently attacking slave-catchers, "they will be wholly unprepared with either equipments or mature plans—all with them will be confusion and terror." Ibid, 193.
26. JB wrote, a "lasso might possibly be applied to a slave catcher for once with good effect." Quoted in DeCaro, *"Fire from the Midst of You:" A Religious Life of John Brown*, 193.
27. According to De Caro, Sumner met with both John Brown and the Gileadites in the back room of Rufus Elmer's shoe store, a frequent covert meeting place for Springfield abolitionists. Sumner reputedly spoke to the assembly and then confidentially told Brown that slavery was doomed "but not in your day or mine." De Caro, *"Fire from the Midst of You:" A Religious Life of John Brown*, 193.
28. Brown successively failed as a ministry student, leather tanner, land speculator, stockman, shepherd, and wool merchant before dedicating himself to the fight against the encroachment of the slave-power full-time in 1855. Oates, *To Purge this Land with Blood: A Biography of John Brown*, 13–81.
29. DeCaro, *"Fire from the Midst of You:" A Religious Life of John Brown*, 191.

30. Most historians note that the overwhelming victory of the Pro-Slavery legislature in 1855 was a result of illegal voting by Pro-Slavery residents of
Missouri. Villard suggests that this was not unexpected. In the first territorial election on 29 November, 1854, 'hundreds of residents of Missouri, on
horseback and in wagons, with guns, bowie knives, revolvers and plenty of
whiskey . . . cast 1729 fraudulent votes" electing their delegate, General J.W.
Whitfield, to Congress. Following the 1854 elections, the Kansas *Herald* proclaimed that with the "triumph of the Pro-Slavery party . . . Kansas is saved."
The second major election in Kansas (for the first territorial legislature) took
place on 30 March, 1855; both Pro-Slavery and Free-State settlers believed
that this election would determine the fate of the territory. Missourians again
flooded into Kansas to ensure overwhelming victory at the polls. Meeting on
Jul.16, 1855, the completely Pro-Slavery legislature adopted Missouri statutes as Kansas law. After adopting Missouri statutes, General Stringfellow,
the Speaker of the House, declared rather poignantly, "It is the duty of the
Pro-Slavery Party, the Union men of Kansas Territory, to know but one issue,
Slavery." Villard, *John Brown: A Biography Fifty Years After*, 98–101.
31. Oates, *To Purge this Land with Blood: A Biography of John Brown*, 100.
32. Ibid.
33. Brown called the resolutions passed by the Pawnee legislature the "Bogus
Legislature." Villard, *John Brown: A Biography Fifty Years After*, 102.
34. Ibid, 104.
35. Ibid, 103–104.
36. Ibid,104.
37. Oates, *To Purge this Land with Blood: A Biography of John Brown*, 102.
38. Ibid.
39. Ibid, 106.
40. Ibid, 106; Villard, 118.
41. JB, letter to MB, 16 Dec. 1855. Villard, *John Brown: A Biography Fifty
Years After*, 118.
42. In response to rumors that Robinson and Lane had accepted the Pro-Slavery
laws as part of the agreement that Pro-Slavery militia would stand down
and Missourians would leave the vicinity of Wakurusa, only two miles from
Lawrence, Brown declared that "Lawrence had been betrayed" asserting
that instead of accepting the terms of the treaty that the Free State leaders
had arranged, they ought to conduct a night attack on the Pro-Slavery enemy
to immediately demonstrate the will of the Free State forces. Villard, *John
Brown: A Biography Fifty Years After*,124.
43. During the conduct of negotiations, Robinson convinced a rather inebriated
Governor Shannon to sign a document specifying that "commanders of the
Enrolled Citizens of Lawrence" had the authority to employ enrolled forces
"for the preservation of peace and the protection of the persons and property
of the people of Lawrence and vicinity." Villard, 125
44. JB,letter to MB, undated. Quoted by Oates, *To Purge this Land with Blood:
A Biography of John Brown*,110.
45. JB, letter to Orson Day, 14 Dec. 1855.
46. Atchison *Squatter Sovereign*, quoted in Villard, *John Brown: A Biography
Fifty Years After*, 129: Kansas *Pioneer*, quoted in Oates, *To Purge this Land
with Blood: A Biography of John Brown*, 114.
47. President Franklin Pierce, "Special Address to Congress," 24 Jan. 1856.
Quoted by Oates, *To Purge this Land with Blood: A Biography of John
Brown*, 115.
48. JB, letter to MB, 20 Feb. 1856.
49. Oates, *To Purge this Land with Blood: A Biography of John Brown*, 115.
50. Ibid, 118.

51. Quoted in Villard, *John Brown: A Biography Fifty Years After*, 135.
52. See Villard for the full text of the 16 Apr. 1856 letter repudiating the author-ity of the Pro-Slavery legislature and establishing the intent of many Ossa-watomie settlers to deny the authority of the laws past at Shawnee. Villard, *John Brown: A Biography Fifty Years After*, 135.
53. Jones had arrested six Free-State men for refusing to help him apprehend the leader of the armed Lawrence citizens who had rescued Branson (from his custody) in December; he had arrested Branson for "disturbing the peace" when he called for a protest meeting after Jones failed to charge Charles Dow's murderer. Incensed, Jones called on Governor Shannon to quell the "open rebellion" with the territorial militia. Noted by Oates, *To Purge this Land with Blood: A Biography of John Brown*, 106.
54. Atchison *Squatter Soveriegn*. 6 May 1856. Quoted by Villard, *John Brown: A Biography Fifty Years After*, 141.
55. In a May 9, 1856 anonymous letter from Ossawatomie printed in *The Inde-pendent*, MAJ Buford's militiamen are described as "a rather sorry set of fel-lows. Many of them are profane, drunken, and unacquainted with business, and with but little money to pay their bills." "Buford's Men," *The Indepen-dent*, Vol. VIII, No. 388, 12 Jun. 1856, 1.
56. Villard, *John Brown: A Biography Fifty Years After*, 142.
57. Oates, *To Purge this Land with Blood: A Biography of John Brown*, 125.
58. Villard, *John Brown: A Biography Fifty Years After*, 137, 145.
59. Oates, *To Purge this Land with Blood: A Biography of John Brown*, 127.
60. Oates notes that news of Brooks's attack on Sumner reached Kansas on the evening of 22 May. He suggests that it is probable that Brown, responding to the developments in Lawrence, and particularly attentive to news from that frontier hub, would almost certainly have heard about Sumner's beat-ing sometime on the 22d. Salmon Brown, in a much later interview, recalled hearing the news from a messenger in the morning, though he could not recall the date. Oates, *To Purge this Land with Blood: A Biography of John Brown*, 129.
61. E.A. Coleman recalled a conversation he had with Brown in 1856 where Brown suggested that killing the men on 24 May was in "God's service;" after being queried by Coleman's wife, Brown acknowledged his belief that God "has used me as an instrument to kill men" further noting that "if I live, I think that he will use me as an instrument to kill a good many more." Quoted in Villard, *John Brown: A Biography Fifty Years After*, 179.
62. Brown's metaphorical reference to Cato's court is interesting. Cato, of course, had departed Dutch Henry's Tavern on Apr. 22, 1856. His court, composed largely of local Pro-Slavery men, however, remained in the area. As Oates incisively notes, Judge Cato located his court at the Sherman tav-ern, indicating the tacit support that both William and Henry Sherman provided to the representative of the Pro-Slavery government; James Doyle served as a jury member and his son William served as a bailiff during the contested grand jury hearings; Allen Wilkinson served as district attor-ney pro tem. Oates, *To Purge this Land with Blood: A Biography of John Brown*, 119: Salmon Brown, "John Brown and his Sons in Kansas Terri-tory," *A John Brown Reader* ed. Louis Ruchames (New York: Abelard-Schuman, 1959) 193.
63. Ibid.
64. Oates, *To Purge this Land with Blood: A Biography of John Brown*, 133.
65. Ibid.
66. Villard notes August Bondi's recollections of Brown's indignant response to the news of the unopposed sacking of Lawrence. Villard, *John Brown: A*

Biography Fifty Years After, 152: James Townsley, "The Pottawatomie Tragedy and John Brown's connection with it," *A John Brown Reader*. ed. Louis Ruchames (New York: Abelard-Schuman, 1959) 198: Oates, *To Purge this Land with Blood: A Biography of John Brown*, 133.

67. Oates notes that this was probably the cabin of J.H. Menting, a juror on Judge Cato's court. Oates, *To Purge this Land with Blood: A Biography of John Brown*, 134.
68. Villard, *John Brown: A Biography Fifty Years After*, 159.
69. Townsley, "The Pottawatomie Tragedy and John Brown's connection with it," 199.
70. Oates, *To Purge this Land with Blood: A Biography of John Brown*, 135.
71. Villard, *John Brown: A Biography Fifty Years After* 163.
72. According to Harris's affidavit, Sherman's "skull was split open in two places and some of his brains was washed out by the water. A large hole was cut in his breast, and his left hand we cut off except a little piece of skin on one side." Villard, 164: The rendition that I have presented has been derived from the plethora of historical accounts. I have inserted excerpts from letters, personal testimony, and affidavits in order to present a reasonable facsimile of the events that occurred on the night of 24 May, 1856. My primary sources are Ruchames, Oates, Villard, and Sanborn. It is important to note that both the testimony of the men who participated in the brutal murders and the statements of those who witnessed Brown's leadership on the Pottawatomie that night are far from consistent. There is, however, no doubt that John Brown lead a group of men along the Pottawatomie and murdered five men on the night of 24 May, 1856.
73. Oates, *To Purge this Land with Blood: A Biography of John Brown*, 138.
74. Salmon Brown. "John Brown and his Sons in Kansas Territory," *A John Brown Reader* ed. Louis Ruchames (London: Abelard-Schuman1959) 196.
75. Jason Brown's recollections of his conversations with his father on his return from Pottawatomie. Villard, *John Brown: A Biography Fifty Years After*, 165.
76. Villard privileges both Jason and Salmon Brown's recollections of the meeting between Adair and their father. Villard, *John Brown: A Biography Fifty Years After*, 167.
77. Resolution adopted on 27 May, 1856 signed by C.H. Price, R. Golding, R. Gilpatrick, W.C. McDow, S.V. Vandaman, A. Castele, John Blunt, and H.H. Williams responding to the murders at Pottawatomie. Interestingly, Salmon Brown's account of the event indicates that H.H. Williams was both the man who identified those to be killed and the man who condemned those who did the killing. Villard, *John Brown: A Biography Fifty Years After*, 168.
78. Ibid, 189–193.
79. Governor Shannon, letter to President Franklin Pierce, 31 May, 1856: Villard, *John Brown: A Biography Fifty Years After*, 192.
80. Oates, *To Purge this Land with Blood: A Biography of John Brown*, 140.
81. Leavenworth *Herald*, 27 May, 1856: Oates, *To Purge this Land with Blood: A Biography of John Brown*, 142.
82. William Hutchinson recorded the treatment of those captured at Ossawatomie on 31 May, 1856 in a letter to the New York *Times*, Jun.23, 1856: Oates, *To Purge this Land with Blood: A Biography of John Brown*, 145.
83. Brown courted the press during his tenure as a guerilla commander in Kansas. Not only did he write accounts of his battles subsequently published in Eastern newspapers like the New York *Tribune*, he met and developed relationships with various correspondents in order to tell his own story. James Redpath, William A. Phillips, Richard J. Hinton, and various other men

served Brown well publishing his accounts in both newspapers and books, thereby feeding eager Eastern audiences with tales of Brown's personal bravery and privation. Oates, *To Purge this Land with Blood: A Biography of John Brown*, 159.

84. In his June, 1856 letter to his family, Brown recounts his success at Black Jack suggesting that through his superior skill as a military leader, with nine men, he was able to capture a force of twenty-three. He neglects to mention that he captured Pate's Missouri force after he had coerced Pate, who had approached him under a flag of truce, to surrender. Quoted in Ruchames, 96.

85. JB, letter to MB, 7 Sep. 1856. Louis Ruchames, ed. *The John Brown Reader*. (New York: Abelard-Schuman, 1959), 99.

86. Brown and his men looted Bernard's Store on June 3, 1856 of $3000 to $4000 worth of supplies and "several horse and cows." Oates, *To Purge this Land with Blood: A Biography of John Brown*, 155.

87. Capt. Pate's account of the battle of Black Jack Point and his abuse at the hand of John Brown appeared in the "Battle of Black-Jack Point—Exploits of Captain Pate and is Southern Company, as Detailed by Himself," New York *Daily Times*, Jun. 17, 1856, 2.

88. Ibid.

89. With the intervention of the U.S. Army at Lawrence in mid-September, and a new agreement to peacefully settle their differences, Pro-Slavery forces retreated back into Missouri and relative calm spread over Kansas. Determining that the atmosphere in Kansas either no longer required his presence or hearing that Governor Geary, who was fairly enforcing the law, intended to arrest him, John Brown left Kansas in October, 1856 with those of his sons who had lived through the civil war. The exact date that he decided to travel East to gain support for the fight for freedom is not known. Oates, *To Purge this Land with Blood: A Biography of John Brown*, 174–77.

90. Richard Boyd, "Models of Power in Harriet Beecher Stowe's Dred." *Studies in American Fiction*, (19 Spring, 1991), 55.

91. Ibid.

92. Ellen Emerson, letter to an unspecified recipient, Jun. 1856; Len Gougeon, *Virtue's Hero: Emerson, Anti-Slavery, and Reform*. (Athens: University of Georgia Press, 1990), 223.

93. Gougeon, *Virtue's Hero: Emerson, Anti-Slavery, and Reform*, 218.

94. Jeffrey Rossbach, *Ambivalent Conspirators: John Brown, the Secret Six, and a Theory of Slave Violence* (Philadelphia: University of Pennsylvania Press, 1992) 52.

95. Rossbach, *Ambivalent Conspirators: John Brown, the Secret Six, and a Theory of Slave Violence*, 53.

96. Henry D. Thoreau, *The Writings of Henry David Thoreau, Journal* IX, ed. Bradford Torrey (Boston: Houghton Mifflin Company, 1906) 36: Robert D. Richardson Jr., *Henry Thoreau: A Life of the Mind* (Berkeley: University of California Press, 1986) 345.

97. Richardson notes that in 1855, Sanborn began boarding in the Thoreau house in Concord. He remained a border for the next three years seeing Henry "almost daily." Robert D. Richardson, Jr. *Henry Thoreau: A Life of the Mind* (Berkeley: University of California Press, 1986) 331.

98. In the fall of 1856, Sanborn sought out and gained the position as secretary for the Massachusetts State Kansas Committee. This was both a more powerful and more influential committee than the Middlesex County Kansas Committee where he had previously worked for the Kansas cause. Sanborn to Theodore Parker, letter dated 28 Nov. 1856. Rossbach, 53.

99. Gougeon, *Virtue's Hero: Emerson, Anti-Slavery, and Reform*, 224.

100. Henry D. Thoreau, "Slavery in Massachusetts," *The Essays of Henry D. Thoreau*, ed. Lewis Hyde (New York: North Point Press, 2002) 182–194.
101. F.B. Sanborn, *Recollections of Seventy Years* (New York: Gorham Press, 1909), 103.
102. Ibid.
103. Edward J. Renehan, *The Secret Six: the True Tale of the Men Who Conspired with John Brown* (New York: Crown Publishers, 1995), 117.
104. Ibid.
105. Ralph Waldo Emerson. *The Journals and Miscellaneous Notebooks of Ralph Waldo Emerson*, Vol. XIV. eds. Susan Sutton Smith and Harrison Hayford (Cambridge: Belknap Press of Harvard University, 1978) 125.
106. Ralph Waldo Emerson, "John Brown," *The Selected Writings of Ralph Waldo Emerson*. ed. Brooks Atkinson (New York: The Modern Library, 1950) 881.
107. Ibid, 879.
108. Phillis Cole "Pain and Protest in the Emerson Family," The *Emerson Dilemma: Essays on Emerson and Social Reform*. ed. T. Gregory Garvey (University of Georgia Press: Athens, 2001) 85.
109. Emerson entertained Brown at his home on one evening during his fundraising trip to Concord in 1857. Brown's convictions were later translated in Emerson's 1859 speech on John Brown. Robert D. Richardson, Jr. *Emerson: The Mind on Fire* (University of California Press: Berkeley, 1995) 499.
110. Rossbach, *Ambivalent Conspirators: John Brown, the Secret Six, and a Theory of Slave Violence*, 84.
111. Despite his clear embrace of the "glory intrinsic in the white man fighting with arms to end slavery" and his conviction that in Kansas, there was a real promise of revolution, Higginson did not commit any funds when he met Brown on Jan. 9, 1857. Tilden G. Edelstein, *Strange Enthusiasm: A Life of Thomas Wentworth Higginson* (New Haven: Yale University Press, 1968) 196.
112. Rossbach, *Ambivalent Conspirators: John Brown, the Secret Six, and a Theory of Slave Violence*, 96–97.
113. Ibid, 111.
114. Ibid.
115. Ibid, 101.
116. Villard, *John Brown: A Biography Fifty Years After*, 275.
117. Ibid, 288.
118. Renehan, *The Secret Six: the True Tale of the Men Who Conspired with John Brown*, 120.
119. United States Sen. *Inquiry into the late invasion and seizure of the public Property at Harper's Ferry* (S. Rpt. 278) (Washington: Government Printing Office, 1860) 227–28: Renehan, *The Secret Six: the True Tale of the Men Who Conspired with John Brown* 120.
120. Rossbach, *Ambivalent Conspirators: John Brown, the Secret Six, and a Theory of Slave Violence*,113.
121. Failing to recognize the over-inflation of land value like many of his contemporaries, Brown went bankrupt during the depression of 1837. Villard, *John Brown: A Biography Fifty Years After*, 291.
122. JB, letters to George Luther Stearns (hereafter GLS), 8 and 10 Aug. 1857: Villard, *John Brown: A Biography Fifty Years After*, 297.
123. Rossbach, *Ambivalent Conspirators: John Brown, the Secret Six, and a Theory of Slave Violence*, 132.
124. Ibid.
125. To add to the disappointing atmosphere in Tabor, Forbes and Brown discovered that the weapons that the Massachusetts Kansas Committee provided

them were not anything close to modern Sharp's Rifles. In fact, most of them were muskets manufactured in 1790, and only one of those was in operational condition. The only worthy weapons were two hundred revolvers that Stearns had recently purchased. Renehan, *The Secret Six: the True Tale of the Men Who Conspired with John Brown,* 127.

126. Ibid, 128.
127. Villard, *John Brown: A Biography Fifty Years After,* 292.
128. JB, letter to GLS, 16 Nov. 1857: Villard, *John Brown: A Biography Fifty Years After,* 305.
129. Villard, *John Brown: A Biography Fifty Years After,* 308.
130. After his capture at Harpers Ferry, John Cook confessed to learning of Brown's plan to begin a rebellion of slaves in Virginia during the journey from Kansas to Ohio in the late fall of 1857. Villard, *John Brown: A Biography Fifty Years After,* 308.
131. John Brown's declaration was recalled in 1908 by L.F. Parsons. Quoted in Villard, *John Brown: A Biography Fifty Years After,* 310.
132. Villard, *John Brown: A Biography Fifty Years After,* 316.
133. Renehan, *The Secret Six: the True Tale of the Men Who Conspired with John Brown,* 128.
134. Hugh Forbes, letter to Dr. S.G. Howe (hereafter SGH), 14 May 1858: Villard, *John Brown: A Biography Fifty Years After,* 313–314.
135. JB, letter to Thomas Wentworth Higginson (hereafter TWH), 2 Feb. 1858: TWH, *Cheerful Yesterdays* (New York: Arno Press, 1968), 216–217.
136. Renehan, *The Secret Six: the True Tale of the Men Who Conspired with John Brown,* 139.
137. Ibid.
138. Franklin B. Sanborn (hereafter FBS), letter to JB, 12 Jan. 1858: Rossbach, *Ambivalent Conspirators: John Brown, the Secret Six, and a Theory of Slave Violence,* 134.
139. Sanborn informed Brown that in the letter he had received from Forbes, the veteran of the Italian Revolution had called "one a cheat and accuses one of lying and other iniquities," referring to Brown's New England supporters. FBS, letter to JB, 12 Jan. 1858: Renehan, *The Secret Six: the True Tale of the Men Who Conspired with John Brown,* 139.
140. Quoted by Renehan, *The Secret Six: the True Tale of the Men Who Conspired with John Brown,* 140.

NOTES TO CHAPTER 3

1. Free State voters had been successful in electing 33 of 52 Free State representatives in the territorial legislature and a Free State representative in Congress. Additionally, they had defeated the effort to advance a Pro-Slavery constitution to the United States Congress. Oates, *To Purge this Land with Blood: A Biography of John Brown,* 217.
2. Brown and Douglass discussed Brown's ideas about a slave insurrection sporadically during the years following their introduction in Springfield, Ohio in 1847. Frederick Douglass, *Life and Times,* 1883, *Autobiographies* (New York: Library of America, 1994) 717–19, 754–55.
3. Ibid, 718.
4. Ibid.
5. Ibid, 719.
6. Ibid, 754.
7. Ibid, 755.

8. Oates, *To Purge this Land with Blood: A Biography of John Brown*, 224.
9. Ibid.
10. Forbes used the term "New England humanitarians" to refer to Brown's primary financial supporters. Villard, *John Brown: A Biography Fifty Years After*, 299.
11. Rossbach, *Ambivalent Conspirators: John Brown, the Secret Six, and a Theory of Slave Violence*, 136.
12. JB, letter to TWH, 2 Feb. 1858. TWH, *Cheerful Yesterdays*. (New York: Arno Press and New York Times, 1968) 218.
13. Higginson had been one of two men to cross the doorway of the courthouse in Boston in a poorly executed attempt to free Anthony Burns, an escaped slave who was being held in the Court House prior to his return to slavery, in accordance with the Fugitive Slave Law. Although Higginson and his fellow conspirators failed to free Burns (and he received a cutlass wound to the chin), Higginson earned both a reputation for radical abolition and inspired others to consider violent opposition to immoral slave laws as a result of his bold efforts at the Boston Court House. Rossbach, *Ambivalent Conspirators: John Brown, the Secret Six, and a Theory of Slave Violence*, 30–35: Higginson includes Brown's two letters appealing for funds in *Cheerful Yesterdays*, 216–18.
14. TWH, letter to JB, 8 Feb. 1858: Tilden G. Edelstein, *Strange Enthusiasm: a Life of Thomas Wentworth Higginson*. (New Haven:Yale University Press, 1968) 208.
15. JB, letter to TWH, 2 Feb. 1858: TWH, *Cheerful Yesterdays*, 216–217.
16. Ibid, 218.
17. Brown explained the details of his plan to Smith, Sanborn, and Edward Morton (Smith's children's tutor and Sanborn's Harvard classmate) at Smith's home in Peterboro, New York on 22 Feb. 1858. Edelstein, 209: TWH, letter to Hawkins (the name Brown assumed while courting those that would become the Secret Six), 8 Feb. 1858: Edelstein, *Strange Enthusiasm: a Life of Thomas Wentworth Higginson*, 208.
18. Rossbach, *Ambivalent Conspirators: John Brown, the Secret Six, and a Theory of Slave Violence*, 144.
19. FBS, letter to Theodore Parker (hereafter TP), 15 Jan. 1858: Oates, *To Purge this Land with Blood: A Biography of John Brown*, 226.
20. In addition to the assurances Frederick Douglass had made him, Brown revealed his plan to Dr. and Mrs. J.N. Gloucester and J.W. Louguen, both affluent free blacks, who assured him of their support. Villard, *John Brown: A Biography Fifty Years After*, 323.
21. In his 3 December 1860 "Address on John Brown's contributions to the Abolitionist Movement," Frederick Douglass celebrates the "John Brown way" of bringing about the end to slavery. *The Frederick Douglass Papers: Series One: Speeches, Debates and Interviews*, Vol. 3., ed. John W. Blassingame (New Haven: Yale University Press, 1985) 413.
22. TP, "The Present Aspect of Slavery and the Immediate Duty of the North," [a speech given in Jan. 29, 1858] in Works (Cobbe Edition), 6: 289: Rossbach, *Ambivalent Conspirators: John Brown, the Secret Six, and a Theory of Slave Violence*, 148–149.
23. Rossbach, *Ambivalent Conspirators: John Brown, the Secret Six, and a Theory of Slave Violence*, 148.
24. From his own experiences during the Anthony Burns' case, Higginson was sure that blacks were both capable of violence and ready to engage in violent action in opposition to slavery; aside a black man, Higginson had attempted to penetrate the Boston Court House to rescue Burn's in the ill-fated 1854 attempt to secure the fugitive before he was returned to South Carolina.

Rossbach, *Ambivalent Conspirators: John Brown, the Secret Six, and a Theory of Slave Violence,* 33, 150.

25. Rossbach, *Ambivalent Conspirators: John Brown, the Secret Six, and a Theory of Slave Violence,* 149–50.

26. Brown acknowledged, during the secret convention in Chatham, that he had been thinking about freeing the slaves in America for the past thirty years. Oates, *To Purge this Land with Blood: A Biography of John Brown,* 244.

27. Martin Delany, *The Condition, Elevation, Emigration, and Destiny of the Colored People of the United States* (1852: rpt, New York: Arno Press and New York Times, 1968) 45.

28. Quoted by Oates, *To Purge this Land with Blood: A Biography of John Brown,* 244.

29. JB, "Provisional Constitution and Ordinances for the People of the United States," *The Life, Trial and Execution of Captain John Brown* (1859: rpt: New York: De Capo Press, 1969) 51–54.

30. Oates, *To Purge this Land with Blood: A Biography of John Brown,* 248.

31. SGH, letter to Senator Henry Wilson, 12 May 1858: Villard, *John Brown: A Biography Fifty Years After,* 341.

32. SGH, letter to Hugh Forbes, 10 May 1858: Rossbach, *Ambivalent Conspirators: John Brown, the Secret Six, and a Theory of Slave Violence,* 163.

33. Villard, *John Brown: A Biography Fifty Years After,* 299.

34. Gerrit Smith (hereafter GS), letter to FBS, 7 May, 1858: Franklin Benjamin Sanborn, *The Life and Letters of John Brown.* (Boston: Roberts Bros., 1885) 448.

35. TWH, letter to TP, 9 May 1858: Renehan, *The Secret Six: the True Tale of the Men Who Conspired with John Brown,* 152: TWH, letter to TP, 18 May 1858: Rossbach, *Ambivalent Conspirators: John Brown, the Secret Six, and a Theory of Slave Violence,* 168.

36. The term stockholder, which I employ to describe the six men who were Brown's primary financiers was used by TWH in a May 7, 1858 letter to John Brown's son, Jason. Higginson laments the fact that the "leading stockholders" had so much influence over Brown, though he understood Brown's reasons for consenting to their wishes. TWH, letter to JB Jr., 7 May, 1858.

37. Rossbach, *Ambivalent Conspirators: John Brown, the Secret Six, and a Theory of Slave Violence,* 173.

38. TWH, memorandum of 1 June 1858 meeting with John Brown: Villard, *John Brown: A Biography Fifty Years After,* 340.

39. Ibid.

40. Mary Thacher Higginson, *Thomas Wentworth Higginson: The Story of His Life* (Boston: Houghton Mifflin Compay, 1914) 192.

41. Following the news of the delay, Realf appealed to several members of the Secret Six for funding to enable him to travel to England and raise money for future operations. Stating that he was intimate with the likes of "Lady Noel Byron, Charles Kingsley, and others of the aristocracy and literati," Realf believed that in a relative short time, he could raise over $2000 for future operations. Richard Realf to FBS, letter dated May 29, 1858: Renehan, *The Secret Six: the True Tale of the Men Who Conspired with John Brown,* 167.

42. Oates, *To Purge this Land with Blood: A Biography of John Brown,* 253.

43. JB, letter to JB Jr., 6 Aug. 1858: Villard, *John Brown: A Biography Fifty Years After,* 354.

44. JB, letter to FBS, 10 & 13 Sep. 1858: Renehan, *The Secret Six: the True Tale of the Men Who Conspired with John Brown,* 171–172.

45. Villard, *John Brown: A Biography Fifty Years After,* 366.

46. Ibid, 367.
47. Ibid.
48. Oates, *To Purge this Land with Blood: A Biography of John Brown*, 263.
49. Ibid.
50. JB, "Old Brown's Parallels," *A John Brown Reader*, ed. Louis Ruchames (New York: Abelard-Schuman, 1959) 115
51. Captain James Montgomery, letter to the Editor of the Lawrence *Republican*, 15 Jan. 1859. Quoted by Villard, *John Brown: A Biography Fifty Years After*, 377.
52. JB, letter to James Montgomery, 2 Jan. 1859: Villard, *John Brown: A Biography Fifty Years After*, 373.
53. JB, letter to the Editor of the Kansas *Trading Post*, January 1859: Villard, *John Brown: A Biography Fifty Years After*, 376.
54. GS, letter to his wife, 10 Jan. 1859: Oates, *To Purge this Land with Blood: A Biography of John Brown*, 262.
55. Oates, *To Purge this Land with Blood: A Biography of John Brown*, 265.
56. Villard notes that after they left Kansas, there was one private attempt to arrest Brown and Kagi in Iowa City. Villard, *John Brown: A Biography Fifty Years After*, 388.
57. Villard, *John Brown: A Biography Fifty Years After*, 377.
58. In his 2 Feb. 1858 note to Higginson, Brown noted that he needed between "$500 to $800" in order perfect "BY FAR the most *important* undertaking of my whole life." Quoted by TWH, *Cheerful Yesterdays*, 217.
59. Oates, *To Purge this Land with Blood: A Biography of John Brown*, 267.
60. Oates, *To Purge this Land with Blood: A Biography of John Brown*, 266.
61. While in Cleveland, Brown lectured on Kansas on his underground railroad mission. During this lecture, he acknowledged the $250 reward that President Buchanon had offered for his capture, characteristically offering a reward of two dollars and fifty cents for capture of the President. Brown's remarks were printed in the 22 March, 1859 Cleveland *Plain Dealer*: Oates, *To Purge this Land with Blood: A Biography of John Brown*, 267.
62. Cleveland *Plain Dealer*, 22 Mar. 1859: Villard, *John Brown: A Biography Fifty Years After*, 392.
63. Villard, *John Brown: A Biography Fifty Years After*, 394.
64. GS, letter to JB, 22 Jan. 1859. Quoted in FBS, *The Life and Letters of John Brown* (Boston: Roberts Bros., 1885) 483.
65. Ibid.
66. Renehan, *The Secret Six: the True Tale of the Men Who Conspired with John Brown*, 182.
67. Bronson Alcott on JB, May 1859. Oates, *To Purge this Land with Blood: A Biography of John Brown*, 269: Ralph Waldo Emerson, "Speech at a Meeting to Aid John Brown's Family," *Emerson's Anti-Slavery Writings*, eds. Len Gougeon and Joel Myerson (New Haven: Yale University Press, 1995) 118.
68. RWE, *JMN* 14:125: Robert D. Jr. Richardson, *Emerson: The Mind on Fire* (University of California Press: Berkeley, 1995) 370.
69. Oates, *To Purge this Land with Blood: A Biography of John Brown*, 270.
70. In a letter to Theodore Parker, John Brown voiced his theory that "[f]emales are susceptible of being carried away entirely by kindness of an intrepid and magnanimous soldier." Evidently, he applied the same theory in appeal to both Mary Preston Stearns and Julia Ward Howe. JB, letter to TP, 7 Mar. 1858: Sanborn, *Life and Letters of John Brown*, 449.
71. Quoted by Oates, *To Purge this Land with Blood: A Biography of John Brown*, 270.

72. In a 13 May letter from Boston, John Brown told his wife Mary that "I feel now very confident of *ultimate success.*" JB, letter to MB, 13 May 1859: Villard, *John Brown: A Biography Fifty Years After,* 398.
73. JB, letter to TWH, 2 Feb. 1858: Higginson, *Cheerful Yesterdays,* 217.
74. Oates, *To Purge this Land with Blood: A Biography of John Brown,* 272.
75. Villard, *John Brown: A Biography Fifty Years After,* 408.
76. In addition to his own efforts to rally men to his standard over the previous two years, Brown tasked his son, John Jr. to actively recruit men for the mission as he traveled east from Ohio. Oates, *To Purge this Land with Blood: A Biography of John Brown,* 273.
77. Recalling the summer of 1859, Annie Brown remarks on a particularly inquisitive neighbor (Mrs. Huffmaster) who made concealment of the men at the Kennedy Farm a difficult task. Villard, *John Brown: A Biography Fifty Years After,* 416–420.
78. Ibid.
79. Oates, *To Purge this Land with Blood: A Biography of John Brown,* 276.
80. Owen Smith's 18 Aug. 1859 letter indicates that Brown recently revealed the full details of his Harpers Ferry plan. Villard, *John Brown: A Biography Fifty Years After,* 416.
81. Oates, *To Purge this Land with Blood: A Biography of John Brown,* 278.
82. Ibid, 279.
83. Ibid, 280.
84. Ibid, 280.
85. Ibid, 280.
86. Owen Smith, letter to JB, 18 Aug. 1859, Villard, *John Brown: A Biography Fifty Years After,* 416.
87. William Leeman, letter to his Mother, 9 Sep. 1859: Oates, *To Purge this Land with Blood: A Biography of John Brown,* 281.
88. On March 30, 1857, Brown commissioned Blair to produce 1000 pikes at one dollar a piece suggesting his intention, as early as 1857 of engaging in the business of a Southern guerilla campaign. With the $2000 that his secret benefactors had provided him, Brown completed payment for the pikes in June 1859. Rossbach, *Ambivalent Conspirators: John Brown, the Secret Six, and a Theory of Slave Violence,* 107, 207.
89. Following the cessation of the preponderance of hostilities in Kansas in 1858, Stearns bought back the 200 Sharps carbines that the Massachusetts State Kansas Committee had originally purchased and supplied to Brown. Stearns chose to give Brown the weapons "with no restrictions" for his raid at Harpers Ferry. Noted by Franklin Benjamin Sanborn, *The Life and Letters of John Brown* (Boston: Roberts Bros., 1885) 465.
90. In his account of the Chatham convention, Brown repeatedly uses the word negro to designate both free African-Americans who "were to constitute the soldiers" of his Provisional Army. Villard, *John Brown: A Biography Fifty Years After* 332.
91. Renehan, *The Secret Six: the True Tale of the Men Who Conspired with John Brown,* 148.
92. FBS, letter to TWH, 4 Jun. 1859: Edelstein, *Strange Enthusiasm: A Life of Thomas Wentworth Higginson,* 218–219.
93. Frederick Douglass, *Life and Times of Frederick Douglass in Autobiographies* (New York: Library of America, 1994) 760.
94. Ibid, 759.
95. Ibid.
96. Ibid.

97. Ibid.
98. In May, Brown left Boston with $2000 that the secret committee had provided him. Renehan, *The Secret Six: the True Tale of the Men Who Conspired with John Brown*, 191.
99. FBS, letter to TWH, 19 Apr. 1859: Edelstein, 217.
100. FBS, letter to JB, 27 Aug. 1859: Renehan, *The Secret Six: the True Tale of the Men Who Conspired with John Brown*, 192.
101. FBS, letter to TWH, 24 Aug. 1859: Edelstein, *Strange Enthusiasm: A Life of Thomas Wentworth Higginson*, 219.
102. Edelstein, 2 *The Secret Six: the True Tale of the Men Who Conspired with John Brown*, 19.
103. Renehan, *The Secret Six: the True Tale of the Men Who Conspired with John Brown*, 193.
104. Anon. (later attributed to David J. Gue), letter to the Hon. Mr. Floyd, Secretary of War, 23 Aug. 1859: Villard, *John Brown: A Biography Fifty Years After*, 410.
105. Ibid.
106. Villard, *John Brown: A Biography Fifty Years After*, 410.
107. Oates, *To Purge this Land with Blood: A Biography of John Brown*, 285.
108. Ibid, 284.
109. GS, letter to John Thomas, Chairman Jerry Rescue Committee, 27 Aug. 1859: New York *Times*, Oct. 20, 1859, 1.
110. Ibid.
111. "Gerrit Smith on Insurrection," The New York *Times*, Oct. 20, 1859, 1.
112. Edelstein, *Strange Enthusiasm: a Life of Thomas Wentworth Higginson*, 215.
113. John A. Alexander, "The Ideas of Lyander Spooner," *New England Quarterly* 23 (June, 1850) 204, 207: Rossbach, *Ambivalent Conspirators: John Brown, the Secret Six, and a Theory of Slave Violence*, 186.
114. TWH, letter to Lysander Spooner, 30 Nov. 1858: Renehan, *The Secret Six: the True Tale of the Men Who Conspired with John Brown*, 175–176.
115. Renehan, *The Secret Six: the True Tale of the Men Who Conspired with John Brown*, 175.
116. TP, letter to Lysander Spooner, 30 Nov. 1858: Renehan, *The Secret Six: the True Tale of the Men Who Conspired with John Brown*, 175. Renehan notes that Francis Jackson also received a letter from Spooner requesting his endorsement for his "Plan for the Abolition of Slavery." Jackson, a Garrisonian, refused to do so due to his belief that the end of slavery could be achieved by peaceful means. Renehan, *The Secret Six: the True Tale of the Men Who Conspired with John Brown*, 194.
117. Lysander Spooner, letter to Octavious Brooks Frothingham, 26 Feb. 1878: Renehan, *The Secret Six: the True Tale of the Men Who Conspired with John Brown*, 175.
118. TWH, *Cheerful Yesterdays*, 222.
119. Edelstein, *Strange Enthusiasm: a Life of Thomas Wentworth Higginson*, 220.
120. Francis Merriam, letter to Wendell Phillips, 22 Sep. 1859: Edelstein, *Strange Enthusiasm: a Life of Thomas Wentworth Higginson*, 219.
121. Oates, *To Purge this Land with Blood: A Biography of John Brown*, 289.
122. Brown left a rear guard of three men (his son Owen, Barclay Coppoc and Francis Merriam) in the Kennedy farmhouse on Oct. 16, 1859 when he initiated his attack on Harpers Ferry. Villard, *John Brown: A Biography Fifty Years After*, 426.

123. Oates, *To Purge this Land with Blood: A Biography of John Brown*, 291.
124. Ibid, 292.
125. Ibid, 291–92.
126. Villard, *John Brown: A Biography Fifty Years After*, 431.
127. Ibid, 432.
128. Ibid, 432.
129. Oates, *To Purge this Land with Blood: A Biography of John Brown*, 292.
130. Villard notes the rapid response of the Jefferson Guards, a militia unit from nearby Charlestown as proof of the real concern that Southern slaveholders had when notified of a slave insurrection. Villard, *John Brown: A Biography Fifty Years After*, 436.
131. The conductor of the train sent a telegraph indicating that 150 insurrectionists were in Harpers Ferry intent on freeing the slaves "at all hazards." Conductor Phelps sent the telegraph to the master of transportation in Baltimore as soon as he reached Monocacy, the first town on his route after Harpers Ferry, and strongly suggested that W.P. Smith "notify the Secretary of War at once." Villard, *John Brown: A Biography Fifty Years After*, 433.
132. Renehan, *The Secret Six: the True Tale of the Men Who Conspired with John Brown*, 201.
133. Oates, *To Purge this Land with Blood: A Biography of John Brown*, 299.
134. Ibid, 295.
135. Villard, *John Brown: A Biography Fifty Years After*, 433.
136. Oates, *To Purge this Land with Blood: A Biography of John Brown*, 295.
137. Ibid.
138. Villard, *John Brown: A Biography Fifty Years After*, 440.
139. Ibid, 445.
140. New York *Times*, 19 Oct. 1859: New York *Tribune*, 19 Oct. 1859: Oates, 298.
141. Villard, *John Brown: A Biography Fifty Years After*, 449.
142. Oates, *To Purge this Land with Blood: A Biography of John Brown*, 297.
143. Villard includes an excerpt of J.E.B. Stuart's letter to his mother from Fort Riley, January, 1860 as a record of the events that occurred between 17 and 18 October, 1859. Villard, *John Brown: A Biography Fifty Years After*, 450–51.
144. Robert E. Lee, letter to "Persons in the Armory Buildings" [John Brown], 18 Oct. 1859, United States Senate. *Inquiry into the late invasion and seizure of the public Property at Harper's Ferry* (S. Rpt. 278), (Washington: Government Printing Office, 1860), 43–44.
145. Robert E. Lee, "Report to the Adjutant General," 19 October 1859. United States Senate. *Inquiry into the late invasion and seizure of the public Property at Harper's Ferry* (S. Rpt. 278), (Washington: Government Printing Office, 1860) 41.
146. J.E.B. Stuart, letter to Mother (from Fort Riley), Jan. 1860: Villard, *John Brown: A Biography Fifty Years After*, 450–451.
147. Robert E. Lee, "Report to the Adjutant General," 19 October 1859. United States Senate, *Inquiry into the late invasion and seizure of the public Property at Harper's Ferry* (S. Rpt. 278), (Washington: Government Printing Office, 1860), 44.
148. Of Brown's twenty-one men, ten were either killed or fatally wounded during the attack; five others were captured and seven escaped (two however, were later captured). Oates, *To Purge this Land with Blood: A Biography of John Brown*, 302.
149. Quoted in Villard, *John Brown: A Biography Fifty Years After*, 456.

150. "A Conversation with Brown," *The Life, Trial, and Execution of Captain John Brown* (New York: De Capo Press, 1969) 45.
151. Ibid.
152. Ibid.
153. Ibid.
154. Ibid.
155. Ibid, 47.
156. Governor Henry Wise, "Speech of 21 Oct. 1859." Quoted in Villard, *John Brown: A Biography Fifty Years After,* 455.
157. Baltimore *American and Commercial Advertiser,* 21 Oct. 1859: Oates, *To Purge this Land with Blood: A Biography of John Brown,* 303.
158. Oates, *To Purge this Land with Blood: A Biography of John Brown,* 322.
159. Ibid, 323.
160. Executive Committee, *Annual Report* of the American Anti-Slavery Society (1861: New York: Negro University Press, 1969) 169.
161. Ibid, 167.
162. Henry Wise, "The John Brown Invasion," The New York *Times*: 8 Dec. 1859: 2
163. Ibid.
164. "Insurrection at the South," The New York *Times,* Oct. 24, 1859.
165. Oates, *To Purge this Land with Blood: A Biography of John Brown,* 310.
166. Ibid.
167. Abraham Lincoln, "Cooper Union Address," Feb. 7, 1860: Oates, *To Purge this Land with Blood: A Biography of John Brown,* 310.
168. Compromising letters from Sanborn, Howe, Smith, and Douglass were discovered at the Kennedy Farm and were published in the 21 Oct. 1859 New York *Tribune.*
169. "Northern Abolitionists Apparently Implicated," The New York *Times,* Oct. 20, 1859, 1; United States Senate, *Inquiry into the late invasion and seizure of the public Property at Harper's Ferry* (S. Rpt. 278), (Washington: Government Printing Office, 1860) 13.
170. Edelstein, *Strange Enthusiasm: A Life of Thomas Wentworth Higginson,* 223.
171. TWH, letter to his Mother, 5 Nov. 1859: Mary Thacher Higginson, ed. *The Letters and Journals of Thomas Wentworth Higginson 1846–1906,* (Boston: Houghton Mifflin Company, 1921) 87.
172. Oates, *To Purge this Land with Blood: A Biography of John Brown,* 301.
173. Governor Henry Wise, "Speech of 21 Oct. 1859": Villard, *John Brown: A Biography Fifty Years After,* 469.
174. Message of Governor Wise to the Virginia Legislature, Dec. 5, 1859: Villard, *John Brown: A Biography Fifty Years After,* 465.
175. "The Trial of John Brown," *The Life Trial, and Execution of Captain John Brown* (New York: De Capo Press, 1969) 55.
176. JB, Statement to the Circuit Court at Charlestown, 27 Oct. 1859, "The Trial of John Brown," *The Life Trial, and Execution of Captain John Brown* (New York: De Capo Press, 1969) 55.
177. Clarence Botts, defense attorney for John Brown, "The Trial of John Brown," *The Life, Trial, and Execution of Captain John Brown* (New York: De Capo Press, 1969) 64.
178. Ibid.
179. Ibid, 64–65.
180. Andrew Hunter, special prosecutor for the Commonwealth of Virginia, "The Trial of John Brown," *The Life, Trial, and Execution of Captain John Brown* (New York: De Capo Press, 1969) 65–66.

181. Twenty-one year old George H. Hoyt was sent to Harpers Ferry by J. W. Le Barnes to provide information about the measures taken to protect Brown. Oates, *To Purge this Land with Blood: A Biography of John Brown,* 316: John Brown, "Statement to the Circuit Court at Charlestown," 29 Oct. 1859, "The Trial of John Brown," *The Life Trial, and Execution of Captain John Brown* (New York: De Capo Press, 1969) 76.

182. Andrew Hunter, Special Prosecutor during trial of John Brown. Quoted in Villard, *John Brown: A Biography Fifty Years After,* 496.

183. "The Trial of John Brown," *The Life, Trial and Execution of Captain John Brown,* (1859 Reprint, New York: Da Capo Press, 1969) 94–95.

184. New York *Journal of Commerce.* Quoted in the *Liberator* Vol. XXIX. No. 44, 4 Nov. 1859: 1.

185. Henry Wise, "Document No. I, Dec. 1859," *Journal of the House of Delegates.* Quoted in Villard, *John Brown: A Biography Fifty Years After,* 505.

186. JB, letter to "Dear Brother" Jeremiah, 12 Nov. 1859: Lawrence *Republican,* 8 Dec. 1859: Ruchames, *The John Brown Reader,* 134.

187. Villard notes that Brown received frequent visitors during his incarceration. Even those who had fought him at Harper's Ferry visited and discovered the freedom fighter cordial and pleasant. Villard, *John Brown: A Biography Fifty Years After,* 544.

188. James Redpath, "Reminiscences of the Insurrection," Boston *Atlas & Bee,* 24 Oct. 1859: Oates, *To Purge this Land with Blood: A Biography of John Brown,* 317.

189. Charlestown *Independent Democrat,* 22 Nov. 1859: Villard, *John Brown: A Biography Fifty Years After,* 545.

190. "John Brown's Speech," New York *Times,* 3 Nov. 1859: 4.

191. JB, letter to his wife and family, 12 Nov. 1859: Oates, *To Purge this Land with Blood: A Biography of John Brown,* 338.

192. JB, letter to Dear Friend E.B. of RI, 1 Nov. 1859: *The Liberator,* 11 Nov. 1859, 1.

193. JB. letter to J B Musgrave Esqr., 17 Nov. 1859: Ruchames, *The John Brown Reader,* 139.

194. Lydia Maria Child, letter to JB, 26 Oct. 26, 1859: *The Liberator,* 11 Nov. 1859, 1.

195. JB, letter to Lydia Maria Child, 4 Nov. 1859: Ruchames, *The John Brown Reader,* 131–132

196. JB, letter to TWH, 4 Nov. 1859; Ruchames, *The John Brown Reader,* 130.

197. JB, letter to Rev. Luther Humphrey, 19 Nov. 1859: Ruchames, *The John Brown Reader,* 139–140

198. RWE, "Speech at a Meeting to Aid John Brown's Family (18 Nov. 1859)," *Emerson's Anti-Slavery Writings,* eds. Len Gougeon and Joel Myerson, (New Haven: Yale University Press, 1995) 117.

199. Ibid, 118.

200. HDT, "A Plea for Captain John Brown," *The Essays of Henry D. Thoreau,* ed. Lewis Hyde (New York: North Point Press, 2002) 262.

201. JB, letter to MB, 10 Nov. 1859: Villard, *John Brown: A Biography Fifty Years After* 540–541.

202. Ibid.

203. After receiving Brown's initial letter indicating that he did not wish her to come to Charlestown on Nov. 5, 1859 (while in the company of T.W. Higginson), Mary Brown decided to stay with abolitionist friends in order to be able to visit her husband if he had a change in heart. Villard, 548: Oates, *To Purge this Land with Blood: A Biography of John Brown,* 340.

204. Aside Henry Ward Beecher's comment, "Let no man pray that Brown be spared. Let Virginia make him a martyr. Now, he has blundered. His soul

was noble: his work miserable. But a cord and gibbet would redeem all that, and round up Brown's failure with success" (New York *Herald*, 31 Oct. 1859 and 22 Nov. 1859)," Brown wrote the single word, "good." Villard, *John Brown: A Biography Fifty Years After*, 518–519.

205. JB, letter to Rev. James Mcfarland, 23 Nov. 1859: Ruchames, *The John Brown Reader*, 145.

206. "Execution of John Brown." New York Times, Dec. 3, 1859. 1.

207. New York *Tribune*, 5 Dec. 1859: Merrill D. Peterson, *John Brown: The Legend Revisited* (Charlottesville: University of Virginia Press, 2002) 21–22, 45–46: James Redpath, *The Public Life of Capt. John Brown, with an Auto-Biography of His Childhood and Youth* (Boston, 1860) 397: Franklin Sanborn, *The Life and Letters of John Brown: Liberator of Kansas, and Martyr of Virginia* (Boston, 1185) 603–605.

208. Henry S. Olcott, New York *Tribune*, 5 Dec. 1859: Benjamin Quarles, *Allies for Freedom: Blacks on John Brown* (New York: De Capo Press, 2001) 121.

209. Ibid.

210. James Redpath, *The Public Life of Capt. John Brown, with an Auto-Biography of His Childhood and Youth* (Boston, 1860) 397.

211. Peterson, *John Brown: the Legend Revisited*, 26.

212. JB, letter to Rev. H. L. Vaill, 14 Nov. 1859: Ruchames, *The John Brown Reader*, 135.

213. JB, letter to MB, 10 Nov. 1859: Villard, *John Brown: A Biography Fifty Years After*, 540.

214. JB, letter to BELOVED WIFE, SONS: & DAUGHTERS, EVERYONE, 30 Nov. 1859: Ruchames, *The John Brown Reader*, 156–158.

215. De Caro, *Fire from the Midst of You: A Religious Life of John Brown*, 276.

216. MB, letter to Governor H.A. Wise, 21 Nov. 1859: Villard, *John Brown: A Biography Fifty Years After*, 549.

217. Dr. Lewis A. Sayr, letter to Governor Henry Wise, 30 Nov. 1859: Oates, *To Purge this Land with Blood: A Biography of John Brown*, 344.

218. Dr. A.E. Petricolas, letter to Andrew Hunter, 1 Nov. 1859: Villard, *John Brown: A Biography Fifty Years After*, 504.

219. "To Arms!" New York *Times*, Nov. 4, 1859: 4.

220. In the October 31, 1859 New York *Herald*, Henry Ward Beecher asserts: "Let no man pray that Brown be spared. Let Virginia make him a martyr. Now, he has only blundered. His soul was noble; his work miserable. But a cord and gibbet would redeem all that, and round up Brown's failure with a heroic success." Villard, *John Brown: A Biography Fifty Years After*, 518–519.

221. Henry D. Thoreau (hereafter HDT) on JB. Noted by Peterson, *John Brown: the Legend Revisited*, 17.

222. Bronson Alcott, Journal entry, 26 Oct. 1859: Sanborn. *Recollections of Seventy Years*. Vol. I, 201.

223. Samuel Longfellow, *Life of Henry Wadsworth Longfellow* (3 vols., Boston: 1891) II, 347: Oates, 319.

224. JB, letter to his Dearly beloved Wife, Sons: & Daughters, every one, 30 Nov. 1859: Ruchames, *The John Brown Reader*, 156–158.

225. Ibid.

226. JB, letter to Brother Jeremiah, 12 Nov. 1859: Ruchames, *The John Brown Reader*, 134.

227. TWH, letter to Lysander Spooner, 28 Nov. 1859.

228. Villard, *John Brown: A Biography Fifty Years After*, 484.

229. John LeBarnes, instructons to George H. Hoyt. Villard, *John Brown: A Biography Fifty Years After*, 484.

230. George H. Hoyt, letter to John A. LeBarnes, 28 Oct. 1859: Villard, *John Brown: A Biography Fifty Years After,* 512.
231. George Hoyt, letter to John Le Barnes, 30 Oct. 1859: Edelstein, *Strange Enthusiasm: A life of Thomas Wentworth Higginson,* 227
232. George Hoyt, letter to John Le Barnes, 30 Oct. 1859, Villard, *John Brown: A Biography Fifty Years After* 512.
233. JB, letter to TWH, 4 Nov. 1859: Ruchames, *The John Brown Reader,* 130.
234. John LeBarnes, letter to TWH, 15 Nov. 1859; Edelstein, *John Brown: A Biography Fifty Years After* 229.
235. Quoted by Oates, *To Purge this Land with Blood: A Biography of John Brown,* 351.
236. "EXECUTION OF JOHN BROWN," New York *Times,* 3 Dec. 1859, 1.
237. William Lloyd Garrison, "Address in Boston's Tremont Temple." 2 Dec. 1859; Villard, *John Brown: A Biography Fifty Years After,* 560.
238. William Lloyd Garrison, letter to Rev. D.H. Furness, 17 Dec. 1859: Louis Ruchames, ed. *The Letters of William Lloyd Garrison,* Vol. IV, *From Disunion to the Brink of War,* 1850–1860 (Cambridge: Belknap Press of Harvard University, 1975) 663.
239. Dean and Hoag note that there are widely varying accounts of Thoreau's presentation on 2 Dec. 1859. John Keyes recalled that Thoreau alone did not follow the program and read from other's works; he asserts that "Thoreau made a long speech of his own ideas and opinions. Redpath included the account I have included in *Echoes of Harper's Ferry.* Bradley P. Dean and Ronald Wesley Hoag, "Thoreau's Lectures after Walden: an Annotated Calendar," *Studies in the American Renaissance 1996,* ed. Joel Meyerson (Charlottesville: University Press of Virginia, 1996) 329.
240. Michael Meyer, "Discord in Concord on the Day of John Brown's Hanging," *Thoreau Society Bulletin,* 146 (Winter, 1979) 2: Gougeon, *Virtues Hero: Emerson, Anti-Slavery, and Reform* 248.
241. Abraham Lincoln, 2 Dec, 1859 remarks in Troy, Kansas. Quoted by Villard, *John Brown: A Biography Fifty Years After,* 564.
242. Ibid.
243. Peterson, *John Brown: the Legend Revisited,* 33.
244. I have included a line from the marching song, "John Brown's Body" to illustrate the connection between the "Battle Hymn of the Republic" and the martyr's effort. Peterson, *John Brown: the Legend Revisited,* 34.
245. John Greenleaf Whittier, "Brown of Ossawatomie," *The Complete Poetical Works of John Greenleaf Whittier* (Boston: 1892) 201.
246. "Report on the Invasion at Harpers Ferry." United States Senate, *Inquiry into the late invasion and seizure of the public Property at Harper's Ferry* (S. Rpt. 278), Washington: Government Printing Office, 1860) 1.
247. *The Liberator,* 22 Jun. 1860.
248. Report on the Invasion at Harpers Ferry. United States Senate, *Inquiry into the late invasion and seizure of the public Property at Harper's Ferry* (S. Rpt. 278), Washington: Government Printing Office, 1860) 22.
249. Ibid, 23.
250. The Mason Committee summoned 36 witnesses to appear before them between December 14, 1859 and June 14, 1860. Four men—Franklin Sanborn, John Brown Jr., Hugh Forbes, and James Redpath refused to appear in Washington and were subsequently indicted. United States Senate, *Inquiry into the late invasion and seizure of the public Property at Harper's Ferry* (S. Rpt. 278), Washington: Government Printing Office, 1860).
251. Following his interview with the Mason Committee, Howe suggested that the investigation "had been conducted 'unskillfully,'" since the questions he

had been asked had been poorly conceived, hence allowed him room for vague or less than truthful responses. Samuel G. Howe, letter to TWH, 16 Feb. 1860. Rossbach, *Ambivalent Conspirators: John Brown, the Secret Six, and a Theory of Slave Violence,* 259.

252. Worcester *Spy*, April 16, 1861; TWH, letter to L. Higginson, 17 Apr. 1861; Edelstein, *Strange Enthusiasm: A Life of Thomas Wentworth Higginson*, 244.

253. Edelstein, *Strange Enthusiasm: A Life of Thomas Wentworth Higginson*, 246.

254. Frederick Douglass, "John Brown's Contributions to the Abolition Movement: an Address Delivered in Boston, Massachusetts on 3 December, 1860," *The Frederick Douglass Papers*, Vol. 3, ed. John W. Blassingame (New Haven: Yale University Press, 1985) 413.

255. Ibid, 414.

256. TP, letter to Francis Jackson, 24 Nov. 1859. Weiss, *The Life and Correspondence of Theodore Parker*, 178.

257. Ralph Waldo Emerson, "Speech at a Meeting to Aid John Brown's Family (18 November, 1859)," *Emerson's Anti-Slavery Writings*, eds. Len Gougeon and Joel Myerson (New Haven: Yale University Press, 1995) 119.

258. Higginson published narrative accounts of Nat Turner, Denmark Vesey, and Gabriel Prosser in the Atlantic during August 1861, June 1861 and September, 1862 respectively. Additionally, in the February and May, 1860 editions of the Atlantic, he published accounts of the militant resistance of the Maroons of Jamaica and Surinam.

NOTES TO CHAPTER 4

1. Henry David Thoreau, "A Plea for Captain John Brown," *The Essays of Henry D. Thoreau*, ed. Lewis Hyde (New York: North Point Press, 2002) 269–70. All subsequent parenthetical references in this chapter originate from this anthology of Thoreau's essays.

2. Franklin Sanborn (hereafter FBS) recalls Thoreau's first meeting with Brown in his *Recollections of Seventy Years*. Vol. I (Boston: Gorham Press, 1909) 103–104.

3. In his 27 March, 1857 *Journal* entry, Thoreau (hereafter HDT) reveals his Journal methodology: "I would fain make two reports in my Journal, first the incidents and observations of today; and by to-morrow I review the same and record what was omitted before, which will often be the most significant and poetic part. I do not know at first what it is that charms me. The men and things of to-day are wont to lie fairer and truer in to-morrow's memory." HDT, *The Writings of Henry David Thoreau. Journal*, IX, ed. Bradford Torrey (Boston: Houghton Mifflin Company, 1906) 306: Sanborn suggests that the conversations that Thoreau, Brown, and Emerson had during the Brown's two day visit provided them with "intimate knowledge of Brown's character and general purpose which qualified them, in October 1859, to make those addresses in his behalf." FBS, *Recollections of Seventy Years*, 105: However, no mention of Brown or his visit in Concord is recorded in Thoreau's extant 1857 journal. The extant entries on March 11 and 12 are brief, but not significantly different from other entries of the same time period to suggest that they are a segment of the Thoreau's musings on the date of Brown's visit. Ibid, 289–90: Harding notes that Thoreau contributed "a trifle" to Brown following his lecture at the Concord Town Hall. Walter Harding, *The Days of Henry Thoreau* (New York: Knopf, 1965) 415–416.

4. HDT, *Journal* XII: 184. Although there is some confusion about the exact date of Brown's last visit to Concord, Bronson Alcott's journal records indicate that May 8, 1859. Sanborn includes Alcott's 8 May journal entry in *Recollections of Seventy Years*, 163–164.
5. Ibid.
6. Thoreau first gave "A Plea for Captain John Brown" in Concord on October 30, 1859, three days before Judge Parker sentenced Brown to death for murder, treason, and insurrection.
7. FBS, *Recollections*, 79: I make this comment conscious of Perry Miller's acknowledgement that the 30 original notebooks were variously used by several authors before Torrey and Allen produced the fourteen volume Walden edition of the journals in 1906. I also acknowledge Miller's assertion that Torrey and Allen "left out . . . portions of the journal in which Thoreau fiddled with paragraphs for which we never found publishable use" (128) and that Thoreau routinely "extract[ed] bits and pieces from the working notebooks for from the "long Red Book" (24) and is of "little use as a historical record, social or intellectual" since it is "perpetually, consumedly preoccupied with Henry Thoreau" (29–30). Perry Miller, *Consciousness in Concord* (Boston: Houghton Mifflin Company, 1958) 24, 29–30, 128.
8. HDT, "Slavery in Massachusetts." *The Essays of Henry D. Thoreau*. Ed. Lewis Hyde. (New York: North Point Press, 2002) 187.
9. Ralph Waldo Emerson noted that the lecture "was heard by all respectfully, by many with a sympathy that surprised themselves." Quoted by Bradley P. Dean and Ronald Wesley Hoag, "Thoreau's Lectures After Walden: An Annotated Calendar," *Studies in the American Renaissance*, ed. Joel Myerson (Charlottesville: University of North Carolina Press, 1996) 312.
10. Len Gougeon. *Virtue's Hero: Emerson, Anti-Slavery, and Reform* (Athens: University of Georgia Press, 1990) 240.
11. "Personal," New York *Daily Tribune*, 4 Nov. 1859, Bradley P. Dean and Ronald Wesley Hoag, "Thoreau's Lectures After Walden: An Annotated Calendar," *Studies in the American Renaissance*, 1996 ed. Joel Meyerson (Charlottesville: University Press of Virginia, 1996) 318.
12. When Thoreau presented his lecture at the Tremont Temple on 1 Nov. 1859, Parker was in Switzerland attempting to address the debilitating effects of tuberculosis. He remained in Europe until his death in May.
13. Ever since his installation in Worcester in September, 1852, Higginson had aggressively appealed to his predominantly Free Soil parishioners to actively engage in reform of their society. During his first year in Worcester, he organized the Worcester Freedom Club, an organization committed to the end of the Fugitive Slave Laws and to "protecting the rights of the men of toil" (134). Subsequently, he was elected president of the Municipal Anti-Slavery Society: his neighbor, Theophilus Brown (Thoreau's good friend) served on the board of directors. In addition to his weekly sermons, he publicly spoke before both the Worcester (1852), Massachusetts (1853), and American Anti-Slavery Societies (1857), spoke on Kansas at the West Indian Emancipation Day Celebration (1856), published "Moral Results of Slavery" (1852), "Romance of Slavery or American Feudalism" (1853), "Massachusetts in Mourning (1854)," "A Ride Through Kansas (1856):" He had taken a key role in the 1854 attempt to free fugitive slave Anthony Burns from the Boston Court House (for which he had been indicted) and was an active member of both the Massachusetts State and Worcester County Kansas Committees, the organizer of the Worcester Disunion Convention (1857), as well as a frequent lecturer on the lyceum circuit. Tilden G. Edelstein, *Strange Enthusiasm: A Life of Thomas Wentworth Higginson* (New Haven: Yale University Press, 1968) 129–236.

14. Higginson's radical abolitionism was well known as was his role in the attempted rescue of Anthony Burns from the Boston Courthouse on May 24, 1854. In *The Liberator* on 28 May, 1858, Higginson acknowledged that slavery was "destined, as it began in blood, so to end."

15. Sanborn asserts that Higginson, Blake, and Theo Brown were present at Thoreau's 3 November, 1859 speech in Worcester. F. B. Sanborn, *The Life of Henry David Thoreau* (Boston: Houghton Mifflin Company, 1917) 287.

16. TP, letter to Francis Jackson, 24 Nov. 1859: Quoted in full by John Weiss, *Life and Correspondence of Theodore Parker*, Vol. II (New York: D. Appleton & Company, 1864) 175.

17. Responding to Senator Mason's question, "How do you justify your acts?" during his first interview on 19 October, 1859 (subsequently published by the New York *Herald*), John Brown responded, "I think, my friend, you are guilty of a great wrong against God and humanity—I say it without wishing to be offensive—and it would be perfectly right in anyone to interfere with you so far as to free those you willfully and wickedly hold in bondage." Quoted in "A Conversation with Brown," *The Life Trial and Execution of Captain John Brown* (1859 rep. New York: De Capo Press, 1969) 45: Thoreau specifically points to Brown's response to Mason in the middle of his lecture: "Read his admirable answers to Mason and others. How they are dwarfed and defeated in contrast." Henry D. Thoreau, "A Plea for Captain John Brown," *The Essays of Henry D. Thoreau*, ed. Lewis Hyde (New York: North Point Press, 2002) 272.

18. Harding, *The Days of Henry Thoreau*, 353

19. Martin Bickman, *Minding American Education: Reclaiming the Tradition of Active Learning* (New York: Teachers College Press, 2004) 67: Harding. *The Days of Henry Thoreau*, 353.

20. Ibid 353.

21. Ibid 354.

22. FBS, *Recollections*, 49.

23. In *The Days of Henry Thoreau*, Harding includes an excerpt of Samuel Stowell Higginson's recollections of afternoon outings with Thoreau during his tenure as a student in Sanborn's school in Concord. Harding, *The Days of Henry Thoreau* 354.

24. Ibid 353.

25. FBS, *Recollections*, 35.

26. TP, letter to Charles Sumner, 14 Jan. 1856: Quoted in full by John Weiss, *Life and Correspondence of Theodore Parker*, Vol. II (1864 rpt., New York: D. Appleton & Company, 1969), 157–60: In *Recollections of Seventy Years*, Sanborn acknowledges both the influence of Parker, whom he credits with much of his political awareness, and members of the Bird Club, which he joined in 1854 while still a student at Harvard. 48–51.

27. Rossbach, *Ambivalent Conspirators: John Brown, the Secret Six, and a Theory of Slave Violence*, 51.

28. Ellen Tucker Emerson. *The Letters of Ellen Tucker Emerson*. Vol. 1, ed. Edith E.W. Gregg (Kent, Ohio: Kent State University Press, 1982) 118: Gougeon, *Virtue's Hero: Emerson, Anti-Slavery, and Reform*, 218.

29. Sanborn's made his August trip along the route that emigrants normally journeyed from Ohio to Kansas on behalf of the Middlesex County Committee. His charter was two-fold: determine if the funds and supplies collected by the committee were actually arriving at specified collection points along the route to Kansas and see what settlers needed in the future. Sanborn never entered the contested territory of Kansas stopping short of what Rossbach terms the "strife torn area" claiming that he "had not the time"

in one account and that his charter did not require that he actually enter the border area in another. Sanborn, *Recollections*, 58: Rossbach, *Ambivalent Conspirators: John Brown, the Secret Six, and a Theory of Slave Violence*, 52.

30. Ibid.
31. FBS, letter to TP, 28 Nov. 1856: Rossbach, *Ambivalent Conspirators: John Brown, the Secret Six, and a Theory of Slave Violence*, 53–54.
32. Harding, *The Days of Henry Thoreau*, 74.
33. Ibid, 317.
34. The ratification of the Kansas-Nebraska Bill (which potentially allowed slavery above the 36'30 latitude previously specified as the northern limit of slavery in the 1820 Missouri Compromise) and the Anthony Burns riot took place on the nearly same date—May 26 and 24, 1854 respectively. The Burns' riot, however, was a response to an attempt to enforce the Fugitive Slave Law in Boston and was not a reaction to the Kansas-Nebraska Act, though the latter (which had been debated in Congress since its introduction by Illinois Senator Stephen Douglass in January, 1854) in all probability fueled the indignation of the participants.
35. In their thorough review of the events that occurred on July 4, 1854 at Harmony Grove's amphitheater in Framingham, Dean and Hoag include the 7 Jul. 1854 *Liberator* comment that "Henry Thoreau, of Concord, read portions of a racy and ably written address, the whole of which will be published in the LIBERATOR." The entire text did appear in the 21 Jul. 1854 edition. Bradley P. Dean and Ronald Wesley Hoag, "Thoreau's Lectures Before Walden," *Studies in the American Renaissance, 1995*, ed. Joel Myerson (Charlottesville: University press of Virginia, 1995) 219.
36. Horace Greeley, "A Higher Law Speech," New York *Daily Tribune*, 2 Aug. 1854. Quoted by Dean and Hoag, "Thoreau's Lectures Before Walden," 219–20.
37. Oates, *To Purge this Land with Blood: A Biography of John Brown*, 198, 236.
38. From 1856 until his death in 1862, Henry Thoreau lived in his family home and took his meals at his mother's table. Harding, *The Days of Henry Thoreau*.
39. FBS, *Recollections*, 103
40. In his 28 Jul. 1856 *Journal* entry, Thoreau notes that he had the opportunity to examine four of the weapons commonly employed in Kansas in 1856—the "Sharp's rifle, a Colt's revolver, a Maynard's, and a Thurber's revolver." *Journal* VIII: 433
41. Ibid.
42. Ibid, 104–05.
43. Ralph Waldo Emerson, *The Journals and Miscellaneous Notebooks of Ralph Waldo Emerson*, Vol. XIV, eds., Susan Sutton Smith and Harrison Hayford (Cambridge: Belknap Press of Harvard University Press, 1978) 125.
44. Ibid, 126.
45. Ibid.
46. Rossbach, *Ambivalent Conspirators: John Brown, the Secret Six, and a Theory of Slave Violence*, 110.
47. Ibid, 108.
48. FBS, letter to JB, 16 Apr. 1857, Rossbach, *Ambivalent Conspirators: John Brown, the Secret Six, and a Theory of Slave Violence*, 114–15.
49. Ibid.
50. FBS, letter to JB, 14 Aug. 1857: Rossbach, *Ambivalent Conspirators: John Brown, the Secret Six, and a Theory of Slave Violence*, 125.
51. FBS, letter to JB, 16 Apr.1857: Rossbach, *Ambivalent Conspirators: John Brown, the Secret Six, and a Theory of Slave Violence*, 114–15.

52. Rossbach, *Ambivalent Conspirators: John Brown, the Secret Six, and a Theory of Slave Violence*, 146.

53. Villard, 248: Renehan, *The Secret Six: the True Tale of the Men Who Conspired with John Brown*, 148.

54. TWH, letter to FBS, 9 May 1858: Renehan, *The Secret Six: the True Tale of the Men Who Conspired with John Brown*, 152.

55. Richardson cites Emerson's *Journals*, XIV: 125. However, this source does not confirm Thoreau's annoyance, nor the amount of his contribution. Robert D. Richardson, Jr., *Henry David Thoreau: A life of the Mind* (Berkeley, University of California Press, 1986) 370.

56. In *The Life of Henry David Thoreau*, Sanborn quotes Whitman's assessment of Thoreau, then diminishes it suggesting that Thoreau's manner of speaking suggested a lack of appreciation for casual acquaintances (that he did not develop), but it was in fact, a "misapprehension" of Thoreau's casual approach to people of all classes. FBS, *Life*, 336–337.

57. HDT, *Journal* XII, 408–409.

58. HDT, *Journal*, XII, 420.

59. Rossbach, *Ambivalent Conspirators: John Brown, the Secret Six, and a Theory of Slave Violence*, 221.

60. Renehan, *The Secret Six: the True Tale of the Men Who Conspired with John Brown*, 206–07

61. FBS, letter to Ralph Waldo Emerson (hereafter RWE), 22 Oct. 1859. Gougeon, *Virtue's Hero: Emerson, Anti-Slavery, and Reform*, 239.

62. Gougeon, *Virtue's Hero: Emerson, Anti-Slavery, and Reform*, 239–40.

63. RWE, letter to Mrs. Forbes, 26 Oct. 1859: Ralph Rusk, ed. *The Letters of Ralph Waldo Emerson*. Vol 5 (New York: Columbia University Press, 1938) 179.

64. RWE, letter to FBS, 26 Oct. 1859; Gougeon, *Virtue's Hero: Emerson, Anti-Slavery, and Reform*, 240.

65. Sanborn returned to Concord on 26 October, 1859. Gougeon, *Virtue's Hero: Emerson, Anti-Slavery, and Reform*, 240.

66. There is no record of this meeting in either Thoreau's nor Emerson's journal. Alcott's journal provides the sole record of the attendees and their 26 October business. Gougeon, *Virtue's Hero: Emerson, Anti-Slavery, and Reform*, 240.

67. Bronson Alcott, *Diary*, 26 Oct. 1859, Evening. Quoted in Sanborn, *Recollections*, I: 201.

68. Sanborn's efforts to inspire the other members of the secret committee to destroy their correspondence probably began with his 21 Oct 1859 letter to Higginson that explained that he was going to leave the country rather than face arrest for his complicity in Brown's attack on Harper's Ferry. He ended the letter by instructing Higginson, "Burn this." In a later (19 Nov. 1859) letter, Sanborn informed Higginson that he had destroyed all letters that might be used against anyone hoping that Higginson would do the same. Edelstein, *Strange Enthusiasm*, 223, 226.

69. Edward Waldo Emerson, *The Complete Works of Ralph Waldo Emerson*, Vol 10 (Boston: Houghton Mifflin Company, 1903–4) 460; Gougeon, *Virtue's Hero: Emerson, Anti-Slavery, and Reform*, 240.

70. Quoted in George W. Cooke, "The Two Thoreaus." *Independent*, 48 (10 December 1896): 1672; Bradley P. Dean and Ronald Wesley Hoag, "Thoreau's Lectures after Walden: An Annotated Calendar," *Studies in the American Renaissance, 1996*. ed. Joel Myerson (Charlottesville: University of Virginia Press, 1996) 311–12.

71. Edward Emerson noted that Thoreau read his lecture "with no oratory . . . as "if it burned him." Quoted by Dean and Hoag, 312: Thoreau, "A Plea for Captain John Brown," 276.

72. Bradley P. Dean and Ronald Wesley Hoag, "Thoreau's Lectures after Walden: an Annotated Calendar," *Studies in the American Renaissance 1996*, ed. Joel Meyerson (Charlottesville: University Press of Virginia, 1996), 311.
73. Ibid.
74. Ibid, 313.
75. Emerson's Monday morning, 31 Oct. 1859 letter to Charles W. Slack is not acknowledged in previous historical accounts of Thoreau's presentations of his address "On the Character and Actions of Captain John Brown." In their very thorough 1996 summary of Thoreau's lectures after Walden, Dean and Hoag suggest that Slack, "apparently having received word of Thoreau's lecture in Concord the day before, sent his telegram to Thoreau" (315). They suggest that Slack gained knowledge of Thoreau's Concord performance in casual conversation with Boston friends. As Emerson's letter indicates, however, this was clearly not the case. Emerson informed Slack of the value of Thoreau's lecture and convinced the chairman (of the Fraternity Lecture Course) to invite Thoreau to speak at Tremont Temple on 1 November. Emerson clearly sought the Parker Fraternity venue before receiving Slack's note, making my earlier assertion that Thoreau sought the opportunity to vicariously confront Parker more likely since Emerson's letter is dated "31 October, 1859/ Morn" and Slack's telegraph arrived, by most accounts, in the "late on 31 October, 1859." Dean and Hoag, *"Thoreau's Lectures After* Walden," 314: RWE , letter to Charles Wesley Slack, *Morn* 31 Oct. 1859. American Antiquarian Society, Worcester, MA. See Appendix A for a complete transcription of Emerson's here-to-fore unpublished letter.
76. Ibid.
77. Parker left Boston for the West Indies and Europe in February, 1859 in order to seek a climate conducive to recovery from the onslaught of tuberculosis, which his doctors indicated was advanced to the point that he only had one chance in ten of recovery. Theodore Parker, letter to FRIENDS IN GERMANY, 18 Jan.1859; Quoted in John Weiss, *Life and Correspondence of Theodore Parker*, Vol. II (1864 rpt., New York: D. Appleton & Company, 1969) 264.
78. Ibid 432.
79. In all probability, the single expression of sympathy for John Brown that Thoreau read was one of James Redpath's articles in the Boston *Atlas & Daily Bee*. Edelstein notes that "three days after Brown's imprisonment, Redpath began a series of articles [extolling Brown's actions in the daily newspaper] variously entitled 'Reminiscences of the Insurrection' and 'Notes on the Insurrection.'" Edelstein, *Strange Enthusiasm*, 226.
80. Dean and Hoag note that Emerson had recommended Thoreau as a speaker for the 28th Congregational Society, 306: Dean Grodzins, "Theodore Parker and the 28th Congregational Society," *Transient and Permanent: The Transcendentalist Movement and Its Contexts*. eds. Charles Capper and Conrad Edick Wright (Boston: Massachusetts Historical Society, 1999) 94.
81. Boston *Altas & Daily Bee*, 10 Oct. 1859. Quoted by Dean and Hoag, "Thoreau's Lectures after Walden: an Annotated Calendar," 305; Emerson privately noted his relief about Thoreau's performance in an 11 Oct 1859 letter to Daniel Ricketson. He noted, "From private reports I infer that he made a just impression." Quoted in Dean and Hoag, "Thoreau's Lectures after Walden: an Annotated Calendar," 306.
82. Frederick Douglass, letter to Charles Wesley Slack, 26 August, 1859. Charles Wesley Slack Papers. Department of Special Collections and Archives, Kent State University Libraries and Media Services. See Appendix C for the full text of Douglass's here-to-fore unpublished letter.

83. In the first Fraternity Course lecture (given on October 6, 1858), Parker spoke on Benjamin Franklin, the man he distinguished as the "greatest man that America ever bore in her bosom or set eyes upon." Theodore Parker, "Benjamin Franklin," *Historic Americans*, ed. Samuel A. Eliot (Boston: American Unitarian Association, 1908) 16; Theodore Parker, "The Effect of Slavery on the American People" *Saint Bernard and Other Papers*. ed. Charles W. Wendte (Boston: American Unitarian Association, 1911) 345.

84. A. Bronson Alcott, letter to William T Harris, 2 April, 1868, Richard L. Hernstadt, ed., *The Letters of A. Bronson Alcott* (Iowa: Iowa State University Press, 1969) 431: In the *Journals and Miscellaneous Notebooks*, Emerson distinguishes between the Music Hall, the site where the 28th Congregational Society conducted Sunday services and the Fraternity, which met on Tuesday evenings during the lecture season in the Tremont Temple. Emerson, *JMN*, XIV: 293, 468–9.

85. In his July 20, 1859 letter to Slack, Parker demonstrates his continued interest in the lectures that Slack scheduled for the Tuesday evening lecture series. He tells Slack, "[y]ou know how dear I hold the Fraternity; I would do all in my power to promote its generous & noble works; but I think it had better let Mr. Sumner *slide* this winter. I shall tell him my opinion when I write him next, & know that you & your friends will appreciate my conduct tho' it is not the ghiste [sic] of your advice.—I rejoice in the evening lectures you have yet laid out. I hope by all means Phillips will speak & that too in his favorite theme. I wish I could give you a lecture on *the Causes & immediate & remote Results of the Present War in Europe,* & and the authors in this *Conflict of Principles in European Politics* as I have *in the conduct of the 5 Great Powers*. But it cannot be. I think Lowell has no deep & hearty interest in the great things the Fraternity aims at that I hope its Lectures will help forward. (Dr.-elided) Holmes is much more on our side today. It will be a fine thing if *Whittier* stands up tall & valiant before you & gives one of his grand poems." TP, letter to Charles Wesley Slack, 20 Jul. 1859. Charles Wesley Slack, Papers. Department of Special Collections and Archives, Kent State University Libraries and Media Services. See Appendix B for the full text of Parker's here-to-fore unpublished letter.

86. Ibid.

87. TP, "Thanksgiving Sermon, 29 Nov. 1838." Dean Grodzins, *American Heretic: Theodore Parker and Transcendentalism* (Chapel Hill: University of North Carolina Press, 2002) 173.

88. TP, "Sermon on Slavery." 1841. Quoted in Grodzins, *American Heretic: Theodore Parker and Transcendentalism,* 334.

89. Ibid, 335.

90. TP, "Another Sermon of Slavery." Quoted in Grodzins, *American Heretic: Theodore Parker and Transcendentalism,* 474.

91. TP, "The Mexican War," *The Slave Power,* ed. James K Hosmer (Boston: American Unitarian Association, 1907) 31.

92. TP, letter to Francis Jackson, 24 Nov. 1859. Quoted By John Weiss, ed. *The Life and Correspondence of Theodore Parker,* 2 Vols. (New York: D. Appleton & Company, 1864) 175.

93. In his essay on the history of the 28th Congregational Society, Grodzins lists some of Parker's more notable Sunday afternoon guests. Grodzins, "Theodore Parker and the 28th Congregational Society," 91.

94. TP, *Journal* Entry, 30 Apr. 1850. Quoted by Weiss, *The Life and Correspondence of Theodore Parker,* 97.

95. Ibid.

96. "Hughes, the Slave-Hunter's Account of his Mission," *Liberator,* Vol. XX. No. 49., 6 Dec. 1850.

97. RWE, *JMN* 11: 323: Gougeon, *Virtues Hero*, 150–51.
98. TP, letter to President Millard Fillmore, 21 Nov. 1850. Quoted by Weiss, *The Life and Correspondence of Theodore Parker*, 100–102.
99. Ibid.
100. Rossbach asserts that Martin Stowell and Thomas Wentworth Higginson hastily revealed their plan to the speakers at Fanueil Hall prior to the beginning of the lectures. Though Parker and Howe were both "incredulous" when they heard the plan, neither voiced objections and Higginson and his cohort left the anteroom believing that they could count on the speakers to send the crowd to the Court House Square at the right time. Parker's journals do not reveal the same awareness. Rossbach, *Ambivalent Conspirators: John Brown, the Secret Six, and a Theory of Slave Violence*, 25–26.
101. Rossbach, *Ambivalent Conspirators: John Brown, the Secret Six, and a Theory of Slave Violence*, 31.
102. TP, letter to President Millard Fillmore, 21 Nov. 1850. Quoted by Weiss, *The Life and Correspondence of Theodore Parker*, 100–102.
103. Weiss, *The Life and Correspondence of Theodore Parker*, 32.
104. Quoted by Gougeon, *Virtue's Hero: Emerson, Anti-Slavery, and Reform*, 200.
105. Renehan, *The Secret Six: the True Tale of the Men Who Conspired with John Brown*, 65.
106. TP, letter to Charles Ellis, 8 Feb. 1859: Rossbach, *Ambivalent Conspirators: John Brown, the Secret Six, and a Theory of Slave Violence*, 144–146.
107. Edelstein, *Strange Enthusiasm: a Life of Thomas Wentworth Higginson*, 172.
108. Renehan, *The Secret Six: the True Tale of the Men Who Conspired with John Brown*, 77.
109. "Who are the Guilty," *Liberator*, Vol XXIV, No. 23, 9 Jun. 1854.
110. Boston *Courier*, 29 May, 1854. Quoted in the *Liberator*, Vol. XXIV, No. 25, 23 Jun. 1854.
111. Harding notes that Thoreau's mother, sisters, and Prudence Ward (who had been a member of the household since 1833)—all members of the Women's Abolition Society, regularly subscribed to anti-slavery periodicals and "made [Henry] particularly aware of the issues" concerning anti-slavery activists. Additionally, he notes that "anti-slavery agitators who visited Concord invariably put up for the night at [Thoreau's] mother's boarding house" and ate at his mother's table. Harding, *The Days of Henry Thoreau*, 201.
112. Parker was at Harvard on and off from August, 1830 to 1836, first devoting himself to undergraduate studies then to graduate work in the Divinity School. Thoreau attended Harvard from August, 1833 to July, 1837, though he did withdraw briefly on account of an illness in 1836 and spend between six and twelve weeks in Canton, Massachusetts teaching in a school where radical Unitarian minister Orestes Brownson served on the School Committee. Harding notes that only "two hundred and fifty students were enrolled at Harvard [in the undergraduate program] in Thoreau's day" (39) and Parker remarks (in a letter to his nephew Columbus Greene) that there were only "thirty scholars, divided into three classes" enrolled in the Divinity School, so it is very likely that the two men often met while in Cambridge. Harding, *The Days of Henry Thoreau*, 39: Weiss, 67.
113. TP, *Journal*, 10 Aug. 1840. Quoted by Raymond R. Borst, *The Thoreau Log: A Documentary Life of Henry David Thoreau 1817–1862* (New York: G.K. Hall & co., 1992) 58–59.

114. Grodzins, *American Heretic: Theodore Parker and Transcendentalism*, 237: Parker's opinion of Thoreau's work was not singular. During her editorship of the *Dial*, Margaret Fuller doesn't seem to have appreciated Thoreau's literary skills any more than Parker. She resisted publishing Thoreau's work often returning it several times for revision before rejecting it. Harding cites both Thoreau's essay "The Service" and his poem "With frontier strength ye stand your ground" as examples of Fuller's rejection of Henry Thoreau's submissions for the *Dial*. Harding, The *Days of Henry Thoreau*, 114–115.

115. RWE, letter to TP, 1 Jun. 1849: TP, letter to Emerson, 15 Jun. 1849, Ralph L. Rusk, ed. *The Letters of Ralph Waldo Emerson*, Vol. IV (New York: Columbia University Press, 1939) 151.

116. James Russell Lowell, "A Fable for Critics," *Nineteenth-Century American Poetry*, eds. William Spengemann with Jessica F. Roberts (New York: Penguin, 1996) 153. Thoreau would later castigate Lowell for editorial license, bigotry, and timidity. Henry D. Thoreau, letter to James Russell Lowell, 22 Jun. 1858. Quoted by Raymond R. Borst, ed., *The Thoreau Log: A Documentary Life of Henry David Thoreau 1817–1862.* (New York: G.K. Hall & Co., 1992) 515–516.

117. J. R. Lowell, Review of *A Week on the Concord and Merrimack* in the *Massachusetts Quarterly Review*, Dec. 1849. Quoted in Kenneth Walter Cameron, ed. *Transcendental Log: Fresh Discoveries in Newspapers Concerning Emerson, Thoreau, Alcott and Others of the American Literary Renaissance* (Hartford: Transcendental Books, 1973) 48.

118. Ibid.

119. Harding, *The Days of Henry Thoreau*, 215.

120. Ibid.

121. Harding, *The Days of Henry Thoreau*, 215: Frothingham notes that in 1850, "the public was not prepared for anything so thorough or so advanced" as the *Review*. He also suggests that the "political urgency [of the times] was pressing too hotly to allow" Parker, who was writing the majority of the articles for the *Review* in the 1850s, the time that the *Review* demanded. Therefore, he ended the three year run of the periodical. Octavius Brooks Frothingham, *Theodore Parker: A Biography* (Boston: James R. Osgood and Company, 1874) 398.

122. Dean Grodzins, "Theodore Parker," 29 Mar. 2005, <http//www.uua.org/uuhs/duub/articles/Theodoreparker.html>.

123. TP, "The Function and Place of Conscience in relation to the Laws (1850)," 15 Mar. 2005, <http://www.pragmatism.org/american/parker_conscience.htm>.

124. Parker's effort on behalf of the Crafts occurred in October, 1850, while his attempts on Sims behalf took place in April, 1851.

125. Weiss, *The Life and Correspondence of Theodore Parker*, 108.

126. In *Emerson: the Mind on Fire*, Richardson notes that during the 1850s, Emerson drew closer to Parker, whom he recognized as one of "four powerful men in the virtuous class in this country," along with Greeley, Mann, and Beecher (RWE, *JMN* 13: 49); Richardson, 510.

127. "Speech of Rev. Theodore Parker" *Liberator*, Vol. XXIV, No. 23. 9 Jun. 1854

128. Attempting to inspire the audience to act on the part of Burns, Parker asked "are we to have deeds as well as words? "Speech of Rev. Theodore Parker" *Liberator*, Vol. XXIV, No. 23. 9 Jun. 1854.

129. TP, letter to Charles Sumner, 14 Jan. 1856. Quoted in Weiss, *The Life and Correspondence of Theodore Parker*, 157–60.

130. Ibid.

131. TP, letter to J. P. Hale, 21 Oct. 1856; Weiss, *The Life and Correspondence of Theodore Parker,* 187.

132. Dean Grodzins, "Why Theodore Parker Backed John Brown: The Political and Social Roots of Support for Abolitionist Violence," Unpublished, (2004) 11.

133. TP, letter to Miss Hunt, 17 Nov. 1856; Quoted in Weiss, 191.

134. Grodzins, "Why Theodore Parker Backed John Brown: The Political and Social Roots of Support for Abolitionist Violence," 12.

135. FBS, *Life of Henry David Thoreau,* 511: Grodzins, "Why Theodore Parker Backed John Brown: The Political and Social Roots of Support for Abolitionist Violence," 3.

136. Renehan, *The Secret Six: the True Tale of the Men Who Conspired with John Brown,* 92: In an April, 1856 journal entry, Parker notes that he bade farewell to a party of about forty Kansas emigrants who had "twenty copies of Sharp's Rights of the People" in their hands, of the new and improved edition, and divers Colt's six-shooters also," intimating that he had a role in their provision. Quoted in Weiss, *The Life and Correspondence of Theodore Parker,* 160.

137. Rossbach, *Ambivalent Conspirators: John Brown, the Secret Six, and a Theory of Slave Violence,* 78.

138. Grodzins, "Why Theodore Parker Backed John Brown: The Political and Social Roots of Support for Abolitionist Violence," 4.

139. Villard, *John Brown: A Biography Fifty Years After,* 272.

140. Grodzins, "Why Theodore Parker Backed John Brown: The Political and Social Roots of Support for Abolitionist Violence," 4.

141. TP, letter to TWH, 18 Jan. 1857: Weiss, *The Life and Correspondence of Theodore Parker,* 192–194.

142. Ibid.

143. TP, letter to TWH, 18 Jan. 1857: Weiss, *The Life and Correspondence of Theodore Parker,* 194.

144. TWH, *Contemporaries* (Boston: Houghton, Mifflin and Company, 1899) 229: Renehan, *The Secret Six: the True Tale of the Men Who Conspired with John Brown,* 146.

145. *Liberator* 12 Mar. 1858. Quoted by Grodzins, "Why Theodore Parker Backed John Brown: The Political and Social Roots of Support for Abolitionist Violence." 10–11.

146. "Speech of Theodore Parker," *The Liberator,* Vol. XXVIII, No. 13., 26 March 1858.

147. Ibid.

148. Parker notes that the Declaration of Independence is the "National PROGRAMME OF POLITICAL PRINCIPLES . . . adopted by the people themselves as their rule of conduct in separating from the mother country." Theodore Parker, "The Relation of Slavery to a Republican Form of Government." *The Liberator,* Vol. XXVIII, No. 23, 4 Jun. 1858.

149. TP, "The Relation of Slavery to A Republican Form of Government (Concluded)," *The Liberator,* Vol. XXVIII, No. 24, 11 Jun. 1858.

150. TP, "The Effect of Slavery on the American People," *Saint Bernard and Other Papers.* ed. Charles W. Wendte (Boston: American Unitarian Association, 1911) 345.

151. TP, "The Relation of Slavery to a Republican Form of Government." Quoted by Weiss, *The Life and Correspondence of Theodore Parker,* 196.

152. TP, "The Effect of Slavery on the American People." [sermon: July 4, 1858]. Quoted by Weiss, *The Life and Correspondence of Theodore Parker,* 196

153. Parker gave his congregation his last sermon on 2 Jan. 1859 and departed the country on 3 Feb. 1859 in the company of Samuel G. Howe, another member

of the Secret Six. He died in Florence on May 10, 1860. Weiss, *The Life and Correspondence of Theodore Parker*, 256–70.

154. John Brown claimed that he had come South to "free the slaves and only that" during the widely reported interview that occurred on 18 Oct., 1859 in the paymaster's office at Harpers Ferry: FS, letter to TP, (received) 13 Nov. 1859. Noted in Parker's 1859 diary. The first mention of Brown in Parker's diary occurs two days later. Dean Grodzins, "Re: Brown and Parker." E-mail to Michael Stoneham, 26 Oct. 04.

155. TP, letter to Francis Jackson, 24 Nov. 1859. Quoted by Weiss, *The Life and Correspondence of Theodore Parker*, 170–178.

156. Ibid.

157. I provide Parker's five maxims here as he presented them, but I do not quote the discussion he provides to elucidate each point: "1. A MAN HELD AGAINST HIS WILL AS A SLAVE HAS A NATURAL RIGHT TO KILL EVERY ONE WHO SEEKS TO PREVENT HIS ENJOYMENT OF LIB-ERTY. . . . 2. IT MIGHT BE A NATURUAL DUTY OF THE SLAVE TO DEVELOP THIS NAUTRAL RIGHT IN A PRACTICAL MANNER, AND ACTUALLY KILL ALL THOSE WHO SEEK TO PREVENT HIS ENJOYMENT OF LIBERTY . . . 3. THE FREEMAN HAS A NATURAL RIGHT TO HELP THE SLAVES RECOVER THEIR LIBERTY, AND IN THAT ENTERPRISE TO DO FOR THEM ALL WHICH THEY HAVE A RIGHT TO DO FOR THEMSELVES . . . 4. IT MAY BE A NATURAL DUTY FOR THE FREEMAN TO HELP THE SLAVES TO THE ENJOY-MENT OF THEIR LIBERTY, AND AS A MEANS TO THAT END, TO AID THEM IN KILLING ALL SUCH AS OPPOSE THEIR NATURAL FREEDOM. . . . 5. THE PERFORMANCE OF THIS DUTY IS TO BE CONTROLLED BY THE FREEMAN'S POWER AND OPPORTUNITY TO HELP THE SLAVES." Weiss, *The Life and Letters of Theodore Parker*, 170–71.

158. TP, letter to Francis Jackson, 24 Nov. 1859; Weiss, *The Life and Correspondence of Theodore Parker*, 172.

159. Ibid, 170.

160. TP, letter to George Ripley, Shrove Tuesday, 1860; Quoted by Weiss, *The Life and Correspondence of Theodore Parker*, 433.

161. HDT, "Civil Disobedience," 126.

162. In "Civil Disobedience," Thoreau uses the phrase a "majority of one" to suggest the righteous power of the individual in opposition to a corrupt state. HDT, "Civil Disobedience," 133.

163. Both Washburn Hall's newness within the Mechanics Hall Building and Alcott's reflections on Thoreau's Worcester presentation are included in Dean and Hoag's summary account of Lecture 67 in "Thoreau's Lectures After Walden," 321.

164. After being "unanimously chosen to head the new Free Church" in Worcester, Higginson moved to the predominantly Free Soil community in September, 1852 preaching his first sermon there on the 15th of September; Edelstein, *Strange Enthusiasm: a Life of Thomas Wentworth Higginson*, 130–31.

165. Newburyport *Union*, 8, 10 Oct. 1850; Edelstein, *Strange Enthusiasm: a Life of Thomas Wentworth Higginson*, 100–101.

166. TWH, "Address to the Voters of the Third Congressional District," Newburyport, 1850. Quoted by Edelstein, *Strange Enthusiasm: a Life of Thomas Wentworth Higginson*, 103.

167. Ibid, 105.

168. Ibid.

169. TWH, "The Crisis Coming Now," Newburyport *Union*, 4, 12, 20 Nov. 1850. Quoted by Edelstein, *Strange Enthusiasm: a Life of Thomas Wentworth Higginson*, 105–106.
170. Ibid.
171. Ibid.
172. Newburyport *Union*, Feb. 18, 1851. Edelstein, *Strange Enthusiasm: a Life of Thomas Wentworth Higginson*, 111.
173. Ibid. Parker similarly suggested that the rescue was the "noblest deed done in Boston since the destruction of tea in 1773." Quoted by Edelstein, *Strange Enthusiasm: a Life of Thomas Wentworth Higginson*, 110.
174. TWH, letter to Mary Curzon, 6 Apr. 1851: Edelstein, *Strange Enthusiasm: a Life of Thomas Wentworth Higginson*, 112, 114 .
175. Edelstein, *Strange Enthusiasm: a Life of Thomas Wentworth Higginson*, 115.
176. Ibid.
177. TWH, "Sermon," *Liberator*, Feb. 17, 1854. Edelstein, *Strange Enthusiasm: a Life of Thomas Wentworth Higginson*, 154.
178. Ibid.
179. Rossbach, *Ambivalent Conspirators: John Brown, the Secret Six, and a Theory of Slave Violence*, 33.
180. TWH, "Massachusetts in Mourning," *Liberator* Vol. XXIV, No. 23, 16 Jun 1854: Edelstein, *Strange Enthusiasm: a Life of Thomas Wentworth Higginson*, 182
181. TWH, "Massachusetts in Mourning," 13.
182. Edelstein, *Strange Enthusiasm: a Life of Thomas Wentworth Higginson*, 164.
183. TWH, letter to TP, 12 Feb. 1855. Noted by Edelstein, *Strange Enthusiasm: a Life of Thomas Wentworth Higginson*, 172.
184. Wendell Phillips, letter to TWH, 14 Jun. 1854. Noted by Edelstein, *Strange Enthusiasm: a Life of Thomas Wentworth Higginson*, 171.
185. In anticipation of his trial, Parker had prepared an elaborate attack on the Fugitive Slave Law. In order to prepare for his own defense, he "attended [Burn's trial] steadily every day." Noted by Higginson, *Cheerful Yesterdays*, 160.
186. Edelstein, *Strange Enthusiasm: a Life of Thomas Wentworth Higginson*, 177.
187. Ibid, 180.
188. Ibid.
189. Quoted by Villard, *John Brown: A Biography Fifty Years After*, 129.
190. Quoted by Villard, *John Brown: A Biography Fifty Years After*, 139.
191. New York *Tribune*. 26 May 1856. Quoted by James C. Malin. "Judge Lecompte and the "Sack of Lawrence," May 26, 1856" *Kansas Historical Society*, 25 Mar. 2005, <http://www/kshs.or/publicat/khq/1953/53_7_amlin.htm>.
192. TWH, *Journal*, 18 Feb. 1856. Quoted by Edelstein in *Strange Enthusiasm: a Life of Thomas Wentworth Higginson*, 180.
193. Edelstein, *Strange Enthusiasm: a Life of Thomas Wentworth Higginson*, 184.
194. Howard N. Meyer, *Colonel of the Black Regiment: The Life of Thomas Wentworth Higginson* (New York: W. W. Norton & Company, 1967) 121.
195. "Letter from T.W. Higginson," *The Liberator*, Vol. XXVI, No. 29, 18 Jul. 1856.
196. Ibid.
197. Ibid.
198. Before leaving Worcester, Higginson "made arrangements to act as a correspondent for the New York *Tribune*, whose readers [, Meyers asserts]

were anxious for sympathetic firsthand accounts of the fight against slavery in Kansas." Meyers, *Colonol of the Black Regiment: The Life of Thomas Wentworth Higginson*, 121, 124.

199. TWH, letter to his Mother, Summer, 1856. Quoted by Meyers, 124.
200. Edelstein notes that in order to equip his emigrant band, TWH bought 91 Sharps rifles, 27 US muskets, 92 revolvers, 161 knives, a 2 ½ pound cannon, and significant amounts of both cartridges and powder for his arsenal. These supplies were in addition to the boots, clothing, blankets and various other supplies the minister purchased to outfit his charges and bring them to Kansas. Edelstein, *Strange Enthusiasm: a Life of Thomas Wentworth Higginson*, 186.
201. Higginson collected the articles that he wrote for the *Tribune*s and the *Democrat* in September and October, 1856 into a pamphlet he entitled *A Ride Through Kansas*, which he issued upon his return from the territory. Edelstein, *Strange Enthusiasm: a Life of Thomas Wentworth Higginson*, 187.
202. TWH, "Nebraska City," *A Ride Through Kansas; Sermons, Essays, and Lectures* (1926), 2.
203. TWH, letter to Mary Higginson, 24 Sep. 1856. Quoted by Mary Thacher Higginson in *Thomas Wentworth Higginson: The Story of His Life* (Boston: Houghton Mifflin Company, 1914) 174.
204. Higginson's 2 Jan. 1857 speech was printed in the January 16 edition of the *Liberator*. Although he had not met Brown at the time, and exaggerated the number of sons (from five to seven) Brown fought with in Kansas in 1856, his recognition of Brown's willingness to fight for the right of Free State settlers at a moments' notice and actively practice his religion as he fought, and killed Pro-Slavery forces, suggests that Higginson's knowledge of Brown's activities, particularly his actions at Pottawatomie, may have been better informed than most historians claim. Quoted in Edelstein, *Strange Enthusiasm: a Life of Thomas Wentworth Higginson*, 195–6.
205. *Liberator*, 2 Jan. 1857: Edelstein, *Strange Enthusiasm: a Life of Thomas Wentworth Higginson*, 196.
206. At the Massachusetts Disunion Convention, which Higginson organized and participated in, state delegates realized that "a long period of deliberation or discussion" would precede any actual disunion movement. Edelstein, *Strange Enthusiasm: a Life of Thomas Wentworth Higginson*, 198.
207. The term stockholder, which I employ to describe the six men who were Brown's primary financiers was used by TWH in a May 7, 1858 letter to John Brown's son Jason. Higginson laments the fact that the "leading stockholders" had so much influence over Brown, though he understood Brown's reasons for consenting to their wishes. TWH, letter to JB Jr., 7 May 1858.
208. In his notes on the conversation he had with Brown on 1 June, 1858, Higginson records that Brown suggested that "G.S. [Smith] he knew to be a timid man, G.L.S. [Stearns] and T.P. [Parker] he did not think abounded in courage, H.[Howe] had more." Quoted by Renehan, *The Secret Six: the True Tale of the Men Who Conspired with John Brown*, 163–64.
209. FS, letter to TWH, 11 May, 1858, Rossbach, *Ambivalent Conspirators: John Brown, the Secret Six, and a Theory of Slave Violence*, 164: Higginson's May 12, 1858 address to the American Anti-Slavery Society was printed in full in the 28 May 1858 *Liberator*. Edelstein, *Strange Enthusiasm: a Life of Thomas Wentworth Higginson*, 211.
210. Ibid.
211. TWH, "Saints, and Their Bodies," *Out-Door Papers*. (Boston: Lee and Shepard, 1879) 10.

212. TWH, letter to JB, 29 Oct. 1858; Edelstein, *Strange Enthusiasm: a Life of Thomas Wentworth Higginson,*, 214.
213. Edelstein, *Strange Enthusiasm: a Life of Thomas Wentworth Higginson*, 225.
214. Ibid, 221.
215. In his 17 Nov. letter to Sanborn, Higginson forthrightly denied Sanborn's request that he burn all correspondence which might be used in the future to prove their complicity in his attack at Harper's Ferry. Confronting the tentative Sanborn with all of the vitriol he had, Higginson asked "Can your clear moral sense be so sophisticated . . . [as] to justify holding one's tongue in face of this lying—and lying under the meanest circumstances—to save ourselves from all share in even the reprobation of society when the nobler man whom we have provoked unto danger is the scapegoat of that reprobation." Quoted by Edelstein, *Strange Enthusiasm: a Life of Thomas Wentworth Higginson*, 226.
216. HDT, letter to HGO Blake, 31 Oct. 1859; *Correspondence*, 563.
217. Higginson's sermon "Massachusetts in Mourning" was published in the 16 June edition of the *Liberator*, the periodical Thoreau had noted was one of two "papers in Boston . . . that made themselves heard in the condemnation of the cowardice and meanness of the authorities of that city" in his lecture "Slavery in Massachusetts," given on 4 July, 1854.
218. Higginson's response to the Anthony Burns's rendition, "Massachusetts in Mourning," was published in the *Liberator* Vol. XXIV, No. 24 on 16 June, 1854. The same edition carried a notice that Higginson had been arrested "as one of the Court Square 'rioters.'" It had previously appeared in the Massachusetts *Spy* on June 8, 1854.
219. FS, letter to TWH, 5 Jan. 1857: Edelstein, *Strange Enthusiasm: a Life of Thomas Wentworth Higginson*, 203–04.
220. TWH, letter to Hawkins (JB), 8 Feb. 1858: Edelstein, *Strange Enthusiasm: a Life of Thomas Wentworth Higginson*, 208.
221. Although Higginson informed Brown that he was "always ready to invest money in treason" but had none to invest in his 8 Feb. 1858 letter to the Kansas veteran, he alluded to a "trifling balance" in the coffers of the Worcester County Kansas Committee leading both Sanborn and Brown to believe that he had funds at his disposal that he might release to Brown if he were suitably impressed (and courted). Rossbach, *Ambivalent Conspirators: John Brown, the Secret Six, and a Theory of Slave Violence*, 136–37.
222. Worcester *Spy*, 20 Oct. 1859: Edelstein, *Strange Enthusiasm: a Life of Thomas Wentworth Higginson*, 222.
223. Quoted by HDT, "A Plea for Captain John Brown," 269.
224. TWH, "Massachusetts in Mourning" Massachusetts *Spy*, 8 Jun. 1854.
225. Edelstein, *Strange Enthusiasm: a Life of Thomas Wentworth Higginson*, 96.
226. TWH, letter to L. Higginson, 5 Jun. 1850; Mary Thacher Higginson, *Thomas Wentworth Higginson: the Story of his Life*, 98.
227. Ibid.
228. TWH, letter to HDT, 3 Dec. 1850: *Correspondence*, 269.
229. Dean and Hoag note that Higginson provided Thoreau with an introduction to Dr. H. C. Perkins, a local naturalist, who showed Thoreau some samples under a microscope. Dean and Hoag, "Thoreau's Lectures before Walden,"188.
230. Higginson, "The Crisis Coming Now." Newburyport *Union*, 4 Nov. 1850.
231. "Civil Disobedience" was published in the *Aesthetic Papers* in January, 1849, only twenty months before Thoreau met with Higginson for his Newburyport lecture. HDT, *The Essays of Henry D. Thoreau*, ed. Lewis Hyde (New York: Northpoint Press, 2002) 124.

232. HDT, *Journal* III: 213: *Log*, 208–209.

233. Ibid.

234. HDT, letter to TWH, 2 Apr. 1852: *Correspondence*, 278–79.

235. HDT, letter to TWH, 3 Apr. 1852: *Correspondence*, 280.

236. In "Short Studies of American Authors," published forty years after Thoreau gave his lecture in Boston, Higginson recalls the evening at Cochituate Hall on 6 Apr. 1852. Quoted by Dean and Hoag, "Thoreau's Lectures Before Walden," 207.

237. A. Fairbanks, letter to HDT, 14 Oct. 1854; *Correspondence*, 345–46.

238. TWH, letter to HDT, 13 Aug. 1854: *Correspondence*, 336.

239. HDT, *Journal*, VII: 79: *Log*, 333.

240. HDT, letter to HGO Blake, 26 Sep. 1855: *Correspondence*, 383–385. Thoreau employs Ktaadn, the Penobscot term for the "greatest mountain" when he refers to Mount Katahdin, Maine's rugged highest point.

241. Ibid.

242. HDT, "Reform and the Reformers," *Reform Papers*. ed. Wendell Glick (Princeton, Princeton University Press, 1973) 185.

243. HDT, letter to Sophia Thoreau, 1 Nov. 1856: *Correspondence*, 438–439: *Log*, 338, 393,409, 423, 470.

244. Harding, *Days*, 338

245. TWH, *Cheerful Yesterdays*, 181.

246. TWH, letter to Mrs. Harriet Prescott Spofford, undated, Mary Thacher Higginson, ed. *Letters and Journals of TWH 1846–1906* (Boston: Houghton Mifflin Company, 1921) 105.

247. Elizabeth Hoar's comment was noted by Ralph Waldo Emerson in his *Journal* (VI: 371); *Log*, 90.

248. Mary Thacher Higginson, *Letters and Journals of TWH, 1846–1906*, 94.

249. JB, letter to TWH, 12 Feb. 1858. Quoted in full by Higginson, *Cheerful Yesterdays*, 218.

250. Responding to Senator Mason's question, "How do you justify your acts?" during his first interview on 19 October, 1859 (subsequently published by the New York *Herald)*, John Brown responded, "I think, my friend, you are guilty of a great wrong against God and humanity—I say it without wishing to be offensive—and it would be perfectly right in anyone to interfere with you so far as to free those you willfully and wickedly hold in bondage." Quoted in "A Conversation with Brown," *The Life Trial and Execution of Captain John Brown* (1859 rep. New York: De Capo Press, 1969) 45: Thoreau specifically points to Brown's response to Mason in the middle of his lecture. "Read his admirable answers to Mason and others. How they are dwarfed and defeated in contrast." Quoted in HDT, "A Plea for Captain John Brown," 272.

251. TWH, "Massachusetts in Mourning," *Liberator* Vol. XXIV, No. 23 16 Jun 1854: TWH, letter to William Lloyd Garrison, 21 Aug. 1855: *Liberator*, 24 Aug. 1855: Edelstein, *Strange Enthusiasm*, 165.

252. TWH, "Massachusetts in Mourning," Massachusetts *Spy*, 8 Jun. 1854.

253. TP, letter to Francis Jackson, 24 Nov. 1859: Quoted by Weiss, *The Life and Correspondence of Theodore Parker*, 175.

254. In all probability, the single expression of sympathy for John Brown that Thoreau read was one of James Redpath's articles in the Boston *Atlas & Daily Bee*. Edelstein notes that "three days after Brown's imprisonment, Redpath began a series of articles [extolling Brown's actions in the daily newspaper] variously entitled 'Reminiscences of the Insurrection' and 'Notes on the Insurrection.'" Edelstein, 226.

NOTES TO CHAPTER 5

1. RWE, "American Slavery (25 Jan. 1855)," *The Later Lectures of Ralph Waldo Emerson 1843–1871*, eds. Ronald A. Bosco and Joel Myerson (Athens: University of Georgia Press, 2001) 10.
2. Len Gougeon, *Virtues Hero*, 218.
3. Ibid.
4. Ibid, 223.
5. Ibid.
6. RWE, "Kansas Relief Meeting (10 Sep. 56),"*Emerson's Anti-Slavery Writings*, eds. Len Gougeon and Joel Myerson, (New Haven: Yale University Press, 1995) 112. All subsequent parenthetical references in this chapter originate from this anthology of Emerson's work.
7. Ibid.
8. Renehan, *The Secret Six: the True Tale of the Men Who Conspired with John Brown*, 117.
9. Oates, *To Purge this Land with Blood: A Biography of John Brown*, 197.
10. Phillis Cole, "Pain and Protest in the Emerson Family," *The Emerson Dilemma: Essays on Emerson and Social Reform*. ed. T. Gregory, Garvey (University of Georgia Press: Athens, 2001) 85.
11. RWE, "Morals (26 April, 1859)," *The Later Lectures of Ralph Waldo Emerson 1843–1871*, eds. Ronald A. Bosco and Joel Myerson (Athens: University of Georgia Press, 2001) 137.
12. Ibid.
13. RWE, letter to William Emerson, 23 October, 1859. Ralph L. Rusk, ed., *The Letters of Ralph Waldo Emerson* Vol. V. (New York: Columbia University Press, 1939) 178.
14. RWE, letter to Sarah Swain Forbes, 26 October, 1859. Ralph L. Rusk, ed., *The Letters of Ralph Waldo Emerson* Vol. V. (New York: Columbia University Press, 1939) 179–180.
15. RWE, letter to Charles Wesley Slack, 31 October, 1859. American Antiquarian Society, Worcester, MA.
16. Ibid.
17. Charles W. Slack, letter to RWE, 31 October, 1859, Walter Harding and Carl Bode, eds., *The Correspondence of Thoreau* (New York: New York University Press, 1958) 564.
18. Gougeon, *Virtue's Hero: Emerson, Anti-Slavery, and Reform*, 241.
19. In addition to signing the public letter encouraging the donation of funds for Brown's defense, Emerson agreed to receive funds on Brown's behalf. Ibid.
20. Gilman Ostrander, "Emerson, Thoreau, and John Brown. *The Mississippi Valley Historical Review*. Vol. XXXIV (1852/1853), 726; Ralph Waldo Emerson, "Courage," *Society and Solitude* (Boston: Houghton Mifflin and Company, 1904) 270, 255.
21. RWE, "Courage," *Society and Solitude* (New York: Boston: Houghton Mifflin, 1904) 255.
22. Jefferson, *Declaration of Independence*, 235.
23. "Brown Meeting in Concord," Boston *Atlas & Daily Bee*, 2 Dec. 1859. Quoted by Kenneth Walter Cameron, ed. *Transcendental Log: Fresh Discoveries in Newspapers Concerning Emerson, Thoreau, Alcott and Others of the American Literary Renaissance* (Hartford: Transcendental Books, 1973) 138.
24. RWE, "Morals (26 April, 1859)," *The Later Lectures of Ralph Waldo Emerson 1843–1871* Vol. 2, eds. Ronald Bosco and Joel Myerson (Athens: University of Georgia Press, 2001) 137.

25. Phillips asserted that Brown's family was "destitute" when he approached Emerson about speaking at the 6 January fund-raiser for Brown's family. Gougeon, *Virtue's Hero: Emerson, Anti-Slavery, and Reform*, 249.

26. John Carlos Rowe, *At Emerson's Tomb: The Politics of Classic American Literature* (New York: Columbia University Press, 1997) 21.

27. RWE, "American Slavery (25 Jan. 1855)," *The Later Lectures of Ralph Waldo Emerson 1843–1871*, eds. Ronald A. Bosco and Joel Myerson (Athens: University of Georgia Press, 2001) 3.

28. RWE, "Self Reliance," *The Selected Writings of Ralph Waldo Emerson*, ed. Brooks Atkinson (New York: The Modern Library, 1950) 160.

29. RWE, "The American Scholar," *The Norton Anthology of American Literature*, Vol. 6. Gen. ed. Nina Baym (New York: W.W. Norton & Company, 2003) 1142.

30. Much to Emerson's embarrassment, Thomas Sims, a fugitive slave, was captured, tried, and sent back to slavery from Boston in 1851 in acquiescence to the Fugitive Slave Law passed in September, 1850. Gougeon, *Virtue's Hero: Emerson, Anti-Slavery, and Reform*, 156.

31. In "The American Scholar," Emerson had asserted that the office of the scholar, is to "cheer, to raise, and to guide men by showing them facts amidst appearances." RWE, "The American Scholar," 1142.

32. Ibid, 1142: RWE, "Fugitive Slave Law" (March 7, 1854), *Emerson's Anti-Slavery Writings*, eds. Len Gougeon and Joel Myerson (New Haven: Yale University Press, 1995) 82.

33. Ibid, 78.

34. Ibid.

35. Ibid, 82.

36. Ibid, 96.

37. Ibid, 102.

38. RWE, "Kansas Relief Meeting," *Emerson's Anti-Slavery Writings*, eds. Len Gougeon and Joel Myerson (New Haven: Yale University Press, 1995) 113.

39. Ibid, 114.

40. RWE, "Assault on Charles Sumner" (23 May 1856), *Emerson's Anti-Slavery Writings*, eds. Len Gougeon and Joel Myerson (New Haven: Yale University Press, 1995) 109.

41. Gougeon, *Virtue's Hero: Emerson, Anti-Slavery, and Reform*, 221.

42. Following Brooks' attack, Sumner withdrew from politics and was not able to "resume his normal Senate duties" until December, 1859," a period of three years time. Gougeon, *Virtue's Hero: Emerson, Anti-Slavery, and Reform*, 221.

43. Robert D. Richardson Jr., *Emerson: The Mind on Fire* (Berkeley: University of California Press, 1995) 498.

44. RWE, "John Brown" (January 6, 1860), *Emerson's Anti-Slavery Writings*, eds. Len Gougeon and Joel Myerson (New Haven: Yale University Press, 1995) 123.

45. RWE, "American Slavery" (25 January, 1855), *The Later Lectures of Ralph Waldo Emerson 1843–1871* Vol. 2, eds. Ronald Bosco and Joel Myerson (Athens: University of Georgia Press, 2001) 10.

46. Ibid, 9.

47. RWE, "American Slavery" (25 January, 1855), *The Later Lectures of Ralph Waldo Emerson 1843–1871*, eds. Ronald A. Bosco and Joel Myerson (Athens: University of Georgia Press, 2001) 9.

48. Gougeon. *Virtue's Hero*, 231,153.

49. JMN 11: 361: Gougeon, *Virtue's Hero: Emerson, Anti-Slavery, and Reform*, 156.

50. JMN 11: 352: Gougeon, *Virtue's Hero: Emerson, Anti-Slavery, and Reform*, 157.
51. RWE, JMN 14: 421
52. In "Nature," Emerson contends that men who virtuously sought truth and unflinchingly proclaimed it, would inevitably gain a true understanding of virtue. RWE, "Nature," 1115.
53. RWE, "Self-Reliance," 148.
54. Emerson had been greatly disappointed by the denigration of New York Senator William H. Seward's March 11, 1850 "Higher Law" speech in the United States Senate. Arguing over the admission of California, Seward asserted that the new territory was governed by a "higher law than the Constitution which regulated the authority of Congress over the national domain—the law of God and thee interest of humanity"—a moral law established by the "creator of the Universe" which denied slavery; he asserted that there was "an irrepressible conflict between opposing and enduring forces," and that the United States must become either entirely slave or entirely free. Emerson agreed with Seward's argument terming what Seward called a "law of nature" a universal or moral law. JMN 11: 248: Gougeon, *Virtue's Hero: Emerson, Anti-Slavery, and Reform*, 139: "William Henry Seward's Higher Law Speech," 31 Mar. 2005, <http://www.furman.edu/~benson/docs/seward.html>.
55. Gougeon, *Virtue's Hero: Emerson, Anti-Slavery, and Reform*, 231: RWE, "American Slavery," 9.
56. Emerson's draft letter to Governor Wise was apparently never sent. His notes for the letter appear to have been employed during composition for his November 18th speech and are extant in his journal. JMN 14: 334.
57. Villard notes that Governor Wise expressed willingness to have his name presented to the National Democratic Convention at Charleston, South Carolina for the presidency a few months after Brown's trial. Since his gubernatorial term was near expiration, Wise was uniquely positioned to capitalize on his recent public exposure or notoriety during the tumultuous election season. Villard, *John Brown: A Biography Fifty Years After*, 527.
58. RWE, "English Traits," *The Selected Writings of Ralph Waldo Emerson*, ed. Brooks Atkinson (New York: The Modern Library, 1950) 523–690: Robert D. Richardson Jr., *Emerson: The Mind on Fire*, 519.
59. Emerson employs the word *stoutness* to describe the English as forthright, full of course strength, bold, loud, plodding, combative, thorough, and utterly assured of their superiority to other races. RWE, "English Traits," 593.
60. RWE, "Morals," *Emerson's Anti-Slavery Writings*, eds. Len Gougeon and Joel Myerson (New Haven: Yale University Press, 1995) 137.
61. RWE, *Representative Men: Seven Lectures*, ed. Douglas Emory Wilson (Cambridge: Harvard UP, 1996) 15.
62. Ibid, x.
63. Ibid, 13.
64. Emerson's claim that John Brown was "happily a representative of the American Republic" cannot fail to recall the informed listener to his exposition of the qualities which made his six representative men, none of whom was American, worthy of recognition. As he explained in the "Uses of Great Men," representative men "teach us the qualities of primary nature, [and] admit us to the constitution of things" (12). He proceeds to intimate that the service that representative do for mankind is to "introduce moral truths into the general mind" (12). The resultant "apprehension . . . of incorruptible goods" (13) liberates the perceiver or creates a "new conscious-

ness" (11). For Emerson, this is Brown's value as a representative man. He fearlessly advocated the moral truth that slavery established an unnatural relation between men, violated virtuous sensibility, and fostered evil in a society based on the notion of liberty, and by his oft quoted "simple, artless" (118, JB) denunciations of slavery and those who defended the corrupt institution, Brown brought slavery and the immoral laws which supported it to the forefront of the national conscience.

65. John Brown's October, 19 1859 response to Senator Mason's query was noted by an anonymous reporter in "A Conversation with Brown," *The Life, Trial, and Execution of Captain John Brown* (New York: De Capo Press, 1969) 45.

66. In 1875, Emerson asserted that Brown and Lincoln were the "two best examples of eloquence" in American History. Harold K. Bush, "Emerson, John Brown, and "Doing the Word," *The Emerson Dilemma: Essays on Emerson and Social Reform*, ed. T. Gregory Garvey, (Athens: University of Georgia Press, 2001) 212.

67. Thomas Jefferson, "Notes on the State of Virginia," ed. William Peden (Chapel Hill: University of North Carolina Press, 1954) 164–165.

68. RWE, "Nature," 1106.

69. Ibid, 1121.

70. RWE, "Nature." 1129.

71. RWE, "Farming," *The Selected Writings of Ralph Waldo Emerson*. ed. Brooks Atkinson. (New York: The Modern Library, 1950) 749.

72. RWE, "Nature," 1121.

73. RWE, "The American Scholar," 1135.

74. RWE, "Self-Reliance," 157.

75. Brown, evidently, was less that scrupulous in his construction of his own past. As many scholars have noted, Peter Brown was not among the original Mayflower passengers or crew who settled in Plymouth. Harold K. Bush, "Emerson, John Brown, and 'Doing the Word.'" *The Emerson Dilemma: Essays on Emerson and Social Reform*. Ed. T. Gregory Garvey (Athens: University of Georgia Press, 2001) 205.

76. In his essay "Character," Emerson suggests that character is moral order seen through the medium of an individual nature. RWE, "Character," *Selected Writings of Ralph Waldo Emerson*, ed. Brooks Atkinson (New York: The Modern Library, 1950) 369.

77. RWE, "Politics," *The Selected Writings of Ralph Waldo Emerson*. ed. Brooks Atkinson. (New York: The Modern Library, 1950) 422.

78. RWE, "Self Reliance," 1147.

79. Ibid, 1142.

NOTES TO CHAPTER 6

1. Harriet Beecher Stowe (hereafter HBS), *The Minister's Wooing* (New Jersey: Gregg Press, 1968) 82.

2. Ibid.

3. Ibid.

4. HBS, *Uncle Tom's Cabin*. ed. Elizabeth Ammons (New York: W.W. Norton & Company, 1994) 385.

5. Ibid, 385.

6. Ibid, 386.

7. Robert S. Levine, "Introduction," *Dred: A Tale of the Dismal Swamp*, ed. Harold S. Levine (New York: Penguin Books, 2000) xii.

8. HBS, *Dred: A Tale of the Dismal Swamp,* ed. Harold S. Levine (New York: Penguin Books, 2000) 530. All subsequent parenthetical references in this chapter originate from this text.

9. In "Violence and Sacrificial Displacement in Harriet Beecher Stowe's *Dred,*" Richard Boyd notes that Northern newspapers reported that widespread "plans for slave revolts dominated the popular consciousness throughout 1856." Quoting historian Harvey Wish, Boyd suggests Stowe's awareness of this panic since it was reported in both the Boston *Liberator* and New York *Tribune* . He also intimates its influence upon her during her construction of *Dred*; Richard Boyd, *Arizona Quarterly,* Vol. 50, 2 (Summer, 1994) 51–52.

10. I think it important to distinguish offensive from defensive acts of personal violence. An individual embraces offensive violence when, unprovoked, he or she arbitrarily exerts physical force to either violate, abuse, or kill a person or damage that person's property with the intent of violating his or her sensibility. I define defensive violence as the limited physical force employed to defend life, limb, or property.

11. RWE, letter to William Emerson, 2 June 1856. Ralph L. Rusk, ed., *The Letters of Ralph Waldo Emerson,* Vol. 5 (New York: Columbia University Press, 1939) 23.

12. Boyd, 55.

13. HBS, letter to Duchess of Argyle, 17 June 1856; Joan Hedrick, *Harriet Beecher Stowe: a Life* (New York: Oxford University Press, 1994) 258.

14. On May 22, 1856, John Brown decided to "strike terror in the hearts of the Pro-Slavery people" of Kansas. Enlisting the aid of seven hand-picked men, four who were related to him by blood, Brown proceeded to Pottawatomie Creek to see a bit of "radical retaliatory" justice done. In the killing spree that followed, Brown and his men brutally murdered five men on the banks of the Pottawatomie in Kansas. In the New York Daily *Times*, Captain Pate forcefully concludes his account of the battle of Black Jack by exposing John "BROWN and his confederates [as the] . . . men [who] were engaged in the Pottawatomie [sic] massacre." Henry C. Pate, "Battle of Black-Jack Point— Exploits of Captain Pate and is Southern Company, as Detailed by Himself," *The New York Daily Times,* 17 June, 1856, 2.

15. Salmon Brown, "John Brown and Sons in Kansas Territory," *A John Brown Reader,* ed. Louis Ruchames (New York: Abelard-Schuman, 1959) 195.

16. George and Henry Grant record John Brown Jr.'s words of caution in their testimony on the Pottawatomie tragedy, "New and Important Testimony . . . What George and Henry Grant Say About It." Ruchames, 205: Salmon Brown records his brother's mental state in "John Brown and Sons in Kansas." He notes that following the raid at Pottawatomie, John Brown Jr. "made his way back to Ossawatomie, where his family had gone, in a very dejected state of mind, bordering on breakdown." Later, he notes that his brother Owen saw John Jr. at Ossawatomie, "but could do nothing for him as his head was still wild." Ruchames, 195: Stephen Oates notes that John Jr. "went completely to pieces . . . he was 'crazed,' 'deranged'" by the time Jason got him to Adair's cabin." Oates, *To Purge this Land with Blood,* 140.

17. Oates notes that in the days following Brown's raid, rumors that "Buford's Southerners were going to kill every free-state settler in the Ossawatomie-Pottawatomie area" soon reached the residents of Southeastern Kansas creating an atmosphere of great anxiety and inspiring fear of violent reprisals. Oates, *To Purge this Land with Blood,* 140.

18. "Resolution" adopted on 27 May, 1856 signed by C.H. Price, R. Golding, R. Gilpatrick, W.C. McDow, S.V. Vandaman, A. Castele, John Blunt, and H.H.

Williams responding to the murders at Pottawatomie. Interestingly, Salmon Brown's account of the event indicates that H.H. Williams was both the man who identified those to be killed and the man who condemned those who did the killing. Villard, *John Brown: A Biography Fifty Years After*, 168.

19. Stowe's brother, Henry Ward Beecher, was well known as a dynamic and demonstrative abolitionist. During the civil war in Kansas, Beecher's Plymouth Church sent boxes of Sharpe's Rifles in boxes marked "Bibles" to the Free-State settlers in Kansas. When this story became known, rifles sent to help the anti-slavery settlers protect themselves against the rampages of Pro-Slavery forces became popularly known as Beecher's Bibles. Hedrick, 258: JB Jr., letters to his father, May 20, 24, and 26. Villard, *John Brown: A Biography Fifty Years After*, 83.

20. Martin Delany, letter to Frederick Douglass, date unspecified. Printed in the *Frederick Douglass Paper*, 1 Apr. 53, 2: Quoted by Robert S. Levine, "*Uncle Tom's Cabin* in *Frederick Douglass Paper*: Analysis of Reception," *Uncle Tom's Cabin*, ed. Elizabeth Ammons (New York: W.W. Norton & Company, 1994) 533.

21. Ibid, 535.

22. Ibid, 533.

23. Stowe's chapter "The Tie Breaks" records Harry's anguish when he learns that the contract that guarantees him freedom on "paying a certain sum" is not legally enforcable. HBS, *Dred: A Tale of the Great Dismal Swamp*, 383–389.

24. Interestingly, in the immediate aftermath of the publication of *Uncle Tom's Cabin*, Stowe was criticized by many African-American critics for writing about slavery, a subject of which she had no intimate knowledge. As Michael J. Meyer asserts, many contemporary critics have espoused the same ideas that Martin Delany articulated in his 1853 letter to Frederick Douglass—that "no white person can truly know a black." Michael J. Meyer, "Toward the Rhetoric of Equality: Reflective and Refractive Images in Stowe's Language," *The Stowe Debate*, eds. Mason I. Lowance Jr., Ellen E. Westbrook, and R.C. De Prospo (Amherst: University of Massachusetts Press, 1994) 238.

25. RWE, "Nature," *The Norton Anthology of American Literature*, 6th Ed., Vol. B, Gen. ed. Nina Baym (New York: W.W. Norton & Company, 2003) 1115.

26. Lisa Whitney, "In the Shadow of Uncle Tom's Cabin: Stowe's Vision of Slavery from the Great Dismal Swamp," *The New England Quarterly*, Vol. LXVI, 4 (December 1993) 566.

27. Stephen B. Oates, *The Fires of Jubilee: Nat Turner's Fierce Rebellion* (New York: Harper & Row, Publishers, 1975) 98, 100.

28. Joan Hedrick notes that Stowe composed *Dred* in a three month period during the summer of 1856. Although she does not suggest the exact date when Stowe began composition, she does note that on June 11, 1856, Calvin Stowe wrote to her publisher indicating that Harriet had already written "one hundred pages of ms." Considering that she regularly completed twelve pages of ms per day, Stowe probably began writing in the beginning of the month. Stowe completed the narrative on 15 Aug. 1856 (following her arrival in London) and had a copies of the book in hand on the 23d. Hedrick, *Harriet Beecher Stowe: A Life*, 260–262.

29. Leavenworth *Herald*, Quoted by Oates, 142.

30. "An Appeal for Kansas," New York *Daily Tribune*. 9 Jun. 1856, 1.

31. A sixteenth-century Spanish noble, the Duke of Alva was sent to the Netherlands to enforce the rule of the Spanish regent in 1567. Upon arrival in Brussels, the duke appointed a counsel to condemn, without trial, twenty-two noblemen suspected of opposing the Spanish rule inspiring widespread

212   *Notes*

terror and masses of refugees. After he had subdued Brussels, Alva commenced a particularly brutal campaign against those sympathetic with the
rebellion. According to one source, during his administration, he sent more
than 18,000 people to the scaffold: "Kansas Bulletin," *The Independent*,
Vol. VIII, No. 391. 29 May 1856, 1.

32. Ibid.
33. "Kansas Bulletin," *The Independent*, Vol. VIII, No. 393. 12 Jun. 1856, 1.
34. "Violence to Women in Kansas," *The Independent*, Vol. VIII, No. 394, 19
    Jun. 1856, 1.
35. HBS, "Mothers of the Men in Kansas," *The Independent*, Vol. VIII, No.
    394, 19 Jun 1856, 1.
36. Ibid.
37. In his *Narrative*, Frederick Douglass famously recalls the turning point of his
    life—his decision to violently resist his brutal owner, Edward Covey. After the
    two hour struggle, Douglass suggests that he was never again a "slave in fact"
    (299) and never experienced his master's wrath again. He achieved, he claims,
    manhood and revived his desire for freedom. Frederick Douglass, *Narrative of
    the Life of Frederick Douglass 1845, The Classic Slave Narratives*, ed. Henry
    Louis Gates Jr. (New York: Mentor Books, 1987) 298–300.
38. Stowe crafts her scene to deliberately confront the reader with Judge Ruffin's
    1829 decision guaranteeing the *"full dominion of the owner over the slave,"*
    even in instances when the owner's cruelty are excessive. She draws attention
    to Ruffin's decision by mentioning it in her "Preface" and liberally quoting
    Ruffin in "The Legal Decision." HBS, *Dred*, 4, 354.
39. Daughters of a third generation slave-owner and leading judge in the
    Supreme Court of South Carolina, Angelina and Sarah Grimke are interest-
    ing figures when considering the Claytons. Born to a slave-owning family
    in South Carolina, in youth, both women rejected the notion that slavery
    was morally justifiable and became some of the most outspoken female abo-
    litionists (and early feminists) of the 1830s and 1840s. When Sarah was
    a young woman, she taught her slave attendant to read and was severely
    punished for her violation of the law by her father. Later, explaining that
    "the sight of [the slaves] condition was unsupportable" (52, Lerner), Sarah
    determined that she could no longer live in a state that embraced slavery
    and moved to Philadelphia. Angelina also revolted against the idea of slav-
    ery and attempted to inspire her mother to liberate all of the slaves on their
    plantation. Unsuccessful, she continued to live in Charleston attempting to
    convince her neighbors of the evils inherent in the system of slavery until
    she too could no longer bear the idea of living in a slave community. Join-
    ing her sister in Philadelphia, she embraced Quakerism and moral suasion
    as the appropriate response to slavery. Inspired to speak out in the cause of
    abolition by their Quaker friends, both Angelina and Sarah fearlessly pre-
    sented abolitionist lectures throughout the North and published abolitionist
    appeals (in 1836, Angelina published *Appeal to the Christian Women of the
    South*, and in 1837 Sarah published her *Appeal to the Women of the Nomi-
    nally Free States*). Within the context of Stowe's work, both women seem
    likely models for Edward and Anne Clayton. The Clayton's father was the
    patriarch of "one of the oldest and most distinguished [slave-owning] fami-
    lies of North Carolina" (16) and the "leading judge of the Supreme Court"
    (350) of North Carolina. Both Anne and Clayton rejected the system of
    slavery that had ensured their social prominence. Edward, trained as a law-
    yer, left the bar when he learned that North Carolina law did not privilege
    higher law; Sarah Grimke aspired to the law (her father claiming that "she
    would have made the greatest jurist in the country" (Lerner, 20)) but never

had the opportunity to study for the bar since she was a woman; like Anne Clayton, Sarah had a "clear judging mind" (28); she rejected the notion that it was wrong to teach slaves to read, openly asserted her equal right to translate her beliefs into reality, and rejected the idea that women had to succumb to the social norm and assume a position subservient to men; like Edward and Anne, both sisters eventually left the South, disgusted with their neighbors' ignorant approval of the system which guaranteed them power, wealth, and position and embraced education (for a time) as the means by which they might advance racial notions of equity. Gerda Lerner, *The Grimke Sisters from South Carolina: Rebels against Slavery* (Boston: Houghton, Mifflin Company, 1967), 11–278.

40. Hedrick's asserts that Stowe's narrative is as much a pointed attack on the inert clergy as a "response to the sectional warfare in Kansas and the increasingly open political struggle between proslavery and antislavery forces." She neglects to mention that that during the composition of *Dred*, the struggle between those two forces was decidedly one-sided. With a Pro-Slavery president (Franklin Pierce) providing overt aid to the empowered Pro-Slavery governor (Wilson Shannon) in Kansas, there seemed little opportunity for the Free State cause in the Kansas territory. Hedrick, *Harriet Beecher Stowe: A Life*, 261.

41. In "An Appeal to the Women of the Free States of America, On the Present Crisis in Our Country," Stowe petitioned the women of America to use all of their influence to ensure that the Kansas-Nebraska Bill did not succeed in Congress. *The Independent*. 6, 23 Feb. 1854: Quoted in *Uncle Tom's Cabin*, ed. Elizabeth Ammons (New York: W.W. Norton & Company, 1994) 428.

42. HBS, letter to William Lloyd Garrison, 18 Feb. 1854. Hedrick, *Harriet Beecher Stowe: A Life*, 257.

43. Henry Ward Beecher, "The Crisis," *The Independent*, 2 Mar.1854: Hedrick, *Harriet Beecher Stowe: A Life*, 256.

44. Hedrick, *Harriet Beecher Stowe: A Life*, 258.

45. Ibid.

46. Charles Edward Stowe, *Life of Harriet Beecher Stowe: Compiled from her Letters and Journals* (Boston: Houghton Mifflin, 1890) 255.

47. Forrest Wilson, *Crusader in Crinoline: The Life of Harriet Beecher Stowe* (Philadelphia: J. B. Lippincott Company, 1941) 333.

48. Charles Sumner, letter to HBS, date not specified. Noted by Wilson, *Crusader in Crinoline: The Life of Harriet Beecher Stowe*,409.

49. Wilson notes that Stowe did not include any mention of Kansas or the troubles there in her *Independent* column during the tumultuous years that following the enactment of the Nebraska Bill. Wilson, *Crusader in Crinoline: The Life of Harriet Beecher Stowe*, 406.

50. TP, "The Present Aspect of Slavery and the Immediate Duty of the North," [a speech given in Jan. 29, 1858] in Works (Cobbe Edition), 6: 289, Rossbach, *Ambivalent Conspirators: John Brown, the Secret Six, and a Theory of Slave Violence*, 148–149.

51. HBS, "Introduction," *The Colored Patriots of the Revolution*. (New York: Arno Press and the New York *Times*, 1968), 5–6

52. Stowe makes explicit reference in *Dred* to two legal decisions—the 1851 decision in the Souther Vs. Commonwealth and the 1829 State vs. Mann decision—both decisions that validated the unlimited power of the master over his slaves.

53. Governor Wilson Shannon, letter to President Franklin Pierce, 31 May 1856, Villard, *John Brown: A Biography Fifty Years After*, 192.

54. New York *Tribune*, 18 Jun. 1856, Villard, *John Brown: A Biography Fifty Years After*, 216.
55. Ibid.
56. "Kansas Bulletin," *The Independent*, Vol. VIII, No. 396, 3 Jul. 1856.
57. Mary Ryan, *Womanhood in America: From Colonial Times to the Present* (New York: New Viewpoints, 1975) 145.
58. Ibid, 165.
59. I specify sentimental women authors in recognition of Jane Tompkins assertion that the chief characteristic of the sentimental novel "is that it is written by, for, and about women." Jane P. Tompkins, "Sentimental Power: *Uncle Tom's Cabin* and the Politics of Literary History," *Uncle Tom's Cabin*, ed. Elizabeth Ammons (New York: W.W. Norton & Company, 1994) 504.
60. Oates notes that when militiamen from Missouri grabbed the "guns and whiskey jugs and rode across the border—a 'swearing, whiskey drinking ruffianly horde' who vowed to exterminate those 'freedom shriekers' in Lawrence with chunks of lead" entered Kansas. On May 22, 1856, these men sacked the town unopposed, "looting stores, destroying the printing presses, and setting fire to the Free-State Hotel." Oates, *To Purge this Land with Blood*, 125, 127: HBS, *Dred*, 536.
61. The opinions expressed in this book are the author's and do not reflect the views of any organizations with which he is associated.

Works Cited

PRIMARY SOURCES

Newspapers:

Atchison *Squatter Sovereign*
Baltimore *American and Commercial Advertiser*
Boston *Atlas & Daily Bee*
Charlestown *Independent Democrat*
Cleveland *Plain Dealer*
Independent
Kansas Herald
Kansas *Trading Post*
Kansas *Pioneer*
Lawrence *Republican*
Leavenworth *Herald*
Liberator
New York *Journal of Commerce*
New York *Daily Times*
New York *Tribune*
Newburyport *Union*

Journals and Texts:

bin Laden, Osama, "letter to the American people (24 Nov. 2002)," *Guardian Observer*, 8 Apr. 2005, http://www.observer.guradian.co.uk/worldview/story/0,11581,845725,00.html>.
———. "Your Security is in your own Hands (29 Oct. 2004)," CNN.com, 8 Apr. 2005, <http://www.cnn.com/2004/WORLD/meast/10/29/bin.laden.transcript/>.
Blassingame, John W., ed. *The Frederick Douglass papers*. Vol. 1–5. New Haven: Yale University Press, 1979–1992.
Borst, Raymond R. *The Thoreau Log: A Documentary Life of Henry David Thoreau 1817–1862*. New York: G. K. Hall & Co., 1992.
Cameron, Kenneth Walter. *Transcendental Log: Fresh Discoveries in Newspapers Concerning Emerson, Thoreau, Alcott and Others of the American Literary Renaissance*. Hartford: Transcendental Books, 1973.
Child, Lydia Maria, ed. "John Brown and the Colored Child." *The Freedman's Journal*. Boston, 1865.
Churchill, Ward, "'Some People Push Back,' On the Justice of Roosting Chickens written by Ward Churchill 9–11–2001." 6 Apr. 2005, http://www.politicalgateway.com/news/read/html?id=2739.

"A Conversation with Brown." *The Life Trial and Execution of Captain John Brown*. 1859. New York: De Capo Press, 1969.

Dean, Bradley P. and Ronald Wesley Hoag. "*Thoreau's Lectures Before* Walden: an Annotated Calendar." *Studies in the American Renaissance, 1995*. Ed. Joel Myerson. Charlottesville: University Press of Virginia, 1995.

———. "*Thoreau's Lectures after* Walden: an Annotated Calendar." *Studies in the American Renaissance 1996*. Ed. Joel Meyerson. Charlottesville: University Press of Virginia, 1996.

Delany, Martin R. *The Condition, Elevation, Emmigration, and Destiny of the Colored People of the United States*. 1852: Reprint. New York: Arno Press and the New York *Times*, 1969.

Douglass, Frederick. *Life and Times*. 1883. *Autobiographies*. New York: Library of America, 1994.

———, *Narrative of the Life of Frederick Douglass*. 1845. *The Classic Slave Narratives*. Ed. Henry Louis Gates Jr. New York: Mentor Books, 1987.

———. "John Brown's Contributions to the Abolition Movement: An Address Delivered in Boston, Massachusetts on 3 December, 1860." *The Frederick Douglass Papers*. Vol. 3., Ed. John W. Blassingame. New Haven: Yale University Press, 1985.

———. Frederick Douglass. Letter to Charles Wesley Slack, 26 August, 1859. Charles Wesley Slack Papers. Department of Special Collections and Archives, Kent State University Libraries and Media Services.

Emerson, Ellen Tucker. *The Letters of Ellen Tucker Emerson*. Vol. 1, Ed. Edith E.W. Gregg. Kent, Ohio: Kent State University Press, 1982.

Emerson, Ralph Waldo. *The Journals and Miscellaneous Notebooks of Ralph Waldo Emerson*, Vol. XIV. Eds. Susan Sutton Smith and Harrison Hayford. Cambridge: Belknap Press of Harvard University, 1978.

———. *The Journals and Miscellaneous Notebooks of Ralph Waldo Emerson*. Vol. XIII. Eds. Ronald Bosco and Glen Jackson. Cambridge: Mass, 1982.

———. *The Letters of Ralph Waldo Emerson*. Vols. IV & V. Ed. Ralph L. Rusk. New York: Columbia University Press, 1939.

———. *The Selected Writings of Ralph Waldo Emerson*. Ed. Brooks Atkinson. New York: The Modern Library, 1950.

———. *The Later Lectures of Ralph Waldo Emerson 1843–1871*. Eds. Ronald A. Bosco and Joel Myerson. Athens: University of Georgia Press, 2001.

———. *Representative Men: Seven Lectures*. Ed. Douglas Emory Wilson. Cambridge: Harvard University Press, 1996.

———. "'Address to the Citizens of Concord" on the Fugitive Slave Law (3 May 1851)," *Emerson's Anti-Slavery Writings*. Eds. Len Gougeon and Joel Myerson. New Haven: Yale University Press, 1995.

———. "American Slavery (25 Jan. 1855)," *The Later Lectures of Ralph Waldo Emerson 1843–1871*. Eds. Ronald A. Bosco and Joel Myerson. Athens: University of Georgia Press, 2001.

———. "Assault on Charles Sumner" (26 May 1856). *Emerson's Anti-Slavery Writings*. Eds. Len Gougeon and Joel Myerson. New Haven: Yale University Press, 1995.

———. "Character,"*Selected Writings of Ralph Waldo Emerson*. Ed. Brooks Atkinson New York: The Modern Library, 1950.

———. "Courage," *Society and Solitude*. Boston: Houghton Mifflin, 1904.

———. "English Traits," *The Selected Writings of Ralph Waldo Emerson*. Ed. Brooks Atkinson, New York: The Modern Library, 1950.

———. "Farming," *The Selected Writings of Ralph Waldo Emerson*. Ed. Brooks Atkinson. New York: The Modern Library, 1950.

———. "Fugitive Slave Law" (7 Mar. 1854), *Emerson's Anti-Slavery Writings*. Eds. Len Gougeon and Joel Myerson. New Haven: Yale University Press, 1995.

———. "John Brown (January 6, 1860)," *Emerson's Anti-Slavery Writings*. Eds. Len Gougeon and Joel Myerson. New Haven: Yale University Press, 1995.

———. "Kansas Relief Meeting (10 Sep. 1856)," *Emerson's Anti-Slavery Writings*. Eds. Len Gougeon and Joel Myerson. New Haven: Yale University Press, 1995.

———. "Morals (26 Apr. 1859)," *The Later Lectures of Ralph Waldo Emerson 1843-1871*. Eds. Ronald A. Bosco and Joel Myerson. Athens: University of Georgia Press, 2001.

———. "Lecture on Slavery" (25 Jan. 1855), *Emerson's Anti-Slavery Writings*. Eds. Len Gougeon and Joel Myerson. New Haven: Yale University Press, 1995.

———. "Nature." *The Norton Anthology of American Literature*, 6th ed., Vol. B. Gen. Ed. Nina Baym. New York: W.W. Norton & Company, 2003.

———. "Self-Reliance." *The Norton Anthology of American Literature*, 6th ed., Vol. B. Gen. Ed. Nina Baym. New York: W.W. Norton & Company, 2003.

———. "Speech at a Meeting to Aid John Brown's Family" (18 Nov. 1859). *Emerson's Anti-Slavery Writings*. Eds. Len Gougeon and Joel Myerson. New Haven: Yale University Press, 1995.

———. Letter to Charles W. Slack, 31 October, 1859. Charles Wesley Slack Papers. Department of Special Collections and Archives, Kent State University Libraries and Media Services.

Executive Committee. *Annual Report* of the American Anti-Slavery Society. New York: American Anti-Slavery Society, 1861.

Fuller, Margaret and Ralph Waldo Emerson, eds., *"The Dial" A Magazine for Literature, Philosophy and Religion*. Boston: Weeks, Jordan, and Company,1840–1844.

Harding, Walter and Carl Bode, eds. *The Correspondence of Henry David Thoreau*. New York: New York University Press, 1958.

Hernstadt, Richard L., ed. *The Letters of A Bronson Alcott*. Iowa: Iowa State University Press, 1969.

Higginson, Thomas Wentworth. *Cheerful Yesterdays*. 1898. Reprint. New York: Arno Press and the New York *Times*, 1968.

———. *Army Life in a Black Regiment*. Alexandria: Time-Life Books, 1982.

———. "The Crisis Coming Now," Newburyport *Union*, 4, 12, 20 Nov. 1850.

———. "Demark Vesey." *Atlantic*, Jun. 1861.

———. "Gabriel's Defeat." *Atlantic* Sep. 1862.

———. "Massachusetts in Mourning." *Liberator* Vol. XXIV, No. 23 16 Jun 1854.

———. "The Maroons of Jamaica" *Atlantic* Feb. *1860*.

———. "The Maroons of Surinam." *Atlantic* May. *1860*.

———. "Nebraska City." *A Ride Through Kansas,1856. Sermons, Essays, and Lectures*, 1926.

———. "Nat Turner's Insurrection." *Atlantic*. Aug. 1861.

———. "Saints, and Their Bodies." *Out-Door Papers*. Boston: Lee and Shepard, 1879.

Higginson, Mary Thacher, ed. *The Letters and Journals of Thomas Wentworth Higginson 1846–1906*. Boston: Houghton Mifflin Company, 1921.

———. *Thomas Wentworth Higginson: The Story of His Life*. Boston: Houghton Mifflin Company,1914.

The Life, Trial and Execution of Captain John Brown. 1859. New York: De Capo Press, 1969.

Lowell, James Russell, "A Fable for Critics" in *Nineteenth-Century American Poetry*. Eds. William Spengemann with Jessica F. Roberts. New York: Penguin, 1996.

———. "Review of *A Week on the Concord and Merrimack*." *Massachusetts Quarterly Review*, Dec. 1849. *Transcendental Log: Fresh Discoveries in Newspapers*

Concerning Emerson, Thoreau, Alcott and Others of the American Literary Renais-sance. Ed. Kenneth Walter Cameron. Hartford: Transcendental Books, 1973.

———. "Judge Lecompte and the 'Sack of Lawrence,' May 26, 1856." *Kansas Historical Society.* 25 Mar. 2005. <http://www/kshs.or/publicat/khq/1953/53_7_amlin.htm>.

Parker, Theodore. "Benjamin Franklin." *Historic Americans.* Ed. Samuel A. Eliot, Boston: American Unitarian Association, 1908.

———. "The Effect of Slavery on the American People." *Saint Bernard and Other Papers.* Ed. Charles W. Wendte. Boston: American Unitarian Association, 1911.

———. "The Function and Place of Conscience in Relation to the Laws (1850)." 15 Mar. 2005.<http://www.pragmatism.org/american/parker_conscience.htm >.

———. "The Mexican War." *The Slave Power.* Ed. James K Hosmer. Boston: American Unitarian Association, 1907.

———. "The Present Aspect of Slavery and the Immediate Duty of the North," [a speech given in Jan. 29, 1858] in Works (Cobbe Edition).

———. "The Relation of Slavery to a Republican Form of Government." *The Liberator,* Vol XXVIII, No. 23., 4 Jun. 1858.

Redpath, James. *Echoes of Harpers Ferry.* Boston: Thayer and Eldridge, 1860.

———. *The Public Life of Captain John Brown, with an Auto-Biography of his Childhood and Youth.* Boston: Thayer and Eldridge, 1860.

Ruchames, Louis, ed. *The John Brown Reader.* New York: Abelard-Schuman, 1959.

———, ed. *The Letters of William Lloyd Garrison,* Vol IV. *From Disunion to the Brink of War, 1850–1860.* Cambridge: Belknap Press of Harvard University, 1975.

Sanborn, F. B., ed. *The Genius and Character of Emerson; Lectures at the Concord School Of Philosophy.* Port Washington, N.Y: Kennikat Press, 1971.

———. *The Life of Henry David Thoreau.* Boston: Houghton Mifflin Company, 1917.

———. *The Life and Letters of John Brown, Liberator of Kansas, and Martyr of Virginia.* Boston, 1885.

———. *Literary studies and Criticism : Evaluations of the Writers of the American Renaissance-with Fresh Approaches to Transcendentalism, Literary Influences, New-England Cultural Patterns, and the Creative Experience.* Ed., Kenneth Walter Cameron, Hartford: Transcendental Books, 1980.

———. *Recollections of Seventy Years.* New York: Gorham Press, 1909.

———. *Transcendental Writers and Heroes: Papers Chiefly on Emerson, Thoreau, Literary Friends and Contemporaries, with Regional and Critical Backgrounds.* Ed. Kenneth Walter Cameron. Hartford: Transcendental Books, 1978.

———. *Transcendental Youth and Age: Chapters in Biography and Autobiography.* Ed. Kenneth Walter Cameron. Hartford: Transcendental Books, 1981.

Seward, Richard Henry. "William Henry Seward's Higher Law Speech," 31 Mar. 2005, <http://www.furman.edu/~benson/docs/seward.html>.

Shakespeare, William. "The Life of King Henry V," Ed. R. J. Dorius. New Haven: Yale University Press, 1955.

Stowe, Harriet Beecher. *Dred: A Tale of the Dismal Swamp.* ed. Harold S. Levine. New York: Penguin Books, 2000.

———. *The Minister's Wooing.* New Jersey: Gregg Press, 1968.

———. *Uncle Tom's Cabin.* Ed. Elizabeth Ammons. New York: W.W. Norton & Company, 1994.

———. "An Appeal to the Women of the Free States of America, On the Present Crisis in Our Country." *Uncle Tom's Cabin,* Ed. Elizabeth Ammons. New York: W.W. Norton & Company, 1994.

——. "Introduction." *The Colored Patriots of the Revolution.* 1855. Reprint. New York: Arno Press and the New York *Times*, 1968.

Stowe, Charles Edward. *Life of Harriet Beecher Stowe: Compiled from her Letters and Journals.* Boston: Houghton Mifflin, 1890.

Thoreau, Henry David. ""Civil Disobedience." *The Essays of Henry D. Thoreau.* Ed. Lewis Hyde. New York: North Point Press, 2002.

——. A Plea for Captain John Brown." *The Essays of Henry D. Thoreau.* Lewis Hyde. Ed. New York: North Point Press, 2002.

——. "Slavery in Massachusetts." *The Essays of Henry D. Thoreau.* Ed. Lewis Hyde. New York: North Point Press, 2002.

——. *Walden.* Ed. J. Lyndon Shanley. Princeton: Princeton University Press, 1988.

——. *The Writings of Henry David Thoreau.* 20 Vols. Ed. Bradford Torrey. Boston: Houghton Mifflin Company, 1906.

Townsley, James. "The Pottowatomie Tragedy and John Brown's connection with it." *A John Brown Reader.* Ed. Louis Ruchames. New York: Abelard-Schuman, 1959.

United States Sen. *Inquiry into the late invasion and seizure of the public Property at Harper's Ferry* (S. Rpt. 278), Washington: Government Printing Office, 1860.

Weiss, John. *The Life and Correspondence of Theodore Parker,* 2 Vols. New York: D. Appleton & Company, 1864.

Whittier, John Greenleaf. "Brown of Ossawatomie." *The Complete Poetical Works of John Greenleaf Whittier.* Boston, 1892.

SECONDARY SOURCES

Abels, Jules. *Man on Fire: John Brown and the Cause of Liberty.* New York: Macmillan, 1971.

Albrecht, R.C. *Theodore Parker.* New York: Twayne Publishers, 1971.

Alcott, Bronson. *The Journals of Bronson Alcott.* 2 Vols. Ed. Odell Shepard. Port Washington: Kennikat Press, 1966.

The Anti-Slavery History of the John Brown Year: Being the 27th Annual Report of the American Anti-Slavery Society. New York: Negro Universities Press, 1969.

Banks, Russell. *Cloudsplitter.* New York: Harper Flamingo, 1998.

Benet, Stephen Vincent. *John Brown's Body.* Ed. Mabel A. Bessey. New York: Rinehart and Winston, 1960

Berwanger, Eugene. *The Frontier Against Slavery.* Urbana: University of Illinois Press, 1967.

Bickman, Martin. *Minding American Education: Reclaiming the Tradition of Active Learning.* New York: Teachers College Press, 2004.

Boyd, Richard. "Models of Power in Harriet Beecher Stowe's Dred." *Studies in American Fiction,* 19 Spring, 1991): 15–30.

——. "Violence and Sacrificial Displacement in Harriet Beecher Stowe's Dred." *Arizona Quarterly* 50 (1994): 51–72.

Bush, Harold K. "Emerson, John Brown, and 'Doing the Word.'" *The Emerson Dilemma: Essays on Emerson and Social Reform.* Ed. T. Gregory Garvey. Athens: University of Georgia Press, 2001.

Brown, Salmon, "John Brown and his Sons in Kansas Territory." *A John Brown Reader.* Ed. Louis Ruchames. New York: Abelard-Schuman, 1959.

Brown, John. "Old Brown's Parallels." *A John Brown Reader,* Ed. Louis Ruchames. New York: Abelard-Schuman, 1959.

Cain, William E. *A Historical Guide to Henry David Thoreau*. New York: Oxford University Press, 2000.

Cole, Phillis. "Pain and Protest in the Emerson Family." The *Emerson Dilemma: Essays on Emerson and Social Reform*. Ed. T. Gregory Garvey. Athens: University of Georgia Press, 2001.

Commager, Henry Steele. *Theodore Parker*. Boston: Beacon Press, 1960.

Cooney, Joan. "Neither Nonresistance nor Violence: Thoreau's Consistent Response to Social Evils." *The Concord Saunterer*, (Fall 1995) 3: 132–39.

Crane, Gregg D. "Dangerous Sentiments: Sympathy, Rights and Revolution in Stowe's Antislavery Novels." *Nineteenth Century Literature* 51 (1996): 176–204.

De Caro, Louis A. Jr. *Fire from the Midst of You: A Religious Life of John Brown*. New York: New York University Press, 2002.

Dubois, W.E. Burghardt. *John Brown*. New York: International Publishers, 1962.

Edelstein, Tilden G. *Strange Enthusiasm: a Life of Thomas Wentworth Higginson*. New Haven:Yale University Press, 1968.

Elkins, Stanley M. *Slavery: a Problem in American Institutional and Intellectual Life*. 2d ed. Chicago: University Of Chicago Press, 1968.

Fields, Anne. *Life and Letters of Harriet Beecher Stowe*. Boston: Houghton Mifflin and Company, 1897.

Finkelman, Paul. *His Soul Goes Marching On: Responses to John Brown and the Harper's Ferry Raid*. Charlottesville: University Press of Virginia, 1995.

Foner, Philip S. *Frederick Douglass*. New York: Citadel Press, 1969.

Frothingham, Octavius Brooks. *Theodore Parker: A Biography*. Boston: James R. Osgood and Company, 1874.

Garvey, T. Gregory, ed. The *Emerson Dilemma: Essays on Emerson and Social Reform*. University of Georgia Press: Athens, 2001.

Genovese, Eugene. *From Rebellion to Revolution: African American Slave Revolts in the Making of the New World*. Baton Rouge: Louisiana State University Press, 1979.

Glick, Wendell, ed. *Henry D. Thoreau: Reform Papers*. Princeton: Princeton University Press, 1973.

Gougeon, Len. *Virtue's Hero: Emerson, Anti-Slavery, and Reform*. Athens: University of Georgia Press, 1990.

Gray, T. R. "Confessions of Nat Turner" Harriet Beecher Stowe in *Dred: a Tale of the Great Dismal Swamp*. Ed. Robert S. Levine. New York: Penguin Books, 2000.

Grodzins, Dean, *American Heretic: Theodore Parker and Transcendentalism*. Chapel Hill: University of North Carolina Press, 2002.

———. "Theodore Parker and the 28th Congregational Society" in *Transient and Permanent: The Transcendentalist Movement and Its Contexts*. Eds. Charles Capper and Conrad Edick Wright. Boston: Massachusetts Historical Society, 1999.

———. "Theodore Parker." 29 Mar. 2005. <http//www.uua.org/uuhs/duub/articles/theodoreparker.html>.

———."Why Theodore Parker Backed John Brown: The Political and Social Roots of Support for Abolitionist Violence." Unpublished, 2004.

———. "Re: Fraternity and Brown." E-mail to Michael Stoneham. 26 Oct. 2004.

Harding, Walter. *The Days of Henry Thoreau*. New York: Knopf, 1965.

———, ed. *Thoreau as Seen by His Contemporaries*. Geneseo: State University College, 1989.

Hedrick, Joan D. *Harriet Beecher Stowe: A Life*. New York: Oxford University Press, 1994.

Herzog, Kristin. "Uncle Tom's Cabin and Incidents in the Life of a Slave Girl: The Issue of Violence." *Approaches to Teaching Stowe's Uncle Tom's Cabin*. Ed. Elizabeth Ammons. New York: Modern Language Association of America; 2000.

Hyde, Lewis. "Henry Thoreau, John Brown, and the Problem of Prophetic Action." *The Raritan: A Quarterly Review*, 22 (Fall, 2002): 125–144.

Jefferson, Thomas. "Declaration of Independence." *The Portable Thomas Jefferson*. Ed. Merrill D. Peterson. New York: Penguin, 1975.

———. *Notes on the State of Virginia*. Ed. William Peden. Chapel Hill: University of North Carolina Press, 1954.

Hovet, Theodore R. *The Master Narrative: Harriet Beecher Stowe's Subversive Story of the Master and the Slave in Uncle Tom's Cabin and Dred*. Lanham, Maryland: University Press of America, 1989.

Krasner, David. *John Brown: Terrible Saint*. New York: Dodd, Mead, and Co., 1934.

Lerner, Gerda. *The Grimke Sisters from South Carolina: Rebels against Slavery*. Boston: Houghton Mifflin Company, 1967.

Levine, Robert S. "Uncle Tom's Cabin in Frederick Douglass's Paper: An Analysis of Reception." *Uncle Tom's Cabin*. Ed. Elizabeth Ammons. New York: W.W. Norton & Company, 1994.

———. "Introduction," *Dred: A Tale of the Dismal Swamp*. Ed. Robert S. Levine. New York: Penguin Books, 2000.

Longfellow, Samuel. *Life of Henry Wadsworth Longfellow*. 3 Vols., Boston, 1891.

Malin, James C. *John Brown and the Legend of Fifty-Six*. Philadelphia: The American Philosophical Society, 1942.

———. "Judge Lecompte and the 'Sack of Lawrence,' May 26, 1856." *Kansas Historical Society*. 25 Mar. 2005. <http://www/kshs.or/publicat/khq/1953/53_7_amlin.htm>.

Mayer, Henry. *All on Fire: William Lloyd Garrison and the Abolition of Slavery*. New York: St. Martin's Press, 1998.

Miller, David C. *Dark Eden: The Swamp in Nineteenth-Century American Culture*. New York: Cambridge University Press, 1989.

Miller, Perry. *Consciousness in Concord*. Boston: Houghton Mifflin Company, 1958.

Meyer, Howard N. *Colonel of the Black Regiment: The Life of Thomas Wentworth Higginson*. New York: W. W. Norton & Company, 1967.

———, ed. *The Magnificent Activist: The Writings of Thomas Wentworth Higginson (1823–1911)*. New York: De Capo Press, 2000.

Meyer, Michael, "Discord in Concord on the Day of John Brown's Hanging." *Thoreau Society Bulletin*. No. 146: (Winter, 1979) 1–6.

———. "Toward the Rhetoric of Equality: Reflective and Refractive Images in Stowe'sLanguage." *The Stowe Debate*. Eds. Mason I. Lowance, Jr, Ellen E. Westbrook, and R.C. De Prospo. Amherst: University of Massachusetts Press, 1994.

Myers, Michael. "Thoreau's Rescue of John Brown from History." *Studies in the American Renaissance*. Ed. Joel Myerson. Charlottesville: University Press of Virginia, 1980.

Nelson, Truman. *The Right of Revolution*. Boston: Beacon Press, 1968.

Oates, Stephen B. *The Fires of Jubilee: Nat Turner's Fierce Rebellion*. New York: Harper & Row, Publishers, 1975.

———. *To Purge this Land with Blood: A Biography of John Brown*. Amherst: University of Massachusetts Press, 1984.

Ostrander, Gillman. "Emerson, Thoreau, and John Brown. *The Mississippi Valley Historical Review*. Vol. XXXIV (1852/1853): 713–726.

Penn-Warren, Robert. *John Brown: The Making of a Martyr*. New York: Payson & Clarke Ltd., 1929.

Peterson, Merril D. *John Brown: the Legend Revisited*. Charlottesville: University of Virginia Press, 2002.

Quarles, Benjamin, ed. *Blacks on John Brown*. Urbana: University of Illinois Press, 1972.

Renehan, Edward J. *The Secret Six: the True Tale of the Men Who Conspired with John Brown*. New York: Crown Publishers, 1995.

Richardson, Robert D. Jr. *Emerson: The Mind on Fire*. University of California Press: Berkeley, 1995.

———. *Henry Thoreau: A Life of the Mind*. Berkeley: University of California Press, 1986.

Rossbach, Jeffery. *Ambivalent Conspirators: John Brown, the Secret Six, and a Theory of Slave Violence*. Philadelphia: University of Pennsylvania Press, 1982.

Rowe, John Carlos. *At Emerson's Tomb: The Politics of Classic American Literature*. New York: Columbia University Press, 1997.

———. "Stowe's Rainbow Sign: Violence and Community in *Dred: A Tale of the Great Dismal Swamp* (1856)." *Arizona Quarterly: A Journal of American Literature, Culture, and Theory*, 58 (Spring, 2002): 37–55.

Rusk, Ralph, ed. *The Letters of Ralph Waldo Emerson*. New York: Columbia University Press, 1938.

Ryan, Mary. *Womanhood in America: From Colonial Times to the Present*. New York: New Viewpoints, 1975.

Stone, Edward, ed. *Incident at Harper's Ferry*. New Jersey: Prentice-Hall, Inc., 1956.

Sunquist, Eric. "Slavery, Revolution and the American Renaissance." *The American Renaissance Reconsidered*. Eds. Walter Ben Michaels and Donald C. Pease. Baltimore:Johns Hopkins University Press, 1985.

Tompkins, Jane P. "Sentimental Power: *Uncle Tom's Cabin* and the Politics of Literary History." *Uncle Tom's Cabin*. Ed. Elizabeth Ammons. New York: W.W. Norton & Company, 1994.

Villard, Oswald Garrison. *John Brown 1800–1859: A Biography Fifty Years Later*. Gloucester: Peter Smith, 1965.

Whitney, Lisa. "In the Shadow of Uncle Tom's Cabin: Stowe's Vision of Slavery from the Great Dismal Swamp." *New England Quarterly* 66 (1993): 552–69.

Wilson, Forrest. *Crusader in Crinoline: The Life of Harriet Beecher Stowe*. Philadelphia: J. B. Lippincott Company, 1941.

Worley, Sam McGuire. *Emerson, Thoreau, and the Role of the Cultural Critic*. Albany: State University of New York Press, 2001.

Yellin, Jean Fagan. *The Intricate Knot: Black Figures in American Literature, 1776–1863*. New York: New York University, 1972.

Index

Printed in the United States
by Baker & Taylor Publisher Services